DMU and EMU Recognition Guide

Colin J. Marsden

First published 2013
ISBN 978 0 7110 3740 3

Published by Ian Allan Publishing.

An imprint of Ian Allan Publishing Ltd, Hersham, Surrey KT12 4RG.
Printed in Bulgaria

Visit the Ian Allan Publishing website at www.ianallanpublishing.com

Distributed in the United States of America and Canada by BookMasters Distribution Services.

Below: *Painted in Regional Railways blue and grey livery, off-set with Wessex Trains bodyside banding, BREL-built Class 150/2 No. 150234 passes Lympstone Village on the Exeter to Exmouth branch on 3 October 2002 forming the 13.18 Paignton to Exmouth service.* CJM

Introduction

The Ian Allan ABC Recognition Series has for many years concentrated on the current operational classes of locomotive, multiple unit or item of rolling stock.

In 2011 we produced the first 'all time' definitive book covering the obsolete and current locomotive classes; this was well accepted and followed a large number of readers' requests. The natural progression from this is the production of the definitive *DMU and EMU Recognition Guide* title.

This product, which has taken huge levels of ground research, includes as full as possible technical details of every class and sub-class of diesel, electric and gas-turbine multiple unit that has operated on the UK rail system.

In a few cases question marks or data are provided in brackets. The information within these may not be fully authenticated, despite extensive research from within the rail industry, historic record files and builder data; we have therefore been unable to prove without doubt the accuracy of these items of information.

In most cases original records from the manufacturers and builders have been consulted and historic reference documents held in archives have been reviewed. In some instances this has resulted in conflicting information between builder and operator emerging; we have tried to resolve this in every case by using the data supplied by the builders.

It is hoped that any reader who can provide any missing information or can provide extra information will provide this by sending an email to the e-mail address below, so that any subsequent editions of this work can be amended.

Illustrations have been selected to feature as many differences as possible, while showing different liveries throughout the life of the class under review.

While covering so many classes and sub-classes in one title, it has not been possible to include every livery and modification, but a fair selection has been included.

For a greater coverage of individual classes reference should be made to *Modern Locomotives Illustrated* magazine, which as a part work is covering all the classes of locomotive and multiple unit to have operated in the UK and is authored by the editor of this title.

The editor of *DMU and EMU Recognition Guide* welcomes any technical updates, new illustrations, detail changes or comments from readers. These should be addressed to me via the Publishers or sent with an illustration if possible by email to cjmarsden@btopenworld.com

Colin J. Marsden
Dawlish, Devon
June 2013

GWR AEC Railcar

Number range:	1	2-4	5-17
Classification:	-	-	-
Introduced:	1933	1934	1935-37
Built by:	AEC, Southall	AEC, Southall	AEC, Southall
Body Supplier:	Park Royal	Gloucester RC&W	Gloucester RC&W
Vehicle length (over body):	63ft 7in (19.38m)	63ft 7in (19.38m)	63ft 7in (19.38m)
Height:	11ft 4in (3.45m)	11ft 8in (3.57m)	11ft 9in (3.58m)
Width:	9ft 0in (2.74m)	9ft 0in (2.74m)	9ft 0in (2.74m)
Bogie wheelbase:	7ft 0in (2.13m)	7ft 0in (2.13m)	7ft 0in (2.13m)
Seating:	69	40 + 4 Buffet	63-70§
Internal layout:	2+2, 2+3	2+2	2+2, 2+3§
Gangway:	Not fitted	Not fitted	Not fitted
Toilets:	1	2	Not fitted (1 on 10-12)
Weight:	20 tons	26ton 4cwt	25ton 6cwt - 29ton 10cwt
Brake type:	Vacuum	Vacuum	Vacuum
Power unit:	1 x AEC 6-cylinder	2 x AEC 6-cylinder	2 x AEC 6-cylinder
Horsepower (total):	121hp (90.2kW)	242hp (180.5kW)	242hp (180.5kW)
Transmission:	Mechanical Vulcan Sinclair flywheel Wilson gearbox	Mechanical Vulcan Sinclair flywheel Wilson gearbox	Mechanical Vulcan Sinclair flywheel Wilson gearbox
Max speed:	45mph (72km/h)	75mph (121km/h)	75mph (121km/h)
Coupling type:	Emergency shackle	Emergency shackle	Emergency shackle
Multiple restriction:	Not fitted	Not fitted	Not fitted
Door type:	Hinged	Hinged	Sliding
Design features:	Streamlined	Streamlined	Streamlined
Notes:			§ No. 17 built for parcels service, no seats, three pairs of bi-parting doors

Right: *Later design Swindon built car No. 34 was built as an Express Parcels vehicle, no passenger seats were provided and the full length luggage area with fold down side tables could accommodate 10 tons of cargo. Access was by three pairs of double hinged doors on each side. Entry to the driving cab was by way of the luggage compartment.* CJM-C

Below: *Car No. 6 is one of 13 built in 1935-37 using a Gloucester RC&W supplied body mounted on an AEC underframe. Seating was provided for between 63-70 depending on configuration, with passenger access in the middle being by manual sliding door. The livery applied is Great Western chocolate and cream.* CJM-C

18	19-33	34	35-38
-	-	-	-
1937	1940-41	1941	1941-42
AEC, Southall	GWR Swindon	GWR Swindon	GWR Swindon
Gloucester RC&W	GWR Swindon	GWR Swindon	GWR Swindon
65ft 8in (20.01m)	65ft 8in (20.01m)	65ft 8in (20.01m)	65ft 8in (20.01m)
12ft 4in (3.76m)	12ft 2½in (3.72m)	12ft 2½in (3.72m)	12ft 1in (3.68m)
8ft 11½in (2.73m)	9ft 0in (2.74m)	9ft 0in (2.74m)	9ft 0in (2.74m)
8ft 6in (2.59m)	8ft 6in (2.59m)	8ft 6in (2.59m)	8ft 6in (2.59m)
49	48	0 (Parcels 10 tons)	Various 44-60
2+2, 2+3	2+2	-	2+2 + buffet
Not fitted	Not fitted	Not fitted	Inner-end
Not fitted	1	Not fitted	1
33ton 12cwt	35ton 13cwt	34ton 18cwt	36ton 14cwt-37ton 12cwt
Vacuum	Vacuum	Vacuum	Vacuum
2 x AEC 6-cylinder	2 x AEC 6-cylinder	2 x AEC 6-cylinder	2 x AEC 6-cylinder
242hp (180.5kW)	242hp (180.5kW)	242hp (180.5kW)	242hp (180.5kW)
Mechanical	Mechanical	Mechanical	Mechanical
Vulcan Sinclair flywheel	Vulcan Sinclair flywheel	Vulcan Sinclair flywheel	Vulcan Sinclair flywheel
Wilson gearbox	Wilson gearbox	Wilson gearbox	Wilson gearbox
75mph (121km/h)	75mph (121km/h)	75mph (121km/h)	75mph (121km/h)
Screw	Screw	Screw	Screw
Not fitted	Not fitted	Not fitted	Not fitted
Sliding	Hinged	Hinged	Sliding
Streamlined	Boxed	Boxed	Boxed
Able to haul trailing load of 60 tons (for Lambourne branch)	Able to haul trailing load	Able to haul trailing load	Single cab to work with intermediate trailer

Ro-Railer - UR 7924

Number:	UR 7924
Classification:	-
Introduced:	1931
Built by:	Karrier Motors, Huddersfield Body - Cravens
Vehicle length:	26ft 0in (7.92m)
Height:	Rail - 9ft 6in (2.89m) Road - 9ft 9¾in (2.99m)
Width:	7ft 5½in (2.27m)
Seating:	26
Internal layout:	2+2
Gangway:	No
Toilets:	No
Weight:	7ton 2cwt
Brake type:	Foot (friction)
Heating:	Hot air
Engine type:	Petrol - 6-cylinder bus
Horsepower (total):	Approx 120hp (89.5kW)
Transmission:	Mechanical
Max speed:	75mph (121km/h)
Coupling type:	Emergency eye
Multiple restriction:	Not fitted
Door type:	Folding
Special features:	-
Notes:	Road/rail vehicle

Below: *Introduced by the LMS in 1931 to operate on either the highway or the railway line, this bus with rail wheels was used between Blisworth and Stratford-upon-Avon in rail mode and at Stratford lifted its rail wheels and used its rubber tyres to continue its journey mainly to the Welcombe Hotel. Built by bus company Karrier Motors of Huddersfield and given the highway number UP 7924. While the unique vehicle did operate with some success it was very rough riding. After commissioning and testing it entered traffic in April 1932 and was withdrawn from joint road/ rail operations in June of the same year. The vehicle is shown from its standard bus cab end.* CJM-C

1932 Michelin Railcar

Number range:	Not issued
Classification:	-
Introduced:	UK 1932
Built by:	Michelin Company, Clermont-Ferrand, France
Length (passenger compartment):	21ft 3in (6.48m)
Length (overall):	44ft 9in (13.64m)
Height:	8ft 1in (2.46m)
Width:	9ft 7in (2.92m)
Wheel arrangement:	10 wheels (3 axle & 2 axle)
Seating:	24
Internal layout:	2+1
Gangway:	No
Toilets:	No
Weight:	5.75 tons
Brake type:	Pedal
Power unit:	Panhard & Levassor, Petrol
Horsepower (total):	27hp (20.13kW)
Transmission:	Mechanical
Max speed:	60mph (97km/h)
Coupling type:	Emergency eye
Multiple restriction:	Not fitted
Door type:	Slam
Special features:	-
Notes:	Rubber tyred

Below: *Following developments in France using rubber tyred railway vehicles, considerably reducing ambient noise, in 1932 designer Edouard Michelin approached the LMS to bring a 24-seat rubber tyred railcar to the UK for trials. The vehicle was carried on 10 wheels all fitted with pneumatic rubber tyres. The 6-wheel leading bogie had a wheelbase of 8ft 6in (2.59m). The middle axle was powered, transferring movement to the forward axle by chains and sprockets. The vehicle had aircraft type water cooled radiators which were mounted either side of the cab at cant rail height. The railcar could not haul a tail load and was designed for mainland European track height access. The French-built car travelled by rail from its factory in Clermont-Ferrand to Dunkirk, where it was shipped to Tilbury, before going to Derby for inspection and commissioning. Testing was carried out over the Bletchley-Oxford line, where speeds of up to 60mph (97km/h) were obtained. In addition to the LMS, the vehicle was used on the Southern Region between Ascot and Alton. Although tested and providing some positive results no firm orders were placed for like vehicles. After tests were complete the unusual train was returned to its builder's factory in France. Two views of the unusual vehicle are shown while testing on LMS metals. Both:* CJM-C

Michelin 'Coventry' Railcars 1 & 2

Number range:	1-2
Classification:	Coventry Railcar
Introduced:	1936
Built by:	Armstrong Siddeley (Parkside), Coventry, UK by the Coventry Pneumatic Railcar Co
Length (overall):	54ft 3½in (16.55m)
Height:	12ft 0in (3.66m)
Width:	9ft 2in (2.79m)
Wheel arrangement:	4-wheel (2-axle)
Seating:	48
Internal layout:	2+2
Gangway:	No
Toilets:	No
Weight:	13¼ tons
Brake type:	Air
Power unit:	Leyland Motors
Horsepower (total):	275hp (205kW)
Transmission:	Mechanical
Max speed:	70mph (116km/h)
Coupling type:	Emergency
Multiple restriction:	Not fitted
Door type:	Sliding (bi-parting)
Special features:	-
Notes:	Rubber tyred

Below: *Two Coventry Railcars based on the Michelin design were introduced in 1936, being constructed by Armstrong Siddeley of Coventry. Each car, delivered by road from the building plant to Coventry goods yard was mounted on two eight wheel pneumatic tyred bogies. The vehicles with a raised cab at one end looked impressive painted in crimson and cream. The vehicles were numbered as No. 1 and No. 2 and labelled on the side as 'Coventry Railcar'. The raised cab gave excellent visibility all round and avoided the need to have a cab at the other end or to turn the vehicle. During 1936 the pair commenced a series of trial runs on the Oxford to Cambridge and Rugby to Market Harborough lines, being kept when not in use at Rugby depot. After press runs and demonstrations where a speed of 72mph (116km/h) was attained the cars entered passenger service on 14 September 1936 working Rugby-Leamington Spa, Rugby-Nuneaton and Rugby-Coventry. When in passenger service the vehicles were drived by Armstrong Siddeley staff with an LMS pilot driver. The cars' performance was described as 'excellent' and a handful of surviving ex-passengers reported the ride to be near silent. However, the railways in the UK were not keen to develop the design. The pair were withdrawn at the end of 1937 and taken to the UK Michelin factory at Stoke-on-Trent where both were broken up in 1945. Car No. 1 is seen in Coventry Yard.* CJM-C

Leyland 4-wheel Railbuses - 29950 – 29952

Number range:	LMS 29950 - 29952
Classification:	-
Introduced:	1933
Built by:	Leyland Motors
Length (overall):	41ft 1in (12.52m)
Height:	11ft 7in (3.53m)
Width:	9ft 8in (2.95m)
Wheel arrangement:	4-wheel cars
Wheelbase:	21ft 0in (6.4m)
Wheel diameter:	3ft 0in (914mm)
Seating:	40
Internal layout:	2+2
Gangway:	No
Toilets:	1
Weight:	13ton 2cwt
Brake type:	Air
Power unit:	Armstrong Siddeley V12, 13 Lit
Horsepower (total):	95hp (70.8kW)
Transmission:	Hydraulic - Lysholm-Smith
Max speed:	56mph (90km/h)
Fuel capacity:	27 gals (123lit)
Coupling type:	Emergency
Multiple restriction:	Not fitted
Door type:	Sliding
Special features:	-

Below: *These three early LMS railbuses were built by Leyland Motors at the end of 1933 and entered service in summer 1934. Each vehicle was powered and they could operate alone or in multiple. Strict operating restrictions were imposed as their light weight was seen as a problem with the operation of signalling equipment. As early as February 1934, vehicle No. 29950 was put on display at Euston station and operated a press and directors special to Watford Junction and return. Reports from the day indicate the ride was good and a top speed of 60mph (97km/h) was attained. By summer 1934 the first of the build was working in the Leicester area, while No. 29951 was introduced on Blackpool Central to St Annes services. By mid summer the third of the build was delivered. All three were allocated to Lower Darwin and were to be found working in the Preston, Accrington, Clitheroe, Blackburn area. By 1939 the three vehicles were transferred to Scotland and operated from Hamilton shed. Reports in 1949 indicate that the ride was now becoming very poor, with a number of complaints from passengers and staff. Soon after two of the three were stored; eventually all three were out of service and went to St Rollox Works in Glasgow, from where they were withdrawn in April 1951. All were broken up. Car No. 29950 is illustrated in early 1934.* CJM-C

English Electric 'Bluebird'

Identity:	*Bluebird*
Classification:	-
Introduced:	1933
Built by:	Dick Kerr, Preston
Vehicle length:	62ft 10½in (19.16m)
Height:	12ft 11½in (3.95m)
Width:	8ft 11¾in (2.74m)
Seating:	53 (design allowed for up to 61)
Internal layout:	2+2
Gangway:	No
Toilets:	Not fitted
Weight:	37¾ tons
Brake type:	Vacuum
Engine type:	1 x English Electric 6HT of 200hp 149kW at 1500rpm, 6in bore x 8in stroke
Horsepower (total):	200hp (149kW)
Generator:	Dick Kerr 135kW
Transmission:	Electric
Traction motors:	2 x Dick Kerr of 100hp (74.5kW)
Max speed:	60mph (97km/h)
Coupling type:	Screw
Multiple restriction:	Not fitted
Door type:	Sliding bi-parting
Train heating:	Steam
Fuel capacity:	60gal (273lit)
Special features:	Ability to haul single trailing load
Notes:	Demonstrator vehicle, owned by Dick Kerr (English Electric), withdrawn 1935

Above and Below: *Built as a demonstrator this single power car, able to haul a vacuum braked trailer, was introduced in 1933, firstly undergoing tests on the Rugby-Market Harborough and Bletchley-Bedford lines. After tests the car entered service on the Warwick-Northampton route. The body mounted high-speed diesel engine was at the No. 1 end, with a power bogie below. In January 1934 the vehicle undertook some main line testing from Euston to Watford, which included hauling a vacuum braked coach over the Watford to St Albans branch. By spring 1934 the vehicle had clocked up around 20,000 miles and was performing well and placed on the Burton-Tutbury line. Although impressive, the design was not furthered and the test vehicle, named* **Bluebird**, *was withdrawn. The view above shows the power end, while the image below shows the non-powered end. On the left is the passenger compartment and driving cab layout. All:* CJM-C

LMSR Leyland Articulated DMU

Number range (vehicles):	80000, 80001, 80002 (3-car set)
Classification:	-
Introduced:	1938
Built by:	LMSR Derby Works
Set length:	184ft 6in (56.24m)
Vehicle length (over body):	63ft 9¾in (19.45m)
Height:	
Width:	
Seating:	Total - 30F/138T DMB - 54T MC - 30F, 24T DMT - 54T
Internal layout:	First 2+2 Second 2+2
Gangway:	Within train
Toilets:	3 (one in each coach)
Weight:	73 tons
Brake type:	Air
Engine type:	2 x Leyland 125hp 93.2kW per car
Horsepower (total):	750hp (559kW)
Transmission:	Hydraulic
Max speed:	75mph (121km/h)
Coupling type:	Emergency only
Multiple restriction:	Not fitted
Door type:	Sliding
Train heating:	Steam
Special features:	-
Notes:	Withdrawn February 1945, driving cars to electrification stock

Below: *By 1937 the LMS had gained considerable knowledge of operating diesel passenger traction from the various trial vehicles operated. With this in mind, they ordered a three-car semi-streamlined articulated train from Derby Works. The train, made up of two driving motors and an intermediate motor, carried the numbers 80000-80002 and underwent tests at Derby Works on 25 January 1938. The set ventured onto the main line as far as Burton on 16 February 1938. Various controlled test runs were conducted in March 1938, including a run to Gloucester for a trial over the Lickey Incline, before more main line testing on the West Coast was undertaken. From May 1938 testing on the Oxford-Cambridge line fell into chaos with numerous failures resulting in the set going to Wolverton for major attention. After modifications the three-car set returned to the Oxford-Cambridge route with far more impressive results. From March 1939 the set commenced operation from Bedford on a St Pancras-Nottingham schedule, running around 350 miles each day. It appears that the three cars were stored during the 1939-45 War. The three-car set never operated again; the driving cars were modified as the end vehicles of a three-car overhead wiring train for the MSJA line, while the intermediate car was scrapped. For their departmental life, the two original cars 80000 and 80002 were renumbered to M198895M and M198896M. The views left and below show the set in action on the LMS in 1938. Both:* CJM-C

LMS 4-car diesel-electric

Below: *Authorisation was granted in July 1927 for a development diesel four-coach train to be built using all four vehicles from the Bury-Holcombe Brook electric scheme. The train was rebuilt as a diesel at Horwich Works under the supervision of Sir Henry Fowler. The set was fitted with a 500hp (373kW) Beardmore engine mounted inside the structure of coach No. 14570. The traction generator was supplied by English Electric, as were the traction motors. The four-car set had a driving motor, driving trailer and two intermediate trailers. The trailer cars were modified for diesel operation at Newton Heath. When originally introduced in July 1928 the set operated between Blackpool Central and Preston, being taken out of traffic in April 1929. After that date the vehicles were stored and the engine supplier had the power equipment returned. The coaches were stored and broken up in 1931. The view below shows the set from its motor coach (DMBT) end.* CJM-C

Number range (vehicles):	14570, 14668, 14669, 14571 (4-car set)
Classification:	-
Introduced:	As electric stock on L&Y - 1916 Converted to DMU - 1928
Converted by:	LMSR Horwich Works & Newton Heath
Formation	DMBT - LMS 14570 x L&Y 3500 TT - LMS 14668 x L&Y 3601 TC - LMS 14669 x L&Y 3600 DTT - LMS 14571 x L&Y 3501
Set length:	254ft 4in (77.52m)
Vehicle length:	63ft 7in (19.38m)
Height:	12ft 7in (3.84m)
Width:	9ft 4in (2.84m)
Seating:	Total - 32F / 265T DMBT 14570 - 60 TT 14668 - 85T TC 14669 - 32F, 45T DTT 14571 - 75T
Internal layout:	First 2+2 Second 2+3
Gangway:	Not fitted
Toilets:	1
Weight:	144 tons
Brake type:	Vacuum
Engine type:	1 x Beardmore of 500hp (373kW) 8 cylinder 8.25in bore/12in stroke
Generator:	English Electric - 340kW, 600V
Traction motors:	2 x English Electric of 280hp (209kW)
Horsepower (total):	560hp (418kW)
Transmission:	Electric
Max speed:	60mph (97km/h)
Coupling type:	Screw
Multiple restriction:	Not fitted
Door type:	Slam
Train heating:	Electric
Special features:	-
Notes:	Withdrawn and broken up in 1931 Converted from 3,500V Bury-Holcombe Brook electric stock, with motor bogies from Euston-Watford stock

Armstrong Whitworth Single Cars

Number range (vehicles):	25	224	232
Name:	*Tyneside Venturer*	*Northumbrian§*	*Lady Hamilton*
Proposed operator:	LNER	LMS	SR
Classification:	-	-	-
Introduced:	1931	1932	1932
Built by:	Armstrong Whitworth	Armstrong Whitworth	Armstrong Whitworth
Body supplied by:	Cravens	Cravens	Cravens
Vehicle length:	63ft 4in (19.3m)	63ft 4in (19.3m)	63ft 4in (19.3m)
Height:	12ft 8in (3.86m)	12ft 8in (3.86m)	12ft 8in (3.86m)
Width:	9ft 4in (2.84m)	9ft 4in (2.84m)	9ft 4in (2.84m)
Seating:	60	60§	60
Internal layout:	2+2, 2+3	2+2, 2+3 § Loose armchairs	2+2, 2+3
Gangway:	Not fitted	Not fitted	Not fitted
Toilets:	1	1	1
Weight:	42½ tons	42½ tons	42½ tons
Brake type:	Vacuum	Vacuum	Vacuum
Engine type:	Sulzer 6LV22 of 250hp (186kW)	Sulzer 6LV22 of 250hp (186kW)	Sulzer 6LV22 of 250hp (186kW)
Transmission:	2 x Electric GEC	2 x Electric GEC	2 x Electric GEC
Max speed:	65mph (105km/h)	65mph (105km/h)	65mph (105km/h)
Coupling type:	Screw	Screw	Screw
Multiple restriction:	Within type	Within type	Within type
Door type:	Sliding bi-parting	Sliding bi-parting	Sliding bi-parting
Train heating:	Steam	Steam	Steam
Special features:			

Notes: § *Northumbria* modified by Wolverton to house 12 luxury seats for operation between Euston and Castle Bromwich in March 1933 - renamed *Armstrong-Shell Express*, then reverted to standard design

Below: *W G Armstrong-Whitworth and Co designed and built three diesel-electric single car vehicles in 1931-32, using bodies supplied by Cravens. Each was fitted with a Sulzer 4-stroke, 6-cylinder diesel engine set to deliver 250hp (186kW).* **Tyneside Venturer**, *the first built vehicle, started a 36 week trial period in April 1932 working in the Newcastle and Middlesbrough area. At the end of 1932 the vehicle was sold to the LNER.* **Tyneside Venturer** *continued to operate in the North East until April 1939 when it was involved in a collision; it was officially withdrawn at the end of April 1939 after operating for around 250,000 miles.* CJM-C

Above and Below: *Vehicle No. 224* **Northumbrian** *introduced in 1932 is seen in pre-delivery condition (above) at its builders works viewed from the power equipment end. After operating commissioning runs in the Newcastle area, the vehicle went to Wolverton Works where it was heavily rebuilt into a luxury saloon to operate between London and Castle Bromwich taking guests to The British Industries Fair. In its luxury form the vehicle carried just 12 passengers and was renamed* **Armstrong-Shell Express**. *The view below shows this car departing from Euston. A third car of near identical design, No. 232 and named* **Lady Hamilton**, *was delivered in 1932 and operated for a period on the Southern Railway before being transferred to the LNER, who purchased it in 1934.* **Lady Hamilton** *was by all accounts a problematic vehicle and spent a lot of time out of service. It was withdrawn in December 1939. After withdrawal all three were stored at Darlington until going to scrap in 1944. Both:* CJM-C

Armstrong Whitworth Single Car LNER 294

Number:	LNER 294
Classification:	-
Introduced:	Built: 1933, to LNER stock Aug 1934
Built by:	Armstrong Whitworth, Scotswood, Newcastle
Body supplier:	Park Royal Vehicles
Length (overall):	53ft 0in (16.15m)
Height:	11ft 10¾ (3.63m)
Width:	8ft 11in (2.72m)
Wheelbase:	37ft 0in (11.28m)
Seating:	57
Internal layout:	3+2
Gangway:	No
Toilets:	1
Weight:	19¾ tons
Wheel diameter:	2ft 9in (838mm)
Brake type:	Air
Power unit:	1 x 6-cyl Saurer of 95hp (71kW)
Horsepower (total):	95hp (71kW)
Transmission:	1 x GEC Electric traction motor
Max speed:	60mph (97km/h)
Coupling type:	Emergency
Door type:	Sliding (bi-parting)
Special features:	
Notes:	Trials vehicle owned by Armstrong Whitworth, used for short period on LNER in North East and then as spare vehicle. Withdrawn Feb-1939

Below: *Another stunning vehicle to emerge from the Armstrong Whitworth factory in Newcastle in 1934 was this single railbus No. 294. This vehicle was not named and originally operated trials on the LNER North Eastern area from May 1933, being taken into capital stock in August 1934. The vehicle, shorter by 10ft than the three vehicles detailed on the previous page, was usually kept as a spare. Its bodywork came from Park Royal Coachworks in London. It had seating for 57 in the 3+2 high-density layout, with passenger access by a pair of central bi-parting sliding doors. Traction was provided by a 95hp diesel engine/generator driving a single electric traction motor. A driving position was provided at both ends of the vehicle. Both:* CJM-C

BR Paxman diesel-electric

Number range:	9821 + 9828
Classification:	-
Introduced:	1956
Built by:	BR Derby, converted from 1926-built LMS all-steel BTO stock
Length (overall):	57ft 1in (17.4m)
Height:	
Width:	
Seating:	Not available for use - test equipment
Internal layout:	-
Gangway:	Within set
Toilets:	No
Weight:	103 tons
Brake type:	Vacuum
Power unit:	2 x Paxman ZHXL450 of 450hp (336kW) Cylinder bore 7in (178mm) stroke 7¾in (197mm)
Horsepower (total):	900hp (671kW)
Transmission:	Electric
Max speed:	90mph (145km/h)
Fuel capacity:	
Coupling type:	Emergency
Multiple restriction:	Screw
Door type:	Slam
Special features:	
Notes:	Bogies from ex-1926 Euston-Watford stock

Below: *In 1956, BR Derby Works built a two-car DMU set from redundant LMS all-steel open brake third vehicles of 1926 vintage. Basic driving cabs were built at each end (one end of each vehicle) and redundant motor bogies salvaged from withdrawn Euston-Watford electric stock. The project was carried out to establish the operating principles of using underfloor mounted diesel-electric engines, rather than taking up passenger space with an above floor mounted engine; this would give extra passenger accommodation as well as a way through an entire train or trains in multiple. BR selected Paxman six-cylinder flat design 450hp (336kW) engines, of a similar type as previously used under the 'Fell' prototype diesel locomotive. The two car set was designed and built as a test bed; although it did have passenger seats it was never intended to carry fare-paying passengers. Records show that during its 17 month operating period from 1956, the set clocked up some 43,000 miles (69,200km). By 1958 it was agreed that with the development of first generation diesel-mechanical stock, the diesel-electric project would be terminated and the set was withdrawn from traffic and broken up. During its test period the set was based at Derby from where it operated all over the LM operating area, being seen as far north as Carlisle, as far south as London and widely in the Midlands, with a number of test runs recorded in the Chinley-Millers Dale area. In the view below the set, complete with its 1950s 'speed whiskers', is seen at Deby in green livery with car No. 9828 leading.* CJM-C

BUT Railbus 79740 – 79750

	1953 set	1955 sets	1957 set
Number range:	DMS - 79740 TS - 79741 DMBS - 79742	DMS - 79745 TS - 79746, 79747 DMBS - 79743, 79744	DMS - 79748 TS - 79749 DMBS - 79750
Classification:	4-wheel Railbus	4-wheel Railbus	4-wheel Railbus
Introduced:	1953	1955	1957
Built by:	AC Vehicles (BUT)	AC Vehicles (BUT)	AC Vehicles (BUT)
Vehicle length (over body):	37ft 6in (11.43m)	37ft 6in (11.43m)	37ft 6in (11.43m)
Height:	11ft 2¾in (3.42m)	11ft 2¾in (3.42m)	11ft 2¾in (3.42m)
Width:	9ft 4in (2.84m)	9ft 4in (2.84m)	9ft 4in (2.84m)
Seating:	DMBS - 28S TS - 46S DMS - 34S	DMBS - 28S TS - 46S DMS - 34S	DMBS - 28S TS - 46S DMS - 34S
Internal layout:	2+2	2+2	2+2
Gangway:	Emergency end doors	Emergency end doors	Emergency end doors
Toilets:	Not fitted	Not fitted	Not fitted
Weight:	DMBS - 15 tons TS - 10 tons DMS - 15 tons	DMBS - 15 tons TS - 10 tons DMS - 15 tons	DMBS - 15 tons TS - 10 tons DMS - 15 tons
Brake type:	Air	Air	Air
Power unit:	1 x BUT (AEC) of 125hp (93.2kW) on each DMBS and DMB	1 x BUT (AEC) of 125hp (93.2kW) on each DMBS and DMB	1 x BUT (AEC) of 125hp (93.2kW) on each DMBS and DMB
Horsepower (total 3-car):	250hp (186.4kW)	250hp (186.4kW)	250hp (186.4kW)
Transmission:	Mechanical	Mechanical	Mechanical
Max speed:	45mph (72km/h)	45mph (72km/h)	45mph (72km/h)
Coupling type:	Shackle	Shackle	Shackle
Multiple restriction:	Within design	Within design	Within design
Door type:	Slam (inward)	Slam (inward)	Slam (inward)
Special features:	Built with full skirt	Built with open underframe	Built with open underframe
Notes:	Withdrawn by 1962	Withdrawn by 1962	Withdrawn by 1962

Private venture, vehicles later sold to BR

Left and Below: *British United Traction built a total of eleven lightweight railbus vehicles for BR between 1953 and 1957; the power cars could operate on their own, in pairs or with an intermediate trailer. The 1953 built set incorporated lower side skirts to allow tramway operation, but these were later removed. The driving cars had a driving position at each end. Passenger accommodation was in the 2+2 layout with a three-car set carrying 108 seated travellers. A three car train weighed just 40 tons tare. The two illustrations show the first set painted in grey livery complete with lower panel skirt sections. Both:* CJM-C

Above: *Three of the 1955-built vehicles painted in green livery without lower body skirts. Nos. M79743, M79745 and M79746 are seen in the St Albans passenger bay at Watford Junction soon after the set was introduced. The DMBS vehicle is nearest the camera.* CJM-C

Below: *Records show that the three sets spent most of their operational days on the St Albans to Watford route. Here the 1957-built set (vehicles M79748, M79749 and M79750) is seen on the approach to Bricket Wood half way along the branch line where a passing place existed.* CJM-C

Bristol 79958 – 79959

Number range:	79958-79959
Classification:	4-wheel Railbus
Introduced:	1956
Built by:	Bristol Commercial Vehicles & Eastern Coach Works
Vehicle length (over body):	42ft 4in (12.9m)
Height:	11ft 7¾in (3.55m)
Width:	9ft 3in (2.82m)
Wheelbase:	22ft 0in (6.71m)
Seating:	56S
Internal layout:	2+3
Gangway:	Not fitted
Toilets:	Not fitted
Weight:	13ton 10cwt
Brake type:	Air Tred
Power unit:	1 x Gardner of 112hp (83.52kW)
Horsepower (total):	112hp (83.52kW)
Transmission:	Mechanical, SCG five speed gearbox
Max speed:	45mph (72.4km/h)
Coupling type:	Eye
Multiple restriction:	Not issued
Door type:	Single sliding

Right: *Two four-wheel railbuses were built in 1958 by Bristol Commercial Vehicles and Eastern Coach Works as part of the 22 vehicle BTC railbus order. This pair were destined for Scotland and perhaps had the most pleasing external appearance, in some respects looking very much like a motor bus. An unusual feature of this design was the single headlight mounted in the front valance. On 20 May 1960 car No. Sc79959 is seen at Strathavon with a service bound for Hamilton Central.* CJM-C

Left: *Driving cab of Bristol Commercial Vehicles / Eastern Coach Work railbus. Switches and door release controls are on the front angled panel, while the power and brake controllers are on the main desk; the power controller or throttle is on the left, with the main brake control valve towards the middle of the desk. The removable master switch is missing from the slot on the right.* CJM-C

Waggon und Maschinenbau 79960 – 79964

Number range:	79960-79964
Classification:	4-wheel Railbus
Introduced:	1958
Built by:	Waggon und Maschinenbau
Vehicle length (over body):	41ft 10in (12.75m)
Vehicle length (overall):	45ft 9¼in (13.95m)
Height:	11ft 9¼in (3.58m)
Width:	8ft 8¼in (2.65m)
Seating:	56S
Internal layout:	2+3
Gangway:	Not fitted
Toilets:	Not fitted
Weight:	15 tons
Brake type:	Air Tred
Power unit:	1 x Büssing of 150hp (112kW)§
Horsepower (total):	150hp (112kW)
Transmission:	Mechanical, carden shaft to ZF electro-magnetic six-speed gearbox
Max speed:	45mph (72km/h)
Coupling type:	Eye
Multiple restriction:	Not issued
Door type:	Single sliding
Special features:	
Notes:	§ Car No. 79961/3/4 later fitted with AEC A220X engine of 150hp (112hp)

Left: *The country with the greatest knowledge of railbus technology was Germany, where a large number of like vehicles operated. In 1957 the Waggon und Maschinenbau company was contracted by the BTC to build five vehicles for use on the Eastern and London Midland Regions. Spare parts were a major problem to this fleet and three, Nos. 79961/63/64, had their original Bussing engines replaced with AEC power units. All were painted in BR green livery, with yellow whiskers later added. Eastern Region car No. E79960 is illustrated. Note the sliding passenger door is open and that traditional buffers were fitted.* CJM-C

Right: *On the railbus vehicles the driver occupied a small, just under half width section at the front end, separated from the passenger saloon by a hinged door. Passenger seats were provided adjacent to the cab offering front seat passengers an excellent view of the line ahead. The guard would occupy the rear driving compartment. Seating was in bus style with two seats one side and three seats the other with a central corridor. These vehicles seated 56. Strung overhead luggage racks were provided, as surprisingly were curtains! With the use of lightweight railbuses being phased out the five German-built cars were withdrawn between November 1966 and April 1967, and thankfully several were saved by preservation groups.* CJM-C

Wickham 79965 – 79969

Number range:	79965-79969
Classification:	4-wheel Railbus
Introduced:	1958
Built by:	D Wickham & Co, Ware
Vehicle length (over body):	38ft (11.58m)
Vehicle length (overall):	39ft 6in (12.04m)
Height:	12ft 6in (3.81m)
Width:	9ft 0in (2.74m)
Wheelbase:	19ft 0in (5.79m)
Seating:	44S
Internal layout:	2+3
Gangway:	Not fitted
Toilets:	Not fitted
Weight:	11½ tons
Brake type:	Air Tred
Power unit:	1 x Meadows 6HDT500 of 105hp (78.3kW)
Horsepower (total):	105hp (78.3kW)
Transmission:	Mechanical, Freeborn-Wickham disc & ring coupling driving SCG four-speed gearbox to final drive
Max speed:	45mph (72km/h)
Coupling type:	Eye
Multiple restriction:	Not fitted
Door type:	Single sliding

Below: *The next batch of five BTC railbuses were ordered from D Wickham of Ware in Hertfordshire for operation in Scotland. These were the lightest of any of the railbus vehicles at just 11½ tons. Seating was also reduced to just 44 in the 2+3 style. This design had a very short life, being introduced in 1958 and phased out of traffic between 1964-66. None were preserved. The last vehicle of the build, No. 79969 (illustrated), was fitted with a prototype pneumatic suspension designed by Andre and Westinghouse, with air bags replacing the more conventional springs. This equipment was often a problem and the vehicle came to an early demise after receiving collision damage in 1963.* CJM-C

Park Royal 79970 – 79974

Below Right: *The five Park Royal built cars were split on allocation between the London Midland and Scottish Regions but by 1960 all five were in Scotland. The design incorporated a two-panel alpha-numeric route display on the front end below the cab window positions, in addition to a roller-blind destination indicator at cant rail height. These vehicles also sported curved cab side windows which looked very pleasing. The Park Royal design incorporated a long body overhang at each end, which often made the design look stumpy and often caused lateral bounce which was not welcomed by the train crew or passengers. The interior design accommodated 50 second class passengers in the traditional 2+3 railbus style. Once in Scotland the five vehicles operated in the Arrochar, Alloa and Ayr areas until withdrawn between November 1966 and February 1968. Car No. SC79970 is illustrated at Craigellachie on the Speyside line between Elgin and Aviemore.* CJM-C

Number range:	79970-79974
Classification:	4-wheel Railbus
Introduced:	1958
Built by:	Park Royal Vehicles, London
Vehicle length (over body):	42ft 0in (12.8m)
Vehicle length (overall):	43ft 4in (13.21m)
Height:	11ft 8¼in (3.56m)
Width:	9ft 3in (2.82m)
Wheelbase:	19ft 8¼in (6.0m)
Seating:	50S
Internal layout:	2+3
Gangway:	Not fitted
Toilets:	Not fitted
Weight:	15 tons
Brake type:	Air Tred
Power unit:	1 x BUT (AEC) of 150hp (112kW)
Horsepower (total):	150hp (112kW)
Transmission:	Mechanical, SCG four-speed gearbox to final drive
Max speed:	45mph (72km/h)
Coupling type:	Eye
Multiple restriction:	Not fitted
Door type:	Single sliding
Special features:	-

Left: *Working in Ayrshire and with a small yellow front end, No. SC79974 is seen at Prestwick with a branch line service to Dalmellington, a branch which closed to passenger traffic on 6 April 1964.* CJM-C

AC Cars 79975 - 79979

Number range:	79975-79979
Classification:	4-wheel Railbus
Introduced:	1958
Built by:	AC Cars Ltd, Thames Ditton
Vehicle length (over body):	36ft 0in (10.97m)
Vehicle length (overall):	37ft 3in (11.36m)
Height:	11ft 7¾in (3.55m)
Width:	8ft 11in (2.72m)
Wheelbase:	18ft 11in (5.77m)
Seating:	46S
Internal layout:	2+3
Gangway:	Not fitted
Toilets:	Not fitted
Weight:	11 tons
Brake type:	Air Tred
Power unit:	1 x BUT (AEC) of 150hp (112kW)
Horsepower (total):	150hp (112kW)
Transmission:	Mechanical, SCG four-speed gearbox to final drive
Max speed:	45mph (72km/h)
Coupling type:	Eye
Multiple restriction:	Not fitted
Door type:	Single sliding

Below: *Built by Associated Commercial Cars (AC Cars) at their small factory in Thames Ditton near Hampton Court, these five cars were the first BTC railbuses to enter service, being allocated to the Western and Scottish Regions. The cars were painted in BR green with speed whiskers on the cab ends. Passenger access was by a single leaf sliding door on each side, with crew access being by the same door. Seating was provided for 46 in the 2+3 configuration. Car No. W79977 is illustrated while operating the Kemble - Cirencester service. After Western Region use in the Swindon area, the WR sets transferred to Bodmin and Yeovil for a short period before moving to Scotland.* CJM-C

Above: No. SC79979 is viewed from the opposite side to that of No. W79977 on the facing page, clearly showing the BUT engine and exhaust pipe. Without speed whiskers, No. 79979 is seen when brand new on delivery to Scotland. It is interesting to record that this car has standard two trumpet air warning horns on the roof. CJM-C

Right: Western Region car No. W79978 is seen departing from Cirencester on 5 August 1963 forming the 14.00 service to Kemble. Another eight months would see the line close and No. 79978 transfer to other Western Region duties before heading north to Scotland. Michael Mensing

Derby Lightweight

Vehicle type:	DMBS	DMBSL	DMS
Original number range:	79008-79046, 79184-79188	79118-79149, 79169-79181	79150-79154
Introduced:	1954-55	1954-55	1954-55
Built by:	BR Derby Works	BR Derby Works	BR Derby Works
Vehicle length (over body):	57ft 6in (17.53m)	57ft 6in (17.53m)	57ft 6in (17.53m)
Height:	12ft 4½in (3.77m)	12ft 4½in (3.77m)	12ft 4½in (3.77m)
Width:	9ft 2in (2.79m)	9ft 2in (2.79m)	9ft 2in (2.79m)
Seating:	79008-79020, 79184-79188 - 61S 79021-79046 - 56S	52S	64S
Internal layout:	Second - 2+3	Second - 2+3	First - 2+1 Standard - 2+3
Gangway:	Not fitted	Not fitted	Not fitted
Toilets:	Not fitted	1	Not fitted
Weight:	27 tons	27 tons	26 tons
Brake type:	Vacuum	Vacuum	Vacuum
Power unit:	2 x BUT (AEC) of 150hp (111.9kW) per vehicle	2 x BUT (AEC) of 150hp (111.9kW) per vehicle	2 x BUT (AEC) of 150hp (111.9kW) per vehicle
Horsepower (total):	300hp (224kW)	300hp (224kW)	300hp (224kW)
Transmission:	Mechanical	Mechanical++	Mechanical
Max speed:	70mph (113km/h)	70mph (113km/h)	70mph (113km/h)
Coupling type:	Screw	Screw	Screw
Multiple restriction:	Yellow Diamond	Yellow Diamond	Yellow Diamond
Door type:	Slam	Slam	Slam
Body structure:	Alloy	Alloy	Alloy
Notes:		++ 79135 fitted with SCG auto four-speed gearbox	

Vehicle type:	DMBS	DMCL
Original number range:	79000-79007	79500-79507
Introduced:	1954	1954
Built by:	BR Derby Works	BR Derby Works
Vehicle length (over body):	57ft 6in (17.53m)	57ft 6in (17.53m)
Height:	12ft 4½in (3.77m)	12ft 4½in (3.77m)
Width:	9ft 2in (2.79m)	9ft 2in (2.79m)
Seating:	61S	12F/53S
Internal layout:	Second - 2+3	First - 2+1, Second - 2+3
Gangway:	Not fitted	Not fitted
Toilets:	Not fitted	1
Weight:	26 tons	27 tons
Brake type:	Vacuum	Vacuum
Power unit:	2 x Leyland of 125hp (93kW)	2 x Leyland of 125hp (93kW)
Horsepower (total):	250hp (186kW)	250hp (186kW)
Transmission:	Hydro-mechanical	Hydro-mechanical
Max speed:	70mph (113km/h)	70mph (113km/h)
Coupling type:	Screw	Screw
Multiple restriction:	Red Triangle	Red Triangle
Door type:	Slam	Slam
Body structure:	Alloy	Alloy
Notes:	Prototype vehicles	Prototype vehicles

■ The first seven Derby Lightweight twin sets were different from the production vehicles. Introduced for use on the Leeds to Bradford route these were little more than an updated version of the 1938 introduced LMS three-car set, using out of date equipment including a troublesome hydro-mechanical torque converter. These sets were very much the prototypes for the squadron introduction and differed in a number of ways, structurally and technically.

DMC	DTCL	TBS	TS
79189-79193*, 79508-79512 79639-79684,	79250-79262, 79600-79625,	79325-79329	79400-79404
1954-55	1954-55	1954-55	1954-1955
BR Derby Works	BR Derby Works	BR Derby Works	BR Derby Works
57ft 6in (17.53m)	57ft 6in (17.53m)	57ft 6in (17.53m)	57ft 6in (17.53m)
12ft 4½in (3.77m)	12ft 4½in (3.77m)	12ft 4½in (3.77m)	12ft 4½in (3.77m)
9ft 2in (2.79m)	9ft 2in (2.79m)	9ft 2in (2.79m)	9ft 2in (2.79m)
79189-79193 - 12F/53S 79508-79512 - 20F/36S 79639-79684 - 9F/53S 79613-79625 - 16F/53S	79250-79262 - 16F/53S 79600-79612 - 9F/53S	45S	61S
First - 2+1 Standard - 2+3	Second - 2+3	Second - 2+2	Second - 2+2
Not fitted	Not fitted	Not fitted	Not fitted
Not fitted	1	Not fitted	Not fitted
27 tons	20 tons	20tons 10cwt	20tons 10cwt
Vacuum	Vacuum	Vacuum	Vacuum
2 x BUT (AEC) of 150hp (111.9kW) per vehicle	-	-	-
300hp (224kW)	-	-	-
Mechanical	-	-	-
70mph (113km/h)	70mph (113km/h)	70mph (113km/h)	70mph (113km/h)
Screw	Screw	Screw	Screw
Yellow Diamond	Yellow Diamond	Yellow Diamond	Yellow Diamond
Slam	Slam	Slam	Slam
Alloy	Alloy	Alloy	Alloy
* 79191-193 modified to DTC and renumbered to 79633-635 - power equipment removed			

Right: *The huge start at modernising the non main line UK railway was the 1954 ordering of new diesel multiple unit stock, a project which revolutionised suburban and outer suburban rail travel. The original Derby Lightweight cars, assembled from alloy sheets and using a diesel-mechanical transmission had a slightly different body design from later built Derby Heavyweight stock. Seven different designs of vehicle were built, including driving power cars with standard class seating, driving power cars with composite seating, driving trailer vehicles and non-driving intermediate coaches with either standard or composite interiors. In original as built condition a four-car set of production vehicles departs from Newcastle in May 1957.* CJM-C

Derby Lightweight

Vehicle type:	DMBS
Original number range:	79900 - 79901
Introduced:	1956
Built by:	BR Derby Works
Vehicle length (over body):	57ft 6in (17.53m)
Height:	12ft 4½in (3.77m)
Width:	9ft 2in (2.79m)
Seating:	52S
Internal layout:	Second - 2+3
Gangway:	Not fitted
Toilets:	Not fitted
Weight:	27 tons
Brake type:	Vacuum
Power unit:	2 x BUT (AEC) of 150hp (111.9kW) per vehicle
Horsepower (total):	300hp (224kW)
Transmission:	Mechanical
Max speed:	70mph (113km/h)
Coupling type:	Screw
Multiple restriction:	Yellow Diamond
Body structure:	Alloy

Below: *When the original Derby Lightweight order was placed this included two single car units with a driving cab at each end. These were introduced specifically for the Banbury (Merton Street) to Buckingham/Bletchley route. The interior configuration was basically the same as a DMBS vehicle with an extra cab at the guards van end. This cab also sported two vertical exhaust pipes running up the vehicle body adjacent to the one third and two third window pillars terminating in a joint exhaust box on the roof line above the marker light. Seating was provided for 52 in the 2+3 style. The vehicles did just 10 years of service before being withdrawn as non-standard. Car No. 79900 was broken up but No. 79901 was transferred to the then growing BR Research division based in Derby, from where it was involved in a number of test projects, most notably radio survey work. It was renumbered as RDB975010 and named* **Iris.** *No. 79900 is seen at Banbury.* Michael Mensing

Vehicle type:	DMBS	DTSL	DTCL
Original number range:	79047-79082	79263-79291	79626-79632
Introduced:	1955	1955	1955
Built by:	Metro-Cammell	Metro-Cammell	Metro-Cammell
Vehicle length (over body):	57ft 0in (17.37m)	57ft 0in (17.37m)	57ft 0in (17.37m)
Height:	12ft 4½in (3.77m)	12ft 4½in (3.77m)	12ft 4½in (3.77m)
Width:	9ft 3in (2.82m)	9ft 3in (2.82m)	9ft 3in (2.82m)
Seating:	79047-79075 - 57S 79076-79082 - 53S	71S	First - 12 Second - 53
Internal layout:	2+2, 2+3	2+2, 2+3	2+1F/2+3S
Gangway:	Inner end	Inner end	Inner end
Toilets:	Not fitted	1	1
Weight:	26tons 10cwt	25 tons	25 tons
Brake type:	Vacuum	Vacuum	Vacuum
Power unit:	2 x BUT (AEC) of 150hp (111.9kW) per vehicle	- - -	-
Horsepower (total):	300hp (224kW)	-	-
Transmission:	Mechanical	-	-
Max speed:	70mph (113km/h)	70mph (113km/h)	70mph (113km/h)
Coupling type:	Screw	Screw	Screw
Multiple restriction:	Yellow Diamond	Yellow Diamond	Yellow Diamond
Door type:	Slam	Slam	Slam
Body structure:	Alloy	Alloy	Alloy

Below: *When the BTC lightweight DMU orders were placed, Metro-Cammell was awarded a contract to supply 36 two-car sets, the first DMU stock of standard design built by an outside contractor. These sets paved the way for the traditional Metro-Cammell body design we saw for many years. With its body mounted jumper sockets, identifying a lightweight rather than a standard vehicle, DMBS No. M79076 is illustrated. Note the Metro-Cammell branding in the destination indicator box, showing this was likely to have been some form of press or demonstration run.* CJM-C

Swindon

Vehicle type:	DMBSL	DMSL	TFBK
Original number range:	79083-79111	79155-79168	79440-79447
Introduced:	1956	1956	1956
Built by:	BR Swindon Works	BR Swindon Works	BR Swindon Works
Vehicle length (over body):	64ft 6in (19.66m)	64ft 6in (19.66m)	64ft 6in (19.66m)
Height:	12ft 9½in (3.82m)	12ft 9½in (3.82m)	12ft 9½in (3.82m)
Width:	9ft 3in (2.82m)	9ft 3in (2.82m)	9ft 3in (2.82m)
Seating:	52S	64S	18F/12U
Internal layout:	Second - 2+2	Second - 2+2	First - 2+1 Unclassified - 2+2
Gangway:	79083-090/095 - Throughout 79091-094/096-111 - Inner end	Throughout	Throughout
Toilets:	1	1	1
Weight:	38 tons	39tons 3cwt	34 tons
Brake type:	Vacuum	Vacuum	Vacuum
Power unit:	2 x BUT (AEC) of 150hp (111.9kW) per vehicle	2 x BUT (AEC) of 150hp (111.9kW) per vehicle	-
Horsepower (total):	300hp (224kW)	300hp (224kW)	-
Transmission:	Mechanical	Mechanical	-
Max speed:	70mph (113km/h)	70mph (113km/h)	70mph (113km/h)
Coupling type:	Outer - buck-eye Inner - screw	Outer - buck-eye Inner - screw	Screw
Multiple restriction:	White Circle	White Circle	White Circle
Door type:	Slam	Slam	Slam
Body structure:	Alloy	Alloy	Alloy
Notes:	Intermediate: 79083-090/095 fitted with side driving cab and gangway end. End: 79091-094/096-111 fitted with full width driving cab		

TFK
79470-79482
1956
BR Swindon Works
64ft 6in (19.66m)
12ft 9½in (3.82m)
9ft 3in (2.82m)
42F
First 2+1
Throughout
1
33tons 9cwt
Vacuum
-
-
-
70mph (113km/h)
Screw
White Circle
Slam
Alloy

Below Left, Above and Below: *Prior to the BTC Modernisation Plan, a 1952 report recommended the design and building of express diesel railcars (DMUs) for use on the Edinburgh to Glasgow route. Swindon produced 21 three-car sets for this purpose on 64ft 6in underframes, based on Mk 1 hauled-stock profile. To enable six car fully gangwayed sets to operate, a number of driving cars, deemed intermediate cab cars, had a small driving cab on one side and a central gangway; thus vehicles of the DMBSL type came in two designs. Passenger seating in second class was in open saloons, while first class passengers had the luxury of side corridor compartments each carrying six passengers. When built, sets were painted in green, offset by a cream body stripe and whisker ends. The whisker ends of the gangway fitted vehicles looked especially attractive. Single stencil letter route indicators were originally fitted. On the left we see a full width driving car at Newport with a stencil route display 'A' on the front end. Above we see an intermediate driving car on the rear of a train. In the view below we see DMBSL 79089 at Birmingham Snow Hill. Above/Left:* CJM-C *Below:* Michael Mensing

Cowlairs

Vehicle type:	DMBS	DTC
Number range:	79998	79999
Introduced:	1958	1958
Original builder:	BR Derby Works	BR Derby Works
Modified as BEMU:	BR Cowlairs Works	BR Cowlairs Works
Vehicle length (over body):	57ft 6in (17.53m)	57ft 6in (17.53m)
Height:	12ft 4½in (3.77m)	12ft 4½in (3.77m)
Width:	9ft 2in (2.79m)	9ft 2in (2.79m)
Seating:	52S	12F/53S
Internal layout:	2+3	2+2F, 2+3S
Gangway:	Inner end	Inner end
Toilets:	1	-
Weight:	37ton 10cwt	32ton 10cwt
Brake type:	Vacuum	Vacuum
Power:	216 lead-acid cells	-
Horsepower (total):	268hp (200kW)	
Transmission:	Electric - 2 x 134hp (100kW) Siemens-Schuckert	-
Max speed:	70mph (113km/h)	70mph (113km/h)
Coupling type:	Screw	Screw
Multiple restriction:	Within type	Within type
Body structure:	Alloy	Alloy
Notes:	Became DB975003 Lab 16 *Gemini*	Became DB975004 Lab 16 *Gemini*

Below Left: *In the late 1950s when the new generation of diesel multiple units was introduced, thoughts turned to developing the Derby Lightweight design into vehicles which could have an electric transmission, with power coming from on-board rechargeable batteries; this followed breakthroughs in battery power retention systems. A pair of Derby Lightweight DMU cars were rebuilt by BR Cowlairs Works in Glasgow to trial battery-electric traction technology. Power was provided by large lead-acid batteries carried in underside pull out boxes which could easily be changed. Traction was provided by two 134hp (100kW) Siemens-Schuckert traction motors mounted under the brake van of the DMBS vehicle. To test the battery-electric system in active service, the Scottish Region agreed to use the Royal Deeside line from Aberdeen to Ballater, where special charging equipment was installed at both ends of the route. As battery technology improved in the 1960s, different designs of battery were tested, with at least one design giving cause for major concern following several small battery related fires. The set was still to be seen in the Aberdeen area up until 1962, but was then officially withdrawn, spending time stored at Aberdeen, Inverurie and Glasgow Hyndland. In 1966 the set was taken over by BR Research at the RTC Derby where it saw use by the Train Control Group at the RTC as well as on the Mickleover Test Track. The pull out battery boxes are seen in the left illustration.* CJM-C

Right Top: *The battery-electric twin-set is seen departing from Aberdeen bound for Ballater in the late 1950s. Why the set is carrying a tail light on the front is not known. Only a limited number of drivers based at Aberdeen were trained on the sets' operation, which by all accounts from those remembering the train is service was described as very quiet, generally smooth but a little rough at speeds in excess of about 35mph (56km/h). The set could hook up to a diesel or steam locomotive but could not operate in multiple with any other stock.* CJM-C

Right Middle: *Taken over by BR Research at Derby in 1966, the battery-electric set was used for train control tests both at the Railway Technical Centre, Derby, as well as on the Mickleover test track, where this illustration was taken. For its Research role, the vehicles were renumbered to RDB975003 and RDB975004, and allocated the name* **Gemini**. *The set remained in test service until 1984 when it was withdrawn and sold for preservation. Firstly it was destined for the ill-fated West Yorkshire Transport Museum and then went to the East Lancashire Railway. In 2001 the set was sold to the Royal Deeside Railway where it is now under restoration.* CJM

Below: *As built, the battery-electric set is seen from its powered end. Note the roof boards giving both route and destination.* CJM-C

Class 100

Vehicle type:	DMBS	DTCL (DTSL)
Original number range:	50339-50358, 51108-51127	56094-56113, 56300-56319
TOPS class number:	100	100
Original classification:	100	143
Revised number range:	Note: 1	Note: 2
Classification:	DMBS	DTCL
Introduced:	1957	1957
Built by:	Gloucester RCW	Gloucester RCW
Vehicle length (over body):	57ft 6in	57ft 6in
Height:	12ft 8½in	12ft 8½in
Width:	9ft 3in	9ft 3in
Seating:	52S	12F/54S
Internal layout:	2+3S	2+2F/2+3S
Gangway:	Inner end	Inner end
Toilets:	Not fitted	1
Weight:	38tons 5cwt	25 tons
Brake type:	Vacuum	Vacuum
Power unit:	2 x BUT (AEC) of 150hp (111.9kW) per vehicle	-
Horsepower (total):	300hp (224kW)	-
Transmission:	Mechanical	-
Max speed:	70mph (113km/h)	70mph (113km/h)
Coupling type:	Screw	Screw
Multiple restriction:	Blue Square	Blue Square
Door type:	Slam	Slam
Special features:	-	-
Body structure:	Steel	Steel
Notes:	1: Only vehicles 50351/353/355/356/358 renumbered to 53351/353/355/356/358	Most later declassified to DTSL. 2: Only vehicles 56106/108/111/113 renumbered to 54106/10

Built by the Gloucester Railway Carriage and Wagon Co of Gloucester, these 40 twin-sets were destined for general branch line use and when originally introduced went to the London Midland and Scottish Regions; in later years a number were transferred to the Eastern Region. When first introduced cars were painted in BR green livery, off-set by a cream mid-height band. Two character route indicators and a destination blind were fitted. Led by DMBS car No. 50354, a Gloucester set leads a Metro-Cammell twin-set into Stechford with the 12.50 Birmingham New Street to Coventry on 8 September 1959. Michael Mensing

Above: *In the days before electrification of Great Northern line services from King's Cross, Finsbury Park had a small allocation of Gloucester Class 100 sets to operate with examples of other builds on outer suburban routes. On 24 July 1971 a BR rail-blue liveried Class 100 DMBS leads Class 101 Metro-Cammell vehicles into one of the suburban bays at London King's Cross with a lunchtime service from Hertford North. By this time the destination indicator appears to have no blind and the alpha-numeric route code shows B2. In King's Cross loco yard we see a Class 31.* J. Rickard

Below: *With a facelifted front end to remove the original alpha-numeric route indicator, Class 100 DMBS No. M51110 arrives at Bath on 1 August 1982 with a Sunday service from Bristol to Weymouth. At the time this was a Tyseley vehicle which had somehow reached Bristol and was pressed into service with a Class 101 Metro-Cammell trailer second No. M59543 and a Cravens Class 105 DMCL (declassified) No. M50812. The last Class 100s were withdrawn in June 1989.* Mike Ware

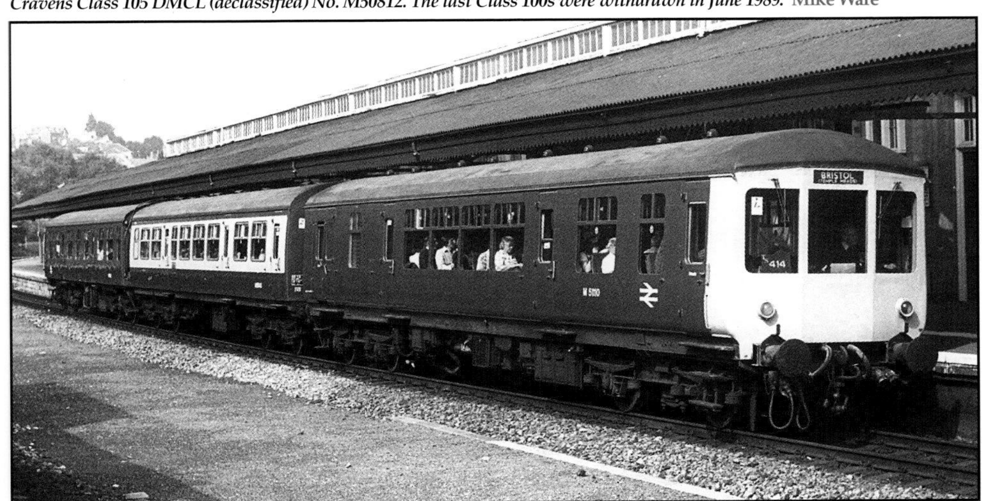

Class 101, 101/1

Original classification:	101/1 (102/1)	101/2 (102/2)	144/147
Revised classification:	101	101	101
Vehicle type:	DMCL ++	DMBS	DTCL +++
Original number range:	50138-50151, 50158-50163, 50168-50197, 50234-50245, 50260-50269, 50321-50338, 51495-51539, 51802-51808	50152-50157, 50164-50167, 50198-50233, 50246-50248, 50250-50259, 50290-50320, 51174-51253, 51425-51470, 51795-51801	56050-56093, 56218-56220, 56332-56411
Revised number range:	50xxx renumbered to 53xxx series	50xxx renumbered to 53xxx series	56xxx renumbered to 54xxx
Introduced:	1956-59	1956-59	1957-58
Built by:	Metro-Cammell	Metro-Cammell	Metro-Cammell
Vehicle length (over body):	57ft 0in (17.37m)	57ft 0in (17.37m)	57ft 0in (17.37m)
Height:	12ft 4½in (3.77m)	12ft 4½in (3.77m)	12ft 4½in (3.77m)
Width:	9ft 3in (2.81m)	9ft 3in (2.81m)	9ft 3in (2.81m)
Seating:	12F/53S or 12F/45S declassified - 57-65S	44-52S	12F/53S or 12F/45S, declassified - 53-57S
Internal layout:	2+1F/2+3S	2+3S	2+1F/2+3S
Gangway:	Inner end	Inner end	Inner end
Toilets:	1	Not fitted	1
Weight:	32.5 tonnes	32.5 tonnes	26.5 tonnes
Brake type:	Vacuum	Vacuum	Vacuum
Power unit:	2 x BUT (AEC) of 150hp (111.8kW) per vehicle	2 x BUT (AEC) of 150hp (111.8kW) per vehicle	- -
Horsepower (total):	300hp (224hp)	300hp (224hp)	
Transmission:	Mechanical	Mechanical	-
Max speed:	70mph (113km/h)	70mph (113km/h)	70mph (113km/h)
Coupling type:	Screw	Screw	Screw
Multiple restriction:	Blue Square	Blue Square	Blue Square
Door type:	Slam	Slam	Slam
Special features:	-	-	-
Body structure:	Steel	Steel	Steel
Notes:	++ Later most were declassified to DMSL	Cars 50290-292 originally fitted with 2 x Rolls Royce 150hp (111.8kW) engines	+++ Later declassified

Left: *One of the largest classes of DMMU constructed under the Modernisation Plan were the Metro-Cammell sets, later classified as 101, many of which remained in service until the end of first generation DMU stock on the main line. Vehicles of some six different types were built in 1956 and 1959 being allocated to all operating areas except the Southern Region. The design was one of the most successful. A four-car Metro-Cammell formation is seen at Birmingham in the late 1950s with a Driving Motor Composite Lavatory (DMCL) leading. The livery is the striking BR green offset by cream bodyside band and whiskers on the front end. The original two character route indicator appears to have slipped and is not showing the correct code.* Michael Mensing

162/164	101	171
101	101	101
TSL	TBS	TCL
59042-59048, 59060-59072, 59086-59091, 59100-59109*, 59302-59306, 59569-59572,	59049-59055, 59073-59085, 59092-59097, 59112-59113	59114-59131, 59523-59568, 59686-59692
-	-	-
-		
1956-59	1956-58	1958-59
Metro-Cammell	Metro-Cammell	Metro-Cammell
57ft 0in (17.37m)	57ft 0in (17.37m)	57ft 0in (17.37m)
12ft 4½in (3.77m)	12ft 4½in (3.77m)	12ft 4½in (3.77m)
9ft 3in (2.81m)	9ft 3in (2.81m)	9ft 3in (2.81m)
61-71S	45-65S	12F/53S, declassified - 65S
2+3	2+3	2+2F/2+3S
Throughout	Throughout	Inner end
1	Not fitted	1
25.5 tonnes	25.5 tonnes	25.5 tonnes
Vacuum	Vacuum	Vacuum
-	-	-
-	-	-
-	-	-
70mph (113km/h)	70mph (113km/h)	70mph (113km/h)
Screw	Screw	Screw
Blue Square	Blue Square	Blue Square
Slam	Slam	Slam
-	-	-
Steel	Steel	Steel
* 59100-109 ex-Class 111 vehicles	Most later declassified to TSL	Most later declassified to TSL

Right: *Repaints of DMMU stock after 1967 saw standard corporate rail blue applied, together with full yellow warning ends. At the same time, underframes were finished in black and in the main buffer beams were painted black, but a number of repaints from Doncaster Works emerged with the buffer beams finished in red. With its front end panel flush after the removal of the redundant alpha-numeric display, a DMCL, declassified to a DMSL, is seen nearest the camera at Hexham.* CJM-C

Class 101, 101/1

Above: *Although a large number of different builders produced DMMU stock under the Modernisation Plan, in the main a standard Blue Square multiple control system was adopted, meaning sets from different classes could be coupled together and operated by one driver. On 31 January 1980, rail blue-liveried No. E51430, a DMBS vehicle, leads a train at Leeds.* CJM

Below: *After rail blue, a number of Class 101s emerged in the all white livery off-set by a broad blue bodyside band, a colour scheme which looked very smart. On 16 May 1980, Class 101 DTCL No. 56057 is seen near Sandy with a Hitchin bound service. To avoid a conflict under TOPS with new Class 56 locomotives, 56xxx DMU numbers were changed to 54xxx in the mid 1980s.* CJM

Above: *For many years the standard livery for the Class 101 sets in either two or three car formation was blue and grey, as shown on set No. P825, led by DMBS No. 53165, the original 50165. The application of set numbers either painted on or on boards started in the 1970s, when it was attempted to operate semi-fixed formations. On the Western Region prefix letters L for London, P for Plymouth, B for Bristol and S for Swansea were used.* CJM

Right Middle: *With the sectorisation of the railways a number of new colour schemes were adopted. One of the brightest was the red, white and blue of Network SouthEast, applied to a handful of sets mainly allocated to Old Oak Common for Thames line operations. Sporting a central headlight, set No. L841, with DMBS No. 53312 nearest the camera, is seen at Old Oak Common depot.* CJM

Right Below: *Sporting Regional Railways grey and two-tone blue, Class 101 twin-set No. 101680, with DMBS No. 53204 leading, departs from Edale on 24 October 1995 on a Sheffield to Manchester service.* CJM

Class 101, 101/1

Left Top: *Class 101 stock operating in Scotland, mainly in and around Edinburgh and Glasgow, emerged in the Glasgow PTE orange and dark brown livery in the 1990s, a striking contrast from the original green and blue colours. With a DMSL vehicle leading, set No. 101693 is seen at Whifflet on 4 June 1996 with a service to Glasgow Central.* CJM

Left Middle: *Interior of a Metro-Cammell Class 101 Driving Motor Composite vehicle, viewed from the second class seating end looking towards the first class and driving cab. The standard seating is in 2+3 bus style, with above seat luggage racks. Forward of the transverse walkway is a sliding door giving access into the first class area with 2+2 seating. In advance of that is a further sliding door giving access to the driving cab.* CJM

Below: *One of the remaining North West operated Class 101 three-car sets was repainted in 1960s green livery during its final years in passenger traffic based in the Manchester and Chester area. Here the Trailer Standard Lavatory No. 59539 is seen at Chester depot. This vehicle was an original Trailer Composite Lavatory, which in later years operated with the first class area declassified and then removed, replaced by standard class seating.* CJM

Original classification:	102/1	102/2
Revised classification:	101	101
Vehicle type:	DMC	DMBS
Original number range:	51495-51540, 51802-51808	51425-51470, 51795-51801
Renumbering:	-	-
Introduced:	1959	1959
Built by:	Metro-Cammell	Metro-Cammell
Vehicle length (over body):	57ft 0in (17.37m)	57ft 0in (17.37m)
Height:	12ft 4½in (3.77m)	12ft 4½in (3.77m)
Width:	9ft 3in (2.81m)	9ft 3in (2.81m)
Seating:	12F/53S	44-52S
Internal layout:	2+1F/2+3S	2+3S
Gangway:	Inner end	Inner end
Toilets:	1	Not fitted
Weight:	32.5 tonnes	32.5 tonnes
Brake type:	Vacuum	Vacuum
Power unit:	2 x Leyland of 150hp (111.8kW) per vehicle	2 x Leyland of 150hp (111.8kW) per vehicle
Horsepower (total):	300hp (224hp)	300hp (224hp)
Transmission:	Mechanical	Mechanical
Max speed:	70mph (113km/h)	70mph (113km/h)
Coupling type:	Screw	Screw
Multiple restriction:	Blue Square	Blue Square
Door type:	Slam	Slam
Special features:	-	-
Body structure:	Steel	Steel
Notes:	Absorbed into Class 101	Absorbed into Class 101

Below: *Later considered part of the standard Metro-Cammell Class 101 fleet, these vehicles were originally constructed with Leyland power units rather than AEC and were thus deemed as a different class being given the identity Class 102. In all other ways the vehicles were standard Class 101s. Vehicle No. 51436, an Eastern Region allocated DMBS, is seen inside the long closed BREL Doncaster DMU repair shop in April 1980. This view is a good guide to the inner end gangway and exhaust arrangement.* CJM

Class 103

Vehicle type:	DMBSL	DTCL
Classification:	103	103
Original classification:	103	145
Original number range:	50395-50414	56150-56169
Revised number range:	-	-
Classification:	DMBSL	DTCL
Introduced:	1957	1957
Built by:	Park Royal Vehicles	Park Royal Vehicles
Vehicle length (over body):	57ft 6in (17.53m)	57ft 6in (17.53m)
Height:	12ft 4½in (3.77m)	12ft 4½in (3.77m)
Width:	9ft 3in (2.82m)	9ft 3in (2.82m)
Seating:	52S	16F/48S
Internal layout:	2+3S	2+2F/2+3S
Gangway:	Inner end	Inner end
Toilets:	1	1
Weight:	33ton 8cwt	26tons 7cwt
Brake type:	Vacuum	Vacuum
Power unit:	2 x BUT (AEC) of 150hp (111.8kW) per vehicle	-
Horsepower (total):	300hp (224kW)	-
Transmission:	Mechanical	-
Max speed:	70mph (113km/h)	70mph (113km/h)
Coupling type:	Screw	Screw
Multiple restriction:	Blue Square	Blue Square
Door type:	Slam	Slam
Special features:	-	-
Body structure:	Alloy and steel	Alloy and steel
Notes:		

Below: *With the London-based Park Royal Vehicles having some previous experience of train building with early Great Western stock and some export carriages to Ireland, the company entered the bidding process in the mid 1950s for part of the huge Modernisation Plan order. The company was awarded a contract to build 20 two-car sets. These closely resembled the structural style of the original Derby Lightweight vehicles. Park Royal provided seating for 52 in the DMBSL and 16 first and 48 second in the DTCL vehicles, using 2+2 for first and 2+3 for second class seats. Painted in green livery but with a small yellow front end warning panel, a Park Royal twin set with a DMBSL vehicle leading approaches Bentley Heath Crossing, Knowle & Dorridge, in August 1966.* Michael Mensing

Right: Showing the original as built livery style with an all green body off-set by a cream bodyside band and cream front end whiskers, a twin-set is seen with DTCL No. M56164 nearest the camera. Although numbered in the series which later clashed with loco numbers in the TOPS period, the Class 103 cars were never renumbered into the 53xxx and 54xxx series. P. J. Sharp

Left: With its unpowered DTCL leading, a Class 103 set passes Mesty Croft near Sandwell on 10 August 1963 with a Walsall to Dudley local service. Two Class 103 vehicles remained in operation after the rest were withdrawn, as vehicles 50396 and 56162 were taken over by BR Research at Derby and modified as Lab Coach No. 5 RDB975089 and RDB975090 or TRIM train used for track instrumentation. Michael Mensing

Right: The Class 103 sets, painted in BR rail blue, were not included in the DMMU refurbishment project, as they were non-standard in many ways. Some vehicles continued working on the London Midland Region until spring 1983. In this 1 November 1980 view, Cars No. M56156 and M50408 are seen at Crewe with a train bound for Chester. Note that the original two-character route indicator display has been plated over. John Tuffs

Class 104

Vehicle type:	DMBS	DMCL	DTCL
Classification:	104	104	104
Original classification:	104/2	104/1	140
Original number range:	50420-50423, 50428-50479, 50532-50541, 50594-50598	50424-50427, 50480-50531, 50542-50593	56175-56189
Revised number range:	50xxx became 53xxx	50xxx became 53xxx	56xxx became 54xxx
Introduced:	1957-58	1957	1958
Built by:	Birmingham RC&W	Birmingham RC&W	Birmingham RC&W
Vehicle length (over body):	57ft 6in (17.53m)	57ft 6in (17.53m)	57ft 6in (17.53m)
Height:	12ft 8¾in (3.88m)	12ft 8¾in (3.88m)	12ft 8¾in (3.88m)
Width:	9ft 3in (2.82m)	9ft 3in (2.82m)	9ft 3in (2.82m)
Seating:	52S	12F/54S, or 12F/51S, declassified - 63-66S	12F/54S, or 12F/51S, declassified - 63-66S
Internal layout:	3+2	3+2	3+2
Gangway:	Inner end	Inner end	Inner end
Toilets:	Not fitted	1	1
Weight:	31.5 tonnes	31.5 tonnes	24.5 tonnes
Brake type:	Vacuum	Vacuum	Vacuum
Power unit:	2 x BUT (Leyland) of 150hp (111.8kW) per vehicle	2 x BUT (Leyland) of 150hp (111.8kW) per vehicle	-
Horsepower (total):	300hp (224kW)	300hp (224kW)	-
Transmission:	Mechanical	Mechanical	-
Max speed:	70mph (113km/h)	70mph (113km/h)	70mph (113km/h)
Coupling type:	Screw	Screw	Screw
Multiple restriction:	Blue Square	Blue Square	Blue Square
Door type:	Slam	Slam	Slam
Body structure:	Steel	Steel	Steel
Notes:		Most later declassified	Most later declassified

Vehicle type:	TSL	TBSL	DHBS
Classification:	104	104	104
Original classification:	160	166	-
Original number range:	59188-59208, 59230-59234	59209-59229, 59240-59244	50446
Revised number range:	-	-	78851
Introduced:	1958	1958	Modified 1982
Built by:	Birmingham RC&W	Birmingham RC&W	Birmingham RC&W
Vehicle length (over body):	57ft 6in (17.53m)	57ft 6in (17.53m)	57ft 6in (17.53m)
Height:	12ft 8¾in (3.88m)	12ft 8¾in (3.88m)	12ft 8¾in (3.88m)
Width:	9ft 3in (2.82m)	9ft 3in (2.82m)	9ft 3in (2.82m)
Seating:	68S	50S	52S
Internal layout:	3+2	3+2	3+2
Gangway:	Throughout	Throughout	Inner end
Toilets:	1	1	Not fitted
Weight:	22.5 tonnes	23.5 tonnes	31.5 tonnes
Brake type:	Vacuum	Vacuum	Vacuum
Power unit:	-	-	1 x BUT (Leyland) of 150hp (111.8kW)
Horsepower (total):	-	-	150hp (111.8kW)
Transmission:	-	-	Mechanical
Max speed:	70mph (113km/h)	70mph (113km/h)	70mph (113km/h)
Coupling type:	Screw	Screw	Screw
Multiple restriction:	Blue Square	Blue Square	Blue Square
Door type:	Slam	Slam	Slam
Body structure:	Steel	Steel	Steel
Notes:			Trial development of single engined vehicle

TCL
104
169
59137-59187

-
1957
Birmingham RC&W
57ft 6in (17.53m)
12ft 8¾in (3.88m)
9ft 3in (2.82m)
12F/54S, declassified 66S

3+2
Throughout
1
22.5 tonnes
Vacuum
-

-
-
70mph (113km/h)
Screw
Blue Square
Slam
Alloy and Steel
Most later declassified

DHC
104
-
50521
78601
Modified 1982
Birmingham RC&W
57ft 6in (17.53m)
12ft 8¾in (3.88m)
9ft 3in (2.82m)
12F/54S - declassified -66S
3+2
Inner end
1
31.5 tonnes
Vacuum
1 x BUT (Leyland) of
150hp (111.8kW)
150hp (111.8kW)
Mechanical
70mph (113km/h)
Screw
Blue Square
Slam
Steel
Trial development of
single engined vehicle

Above: *After BR's own works and Metro-Cammell, Birmingham RC&W was the next largest manufacturer of DMMU stock, with 300 vehicles later to become Class 104. A three-car set is seen near Cannock in September 1963 forming a Stoke to Birmingham service.* Michael Mensing

Below: *Originally second class and later standard class seating on the BRC&W fleet was in the 2+3 layout, except by end doors where it was in the 2+2 style. This interior shows the later BR blue/green moquette.* CJM

Class 104

Above: *Built as a DMCL and later reclassified for all standard class occupancy as a DMSL, vehicle No. 53531 is seen from its gangway end. Note the bars on the passenger door windows to stop people hanging out.* CJM

Left: *With its distinctive front end shaping and ventilation grille under the non-driving window, a Class 104 twin-set, led by a DMSL approaches Willesden Junction after working a Barking service.* CJM

Below: *DMBS M53459 is seen at Buxton running as set BX492. In the middle road is a Class 104 TS clearly showing the large end windows fitted to this design.* CJM

Above and Below: *The Class 104s remained in service well into sectorisation with a handful allocated to Network SouthEast being repainted in the operator's red, white and blue livery. The sets operated from Old Oak Common on Thames and North London services frequently with vehicles from other design classes. Having standard Blue Square controls this allowed huge flexibility in cross coupling. In the above view recorded at Acton on 13 July 1990 set No. L703 heads west with a Paddington to Slough service with a DMBS vehicle at the front. In the view below set No. L492 stands 'on shed' at Old Oak Common with vehicle No. 53459 nearest the camera. Both:* CJM

Class 105 / 106

Vehicle type:	DMBS	DMCL	DTCL
Classification:	105	105	105
Original classification:	105/2 or 106+	105/1	141
Original number range:	50249, 50359-50394, 50752-50784, 51255-51301 51472-51493	50785-50817	56114-56149, 56412-56483
Revised number range:	53249, 53359-53394, 53752-53784	53785-53817	54114-54149, 54412-54483
Classification:	DMBS	DMC	DTC
Introduced:	1956-59	1957	1956-58
Built by:	Cravens RC&W	Cravens RC&W	Cravens RC&W
Vehicle length (over body):	57ft 6in (17.53m)	57ft 6in (17.53m)	57ft 6in (17.53m)
Height:	12ft 7in (3.84m)	12ft 7in (3.84m)	12ft 7in (3.84m)
Width:	9ft 3in (2.82m)	9ft 3in (2.82m)	9ft 3in (2.82m)
Seating:	52S	12F/51S or declassified - 63S	12F/51S or declassified - 63S
Internal layout:	2+3	2+3	2+3
Gangway:	Inner end	Inner end	Inner end
Toilets:	Not fitted	1	1
Weight:	29.5 tonnes	30.5 tonnes	23.5 tonnes
Brake type:	Vacuum	Vacuum	Vacuum
Power unit:	2 x BUT (AEC) of 150hp (111.8kW) per vehicle	2 x BUT (AEC) of 150hp (111.8kW) per vehicle	-
Horsepower (total):	300hp (224kW)	300hp (224kW)	-
Transmission:	Mechanical	Mechanical	-
Max speed:	70mph (113km/h)	70mph (113km/h)	70mph (113km/h)
Coupling type:	Screw	Screw	Screw
Multiple restriction:	Blue Square	Blue Square	Blue Square
Door type:	Slam	Slam	Slam
Special features:	-	-	-
Body structure:	Steel	Steel	Steel
Notes:	+ Class 106 originally allocated to cars fitted with Leyland engines	Later declassified to DMSL	Later declassified to DTSL

Left: *Cravens of Sheffield was awarded several contracts by the BTC for two- and three-car DMMU vehicles, introduced between 1956 and 1959, with four types of vehicle produced. The distinctive Cravens front end body styling of this and the Class 112/113 fleets always rendered the Cravens design recognisable. A twin-set, with DTCL No. SC52463 nearest the camera, departs from Aberdeen for Ballater in spring 1959 painted in green with cream body bands and speed whiskers.* CJM-C

Right: *After withdrawal, preservation beckoned for several Class 105 vehicles. Here a two-car set with DTCL No. 56121 nearest the camera is seen at Crowcombe Heathfield on the West Somerset Railway. This set shows a non-authentic livery, as in green the set would have retained its two-character route indicator and would not have had a roof mounted marker light.* CJM

TCL
105
170
59307-59325

-

TCL
1956
Cravens RC&W
57ft 6in (17.53m)
12ft 7in (3.84m)
9ft 3in (2.82m)
12F/54S or 69S

2+3
Throughout
1
23 tonnes
Vacuum
-

-
-
70mph (113km/h)
Screw
Blue Square
Slam
-
Steel
Later declassified
to TSL

Top: *Displaying rail blue livery with a sealed up route indicator, a Class 105 twin set with DMBS No. 51284 leading departs from Doncaster on 20 November 1984 bound for Sheffield.* CJM

Above: *Led by DTCL 56419, a rail blue two-car set arrives at Stewartby with a service from Bedford to Bletchley.* CJM

Class 107

Vehicle type:	DMBS	DMCL, later DMSL	TSL
Classification:	107	107	107
Original classification:	107/1	107/2	161
Original number range:	51985-52010	52011-52036	59782-59807
Revised number range:	-	-	-
Classification:	DMBS	DMCL	TSL
Introduced:	1960-61	1960-61	1960-61
Built by:	BR Derby Works	BR Derby Works	BR Derby Works
Vehicle length (over body):	58ft 1in (17.7m)	58ft 1in (17.7m)	58ft 1in (17.7m)
Height:	12ft 4½in (3.77m)	12ft 4½in (3.77m)	12ft 4½in (3.77m)
Width:	9ft 3in (2.82m)	9ft 3in (2.82m)	9ft 3in (2.82m)
Seating:	52S	12F/53S or declassified - 65S	71S
Internal layout:	2+3S	2+2F/2+3S	2+3S
Gangway:	Inner end	Inner end	Throughout
Toilets:	Not fitted	1	1
Weight:	35 tonnes	35.5 tonnes	28.5 tonnes
Brake type:	Vacuum	Vacuum	Vacuum
Power unit:	2 x BUT (Leyland) of 150hp (111.8kW) per vehicle	2 x BUT (Leyland) of 150hp (111.8kW) per vehicle	-
Horsepower (total):	300hp (224kW)	300hp (224kW)	-
Transmission:	Mechanical	Mechanical	-
Max speed:	70mph (113km/h)	70mph (113km/h)	70mph (113km/h)
Coupling type:	Screw	Screw	Screw
Multiple restriction:	Blue Square	Blue Square	Blue Square
Door type:	Slam	Slam	Slam
Special features:	-	-	-
Body structure:	Steel	Steel	Steel

Below: *Often deemed as the Derby Heavyweight DMMUs, this fleet of Derby products on short 58ft underframes were some of the heaviest emerging from Derby Works. Having the standard Derby front style, these 26 three-car sets were introduced in 1960-61 for Glasgow area services. Originally in green the sets were repainted in rail blue and then blue-grey, as shown on set No. 107433 which also carries the short-lived 'Trans-Clyde' bodyside branding. The DMBS car which seated 52 second class passengers is nearest the camera.* CJM

Above: *Repaints after the application of blue and grey saw the Class 107s emerge in Strathclyde PTE orange, complete with black window surrounds. Set No. 107747 is seen passing through Edinburgh Princes Street Gardens in autumn 1989 with the set's DMSL nearest the camera.* CJM

Below: *By 1990 several of the intermediate trailer seconds had been withdrawn and to cover for new stock on delivery a number of power twin sets were formed for operation in the Edinburgh local area. With its DMBS nearest the camera, set No. 107026 awaits its next duty at Edinburgh Waverley on 12 September 1990.* CJM

Class 108

Vehicle type:	DMBS	DMCL	DTCL
Classification:	108	108	108
Original classification:	108/1	108/2	142
Original number range:	50599-50629, 50924-50935, 50938-50987, 51416-51424, 51901-51950	50630-50646, 51561-51572, 52037-52065	56190-56215
Revised number range:	50xxx renumbered to 53xxx	50xxx renumbered to 53xx	56xxx renumbered to 54xxx
Classification:	DMBS	DMCL	DTCL
Introduced:	1958-60	1958-60	1958-60
Built by:	BR Derby Works	BR Derby Works	BR Derby Works
Vehicle length (over body):	57ft 6in (17.53m)	57ft 6in (17.53m)	57ft 6in (17.53m)
Height:	12ft 4½in (3.77m)	12ft 4½in (3.77m)	12ft 4½in (3.77m)
Width:	9ft 2in (2.79m)	9ft 2in (2.79m)	9ft 2in (2.79m)
Seating:	52S	12F/53S or declassified - 65S	12F/53S or declassified - 65S
Internal layout:	2+3	2+3	2+3
Gangway:	Inner end	Inner end	Inner end
Toilets:	Not fitted	1	1
Weight:	29.5 tonnes	29.5 tonnes	21.5 tonnes
Brake type:	Vacuum	Vacuum	Vacuum
Power unit:	2 x BUT (Leyland) of 150hp (111.8kW) per vehicle	2 x BUT (Leyland) of 150hp (111.8kW) per vehicle	-
Horsepower (total):	300hp (224kW)	300hp (224kW)	-
Transmission:	Mechanical	Mechanical	-
Max speed:	70mph (113km/h)	70mph (113km/h)	70mph (113km/h)
Coupling type:	Screw	Screw	Screw
Multiple restriction:	Blue Square	Blue Square	Blue Square
Door type:	Slam	Slam	Slam
Special features:	-	-	-
Body structure:	Steel	Steel	Steel
Notes:		Later declassified to DMSL	Later declassified to DTSL

TBSL	TSL
108	108
167	161++
59245-59250	59380-59390
TBSL	TSL++
1958	1958
BR Derby Works	BR Derby Works
57ft 6in (17.53m)	57ft 6in (17.53m)
12ft 4½in (3.77m)	12ft 4½in (3.77m)
9ft 2in (2.79m)	9ft 2in (2.79m)
50S	68S
2+3	2+3
Throughout	Throughout
1	1
23.5 tonnes	22.5 tonnes
Vacuum	Vacuum
-	-
-	-
-	-
70mph (113km/h)	70mph (113km/h)
Screw	Screw
Blue Square	Blue Square
Slam	Slam
-	-
Steel	Steel
	++ Same classified as Class 107 TS vehicles

Below Left: *A total of 333 vehicles of this design, classified as 108, were constructed by Derby Works between 1958 and 1960, mainly for branch line work on the Eastern and London Midland Regions. Five different vehicle types were constructed, enabling two, three or four-car formations to be operated. Class 108s stayed in service until the end of 1993 and a large number entered the world of preservation. Painted in green livery with a small yellow panel and still retaining its two-character route display, a four-car set is seen in the Liverpool suburban area with a DMBS vehicle nearest the camera.* CJM-C

Below: *Painted in all-over rail blue with a full yellow warning end and an out of use two-character route display, an original Driving Motor Composite Lavatory (DMCL), now declassified to a Driving Motor Standard Lavatory, No. 50634 of the Eastern Region fleet is seen at Leeds in November 1980. On the right is a Metro-Cammell Class 101, clearly showing the builder differences between these two designs.* CJM

Class 108

Left Top: *The Class 108 fleet was included in the DMMU refurbishment plan of the 1970s, with a large number of vehicles passing through main works for classified attention; this was mainly carried out at BREL Derby Litchurch Lane and Doncaster sites. Painted in blue and grey livery, a two-car Class 108 set formed of a DMBS (53956) and a DTCL (54238) is seen on the Cumbrian Coast route near Netherton on 17 July 1986 forming the 10.35 Preston to Carlisle service.* CJM

Left Middle: *Again with its DMBS nearest the camera, a Class 108 two-car set stops at Long Preston on 15 July 1986 forming the 09.00 Carlisle to Leeds service via the Settle and Carlisle route. At the time some of the trains on this route were marketed under 'The Dalesman' banner, hence the tailboard on the train. The DMBS vehicles of Class 108 seated 52 second class passengers.* CJM

Below: *A number of the Class 108s operating in the Leeds area, together with vehicles from other classes, and were operated in the 1980s under the Metro Train brand, with South Yorkshire branding applied to the bodyside. Still retaining first class accommodation, Class 108 DTCL No. E56189, together with DMBS No. E50603, is seen at Leeds City station on 21 May 1982.* CJM

Above: *In the 1980s a number of Class 108s were transferred to the Western Region, where they were deployed in the West of England on Devon and Cornish branch line operations. The WR soon applied semi-permanent set numbers, as shown here on set No. P955 approaching Newton Abbot at Aller Junction on 18 May 1989 with a Paignton to Exeter service. The set's DMBS vehicle is leading.* CJM

Right Middle: *In the Manchester area some Class 108s were allocated to Longsight depot and these were given sets numbers prefixed with the depot code LO. In this 27 February 1990 view set No. LO350, a three car set, is seen inside the main shed at Longsight from its DMBS end, and displays standard blue grey livery.* CJM

Right Below: *In the days before the first class seating was declassified to standard class occupancy, the first class portion of the of the DMCL or DTCL vehicles seated 12 in the 2+2 configuration in two seating bays directly behind the driving cab. The window curtains and later brown moquette seating with dark red carpets are shown on a set allocated Leeds Neville Hill.* CJM

Class 109

Vehicle type:	DMBS	DTCL
Tops class number:	109	109
Former class number:	109	146
Original number range:	50415-50419	56170-56174
Revised number range:	-	-
Classification:	DMBS	DTCL
Introduced:	1957	1957
Built by:	D Wickham & Co	D Wickham & Co
Vehicle length (over body):	57ft 0in (17.37m)	57ft 0in (17.37m)
Height:	12ft 4½in (3.77m)	12ft 4½in (3.77m)
Width:	8ft 3in (2.51m)	8ft 3in (2.51m)
Seating:	59S	16F/50S
Internal layout:	2+3S	2+2F/2+3S
Gangway:	Inner end	Inner end
Toilets:	Not fitted	1
Weight:	37tons 10cwt	20tons 10cwt
Brake type:	Vacuum	Vacuum
Power unit:	2 x BUT (Leyland) of 150hp (111.8kW) per vehicle	-
Horsepower (total):	300hp (224kW)	-
Transmission:	Mechanical	-
Max speed:	70mph (113km/h)	70mph (113km/h)
Coupling type:	Screw	Screw
Multiple restriction:	Blue Square	Blue Square
Door type:	Slam	Slam
Special features:	-	-
Body structure:	Steel	Steel

Notes: Cars 50415, 50419, 56170 and 56174 sold by BR to Wickham in 1961 to fulfill an export order for Trinidad Government Railway.

Below: *Just five two-car sets were ordered from D Wickham of Ware. These vehicles were of lightweight design and drew on the Wickham expertise of building vehicles of Skeletal design. The weight reduction was traded against high maintenance and repair costs if the body became damaged. The high quality interior design and unique body design soon rendered these sets as redundant. Originally allocated to the Eastern Region for Suffolk branch line use, two sets (four vehicles) were withdrawn as early as September 1961, being sold back to their builders for modification and re-sale to the Trinidad Government Railway. The other three sets remained on BR's books until 1971 when two were withdrawn and one - formed of vehicles 50416 and 56171 - was converted into the Eastern Region Generals Manager's Saloon. Thankfully as the set remained with BR for a number of years when it was eventually withdrawn it was saved by a preservation group and is now at the Llangollen Railway. DMBS No. E50415 is illustrated.* CJM-C

Class 110

Vehicle type:	DMBC	DMCL	TSL
Classification:	110	110	110
Original classification:	110/1	110/2	163
Original number range:	51809-51828, 52066-52075	51829-51848, 52076-52085	59693-59712, 59808-59817
Revised number range:	-	-	-
Classification:	DMBC	DMCL	TSL
Introduced:	1961	1961	1961
Built by:	Birmingham RC&W	Birmingham RC&W	Birmingham RC&W
Vehicle length (over body):	57ft 6in (17.53m)	57ft 6in (17.53m)	57ft 6in (17.53m)
Height:	12ft 8¾in (3.88m)	12ft 8¾in (3.88m)	12ft 8¾in (3.88m)
Width:	9ft 3in (2.82m)	9ft 3in (2.82m)	9ft 3in (2.82m)
Seating:	12F/33S or declassified - 45S	12F/54S or declassified - 66S	72S
Internal layout:	2+2F/2+3S	2+2F/2+3S	2+3S
Gangway:	Inner end	Inner end	Throughout
Toilets:	Not fitted	1	1
Weight:	33.5 tonnes	33 tonnes	25.5 tonnes
Brake type:	Vacuum	Vacuum	Vacuum
Power unit:	2 x Rolls Royce of 180hp (134kW) per vehicle	2 x Rolls Royce of 180hp (134kW) per vehicle	-
Horsepower (total):	360hp (268kW)	360hp (268kW)	-
Transmission:	Mechanical	Mechanical	-
Max speed:	70mph (113km/h)	70mph (113km/h)	70mph (113km/h)
Coupling type:	Screw	Screw	Screw
Multiple restriction:	Blue Square	Blue Square	Blue Square
Door type:	Slam	Slam	Slam
Special features:	-	-	-
Body structure:	Steel	Steel	Steel
Notes:	Later declassified to DMBS	Later declassified to DMSL	

Below: *Built for use on the Calder Valley route between Manchester and Leeds via Todmorden, these 30 three-car sets emerged from the BRC&W Works in 1961 and to cope with the arduous route were fitted with two 180hp (134kW) Rolls Royce engines under each driving car. The front end, required to house a standard four-character route indicator, was different from the previous BRC&W DMMU design (Class 104) with curved tops to the main front windows and a reduced height central window to house a destination indicator. A three-car set is seen in as delivered condition led by DMCL No. 51840.* CJM-C

Class 110

Left: *Vehicles which passes through depots and workshops for classified attention after mid 1967 emerged carrying standard BR rail blue, complete with full yellow warning end and a black underframe. By the 1970s with the demise of the four character route code, these roof mounted boxes were plated over. Driving Motor Brake Composite No. E52071 is seen in the yard at BREL Doncaster Works.* CJM

Right: *Over the years seating changes were made to the design, with the original first class areas, located behind the driving cabs of both driving motor cars, being downgraded to provide extra second (standard) class seating. Originally this used the former first class seats, but in some sets standard design bus style seats were installed. A three car set, led by DMBC No. E51827, passes over Hall Royd Junction on 6 July 1979 forming a Blackpool to Leeds service.* CJM-C

Left: *The Class 110 fleet was included in the DMMU refurbishment contract, with vehicles upgraded at BREL Doncaster Works. At the same time the then standard BR blue and grey colour scheme was applied, again with full yellow front ends. In this view we see two blue and grey liveried and one rail blue coloured vehicle depart from Manchester Victoria bound for Blackpool, led by DMCL No. E51839.* CJM

Above: *Posed under the overall roof at York, a three-car Class 110 formation, led by car No. E51822, awaits an evening departure to Manchester via Leeds on 16 May 1982. The Class 110s remained in front line service until replaced by new stock in 1992. However, most of the intermediate trailer vehicles were withdrawn in the 1980s, with the remaining '110s' operating as power twins.* CJM

Below: *The preservation movement managed to save two power twin sets and one intermediate vehicle, and these are now restored to operational state. For several years cars E51813 and 51842 operated on the East Lancashire Railway, before transferring to the Wensledale Railway. The pair are seen at Bury Bolton Street.* CJM

Class 111

Vehicle type:	DMBS	DMCL
Classification:	111	111
Original classification:	111/2	111/1
Original number range:	50134-50137, 50280-50292, 51541-51550	50270-50279, 50745-50747, 51551-51560
Revised number range:	50xxx renumbered to 53xxx	50xxx renumbered to 53xxx
Introduced:	1957-58	1957-58
Built by:	Metro-Cammell	Metro-Cammell
Vehicle length (over body):	57ft 0in (17.37m)	57ft 0in (17.37m)
Height:	12ft 4½in (3.77m)	12ft 4½in (3.77m)
Width:	9ft 3in (2.81m)	9ft 3in (2.81m)
Seating:	44-52S	12F/53S or 12F/45S, declassified - 57-65S
Internal layout:	2+3S 2+2F/2+3S	2+2F/2+3S
Gangway:	Inner end	Inner end
Toilets:	Not fitted	1
Weight:	33 tons	33 tons
Brake type:	Vacuum	Vacuum
Power unit:	2 x Rolls Royce of 180hp (134kW) per vehicle	2 x Rolls Royce of 180hp (134kW) per vehicle
Horsepower (total):	360hp (268kW)	360hp (268kW)
Transmission:	Mechanical	Mechanical
Max speed:	70mph (113km/h)	70mph (113 km/h)
Coupling type:	Screw	Screw
Multiple restriction:	Blue Square	Blue Square
Door type:	Slam	Slam
Special features:	-	-
Body structure:	Steel	Steel
Notes:	Some cars re-engined and transferred to Class 101	Some cars re-engined and transferred to Class 101

Below: *Built as part of the main Metro-Cammell DMMU order, a number of vehicles were constructed with more powerful Rolls Royce engines for Trans Pennine operations; these were under the numeric classification system allocated Class 111. The exterior of and internal accommodation in these sets were the same as on the 101s. Car No. E50282 is seen at Doncaster.* CJM

DTCL	TBSL	TSL
111	111	111
147	165	164
56090-56093	59573-59578	59100-59109, 59569-59572
56xxx renumbered to 54xxx	-	-
1957-58	1957-58	1957-58
Metro-Cammell	Metro-Cammell	MetroCammell
57ft 0in (17.37m)	57ft 0in (17.37m)	57ft 0in (17.37m)
12ft 4½in (3.77m)	12ft 4½in (3.77m)	12ft 4½in (3.77m)
9ft 3in (2.81m)	9ft 3in (2.81m)	9ft 3in (2.81m)
12F/53S or 12F/45S, declassified - 57-65S	45-65S	61-71S
2+3S	2+3S	2+3S
Inner end	Throughout	Throughout
1	1	1
25 tons	25 tons	24tons 10cwt
Vacuum	Vacuum	Vacuum
-	-	-
-	-	-
-	-	-
70mph (113 km/h)	70mph (113 km/h)	70mph (113 km/h)
Screw	Screw	Screw
Blue square	Blue square	Blue square
Slam	Slam	Slam
-	-	-
Steel	Steel	Steel
Later went to 101 fleet		Later went to 101 fleet

Below: *The final batch of Metro-Cammell/Rolls Royce sets were fitted with roof line four-character headcode boxes for Calder Valley line use, and thus required the destination indicator to be lowered, resulting in the centre front window being smaller. With roof box removed car No. E51555 shows this modification at Doncaster. The middle coach is of Class 101 TC design.* CJM

Class 111

Above: *The vast majority of Metro-Cammell vehicles from Class 101 and 111 were included in the DMMU refurbishment project with work undertaken at BREL Derby Litchurch Lane and Doncaster workshops. During this work several Class 111 vehicles were absorbed into the Class 101 fleet. In this view we see Class 111 Trailer Standard No. E59107 under overhaul at BREL Doncaster.* CJM

Below: *A four-car Class 111 formation formed of DMCL, TSL, TBSL and DMCL vehicles arrives at Doncaster from Leeds on 23 April 1981. By this time it was quite unusual to find correctly formed four car Class 111 sets still in use. In the background is the massive Doncaster Works site with West Yard located between the works and the station, housing wagons, DMUs and a Class 37.* CJM

Vehicle type:	DHMBS	DHMCL
Classification:	111	111
Original classification:	111 / DMBS	111 / DMCL
Number range:	78706-78724	78956-78974
Revised range:	-	-
Introduced:	1957-58	1957-58
Modified:	1982-85	1982-85
Built by:	Metro-Cammell	Metro-Cammell
Modified:	BREL Doncaster	BREL Doncaster
Vehicle length (over body):	57ft 0in (17.37m)	57ft 0in (17.37m)
Height:	12ft 4½in (3.77m)	12ft 4½in (3.77m)
Width:	9ft 3in (2.81m)	9ft 3in (2.81m)
Seating:	44-52S	12F/53S or 12F/45S declassified - 57-65S
Internal layout:	2+3S	2+2F/2+3S
Gangway:	Inner end	Inner end
Toilets:	Not fitted	1
Weight:	33 tons	33 tons
Brake type:	Vacuum	Vacuum
Power unit:	1 x Rolls Royce of 180hp (134kW) per vehicle	1 x Rolls Royce of 180hp (134kW) per vehicle
Horsepower (total):	180hp (134kW)	180hp (134kW)
Transmission:	Mechanical	Mechanical
Max speed:	70mph (113km/h)	70mph (113km/h)
Coupling type:	Screw	Screw
Multiple restriction:	Blue Square	Blue Square
Door type:	Slam	Slam
Special features:	Half motored	Half motored
Body structure:	Steel	Steel
Rebuilt from:	50286/287/281/288/282/280/283/289/284, 51546/542/543/544/541/549/545/548/550	50279/274/271/273/276/275/278/272/277, 51554/552/557/553/551/559/555/556/558

Below: *Between 1982-85 as a cost cutting exercise, 36 Class 111 power cars had one of their Rolls Royce engines and associated transmissions removed and were reclassified as Driving Half Motors. The modified sets were renumbered from the traditional 5xxxx number series to a new 787xx and 789xx series. Viewed from its inner end DHMBS No. E78966 is seen at Doncaster; this vehicle was converted from DMBS No. 51546. Note that it also sports South Yorkshire MetroTrain branding on the bodyside and clearly shows the end window position provided in brake vehicles.* CJM

Class 112

Vehicle type:	DMBS	DMCL
Classification:	112	112
Original classification:	112/2	112/1
Original number range:	51681-51705	51706-51730
Revised number range:	-	-
Introduced:	1959	1959
Built by:	Cravens RC&W	Cravens RC&W
Vehicle length (over body):	57ft 6in (17.53m)	57ft 6in (17.53m)
Height:	12ft 4in (3.76m)	12ft 4in (3.76m)
Width:	9ft 2in (2.79m)	9ft 2in (2.9m)
Seating:	52S	12F/51S
Internal layout:	2+3S	2+2F/2+3S
Gangway:	Inner end	Inner end
Toilets:	Not fitted	1
Weight:	29ton 10cwt	29 tons
Brake type:	Vacuum	Vacuum
Power unit:	1 x Rolls Royce of 238hp (177.4 kW) per vehicle	1 x Rolls Royce of 238hp (177.4 kW) per vehicle
Horsepower (total):	238hp (177.4 kW)	238hp (177.4 kW)
Transmission:	Mechanical	Mechanical
Max speed:	70mph (113km/h)	70mph (113 km/h)
Coupling type:	Screw	Screw
Multiple restriction:	Blue Square	Blue Square
Door type:	Slam	Slam
Special features:	-	-
Body structure:	Steel	Steel

Below: *In 1959 Sheffield-based Cravens delivered 50 Rolls Royce power twin sets for London Midland Region operation. The first 25, later identified as Class 112, were fitted with a mechanical transmission which proved to be very troublesome. With DMCL No. 51711 nearest the camera one of the twin-sets is seen at Blackburn on 1 September 1962 forming a Colne to Blackpool Central service. This batch has the distinctive upsweep of the gutter either side of the destination indicator.*
Michael Mensing

Below: *As part of the order described on the left, the final 25 twin-sets of the Cravens order were fitted with Rolls Royce engines and a hydraulic transmission. These sets were very problematic and reports indicate a tendency to catch fire. These sets were fitted with an unusual four-character headcode box which also incorporated a destination indicator. DMBS 51755 is seen nearest the camera in this view of a twin set at Carlisle. Although on paper these and the Class 112s were given TOPS numeric classification these were seldom used as all were withdrawn by November 1969.* Michael Mensing

Vehicle type:	DMBS	DMCL
Classification:	113	113
Original classification:	113/2	113/1
Original number range:	51731-51755	51756-51780
Revised number range:	-	-
Introduced:	1959	1959
Built by:	Cravens RC&W	Cravens RC&W
Vehicle length (over body):	57ft 6in (17.53m)	57ft 6in (17.53m)
Height:	12ft 4in (3.76m)	12ft 4in (3.76m)
Width:	9ft 2in (2.79m)	9ft 2in (2.79m)
Seating:	52S	12F/51S
Internal layout:	2+3S	2+2F/2+3S
Gangway:	Inner end	Inner end
Toilets:	Not fitted	1
Weight:	29ton 10cwt	29 tons
Brake type:	Vacuum	Vacuum
Power unit:	1 x Rolls Royce of 238hp (177.4 kW) per vehicle	1 x Rolls Royce of 238hp (177.4 kW) per vehicle
Horsepower (total):	238hp (177.4 kW)	238hp (177.4 kW)
Transmission:	Hydraulic	Hydraulic
Max speed:	70mph (113km/h)	70mph (113km/h)
Coupling type:	Screw	Screw
Multiple restriction:	Blue Square	Blue Square
Door type:	Slam	Slam
Special features:	-	-
Body structure:	Steel	Steel

Class 114

Vehicle type:	DMBS	DTCL
Classification:	114	114
Original classification:	114	148
Original number range:	50000-50049	56001-56049
Revised number range:	53001-53049	54001-54049
Introduced:	1956	1956
Built by:	BR Derby Works	BR Derby Works
Vehicle length (over body):	64ft 6in (19.66m)	64ft 6in (19.66m)
Height:	12ft 4½in (3.77m)	12ft 4½in (3.77m)
Width:	9ft 3in (2.82m)	9ft 3in (2.82m)
Seating:	62S	12F/62S
Internal layout:	2+3S	2+2F/2+3S
Gangway:	Inner end	Inner end
Toilets:	Not fitted	1
Weight:	35 tons 10 cwt	29-31 tons
Brake type:	Vacuum	Vacuum
Power unit:	2 x BUT (Leyland) of 230hp (171kW) per vehicle	-
Horsepower (total):	460hp (343kW)	-
Transmission:	Mechanical	-
Max speed:	70mph (113km/h)	70mph (113km/h)
Coupling type:	Screw	Screw
Multiple restriction:	Blue Square	Blue Square
Door type:	Slam	Slam
Special features:	-	-
Body structure:	Steel	Steel
Notes:	50000 originally fitted with two experimental Rolls Royce 238hp (177kW) engines and hydraulic transmission	

Below: *This class of 49 two-car sets was the first production run of DMMUs under the Modernisation Plan and was constructed from steel on longer underframes than the original Derby Lightweight sets built slightly earlier. These sets became known as the Derby Heavyweights and were the first with the standard Derby three window front end seen on many other designs. Introduced for Eastern Region use the sets worked in the Lincoln area and were in front line service for over 30 years. The first production DMBS, No. 50000, was originally fitted with a trial Rolls Royce engine and hydraulic transmission which was later removed in favour of the Leyland engine and mechanical transmission, the vehicle was later withdrawn before renumbering. In original as delivered condition a two car set is seen with its DTCL vehicle nearest the camera, identifiable by its empty underframe and lack of a guards brake van at the inner end.* CJM-C

Above: *By the late 1960s BR green livery had given way to rail blue with full yellow ends and by the mid 1970s the original alpha-numeric route indictors were set to display two white dots and were quickly removed. With DMBS No. E50014 nearest the camera a two-car set is seen stabled in the middle road at Sheffield on 28 January 1980.* CJM

Below: *The Class 114 fleet was included in the DMMU refurbishment programme and sets emerged in the new white livery off-set by a broad rail blue waist height band. Displaying this livery, DTCL No. E56027 leads DMBS No. 50002 through Kiveton Park on 13 December 1979.* CJM

Class 115

Vehicle type:	DMBS	TS	TCL
Classification:	115	115	115
Original classification:	115	173	177
Original number range:	51651-51680, 51849-51900	59649-59663, 59713-59718, 59725-59744	59664-59678, 59719-59724, 59745-59764
Revised number range:	-	-	-
Introduced:	1960	1960	1960
Built by:	BR Derby Works	BR Derby Works	BR Derby Works
Vehicle length (over body):	64ft 0in (19.51m)	63ft 8½in (19.42m)	63ft 8½in (19.42m)
Height:	12ft 4½in (3.77m)	12ft 4½in (3.77m)	12ft 4½in (3.77m)
Width:	9ft 3in (2.82m)	9ft 3in (2.82m)	9ft 3in (2.82m)
Seating:	78S	106S	30F/40S
Internal layout:	2+3S	3+2	2+1F/2+3S
Gangway:	No	No	No
Toilets:	Not fitted	Not fitted	1
Weight:	38 tons	29 tons	30 tons
Brake type:	Vacuum	Vacuum	Vacuum
Power unit:	2 x BUT (Leyland) of 230hp (171.5kW) per vehicle	-	-
Horsepower (total):	460hp (343kW)	-	-
Transmission:	Mechanical	-	-
Max speed:	70mph (113km/h)	70mph (113km/h)	70mph (113km/h)
Coupling type:	Screw	Screw	Screw
Multiple restriction:	Blue Square	Blue Square	Blue Square
Door type:	Slam	Slam	Slam
Special features:	-	-	-
Body structure:	Steel	Steel	Steel

Below: *Based on the standard Modernisation Plan Derby design, 82 four-car diesel-mechanical sets were built in 1960 for the domestic services radiating from London Marylebone and were very much a suburban unit with 2+3 seating. The vehicles were not gangwayed and the only toilets were provided in the TCL coach, so those needing facilities needed to travel in the correct coach. When built the stock was finished in green; this gave way to BR rail blue in the mid 1960s and blue and grey in later years. A four-car set is seen under the Great Central roof at Marylebone led by DMBS No. 51862.* CJM

Right: *A fleet of 82 Trailer Second (TS) and 82 Trailer Composite Lavatory (TCL) vehicles was built; these seated 106 second and 30 first and 40 second respectively. These were non gangwayed with seating in the 2+3 (second) and 2+2 (first) areas, and doors were provided by each seating bay. TS 59740 is illustrated painted in blue/grey livery.* CJM

Below: *The Class 115s remained in service into the Network SouthEast era with NSE red, white and blue livery applied. The sets were replaced in the early 1990s by Class 165 two- and three-car sets. When in service a Class 115 four-car set could carry 224 second and 30 first class passengers, plus at least 100 standees if needed.* CJM

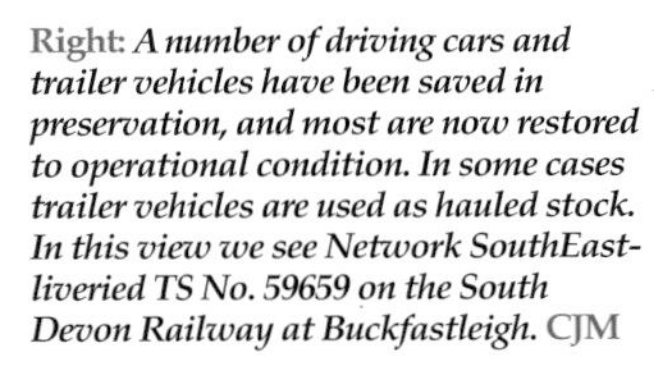

Right: *A number of driving cars and trailer vehicles have been saved in preservation, and most are now restored to operational condition. In some cases trailer vehicles are used as hauled stock. In this view we see Network SouthEast-liveried TS No. 59659 on the South Devon Railway at Buckfastleigh.* CJM

Class 116 & 130

Vehicle type:	DMBS	DMS	TS
Classification:	116	116	116
Original classification:	116/2	116/1	172
Original number range:	50050-50091, 50818-50870, 51128-51140	50092-50133, 50871-50923, 51141-51153	59032-59041
Revised number range:	50xxx renumbered 53xxx	50xxx renumbered 53xxx	-
Introduced:	1957	1957	1957
Built by:	BR Derby Works	BR Derby Works	BR Derby Works
Vehicle length (over body):	64ft 0in (19.51m)	64ft 0in (19.51m)	63ft 8½in (19.42m)
Height:	12ft 4½in (3.77m)	12ft 4½in (3.77m)	12ft 4½in (3.77m)
Width:	9ft 3in (2.82m)	9ft 3in (2.82m)	9ft 3in (2.82m)
Seating:	65S	95S, reduced to 89 after gangways fitted	103S, reduced to 89 after gangways fitted
Internal layout:	2+3S	2+3S	2+3S
Gangway:	As built - No Modified - Inner end	As built - No Modified - Inner end	As built - No Modified - Throughout
Toilets:	Not fitted	Not fitted	As built - Not fitted Modified - some - 1
Weight:	38ton 10cwt	35ton 10cwt	28ton 10cwt
Brake type:	Vacuum	Vacuum	Vacuum
Power unit:	2 x BUT (Leyland) of 150hp (111.8kW) per vehicle	2 x BUT (Leyland) of 150hp (111.8kW) per vehicle	- -
Horsepower (total):	300hp (224kW)	300hp (224kW)	-
Transmission:	Mechanical	Mechanical	-
Max speed:	70mph (113km/h)	70mph (113km/h)	70mph (113km/h)
Coupling type:	Screw	Screw	Screw
Multiple restriction:	Blue Square	Blue Square	Blue Square
Door type:	Slam	Slam	Slam
Special features:	-	-	-
Body structure:	Steel	Steel	Steel
Notes:			

Below: *A total of 216 power cars and 104 trailers of this Derby design were constructed in 1957 to modernise suburban operations in the Cardiff and Birmingham areas. These were basic suburban sets with no gangways, no toilets and a door by each seating bay; they were cramped and not very comfortable. Originally sets were painted in green, which gave way to BR blue in the mid 1960s. As part of the DMMU refurbishment project most sets were overhauled and gangways were installed as were toilets in the TC and TS vehicles. After overhaul sets were finished in white with a broad blue waist band. Eventually blue/grey livery was applied. A three-car set with DMBS No. 50050 nearest the camera is shown, painted in as delivered green livery with cream bodyside strip and whiskers.* CJM

TC	DMPV ++
116	130
175 (190*)	116
59000-59031, 59326-59376, 59438-59448	50819, 50862, 50872, 50915, 51137, 51150
-	50xxx renumbered 53xxx
1957	1957 as DPMV - 1969, 1981
BR Derby Works	BR Derby Works
63ft 8½in (19.42m)	64ft 0in (19.51m)
12ft 4½in (3.77m)	12ft 4½in (3.77m)
9ft 3in (2.82m)	9ft 3in (2.82m)
As built - 28F/74S Declassified - 102S, reduced to 89 after gangways fitted	None
2+2F/2+3S	Luggage space
As built - No Modified - Throughout	No
As built - Not fitted Modified - some - 1	Not fitted
28ton 10cwt	35ton 10cwt - 38tons 10cwt
Vacuum	Vacuum
-	2 x BUT (Leyland) of 150hp (111.8kW)
-	per vehicle
-	300hp (224kW)
-	Mechanical
70mph (113km/h)	70mph (113km/h)
Screw	Screw
Blue Square	Blue Square
Slam	Slam
-	-
Steel	Steel
Declassified to TS * 59447 modified as TPMV and reclassified 190	++ Worked with modified through-wired GUV vans

Below: *An interesting modification was that made to six redundant driving motor vehicles. In 1969 Nos. 51137 and 51150 were stripped of all seating and adapted to carry parcel traffic and branded Railair Express Parcels, the modification work being done at Newton Abbot. The vehicles were then used on an Airfreight Parcels Service between Bristol and Hayes near London Heathrow Airport, marshalled either end of a pair of Blue Square through wired loco-hauled GUVs. The four-car set was withdrawn in 1972. Car No.W51150 leads the four-car set at Reading. A further four driving cars were modified for parcels carrying.* CJM

Class 117

Vehicle type:	DMBS	DMS	TCL
Classification:	117	117	117
Original classification:	117/2	117/1	176
Original number range:	51332-51373	51374-51415	59484-58522
Revised number range:	-	-	-
Introduced:	1959-60	1959-60	1959-60
Built by:	Pressed Steel Co	Pressed Steel Co	Pressed Steel Co
Vehicle length (over body):	64ft 0in (19.51m)	64ft 0in (19.51m)	63ft 10in (19.46m)
Height:	12ft 8½in (3.97m)	12ft 8½in (3.97m)	12ft 8½in (3.97m)
Width:	9ft 3in (2.82m)	9ft 3in (2.82m)	9ft 3in (2.82m)
Seating:	65S	As built - 91S Gangwayed - 89S	As built - 24F/50S, Gangwayed - 22F/48S
Internal layout:	2+3S	3+2	2+1F/2+3S
Gangway:	As built - No Modified - Inner end	As built - No Modified - Throughout	As built - No Modified - Throughout
Toilets:	Not fitted	Not fitted	2
Weight:	36 tons	36 tons	30 tons
Brake type:	Vacuum	Vacuum	Vacuum
Power unit:	2 x BUT (Leyland) of 150hp (111.8kW) per vehicle	2 x BUT (Leyland) of 150hp (111.8kW) per vehicle	-
Horsepower (total):	300hp (224kW)	300hp (224kW)	-
Transmission:	Mechanical	Mechanical	-
Max speed:	70mph (113km/h)	70mph (113km/h)	70mph (113km/h)
Coupling type:	Screw	Screw	Screw
Multiple restriction:	Blue Square	Blue Square	Blue Square
Door type:	Slam	Slam	Slam
Special features:	-	-	-
Body structure:	Steel	Steel	Steel

Left: *For the modernisation of the London Division of the Western Region, Pressed Steel of Linwood, Scotland (a part of the British Motor Corporation), produced 84 driving cars of two different designs and 39 intermediate trailers between November 1959 and October 1960. These were true suburban sets with 2+3 seating and doors to each seating bay. The front ends followed the standard Derby design. The intermediate trailer was a composite vehicle with first class seating at one end. Two intermediate toilets were provided (one for first and one for second class travellers). However, no between vehicle gangways existed so you had to be careful to travel in the correct portion of the train. Gangways were later fitted, reducing the seating capacity. As built the sets were finished in green with cream bodyside bands and whiskers; this later gave way to blue and later blue and grey. Network SouthEast and Regional Railways colours were subsequently applied. Blue and grey-liveried set No. L417 is seen near West Drayton with its DMS vehicle leading.* CJM

Above: *The Class 117s were part of the DMMU modernisation programme, resulting in some sets emerging in white livery with a broad rail blue waist band, as demonstrated on set No. L400 from its DMBS end.* CJM

Below: *Although built for the Western Region, the '117s' later spread their wings working in the Birmingham area and Scotland for the Regional Railways sector, following displacement by new stock. Set No. 117311 in Regional Railways livery is seen at Birmingham New Street when deployed on Birmingham cross-city services.* CJM

Class 118

Vehicle type:	DMBS	DMS	TCL
Classification:	118	118	118
Original classification:	118/2	118/1	174
Original number range:	51302-51316	51317-51331	59469-59483
Revised number range:	-	-	-
Introduced:	1960	1960	1960
Built by:	Birmingham RC&W	Birmingham RC&W	Birmingham RC&W
Vehicle length (over body):	64ft 0in (19.51m)	64ft 0in (19.51m)	63ft 10in (19.46m)
Height:	12ft 8½in (3.97m)	12ft 8½in (3.97m)	12ft 8½in (3.97m)
Width:	9ft 3in (2.82m)	9ft 3in (2.82m)	9ft 3in (2.82m)
Seating:	65S	As built - 91S Gangwayed - 89S	As built - 24F/50S, Gangwayed - 22F/48S
Internal layout:	2+3S	3+2	2+1F/2+3S
Gangway:	As built - No Modified - Inner end	As built - No Modified - Inner end	As built - No Modified - Throughout
Toilets:	Not fitted	Not fitted	2
Weight:	36 tons	36 tons	30 tons
Brake type:	Vacuum	Vacuum	Vacuum
Power unit:	2 x BUT (Leyland) of 150hp (111.8kW) per vehicle	2 x BUT (Leyland) of 150hp (111.8kW) per vehicle	-
Horsepower (total):	300hp (224kW)	300hp (224kW)	-
Transmission:	Mechanical	Mechanical	-
Max speed:	70mph (113km/h)	70mph (113km/h)	70mph (113km/h)
Coupling type:	Screw	Screw	Screw
Multiple restriction:	Blue Square	Blue Square	Blue Square
Door type:	Slam	Slam	Slam
Special features:	-	-	-
Body structure:	Steel	Steel	Steel

Below: *The Birmingham Railway Carriage & Wagon Co produced a fleet of 15 three-car DMMU sets for the Western Region between April and July 1960. The body design followed the standard Derby style. These sets were high-density with 3+2 seating and a door by each seating bay. The three-car sets were not gangwayed, and thus passengers could not move between carriages. In as delivered condition, a set with DMS No. 51319 leading arrives at Plymouth in October 1960. The set is painted in green livery with cream whisker strips on the end.* CJM-C

Above: *From the late 1960s BR rail blue with full yellow ends was progressively applied, as were gangways at the inner ends of driving cars and both ends of intermediate trailers. With its two driving cars displaying rail blue livery, Plymouth set No. P461 is seen at Exeter St David's with a blue and grey-liveried TCL in this August 1982 illustration. DMBS No. 51303 is nearest the camera.* CJM

Below: *By the mid 1980s a number of Class 118s were operating as power twin-sets, especially on Devon and Cornwall branch lines. In this view set No. P461 with DMBS 51303 nearest the camera (the same vehicle as illustrated above) is seen at Newquay on 30 April 1985 with the 16.10 service to Par. Towards the end of use some cars were transferred to Tyseley for Birmingham area use, from where the last sets were withdrawn in 1995.* CJM

Class 119

Vehicle type:	DMBC	DMSL	TBSL modified to TSL
Classification:	119	119	119
Original classification:	119/1	119/2	178
Original number range:	51052-51079	51080-51107	59413-59437
Revised number range:	-	-	-
Introduced:	1958	1958	1958
Built by:	Gloucester RC&W	Gloucester RC&W	Gloucester RC&W
Vehicle length (over body):	64ft 6in (18.74m)	64ft 6in (18.74m)	64ft 6in (18.74m)
Height:	12ft 8¼in (3.87m)	12ft 8¼in (3.87m)	12ft 8¼in (3.87m)
Width:	9ft 3in (2.82m)	9ft 3in (2.82m)	9ft 3in (2.82m)
Seating:	18F/16S	68S	As TBSL - 60S/4U Modified as TSL - 60S
Internal layout:	2+1F/2+2S CrossCountry	2+2S CrossCountry	2+2S/U CrossCountry
Gangway:	As built - No Modified - Inner end	As built - No Modified - Inner end	As built - No Modified - Throughout
Toilets:	Not fitted	1	1
Weight:	36ton 19cwt	37ton 10cwt	31ton 8cwt
Brake type:	Vacuum	Vacuum	Vacuum
Power unit:	2 x BUT (Leyland) of 150hp (111.8kW) per vehicle	2 x BUT (Leyland) of 150hp (111.8kW) per vehicle	-
Horsepower (total):	300hp (224kW)	300hp (224kW)	-
Transmission:	Mechanical	Mechanical	-
Max speed:	70mph (113km/h)	70mph (113km/h)	70mph (113km/h)
Coupling type:	Screw	Screw	Screw
Multiple restriction:	Blue Square	Blue Square	Blue Square
Door type:	Slam	Slam	Slam
Special features:	-	-	-
Body structure:	Steel	Steel	Steel
Notes:	Passenger Luggage Stowage Area later formed in brake for Gatwick Airport services		

Below: *The 1955 Modernisation Plan called for a fleet of DMMU sets to be built specifically for CrossCountry longer-distance operations. These were to incorporate a small buffet and have low-density 2+2 seating with passenger doors fed from transverse walkways at the one third and two third positions. Gloucester Railway Carriage & Wagon built a fleet 28 three-car sets with a Derby outline in 1958. Three designations of vehicle were introduced: DMBC, TBSL and DMSL. Sets were painted green with cream body strips and end whiskers. DMSL No. 51088 is illustrated from its non-driving side at Swindon.* CJM-C

Above: *After the fleet's days on CrossCountry duties were over, it operated alongside the Western Region core DMU fleet, with a number of sets based at Cardiff and Reading. The buffet area was removed and standard seating installed, while the large guards van remained. With its DMBC leading, Cardiff set No. C595 approaches South Brent on 27 June 1980 with a semi-fast service from Bristol to Plymouth.* CJM

Right Middle: *The intermediate vehicle of the Gloucester Railway Carriage & Wagon sets was a Trailer Buffet Second Lavatory (TBSL) seating 60 second (standard) and four in the buffet area. This view of car No. W59424 shows the main seating side, with the lavatory compartment at the far end.* CJM-C

Right Bottom: *In the 1970s, the expanding traffic on the Reading to Gatwick Airport route required trains with extra luggage space. This was met by the conversion of Class 119s, with luggage racks provided in the brake vans of DMBS cars and the fitting of luggage stacks in the space of the original buffet in the intermediate coaches. By now painted in blue grey livery, the luggage space was branded on the outside as 'Passenger Luggage Stowage Area'. Car No. 59429 is illustrated.* CJM

Class 120

Vehicle type:	DMBCL	DMSL	DMBFL
Classification:	120	120	120
Original classification:	120/1	120/2	120/1
Original number range:	50696-50744, 51573-51581,	50647-50695, 51582-51590, 51781-51787+	51783-51786 (from DMBCL fleet)
Revised number range:	50xxx renumbered 53xxx	50xxx renumbered 53xxx	-
Introduced:	1957-59	1957-60	1960
Built by:	BR Swindon Works	BR Swindon Works	BR Swindon Works
Vehicle length (over body):	64ft 6in (19.66m)	64ft 6in (19.66m)	64ft 6in (19.66m)
Height:	12ft 4½in (3.77m)	12ft 4½in (3.77m)	12ft 4½in (3.77m)
Width:	9ft 3in (2.82m)	9ft 3in (2.82m)	9ft 3in (2.82m)
Seating:	18F/16S	68S	34F
Internal layout:	2+1F/2+2S CrossCountry	2+2S CrossCountry	2+1F CrossCountry
Gangway:	Inner end	Inner end	Inner end
Toilets:	1	1	1
Weight:	36ton 7cwt	36ton 10cwt	36 ton
Brake type:	Vacuum	Vacuum	Vacuum
Power unit:	2 x BUT (AEC) of 150hp (111.8kW) per vehicle	2 x BUT (AEC) of 150hp (111.8kW) per vehicle	2 x BUT (AEC) of 150hp (111.8kW) per vehicle
Horsepower (total):	300hp (224kW)	300hp (224kW)	300hp (224kW)
Transmission:	Mechanical	Mechanical	Mechanical
Max speed:	70mph (113km/h)	70mph (113km/h)	70mph (113km/h)
Coupling type:	Screw	Screw	Screw
Multiple restriction:	Blue Square	Blue Square	Blue Square
Door type:	Slam	Slam	Slam
Special features:	-	-	-
Body structure:	Steel	Steel	Steel
Notes:		+ 51783-51786 modified to DMBFL	

Below: *The BR Swindon Works input to the BTC CrossCountry train order was a fleet 130 power cars and 64 intermediate trailers, formed as three-car sets. These were again low-density, with 2+2 seating, and a small buffet was provided in the intermediate coach. Three designs of driving car were built. Sets were introduced between 1957 and 1960 and originally all were outshopped in green with cream bands and whiskers; later BR blue grey was applied. Two different designs of front end were to be found; the majority had the standard Swindon bodywork as applied to the 1950s InterCity sets, but a handful were fitted with four-character headcode boxes. Sets were originally allocated to the Western and Scottish Regions. In this view we see three three-car sets working in multiple, with a DMBCL vehicle nearest the camera.* CJM

TBSL , modified to TSL
120
179
59255-59301, 59579-59588
59679-59685
-
1958-60
BR Swindon Works
64ft 6in (19.66m)
12ft 4½in (3.77m)
9ft 3in (2.82m)
As TBSL - 60S/4U
Modified as TSL - 60S-68S
2+2S CrossCountry
Throughout
1
30ton 12cwt
Vacuum
-
-
-
70mph (113km/h)
Screw
Blue Square
Slam
-
Steel

Above: *Led by DMBCL No. 51573, a three-car Class 120 formation is seen at Derby bound for Lincoln in summer 1982. By the time this illustration was taken the standard BR blue/grey livery was applied and the original middle marker light directly above the buffer beam had been removed. The two remaining marker lights had been modified to show both white (front) and red (rear) illumination. All Class 120 CrossCountry sets were withdrawn by 1984.* CJM

Below: *After their demise from full CrossCountry passenger operations, the Class 120 fleet operated longer distance domestic services, such as this set, operating as Western Region set No. 553, stopping at Lostwithiel on 27 June 1978 forming the 16.40 Plymouth to Penzance service. Car No. 51585, a Driving Motor Second Lavatory (DMSL), is leading, seating 68 in the 2+2 mode, a former Trailer Buffet Second Lavatory (TBSL) is marshalled in the middle but with the buffet equipment isolated, while a Driving Motor Brake Composite Lavatory brings up the rear.* CJM

Class 121

Vehicle type:	DMBS	DTS
Original number range:	55020-55034	56280-56289
Revised number range:	-	54280-54289
TOPS classification:	121	121
Original classification:	121	149
Introduced:	1960	1960
Built by:	Pressed Streel	Pressed Streel
Vehicle length (over body):	64ft 6in (19.66m)	64ft 0½ (19.51m)
Height:	12ft 4½in (3.77m)	12ft 4½in (3.77m)
Width:	9ft 2½in (2.81m)	9ft 2½in (2.81m)
Seating:	65S	91S
Internal layout:	2+3	2+3
Gangway:	Not fitted	Inner end
Toilets:	Not fitted	Not fitted
Weight:	38 tonnes	30 tonnes
Brake type:	Vacuum	Vacuum
Power unit:	2 x Leyland of 150hp (111.8kW) per vehicle	-
Horsepower (total):	300hp (224kW)	-
Transmission:	Mechanical	-
Max speed:	70mph (113km/h)	70mph (113km/h)
Coupling type:	Screw	Screw
Multiple restriction:	Blue Square	Blue Square
Door type:	Slam	Slam
Special features:	-	-
Body structure:	Steel	Steel

Left: *Pressed Steel built 10 single-car double-cab vehicles to a Derby exterior design in 1960 for Western Region branch line use. They were designed to haul a single vehicle, and to satisfy this a fleet of 10 unpowered driving trailers was built with a single cab to a like profile. Originally painted green with cream bands and whiskers, these vehicles were later painted rail blue and blue and grey, ending their days in NSE red, white and blue. Viewed from its brake end, with exhaust pipes on the front bodywork, car No. 55028 is seen near Iver on 30 August 1979.* CJM

Right: *Under privatisation two main Train Operating Companies used Class 121 single cars, more usually known as 'Bubble Cars', for short branch line duties, these are Chiltern Railways and until summer 2013 Arriva Trains Wales. The car operated by Arriva Trains Wales was allocated to Cardiff Canton and used on the Cardiff Queen Street to Cardiff Bay shuttle. To meet the latest safety standards the vehicles now have central door locking and a headlight and have some of their doors sealed up. Viewed from its non-brake end, car No. 55032 is seen departing from Cardiff Queen Street on 5 November 2007 bound for Cardiff Bay. Note the modern LED marker/tail lights.* CJM

Number range:	55000-55019	56291-56299
Vehicle type:	DMBS	DTS
TOPS classification:	122+	122
Original classification:	122	150
Introduced:	1958	1958
Built by:	Gloucester RC&W	Gloucester RC&W
Vehicle length (over body):	64ft 6in (19.66m)	64ft 0½ (19.51m)
Height:	12ft 8¼in (3.87m)	12ft 8¼in (3.87m)
Width:	9ft 3in (2.82m)	9ft 3in (2.82m)
Seating:	68S	Original - 95S, Modified - 91S
Internal layout:	2+3	2+3
Gangway:	Not fitted	No fitted
Toilets:	Not fitted	Not fitted
Weight:	36 tons 10 cwt	27 tons
Brake type:	Vacuum	Vacuum
Power unit:	2 x AEC of 150hp (111.8kW) per vehicle	-
Horsepower (total):	300hp (224kW)	-
Transmission:	Mechanical	-
Max speed:	70mph (113km/h)	70mph (113km/h)
Coupling type:	Screw	Screw
Multiple restriction:	Blue Square	Blue Square
Door type:	Slam	Slam
Special features:	-	-
Body structure:	Steel	Steel
Notes:	+ Some vehicles modified for parcels use, reclassified as Class 131	

Right: *A further 29 single-car vehicles were constructed by Gloucester Railway Carriage & Wagon Co; these comprised 13 double-ended powered cars and nine single-ended driving trailer vehicles. These were allocated to the Western and London Midland Regions. The front body style followed the Gloucester-built CrossCountry stock, but incorporated a high-density Derby style vehicle body. All were fitted with blue square controls. This view shows one of the nine Driving Trailer Seconds No. W56293, coupled to a double ended DMBS coach.* CJM-C

Left: *The first of the DMBS build, No. W55000, or set No. 122100 as it became, poses at Laira depot on 10 November 1993, painted in full BR Regional Railways livery, a colour scheme applied in the early 1990s during the sectorisation of the UK railways leading up to privatisation. This view shows the saloon end of the coach without the exhaust stacks, but does show the addition of a fixed beam headlight in the middle of the front end.* CJM

Class 123 Inter-City

Vehicle type:	DMBSL	DMSK	TSL
Classification:	123	123	123
Original classification:	123/2	123/1	182
Original number range:	52086-52095	52096-52105	59235-59239
Revised number range:	-	-	-
Introduced:	1963	1963	1963
Built by:	BR Swindon Works	BR Swindon Works	BR Swindon Works
Vehicle length (over body):	64ft 11¼in (19.79m)	64ft 11¼in (19.79m)	64ft 6in (19.66m)
Height:	12ft 9½in (3.90m)	12ft 9½in (3.90m)	12ft 9½in (3.90m)
Width:	9ft 3in (2.82m)	9ft 3in (2.82m)	9ft 3in (2.82m)
Seating:	32S	56S	64S
Internal layout:	2+2 (Inter-City)	Comp (Inter-City)	2+2 (Inter-City)
Gangway:	Throughout	Throughout	Throughout
Toilets:	1	1	1
Weight:	41ton 14cwt	41ton 9cwt	31ton 9cwt
Brake type:	Vacuum	Vacuum	Vacuum
Power unit:	2 x BUT (Leyland Albion) of 230hp (171.5kW) per vehicle	2 x BUT (Leyland Albion) of 230hp (171.5kW) per vehicle	-
Horsepower (total):	460hp (343kW)	460hp (343kW)	-
Transmission:	Mechanical	Mechanical	-
Max speed:	70mph (113km/h)	70mph (113 km/h)	70mph (113 km/h)
Coupling type:	Buck-eye	Buck-eye	Buck-eye
Multiple restriction:	Blue Square	Blue Square	Blue Square
Door type:	Slam	Slam	Slam
Special features:	-	-	-
Body structure:	Steel	Steel	Steel
Notes:	Front doors later sealed	Front doors later sealed	

TCKL	TSLRB
123	123
183	184
59818-59827	59828-59832
-	-
1963	1963
BR Swindon Works	BR Swindon Works
64ft 6in (19.66m)	64ft 6in (19.66m)
12ft 9½in (3.90m)	12ft 9½in (3.90m)
9ft 3in (2.82m)	9ft 3in (2.82m)
24F/24S -compartments	32S
(Inter-City)	2+2 (Inter-City)
Throughout	Throughout
1	1
32ton 3cwt	32 tons
	Vacuum
-	-
-	-
-	-
70mph (113 km/h)	70mph (113 km/h)
Buck-eye	Buck-eye
Blue Square	Blue Square
Slam	Slam
-	-
Steel	Steel

Left Below: *By the spring/summer of 1963 when BR Swindon Works produced this fleet of Inter-City DMMUs a new standard had been devised, based on the Mk1 hauled coach. A total of just 40 vehicles were built, comprising 20 powered driving cars of two different internal layouts and 20 intermediate vehicles, 10 Trailer Composites, five Trailer Seconds and five Trailer Seconds with Buffet. The stock operated in three or four car formations. They were delivered for Western Region use working Swansea-Derby, South Wales to Plymouth and Bristol area duties. Later the sets were deployed on Bristol-Portsmouth services and in the London area on outer-suburban duties. Painted in blue/grey livery set No. L714 is seen under the Brunel roof at Paddington on 2 January 1976 with DMSK W52102 nearest the camera.* CJM

Below: *After finishing duties on the Western Region, the Inter-City sets were transferred to Botanic Gardens, Hull, to operate alongside the Trans-Pennine stock on East Coast to Manchester duties. With a revised sealed up front corridor connection and marker lights rather than headcode box displays, a four-car set passes Rotherham on 9 July 1983 led by Driving Motor Brake Standard Lavatory No. E52092 forming the 10.14 Hull to Manchester service. All Class 123 sets were withdrawn by the summer of 1984.* CJM

Class 124 Trans-Pennine

Vehicle type:	DMC	MBSK (TBSK)
Classification:	124	124
Original classification:	124/1	124/2
Original number range:	51951-51967	51968-51984
Revised number range:	-	59833-59842
Introduced:	1960	1960
Built by:	BR Swindon Works	BR Swindon Works
Vehicle length (over body):	64ft 6in (19.66m)	64ft 6in (19.66m)
Height:	12ft 9½in (3.90m)	12ft 9½in (3.90m)
Width:	9ft 3in (2.82m)	9ft 3in (2.82m)
Seating:	21F/36S	48S
Internal layout:	2+1 (Trans-Pennine)	Compartments (Trans-Pennine)
Gangway:	Inner end	Throughout
Toilets:	No	2
Weight:	40 tons	41 tons
Brake type:	Vacuum	Vacuum
Power unit:	2 x BUT (Leyland Albion) of 230hp (171.5kW) per vehicle	2 x BUT (Leyland Albion) of 230hp (171.5kW) per vehicle Later removed
Horsepower (total):	460hp (343kW)	460hp (343kW) Later removed
Transmission:	Mechanical	Mechanical Later removed
Max speed:	70mph (113km/h)	70mph (113km/h)
Coupling type:	Screw	Screw
Multiple restriction:	Blue Square	Blue Square
Door type:	Slam	Slam
Special features:	-	-
Body structure:	Steel	Steel
Notes:		Later modified with engines removed and reclassified as TBSK

Left: *Another fleet of main line DMMU stock built at Swindon Works were the attractive Trans-Pennine six-car sets introduced in 1960, with curved glass cab ends and including an intermediate non-driving power car. The pioneer DMC vehicle No. E51951 is illustrated coupled to a Motor Brake Second Corridor, a Trailer Buffet First Lavatory and a further DMC. The set is painted in green livery with a white cab canopy and cream lining.* CJM-C

Right: *A total of 51 carriages made up the Trans-Pennine fleet, of which 17 were non driving Motor Brake Second Corridor vehicles, as illustrated by vehicle No. E51969 from its guards van end. Note the cant rail height destination boards and the fuel tank and power unit below an intermediate vehicle. The pleasing design of the Trans-Pennine sets was the result of the then BR Design Panel trying to establish a more pleasing profile of rolling stock.* CJM-C

TSL	TBFL
124	124
180	181
59765-59773	59774-59781
-	-
1960	1860
BR Swindon Works	BR Swindon Works
64ft 6in (19.66m)	64ft 6in (19.66m)
12ft 9½in (3.90m)	12ft 9½in (3.90m)
9ft 3in (2.82m)	9ft 3in (2.82m)
64S	18F/8U
2+2 (Trans-Pennine)	2+1 (Trans-Pennine)
Throughout	Throughout
2	1 (staff)
32 tons	34 tons
Vacuum	Vacuum
-	-
-	-
-	-
70mph (113km/h)	70mph (113km/h)
Screw	Screw
Blue Square	Blue Square
Slam	Slam
-	-
Steel	Steel

Below: *After BR green livery the Trans-Pennine stock was repainted into blue and grey main line colours together with a full yellow warning end. The sets sported a standard four character route indicator but no destination blind. Driving Motor Composite vehicles, as illustrated by No. E51955 at Leeds on a Manchester service, had their first class seating for 21 in the three bays directly behind the driving area. This vehicle has gained an early design quartz headlight.* **CJM**

Class 125

Vehicle type:	DMS	DMBS	TS
Classification:	125	125	125
Original classification:	125/2	125/1	185
Original number range:	50988-51007	51154-51173	59449-59468
Revised number range:	-	-	-
Introduced:	1958	1958	1958
Built by:	BR Derby Works	BR Derby Works	BR Derby Works
Vehicle length (over body):	64ft 0in (19.51m)	64ft 0in (19.51m)	63ft 8¾in (19.42m)
Height:	12ft 9½in (3.90m)	12ft 9½in (3.90m)	12ft 9½in (3.90m)
Width:	9ft 4½in (2.86m)	9ft 4½in (2.86m)	9ft 4½in (2.86m)
Seating:	95S	65S	110S
Internal layout:	2+3	2+3	2+3
Gangway:	Not fitted	Not fitted	Not fitted
Toilets:	No	No	No
Weight:	39ton 10cwt	39ton 10cwt	28ton 10cwt
Brake type:	Vacuum	Vacuum	Vacuum
Power unit:	2 x Rolls Royce of 238hp (177.5kW) per vehicle	2 x Rolls Royce of 238hp (177.5kW) per vehicle	-
Horsepower (total):	476hp (355kW)	476hp (355kW)	-
Transmission:	Hydraulic	Hydraulic	-
Max speed:	70mph (113km/h)	70mph (113km/h)	70mph (113km/h)
Coupling type:	Screw	Screw	Screw
Multiple restriction:	Orange Star	Orange Star	Orange Star
Door type:	Slam	Slam	Slam
Special features:	-	-	-
Body structure:	Steel	Steel	Steel

Below: *Often known as the Lea Valley sets, these 20 three-car Derby-built Rolls Royce powered sets were introduced from December 1958 over a nine month period, allocated to the Eastern Region and working over the London Liverpool Street to Broxbourne route. They were powered by a Rolls Royce 238hp (177.5kW) engine driving a hydraulic transmission. The sets were very unreliable and after being displaced by electrification from the Lea Valley were deployed on other Eastern Region routes including King's Cross suburban. The sets had a unique Orange Star coupling code. All were withdrawn by 1977.* CJM-C

Vehicle type:	DMSL	DMBSL	TFK
Classification:	126	126	126
Original classification:	126/1	126/2	189
Original number range:	50936, 51008-51029	51030-51051	59391-59400
Revised number range:	-	-	-
Introduced:	1959	1959	1959
Built by:	BR Swindon Works	BR Swindon Works	BR Swindon Works
Vehicle length (over body):	64ft 6in (19.66m)	64ft 6in (19.66m)	64ft 6in (19.66m)
Height:	12ft 9½in (3.90m)	12ft 9½in (3.90m)	12ft 9½in (3.90m)
Width:	9ft 3in (2.82m)	9ft 3in (2.82m)	9ft 3in (2.82m)
Seating:	64S	52S	42F
Internal layout:	2+2	2+2	Compartment
Gangway:	Intermediate -Throughout	Intermediate -Throughout End - Inner end	Throughout
Toilets:	2	1	1
Weight:	38 tons	38 tons	32 tons
Brake type:	Vacuum	Vacuum	Vacuum
Power unit:	2 x BUT (AEC) of 150hp (111.8kW) per vehicle	2 x BUT (AEC) of 150hp (111.8kW) per vehicle	-
Horsepower (total):	300hp (224kW)	300hp (224kW)	-
Transmission:	Mechanical	Mechanical	-
Max speed:	70mph (113km/h)	70mph (113km/h)	70mph (113km/h)
Coupling type:	Buck-eye	Buck-eye	Buck-eye
Multiple restriction:	White Circle	White Circle	White Circle
Door type:	Slam	Slam	Slam
Special features:	-	-	-
Body structure:	Steel	Steel	Steel

Vehicle type:	TCL	TBFKL
Classification:	126	126
Original classification:	189	187
Original number range:	59402-59412	59098-59099
Revised number range:	-	-
Introduced:	1959	1959
Built by:	BR Swindon Works	BR Swindon Works
Vehicle length (over body):	64ft 6in (19.66m)	64ft 6in (19.66m)
Height:	12ft 9½in (3.90m)	12ft 9½in (3.90m)
Width:	9ft 3in (2.82m)	9ft 3in (2.82m)
Seating:	18F/32S	18F, 12U buffet
Internal layout:	Compartment	First - Compartment, Buffet - Open
Gangway:	Throughout	Throughout
Toilets:	1	1 + 1 staff
Weight:	30 tons	33 tons
Brake type:	Vacuum	Vacuum
Power unit:	-	-
Horsepower (total):	-	-
Transmission:	-	-
Max speed:	70mph (113km/h)	70mph (113km/h)
Coupling type:	Buck-eye	Buck-eye
Multiple restriction:	White Circle	White Circle
Door type:	Slam	Slam
Special features:	-	-
Body structure:	Steel	Steel

Class 126

Left: *The main production run of Swindon Inter-City DMMUs for Scotland followed the same basic style at the original 7xxxx numbered sets of the mid 1950s, with two different styles of driving car, one having a gangway connection and the other a full width cab, thus enabling either three- or six-car operation. A total of 45 vehicles made up the order; 45 driving cars, 10 corridor firsts, 11 trailer composites and two buffet cars. Sc50936, one of the DMSL vehicles, is illustrated at Kilwinning.* CJM-C

Right: *Twenty-three of the driving cars were deemed as intermediate with end corridor connections and 22 had a full width driving cab with two front windows. Two-section four-character route displays were fitted, towards the centre on full width cab cars and either side of the gangway connection on intermediate vehicles. Full width cab car No. Sc51032 is illustrated at Prestwick. These sets were cascaded to the Ayrshire routes after being displaced from the Edinburgh-Glasgow corridor by the introduction of Class 27s on push-pull trains.* Brian Morrison

Left: *The follow-on order for Inter-City DMMUs for Scotland comprised 23 intermediate vehicles, 11 Trailer Composite Corridor, 10 Trailer First Corridor and two Trailer First Corridor Restaurant Buffet. When built all were painted in BR green, off-set by cream bodyside bands. This gave way to rail blue from the mid 1960s. TCK No. Sc59404 is illustrated, viewed from its corridor side. These vehicles had a toilet compartment at each end with three compartments of eight second class seats and four compartments with six first class seats.* CJM-C

Right: *Painted in BR 1960s BR rail blue with a full yellow warning end and still with operational four character route indicator, DMSL No. Sc51015 leads a three-car set into Prestwick on 2 June 1977 forming the 12.35 Glasgow Central to Ayr service. These DMSL vehicles seated 64 in the 2+2 low-density configuration with a central corridor. Note that the drop-head buckeye coupling is in the raised position.* Brian Morrison

Class 127

Vehicle type:	DMBS	TSL	TS
Classification:	127	127	127
Original classification:	-	186	186
Original number range:	51591-51650	59589-59618	59619-59649
Revised number range:	-	-	-
Introduced:	1959	1959	1959
Built by:	BR Derby Works	BR Derby Works	BR Derby Works
Vehicle length (over body):	64ft 0in (19.5,)	63ft 10in (19.46m)	63ft 10in 63ft 10in (19.46m)
Height:	12ft 4½in (3.77m)	12ft 4½in (3.77m)	12ft 4½in (3.77m)
Width:	9ft 3in (2.82m)	9ft 3in (2.82m)	9ft 3in (2.82m)
Seating:	78S	90S	106S
Internal layout:	2+3	2+3	2+3
Gangway:	No	No	No
Toilets:	No	1	No
Weight:	40 tons	30 tons	29 tons
Brake type:	Vacuum	Vacuum	Vacuum
Power unit:	2 x Rolls Royce of 238hp (177kW) per vehicle	-	-
Horsepower (total):	476hp (355kW)	-	-
Transmission:	Hydraulic	-	-
Max speed:	70mph (113km/h)	70mph (113km/h)	70mph (113km/h)
Coupling type:	Screw	Screw	Screw
Multiple restriction:	Red Triangle	Red Triangle	Red Triangle
Door type:	Slam	Slam	Slam
Special features:	-	-	-
Body structure:	Steel	Steel	Steel
Notes:	A number of DMBS vehicles were rebuilt as motor parcels cars and renumbered in the 559xx series.		

Left: *As a stop gap from steam to electrification on the St Pancras to Bedford route a fleet of 30 four-car diesel hydraulic sets was introduced to Cricklewood depot between May and December 1959. The high-density sets, built to the standard Derby design, were not gangway fitted and did not have first class seating. One toilet was provided in the TSL vehicle, but passengers had to travel in the correct coach to avail themselves of the facility. Painted in green livery with a small yellow panel, a four car hydraulic set is seen near Hendon in 1961.* CJM-C

Right: *By the late 1960s BR rail blue livery was being applied and towards the end some sets emerged in blue/grey colours. In this view we see a rail blue liveried set led by DMBS No. M51621 passing Cricklewood during the period of route electrification. After withdrawal 22 driving vehicles were converted to parcels use and fitted with roller shutter doors. After final disposal some vehicles have entered the world of preservation.* CJM

Class 128

Number range:	55987-55996
Classification:	DMLV
Introduced:	1959
Built by:	Gloucester RC&W
Vehicle length (over body):	64ft 5½in (19.65m)
Height:	12ft 8¼in (3.87m)
Width:	9ft 2½in (2.81m)
Seating:	None
Internal layout:	Luggage space
Gangway:	Yes, removed on cars 55989/90 in 1970s
Toilets:	Not fitted
Weight:	40-41 tonnes
Brake type:	Vacuum
Power unit:	2 x Leyland Albion of 230hp (171.5kW) per vehicle
Horsepower (total):	460hp (343kW)
Transmission:	Mechanical
Max speed:	70mph (113km/h)
Coupling type:	Screw
Multiple restriction:	Blue Square
Door type:	Slam for cab, sliding for luggage
Special features:	-
Body structure:	Steel

Below Left: *The British Transport Commission ordered 10 Driving Motor Luggage Vans from the Gloucester Railway Carriage & Wagon Co for delivery between January and April 1960. Two different designs of vehicle made up the order. The first four, Nos. M55987-M55990, were built without end gangways and had a full width driving cab incorporating a solid four character route indicator. The six vehicles built for the Western Region, Nos. W55991 - W55996, were gangway fitted to enable coupling together or with passenger stock. Access to the full length luggage compartment was by three pairs of bi-parting manual sliding doors on each side; a separate hinged door gave access to the one third width driving compartment. When first introduced the DMLVs were painted in green livery offset with cream bodyside bands and whiskers branding on the cab ends. Later BR rail blue was applied and some vehicles which remained in traffic in the Royal Mail era were painted in Royal Mail red and were given red/ yellow wasp banded luggage doors. Painted in BR rail blue, Western Region car No. W55991 awaits departure from Paddington on 10 November 1981 carrying Parcels Service bodyside branding. The former route indicator has been adjusted to display white dots, while the front gangway connection is still intact.* CJM

Right: *Former Western Region car No. 55993 was transferred to the London Midland operating area after the mail services ceased using the single cars on the Western Region. On 19 May 1988 the vehicle is seen at Derby in the bay platform with a Royal Mail service from Nottingham. The vehicle is painted in Royal Mail red livery and has had its gangway connection removed but still retains the shaped exhaust stacks. Marker/tail lights have been fitted in place of the route display boxes and the vehicle is operating as set No. 003.* CJM

Number range:	55997-55999
Classification:	DMLV
Introduced:	1958
Built by:	Cravens RC&W
Vehicle length (over body):	57ft 6in (17.53m)
Height:	12ft 9in (3.89m)
Width:	9ft 3in (2.82m)
Seating:	None
Internal layout:	Luggage space
Gangway:	Not fitted
Toilets:	Not fitted
Weight:	30 tons
Brake type:	Vacuum
Power unit:	2 x BUT (AEC) of 150hp (111.8kW) per vehicle
Horsepower (total):	300hp (224kW)
Transmission:	Mechanical
Max speed:	70mph (113km/h)
Coupling type:	Screw
Multiple restriction:	Yellow Diamond
Door type:	Slam
Special features:	-
Body structure:	Steel

Below Right: *The BTC ordered three Driving Motor Luggage Vans from Cravens of Sheffield for use on the London Midland Region. These were delivered in July/August 1958 and based at Manchester Newton Heath depot. These vehicles did not have a gangway connection and operated north from Manchester to Carlisle and to the Birmingham/Wolverhampton area in the south. Like the Gloucester design opposite, these vehicles were authorised to haul a trailing load, usually one or two vans. Access to the van stowage area was by three pairs of hinged doors on either side, with a separate door for the driving cab. Under the TOPS numeric classification system these cars became Class 129, but none remained in traffic long enough to carry a six digit TOPS number. Two were withdrawn in 1972/73, while No. M55997 was transferred to the BR Research Division based at Derby. This view shows car No. 55998 at Birmingham New Street in 1959, painted in green livery with cream banding and whisker ends. Later BR rail blue was applied with full yellow ends.* R. S. Carpenter

Left: *After withdrawal from parcels use, car No. M55997 was transferred to BR Research at Derby where it was involved in hydraulic transmission development, with special equipment installed on a modified B4 bogie. The vehicle was modified at the RTC Derby and then transferred by rail to the Old Dalby test track where this illustration was captured. For its departmental role, the vehicle was painted in Research red and blue and given the name* **Hydra**, *the Research number RDB975385 and the identity Laboratory 9. It was finally withdrawn after the development work was complete in 1985 and broken up by Vic Berry, Leicester, in 1986.* CJM

For Class 130, see First Generation DMMU Class 116
For Class 131, see First Generation DMMU Class 122
For Class 140, see First Generation DMMU Class 104
For Class 141, see First Generation DMMU Class 105
For Class 142, see First Generation DMMU Class 108
For Class 143, see First Generation DMMU Class 100
For Class 144, see First Generation DMMU Class 101
For Class 145, see First Generation DMMU Class 103
For Class 146, see First Generation DMMU Class 109
For Class 147, see First Generation DMMU Class 111
For Class 148, see First Generation DMMU Class 114
For Class 149, see First Generation DMMU Class 121
For Class 150, see First Generation DMMU Class 122
For Class 160, see First Generation DMMU Class 104
For Class 161, see First Generation DMMU Class 107, 108
For Class 162, see First Generation DMMU Class 101
For Class 163, see First Generation DMMU Class 110
For Class 164, see First Generation DMMU Class 101
For Class 165, see First Generation DMMU Class 111
For Class 166, see First Generation DMMU Class 104
For Class 167, see First Generation DMMU Class 108
For Class 168, see First Generation DMMU Class 101

Below: *On 10 September 1960, a Midland Region St Pancras - Bedford suburban unit was used to form a seaside relief service from Kentish Town to Southend Central and is seen passing Pitsea led by DMBS No. 51644. At that time domestic suburban units were frequently used for relief and special services during the day after the morning rush hour, being back in position for a late teatime departure with London workers returning home. This four-car formation of what was to become Class 127 stock would have carried 352 second class passengers.* CJM-C

For Class 169, see First Generation DMMU Class 104
For Class 170, see First Generation DMMU Class 105
For Class 171, see First Generation DMMU Class 101
For Class 172, see First Generation DMMU Class 116
For Class 173, see First Generation DMMU Class 115
For Class 174, see First Generation DMMU Class 118
For Class 175, see First Generation DMMU Class 116
For Class 176, see First Generation DMMU Class 117
For Class 177, see First Generation DMMU Class 115
For Class 178, see First Generation DMMU Class 119
For Class 179, see First Generation DMMU Class 120
For Class 180, see First Generation DMMU Class 124
For Class 181, see First Generation DMMU Class 124
For Class 182, see First Generation DMMU Class 123
For Class 183, see First Generation DMMU Class 123
For Class 184, see First Generation DMMU Class 123
For Class 185, see First Generation DMMU Class 125
For Class 186, see First Generation DMMU Class 127
For Class 188, see First Generation DMMU Swindon - 79470-79479
For Class 189, see First Generation DMMU Class 126
For Class 190, see First Generation DMMU Class 126

Below: *An interesting period picture just north of Liverpool on what is now the Merseyrail system at Sandhills, showing Sandhills No. 2 signal box on the left, the tracks to Bank Hall motive power depot just a little further on and then Kirkdale carriage sidings, which is now the location of Kirkdale EMU depot. The train approaching forming a Harrogate to Liverpool Exchange service is a three-car Birmingham RC&W, (later Class 104), set painted in green livery with small yellow warning ends.* Ian G. Holt

Class 201 – 6S

Alpha code :	6S
TOPS class:	201
Number range:	1001-1007
Introduced:	1957
Built by:	BR Eastleigh Works
Formation:	DMBS+TS+TC+TS+TS+DMBS
Vehicle numbers:	DMBS - 60000-60013 TS - 60500-60519 TC - 60700-60707
Vehicle length:	DMBS - 58ft (17.68m) TS, TC- 58ft (17.68m)
Height:	12ft 6¾in (3.82m)
Width:	9ft (2.74m)
Seating:	Total - 36F/206S DMBS - 22S TS - 52S TC - 36F/6S
Internal layout:	Standard - 2+2 or - Compartment First - Compartment
Gangway:	Within set
Toilets:	TS, TC - 1
Weight:	Total - 225 tonnes DMBS - 54 tonnes TS - 29 tonnes TC - 30 tonnes TS - 29 tonnes TS - 29 tonnes DMBS - 54 tonnes
Brake type:	Air, EP/Auto
Power unit:	1 x EE4SRKT of 500hp (373kW) per DMBS
Transmission:	Electric
Main generator:	EE
Traction motor type:	EE
Horsepower:	1,000hp (746kW)
Max speed:	75 mph (121km/h)
Coupling type:	Buck-eye
Multiple restriction:	200 series SR DEMUs
Door type:	Slam
Special features:	-

Below: *By the 1950s traffic levels on the London to Hastings route were such that some form of improvement over 'Schools' class steam locos hauling Hastings profile stock was needed. The answer came in the form of a fleet of six-car diesel electric multiple unit trains (DEMUs), built at Eastleigh and incorporating an above floor mounted English Electric 500hp (373kW) engine in each driving car. 32 vehicles of the 6S design, later TOPS Class 201, were built. They were based on short underframes of 58ft and built to a narrow profile, just 9ft to fit within the restricted gauge of the Hastings line south of Tonbridge. The sets, which were internally gangwayed, seated 36 first and 206 standard class passengers in the 2+2 outer-suburban style. When built sets were finished in SR multiple unit green, but this later gave way to BR blue and grey with full yellow ends. These sets were fitted from new with electro-pneumatic air brakes and Southern Region style waist height brake and multiple control jumper cables. Buck-eye couplings were fitted throughout. 6S set No. 1005 is seen painted in original green livery with large size headcode numerals at Sevenoaks in late 1957 soon after introduction* CJM-C

Right: *With the classic London Charing Cross headcode of '22' on the front end, now in standard smaller numerals, the first of the build, No. 1001, passes Chelsfield on 4 June 1982 forming a morning Hastings to Charing Cross service. By the time this image was recorded the set was painted in standard BR rail blue and grey with a full yellow warning end. All the 'Hastings' route DEMU stock was allocated to purpose built accommodation at St Leonards, Hastings, with out-base maintenance available in the London area if needed. Classified overhauls were undertaken at Eastleigh Works.* CJM

Below: *On 9 October 1982, set No. 1002 passes through Hither Green on the down main line with a '22' service bound for Hastings. Three of the 6S sets were disbanded in 1964 and gave one power car to each of six 'Tadpole' units formed with redundant EMU stock to operate on the Reading to Tonbridge line (3R stock). The Hastings line stock remained in operation until the route was electrified. Sets were then withdrawn and broken up. Thankfully the Hastings Diesel Group has saved a full set for preservation, which currently has a main line operating agreement with Network Rail.* CJM

Class 202 – 6L

Alpha code :	6L
Number range:	1011-1019§
Introduced:	1957
Built by:	BR Eastleigh
Formation:	As built: DMBS+TS+TC+TS+TS+DMBS Modified: DMBS+TS+TC+TS+TS+DMBS
Vehicle numbers:	DMBS - 60014-60031 TS - 60521-60547 TF - 60707-60715 - As built TC - 60707-60715 - Modified
Vehicle length:	DMBS - 64ft 6in (19.67m) TS, TC - 64ft 6in (19.67m)
Height:	12ft 6¾in (3.82m)
Width:	9ft (2.74m)
Seating:	As built / Modified Total: 48F/240S / 36F/252S DMBS - 30S / DMBS - 30S TS - 60S / TS - 60S TF - 48F / TC - 36F/12S
Internal layout:	Standard - 2+2 or Compartment First - Compartment
Gangway:	Within set
Toilets:	TS, TC - 1
Weight:	Total - 231 tonnes DMBS - 55 tonnes, TS - 30 tonnes TF (TC) - 31 tonnes, TS - 30 tonnes TS - 30 tonnes, DMBS - 55 tonnes
Brake type:	Air, EP/Auto
Power unit:	1 x EE4SRKT of 500hp (373kW) per DMBS
Transmission:	Electric
Generator:	EE
Traction motor type:	EE
Horsepower:	1,000hp (746kW)
Max speed:	75 mph (121km/h)
Coupling type:	Buck-eye
Multiple restriction:	200 series SR DEMUs
Door type:	Slam
Notes:	§ Fleet later extended by reforming ex-6B sets, 1031-1032

Above: *Between May 1957 and March 1958 a further nine six-car DEMUs were built for the Hastings line, and this time a standard Mk1 underframe was used increasing the vehicle length to 64ft 6in. These sets, numbered 1011-1019, were classified as 6L (6 car long). Set No. 1018 is seen departing from Tonbridge bound for Hastings soon after delivery.* **CJM-C**

Left: *Originally built as a 6L Trailer First Corridor but later reclassified as a Trailer Composite Corridor with two second class compartments, Car No. S60709 is illustrated.* **CJM**

Right: *On 10 August 1982, 6L Class 202 No. 1012 pulls into the staggered platforms at Stonegate with a 'down' Charing Cross to Hastings service. One of the problems with the SR DEMU stock was that it could not operate in multiple with like fitted SR EMU stock.* **CJM**

1018
22

1012
22

Class 203 – 6B, 4L

Alpha code :	6B		4L
Number range:	1031-1037		1036
Introduced:	1957		Reformed - 1985
Built by:	BR Eastleigh		BR Eastleigh
Formation:	As built: DMBS+TS+TF+TRB+TS+DMBS Modified: DMBS+TS+TC+TRB+TS+DMBS		DMBS+TS+TC+DMBS
Vehicle numbers:	DMBS - 60032-60045 TS - 60548-60561 TF - 60716-60722 TRB - 60750-60756	DMBS - 60036-60045 TS - 60554-60561 TC - 60718-60722 TRB - 60751-60756	DMBS - 60042-60043 TS - 60558 TC - 60721 -
Vehicle length:	DMBS - 64ft 6in(19.67m) TS, TC - 64ft 6in(19.67m)		DMBS - 64ft 6in(19.67m) TS, TC- 64ft 6in(19.67m)
Height:	12ft 6¾in (3.82m)		12ft 6¾in (3.82m)
Width:	9ft (2.74m)		9ft (2.74m)
Seating:	As built - Total - 48F/180S/21U Modified - Total - 36F/192S/21U DMBS - 30S TS - 60S TF - 48F TRB - 21U	 DMBS - 30S TS - 60S TC - 36F/12S TRB - 21U	 Total - 36F/132S DMBS - 30S TS - 60S TC - 36F/12S -
Internal layout:	Standard 2+2 or Compartment First - Compartment		Standard 2+2 or Compartment First - Compartment
Gangway:	Within set		Within set
Toilets:	TS, TC - 1		TS, TC - 1
Weight:	Total - 236 tonnes DMBS - 55 tonnes, TS - 30 tonnes TC - 31 tonnes, TRB - 35 tonnes TS - 30 tonnes, DMBS - 55 tonnes		Total - 171 tonnes DMBS - 55 tonnes TS - 30 tonnes TC - 31 tonnes DMBS - 55 tonnes
Brake type:	Air, EP/Auto		Air, EP/Auto
Power unit:	1 x EE4SRKT of 500hp (373kW) per DMBS		1 x EE4SRKT of 500hp (373kW) per DMBS
Transmission:	Electric		Electric
Main generator:	EE		EE
Traction motor type:	EE		EE
Horsepower:	1,000hp (746kW)		1,000hp (746kW)
Max speed:	75mph (121km/h)		75mph (121km/h)
Coupling type:	Buck-eye		Buck-eye
Multiple restriction:	200 series SR DEMUs		200 series SR DEMUs
Door type:	Slam		Slam
Notes:	TRBs later removed, replaced by TS		

Left Below: *To complete the dieselisation of the Hastings line, a fleet of seven , six-car long frame sets with a buffet car were built at Eastleigh Works in 1957. The buffet car took the place of one of the trailer second vehicles in a normal 6L set. The 6B or 6 car Buffet sets were numbered in the 1031-037 series and originally seated 48 first, 180 second and 21 unclassified in the buffet car; later seating modifications reduced the first class accommodation to 36 and increased the second class seating to 192. The buffet service on the Hastings route was never a major success and two cars were withdrawn in 1964 from sets 1031 and 1032 which were reformed as 6L sets. The remaining buffet cars were withdrawn in 1980. Set No. 1037 complete with buffet car is seen arriving at Salisbury on 19 September 1970.* **Geoff Gillham**

Right: *After it was agreed to withdraw the remaining buffet cars, most sets operated with just five coaches, as shown here with set No. 1037 forming a Charing Cross to Hastings service on Hildenborough Bank on 4 June 1982.* **CJM**

Below: *In 1985 the Southern Region rolling stock engineers formed a four-car 'long' set of vehicles from set No. 1036 and reclassified is as a 4L. On 5 November 1985, the set rounds the curve into Tonbridge with a down Hastings line service. As a four-car set, it seated 36 first and 132 standard (second) class passengers.* **CJM**

Class 204 – 3T

TOPS class:	204
Alpha code :	3T
Original number range:	1401-1404
TOPS number range:	-
Introduced:	1979 (from Class 205, 206)
Built by:	Originally and reformed - BR Eastleigh
Formation:	DMBS+TS+DTCL
Vehicle numbers:	DMBS - 60102, 60103, 60107, 60121 TS - 77500, 77503, 77507, 77508 DTCL - 60802, 60803, 60807, 60821
Vehicle length:	DMBS, DTCL - 64ft 0in (19.50m) TS - 63ft 11½in (19.51m)
Height:	12ft 6¾in (3.83m)
Width:	9ft 3in (2.82m)
Seating:	Total - 24F/160S DMBS - 52S TS - 66S DTC - 50S/13F
Internal layout:	Standard - 2+2, First - Compartment
Gangway:	No
Toilets:	DTC - 1
Weight:	Total - 118 tonnes DMBS - 56 tonnes TC - 30 tonnes DTS - 32 tonnes
Brake type:	Air, EP/Auto
Bogie type:	SR/BR Mk4
Power unit:	1 x EE4SRKT of 500hp (373kW) per DMBS
Transmission:	Electric
Main generator:	EE
Traction motor type:	EE507
Horsepower:	500hp (373kW)
Max speed:	75 mph (121km/h)
Coupling type:	Buck-eye
Multiple restriction:	200 series SR DEMUs
Door type:	Slam
Notes:	The TS vehicle was a former 2EPB DTS with the driving controls isolated, previously formed in 3R Class 206 stock

Left Below: *In 1979 BR Eastleigh formed four three-car DEMU sets classified as 3T (Three car Hampshire sets with an additional Trailer). The sets were formed of two-car Hampshire Class 205s with the spare ex EPB driving trailer recovered from the disbanded 'Tadpole' Class 206 stock which was through wired and marshalled between. The four sets were based at Eastleigh and operated over Berkshire, Hampshire and Wiltshire non-electrified lines. The old EPB driving cab was isolated and sealed out of use and the buffer heads at the driving end were removed to stop fouling on the attached vehicle. The unused cab of car No. S77503 from set 1404 is illustrated.* CJM

Right Top: *With its Driving Trailer Composite leading, still retaining two first class compartments, set No. 1401 departs St Denys towards Southampton with a service from Portsmouth Harbour on 7 July 1981. The set still retains standard rail blue livery.* CJM

Right Below: *Set No. 1403, again viewed from its Driving Trailer Composite vehicle, shows the BR blue and grey livery. The 3T sets remained on the operating register until 1987 when they were withdrawn. During the final months of service some were reduced to two-car form, with the original EPB driving trailer removed and scrapped. Set No. 1403 is seen at Southampton during a shunt move from one platform to another on 25 September 1980.* CJM

1401
88
20

1403

Class 205 – 3H, 2H

	Original layout		Trial refurbishment
Alpha code :	3H	2H	3H(M)
TOPS classification:	205	204, changed to 205 as 3-car	205/1
Number range:	205001-205033	205019-205022 (not carried)	205101
Original number range:	1101-1133	1119-1122	1111
Introduced:	1958 *	1959	1979
Built by:	BR Eastleigh	BR Eastleigh	Refurb - BREL Eastleigh
Formation:	DMBS+TS+DTC	DMBS+DTC	DMBS+TS+DTS
Vehicle numbers:	DMBS - 60100-60125, 60145-60151 TS - 60650-60678 DTC - 60800-60832	DMBS - 60118-60121 DTC - 60818-60821 -	DMBS - 60110 TS - 60660 DTS - 60810
Vehicle length:	DMBS, DTS - 64ft (19.51m) TS - 63ft 6in (19.34m)	DMBS, DTS - 64ft (19.51m) TS - 63ft 6in (19.34m)	DMBS, DTS - 64ft (19.51m) TS - 63ft 6in (19.34m)
Height:	12ft 8in (3.86m)	12ft 8in (3.86m)	12ft 8in (3.86m)
Width:	9ft 3¼in (2.82m)	9ft 3¼in (2.82m)	9ft 3¼in (2.82m)
Seating:	Total - 13F/218S DMBS - 52S TS - 104S DTC - 13F/62S	Total - 13F/114S DMBS - 52S DTC - 13F/62S -	Total - 213S DMBS - 39S TS - 98S DTS - 76S
Internal layout:	Standard - 2+3 or Compartment First - Compartment	Standard - 2+3 or Compartment First - Compartment	2+2/2+3S
Gangway:	No	No	Within set
Toilets:	DTC - 1	DTC - 1	DTS - 1
Weight:	Total - 119 tonnes DMBS - 56 tonnes TS - 31 tonnes DTC - 32 tonnes	Total - 87 tonnes DMBS - 55 tonnes DTC - 32 tonnes DTS - 32 tonnes	Total - 119 tonnes DMBS - 56 tonnes TS - 31 tonnes DTS - 32 tonnes
Brake type:	Air, EP/Auto	Air, EP/Auto	Air, EP/Auto
Bogie type:	SR/BR Mk4	SR/BR Mk4	SR/BR Mk4
Power unit:	1 x EE4SRKT of 500hp (373kW) in DMBS	1 x EE4SRKT of 500hp (373kW) in DMBS	1 x EE4SRKT of 500hp (373kW) in DMBS
Transmission:	Electric	Electric	Electric
Main generator:	EE	EE	EE
Traction motor type:	EE507	EE507	EE507
Horsepower:	500hp (373kW)	500hp (373kW)	500hp (373kW)
Max speed:	75mph (121km/h)	75mph (121km/h)	75mph (121km/h)
Coupling type:	Buck-eye	Buck-eye	Buck-eye
Multiple restriction:	200 series SR DEMUs	200 series SR DEMUs	200 series SR DEMUs
Door type:	Slam	Slam	Slam
Notes:	* TS built 1959		

Left: *After the green-livery era, the Hampshire sets were painted in standard rail blue, with a yellow warning end. On the brake vehicles a black triangle was applied to identify to station platform staff which end the brake van was. Viewed from its DTC end, set No. 1124 is seen near Oakley between Andover and Basingstoke in 1979 forming a Salisbury to Reading service.* CJM

Refurbished 3H	
205/0	205/2
205001-205033, 2052xx	205205
1101-1133	1111 (205101)
1970-80s	1995
Selhurst Depot	St Leonards Depot
DMBS+TS+DTS	DMBS+TS+DTS
DMBS - 60100-60125, 60145-60151 TS - 60650-60678 DTC - 60800-60832	DMBS - 60110 TS - 71634 (ex CEP) DTS - 60810
DMBS, DTS - 64ft (19.51m) TS - 63ft 6in (19.34m)	DMBS, DTS - 64ft (19.51m) TS - 63ft 6in (19.34m)
12ft 8in (3.86m)	12ft 8in (3.86m)
9ft 3¼in (2.82m)	9ft 3¼in (2.82m)
Total - 13-19F/190-218S+ DMBS - 42-52S TS - 98-104S DTC - 13-19F/50-62S	Total - 179S DMBS - 39S TS - 64S DTS - 76S
Standard - 2+3 or Compartment First - Compartment	2+2/2+3
Within set	Within set
DTS - 1	DTS - 1
Total - 119 tonnes DMBS - 56 tonnes TS - 31 tonnes DTS - 32 tonnes	Total - 119 tonnes DMBS - 56 tonnes TS - 31 tonnes
Air, EP/Auto	Air, EP/Auto
SR/BR Mk4	SR/BR Mk4
1 x EE4SRKT of 500hp (373kW) in DMBS	1 x EE4SRKT of 500hp (373kW) in DMBS
Electric	Electric
EE	EE
EE507	EE507
500hp (373kW)	500hp (373kW)
75mph (121km/h)	75mph (121km/h)
Buck-eye	Buck-eye
200 series SR DEMUs	200 series SR DEMUs
Slam	Slam
+ Seats vary depending of layout; some DTC vehicles have luggage compartments	

Above: *The 'Hampshire' DEMUs started to appear in 1958, firstly as two-car sets. Viewed from its DMBS vehicle, set No. 1103 is seen at Eastleigh soon after delivery, still with large size headcode numbers.* CJM-C

Above: *By 1959 the two-car sets were being strengthened to three by the addition of a TS coach. Set No. 1103 is now seen at Woking, again from its DMBS end, in 1961 as a three car formation with a 'V' form yellow warning panel.* CJM-C

Right Middle: *The 'Hampshire' sets being suburban stock had seating in the 2+3 style, with doors to each seating bay. Originally strung luggage racks were provided, later changed to metal fittings. This view shows the 1980s blue/green moquette.* CJM

Right Bottom: *In 1979 a trial refurbishment of Hampshire set No. 1111 was carried out at Eastleigh, to open out compartments and bring fittings up to date. The blue/grey-liveried unit is seen at Rye in 1983 from its DTS end.* C. Hall

Class 205 – 3H, 2H

Above: *The 3H or 'Hampshire' units did spread their operating range in the 1970s and 80s to work some Sussex routes. With its DMBS leading, clearly showing the black triangle indicating the brake van and power car end, set No. 1114 is seen at Oxted on 3 November 1984 with a service bound for East Grinstead.* CJM

Left Middle: *A number of the original Hampshire sets, now classified as Class 205, remained working into the Network SouthEast and even the privatised era. One of these was set No. 205205; this was the original set No. 1111 which was trial refurbished in 1979. In the NSE era it was modified at Selhurst to operate with an intermediate TS No. 71634 from a Class 411 set for use on the Ashford-Hastings line. Viewed from its power car end, the set is seen at Selhurst. Note that a headlight has now been applied.* CJM

Left Below: *Under privatisation the remaining Hampshire sets were taken over by Connex, who applied their off-white, blue and yellow livery to some sets. No. 205033 is shown at Selhurst from its DMBS end; in this livery it was decided not to apply the yellow brake van end triangle* CJM

Class 206 – 3R

Below: *In the 1960s, the growth of business on the Reading to Tonbridge via Guildford and Redhill cross-country connection was growing and modernisation was needed. However, little or no money was available for new trains for the line so the Southern Region had to work out the best option. This came from the withdrawing of three six-car short Hastings sets and using the six DMBS vehicles to provide power cars for six three-car DEMU sets. Each set was formed with one Class 201 DMBS and one TS, with the remote driving facility provided by six spare Class 416 EMU Driving Trailer Seconds in the 775xx series. The six units had the odd appearance of two narrow bodied vehicles and one standard width car - hence the 'Tadpole' name being given. Originally painted in green livery, the sets were then dressed in all-over BR rail blue before blue and grey colours were adopted. In the view below set No. 1206 is seen at Ham Street on 27 July 1982 after being displaced from the Reading-Tonbridge route, working a service from Hastings to Ashford. The wide bodied EPB vehicle is at the rear.* CJM

TOPS class	206
Alpha code:	3R
Original number range:	1201-1206
TOPS number range:	-
Introduced:	1964 (from Class 201, 416)
Built by:	Originally and reformed - BR Eastleigh
Formation:	DMBS+TSL+DTS
Vehicle numbers:	DMBS - 60002-60007 TSL - 60503-506/509/510 DTS - 77500/503/507-510
Vehicle length:	DMBS, TSL - 58ft 0in (17.68m) DTS - 63ft 11½in (19.49m)
Height:	12ft 6¾in (3.83m)
Width:	DMBS, TSL - 9ft 0in (2.74m) DTS - 9ft 3in (2.82m)
Seating:	Total - 176S DMBS - 22S TSL - 52S DTS - 102S (some declassified for luggage)
Internal layout:	Standard - 2+2, 2+3 and Compartment
Gangway:	No
Toilets:	TSL - 1
Weight:	Total - 113tons 2cwt DMBS - 54tons 2cwt TSL - 29 tons DTS - 30 tons
Brake type:	Air, EP/Auto
Bogie type:	SR/BR Mk4
Power unit:	1 x EE4SRKT of 500hp (373kW) per DMBS
Transmission:	Electric
Generator:	EE
Traction motor type:	EE507
Horsepower:	500hp (373kW)
Max speed:	75mph (121km/h)
Coupling type:	Buck-eye
Multiple restriction:	200 series SR DEMUs
Door type:	Slam
Notes:	'Tadpole' stock

Class 207 – 3D, 2D

	Original form	Facelifted	Facelifted
TOPS class:	207	207/0	207/1
Alpha code:	3D	3D	2D
Original number range:	1301-1319	-	-
TOPS number range:	207001-207019	207001-207019	207101-207103
Introduced:	1962	Facelifted: 1985-90	
Built by:	BR Eastleigh	BR Eastleigh	
Formation:	DMBS+TC+DTS	DMBS+TC+DTS	DMBS+DTS
Vehicle numbers:	DMBS - 60126-60144 TC - 60600-60618 DTS - 60900-60918	DMBS - 60126-60144 TC - 60600-60618 DTS - 60900-60918	DMBS -60127/29/30 DTS - 60901/03/04 -
Vehicle length:	DMBS, DTS - 64ft 0in (19.51m) TC - 63ft 6in (19.35m)	DMBS, DTS - 64ft 0in (19.51m) TC - 63ft 6in (19.35m)	DMBS, DTS - 64ft 0in (19.51m)
Height:	12ft 6¾in (3.83m)	12ft 6¾in (3.83m)	12ft 6¾in (3.83m)
Width:	9ft (2.74m)	9ft (2.74m)	9ft (2.74m)
Seating:	Total - 24F/160S DMBS - 42S TC - 24F/42S DTS - 76S	Total - 24F/160S DMBS - 42S TC - 24F/42S DTS - 76S	Total - 118S DMBS - 42S DTS - 76S -
Internal layout:	Standard - 2+3 First - Compartment	Standard - 2+3 First - Compartment	Standard - 2+3 First - Compartment
Gangway:	No	No	Within set
Toilets:	TC - 1	TC - 1	
Weight:	Total - 119 tonnes DMBS - 56 tonnes TC - 31 tonnes DTS - 32 tonnes	Total - 119 tonnes DMBS - 56 tonnes TC - 31 tonnes DTS - 32 tonnes	Total - 88 tonnes DMBS - 56 tonnes DTS - 32 tonnes -
Brake type:	Air, EP/Auto	Air, EP/Auto	Air, EP/Auto
Bogie type:	SR/BR Mk4	SR/BR Mk4	SR/BR Mk4
Power unit:	1 x EE4SRKT of 500hp (373kW) per DMBS	1 x EE4SRKT of 500hp (373kW) per DMBS	1 x EE4SRKT of 500hp (373kW) per DMBS
Transmission:	Electric	Electric	Electric
Main generator:	EE	EE	EE
Traction motor type:	EE507	EE507	EE507
Horsepower:	500hp (373kW)	500hp (373kW)	500hp (373kW)
Max speed:	75mph (121km/h)	75mph (121km/h)	75mph (121km/h)
Coupling type:	Buck-eye	Buck-eye	Buck-eye
Multiple restriction:	200 series SR DEMUs	200 series SR DEMUs	200 series SR DEMUs
Door type:	Slam	Slam	Slam
Sub class detail:	As built	Facefilted/2-car	

Left: *In keeping with other DEMU classes the 'East Sussex' or Class 207s carried a black triangle on the end of the DMBS vehicle indicating the location of the brake van and power unit. After carrying all-over BR green the Class 207s were repainted in standard blue and grey colours with full yellow ends, black underframes and dark grey roofs. Set No. 1305 is seen departing from Groombridge on 24 April 1985 forming the 16.09 Tonbridge to Eridge service. These units were fully compatible with all 2xx class SR DEMUs.* CJM

Reformed
207/1
3D
-
207201-207203
Reformed - 1996
Rebuilt - BR Selhurst
DMBS+TS+DTS
DMBS - 60127/29/30
TS - 70286, 70544, 70549 **
DTS - 60901/03/04
DMBS, DTS - 64ft 0in (19.51m)
TS - 64ft 9½in (19.75m)
12ft 6¾in (3.83m)
9ft (2.74m)
Total - 179S
DMBS - 40S
TS - 64S
DTS - 75S
2+3

Within set
TS - 1
Total - 121.7 tonnes
DMBS - 56 tonnes
TS - 33.7 tonnes
DTS - 32 tonnes
Air, EP/Auto
DMBS/DTS - SR/BR Mk4
TS - Commonwealth
1 x EE4SRKT of 500hp (373kW) per DMBS

500hp (373kW)
75mph (121km/h)
Buck-eye
200 series SR DEMUs
Slam
** Refurbished, with gangway within set and ex 4-CEP TS centre car

Above: *BR Eastleigh Works produced a fleet of 19 three-car 'East Sussex' DEMU sets in 1962 in a slightly more rounded design than previous builds using a fibre glass cab front. The sets were to operate from London to East Grinstead, Tunbridge Wells and Brighton via Eridge. Painted in green livery, set No. 1319 is shown from its DTS end.* **Brian Stephenson**

Below: *By the late 1960s BR rail blue was applied with full yellow warning ends. With its 76 seat DTS nearest the camera, set No. 1305 is seen at Oxted in July 1978. First class seating on these sets was provided in the middle TC vehicle.* **CJM**

Right: *Class 207s which remained in service into the Network SouthEast era were repainted when painting fell due into the NSE red, white and blue colours, as shown here on TOPS renumbered set No. 207010. This view clearly shows the power car design with its removable roof section to provide access to the English Electric 6K engine. These high density sets has seating in the 2+3 style with a door position by each seating bay.* **CJM**

Class 251 & 261 'Blue Pullman'

Vehicle type:	DMBFL	DMBS	MPSL	MKFL
Formation type:	6-car	8-car	8-car	6-car
Classification:	251/1	251/2	261/1	261/1
Number range:	60090-60093	60094-60099	60644-60649	60730-60733
Introduced:	1959-60	1959-60	1959-60	1959-60
Built by:	Metro-Cammell	Metro-Cammell	Metro-Cammell	Metro-Cammell
Vehicle length:	66ft 5½in (20.26m)	66ft 5½in (20.26m)	65ft 6in (19.96m)	65ft 6in (19.96m)
Height:	12ft 4½in (3.77m)	12ft 4½in (3.77m)	12ft 4½in (3.77m)	12ft 4½in (3.77m)
Width:	9ft 3in (2.82m)	9ft 3in (2.82m)	9ft 3in (2.82m)	9ft 3in (2.82m)
Seating:	12F	18S	42S	18F
Internal layout:	2+1	2+2	2+2	2+1F
Gangway:	Inner end	Inner end	Throughout	Throughout
Toilets:	1	1	1	1
Weight:	67ton 10cwt	67ton 10cwt	45ton 10cwt	49ton
Brake type:	Air (Westinghouse)	Air (Westinghouse)	Air (Westinghouse)	Air (Westinghouse)
Traction Power unit:	1 x NBL/MAN L12V18-21BS of 1,000hp (746kW)	1 x NBL/MAN L12V18-21BS of 1,000hp (746kW)	Power from DM	Power from DM
Traction motors:	4 x GEC 199hp (148kW) driven through Brown Boveri spring drive	4 x GEC 199hp (148kW) driven through Brown Boveri spring drive	2 x GEC 199hp (148kW) driven through Brown Boveri spring drive	2 x GEC 199hp (148kW) driven through Brown Boveri spring drive
Horsepower (total) traction :	Per car - 796hp (571kW)	Per car - 796hp (571kW)	Per car - 398hp (297kW)	Per car - 398hp (297kW)
Transmission:	Electric	Electric	-	-
Generators:	GEC	GEC	-	-
Traction motors:	GEC	GEC	-	-
Auxiliary engine:	-	-	1 x Rolls Royce C8N of 190hp (142kW)	1 x Rolls Royce C8N of 190hp (142kW)
Maximum speed:	90mph (145km/h)	90mph (145km/h)	90mph (145km/h)	90mph (145km/h)
Gear ratio:	19:67	19:67	19:67	-
Coupling type:	Screw	Screw	Screw	Screw
Multiple restriction:	Not issued, within type only+	Not issued, within type only+	Not issued, within type only+	Not issued, within type only+
Door type:	Slam	Slam	Slam	Slam
Fuel tank capacity:	500gal (2,273lit)	500gal (2,273lit)		
Aux fuel tank capacity:	100gal (455lit)	100gal (455lit)	100gal (455lit)	100gal (455lit)
Body structure:	Steel	Steel	Steel	Steel
Notes:	+ When introduced, no multiple operation facility was fitted nose end jumpers to allow double set operation were later installed			

TFKL	TPFL
8-car	60740-60743 - 6-car 60744-60749 - 8-car
261/2	261/2
60734-60739	60740-60749
1959-60	1959-60
Metro-Cammell	Metro-Cammell
65ft 6in (19.96m)	65ft 6in (19.96m)
12ft 4½in (3.77m)	12ft 4½in (3.77m)
9ft 3in (2.82m)	9ft 3in (2.82m)
18F	36F
2+1F	2+1F
Throughout	Throughout
1	1
36ton	33ton
Air (Westinghouse)	Air (Westinghouse)
-	-
-	-
-	-
-	-
-	-
-	-
-	-
90mph (145km/h)	90mph (145km/h)
-	-
Screw	Screw
Not issued, within type only+	Not issued, within type only+
Slam	Slam
-	-
-	-
Steel	Steel

Far Left: *One of the most impressive unit trains of all time must be the Metro-Cammell 'Blue Pullman' sets introduced in 1959 originally for the Midland Pullman service between St Pancras and Manchester with follow-on sets being introduced for use on the Western Region Birmingham Pullman and later used on London to Bristol/Swansea routes. Originally the six car sets were used on the Midland Pullman and the eight-car sets on the Birmingham route. Later the Midland sets were transferred to the Western Region. One of the eight-car Western Region sets is seen when brand new.* CJM-C

Top: *Interior of The Midland Pullman, showing the luxury first class layout in a parlour car, set out for evening dinner.* CJM-C

Above: *Blue Pullman driving cab, located on the left side of the full width cab layout, with brake controller operated by the driver's left hand, and the power controller operated by the driver's right hand. The hand brake wheel is on the right.* CJM-C

Below: *Blue Pullman Trailer Parlour First No. M60741 from the Midland Pullman set.* CJM-C

Class 251 & 261 'Blue Pullman'

Above: *Originally the eight-car Blue Pullman sets, painted in Nankin blue, operated on the Western Region between London Paddington and Birmingham, offering a first and second class at seat high-quality Pullman catering service, operating two out and back diagrams each day. With DMBS No. 60098 nearest the camera, an eight-car set awaits departure from London Paddington soon after introduction.* CJM-C

Below: *The Midland Pullman from St Pancras to Manchester commenced revenue operation on 4 July 1960, with each of two trains in each direction each weekday formed of one six-car all first class Pullman set. In this view at Leicester, the inaugural 'up' train bound for St Pancras heads south under clear signals.* Alec Swain

Above: *By the mid 1960s and the desire to apply yellow panels and then full yellow ends to all modern traction locomotives and multiple units, the majestic body profile of the Blue Pullman stock was given full yellow ends, losing the wonderful Pullman motif from the front end. One of the Western Region eight car-sets is seen at Cardiff with DMS No. W60098 nearest the camera on 4 September 1967, during the period the fleet was working Cardiff/Bristol to Paddington services.* CJM-C

Below: *The quest for the BR corporate image saw a new Pullman colour scheme introduced in the late 1960s, using the reverse paint application to the usual blue grey scheme, with the main body colour being light grey and the window banner finished in rail blue, which did actually look very smart, but did little for the body styling of the Blue Pullman stock. One of the Western Region eight-car sets is seen approaching Paddington showing the revised scheme.* John Cooper-Smith

APT-E

Vehicle:	PC1, PC2	TC1, TC2
Builder (body shell):	Metro-Cammell Birmingham	GEC Engineering Accrington
Builder (fitting out):	Derby RTC	Derby RTC
Built:	Apr-1971	Feb-1971
Wheel arrangement:	Bo-Artic (type E1)	Artic (type SA)
Height:	12ft 10in (3.91m)	12ft 10in (3.91m)
Length:	73ft.8in (22.50m)	69ft 7in (21.25m)
Total train length:	288ft (87.8m)	-
Width:	8ft 6in (2.59m)	8ft 6in (2.59m)
Wheelbase (powercar):	50ft 8in (15.5m)	-
Bogie wheelbase (power):	10ft 4in (3.17m)	7ft 8in (2.40m)
Wheel diameter:	3ft 0in (915mm)	3ft 0in (915mm)
Maximum speed (design):	195mph (312km/h)	195mph (312km/h)
(operational):	155mph (249.4km/h)	155mph (249.4km/h)
Gas turbine type:	British Leyland 350	-
Gas turbine output:	298hp (222kW)§	-
Number of turbine units:	5*	-
Alternator type:	Houchin 400Hz	-
Traction motor type:	GEC 253AY	-
Number of traction motors:	4	-
Traction output:	2400hp (1789kW) ●	-
Brake type:	Air, dynamic hydrokinetic	Air, dynamic hydrokinetic
Heating type:	Electric, air con	Electric, air con
Fuel tank capacity:	300gal (1136lit)	-
Seating:	-	8 (VIP bay)
Loading gauge:	C1	C1

Figures given are per vehicle

Notes:
§ Output upgraded in spring 1974 to 330hp (246kW)
* Originally only 4 gas-turbine units were used for traction, and one was used for auxiliary power; from spring 1974 all five gas turbines were turned over to traction
● Increased to 3,000hp (2237kW)

Below: *The Advanced Passenger Train - Experimental (APT-E) was without doubt one of the most stunning trains to ever grace the rail tracks in the UK. Gas-turbine powered and built as a development tool for high speed rail travel, the four-car articulated set emerged in 1971 and performed running tests over the Midland Main Line from Derby to the north and south to St Pancras. Major testing was conducted on the Old Dalby test track, where the illustration below was recorded. Further high speed main line testing was then carried out on the Western Region.* CJM

Above: *In August 1975 the APT-E was tested at very high speed on the Western Region between Swindon and Reading, usually peaking its speed at milepost 46¾. On 3 August 1975, a series of runs were undertaken where a maximum speed of 150mph (241km/h) was authorised; in the event a speed of 151.3mph (242km/h) was achieved. This view shows the set returning to Old Oak Common after this run. The following week on 10 August the set attained a speed record when it reached 152.3mph (245km/h).* CJM-C

Right Middle: *The stunning train is seen stabled between test runs in the middle road at Swindon on 7 August 1975, during one of its mid-week proving runs between Old Oak Common and Swindon. This view clearly shows the stunning front end style, with a small cab window and bullet shaped nose, housing two quite small white and red marker lights, but no proper headlight. Usually when APT-E was undertaking high speed trials, all on track railway staff were made well aware of its presence and frequently testing was carried out within a special possession of the track.* CJM

Right Bottom: *After APT-E was withdrawn from development service it was presented to the National Railway Museum, York, where it arrived on 11 June 1976. After a period at York, APT-E was transferred to the NRM outbase at Shildon where it is currently to be found. This view shows the set stabled in the Museum yard at York.* CJM

LEV 1

Vehicle type:	Single DMS
Number range:	LEV1 - RDB975874
Introduced:	1978
Built by:	BR Research/Leyland Bus
Vehicle length (over body):	39ft 4.5in (12m)
Height:	12ft 9.5in (3.9m)
Width:	8ft 2.5in (2.5m)
Seating:	40S
Internal layout:	2+2
Gangway:	None
Toilets:	None
Weight:	22 tonnes
Brake type:	Air / cable
Power Unit:	Leyland 510
Horsepower (total):	200hp (149kW)
Transmission:	Mechanical
Max speed:	75mph (121km/h)
Coupling type:	Emergency eye
Multiple restriction:	Not fitted
Door type:	Jack-knife folding
Body structure:	Steel
Owner/Operator:	BR Research/ Leyland Bus

Below & Inset: *The quest to build new lightweight railbus type passenger carrying vehicles was originally a BR Research project, who with the assistance of Leyland produced a small unpowered vehicle in 1977 to establish the development possibilities of using bus technology for the building of lightweight rail vehicles. After many tests and various modifications Leyland Experimental Vehicle No. 1 (LEV 1), also numbered RDB975874, emerged in 1978 for active testing, firstly at the Railway Technical Centre, Derby, and then on the Old Dalby test track before entering passenger carrying service on the East Suffolk line. At the end of 1980 the vehicle was modified and shipped to the USA for testing and branch line use. The vehicle returned to the UK the following year and was again tested on various branch and rural lines. LEV 1 was officially withdrawn in 1987 and was taken over by the National Railway Museum in York. The view below shows the vehicle in the yard of BREL Derby Litchurch Lane Works. The inset image shows LEV 1 at Lowell in Massachusetts on a demonstration run to Nashua in New Hampshire.* **CJM / CJM-C**

Below & Inset: *The 15.3m long vehicle known as LEV2, or R3/1 as it was recorded in official documentation, was built by D Wickham of Ware, Hertfordshire, and emerged in the third quarter of 1980, visiting the RTC, Derby, for type testing and then spending a short time on the Old Dalby test track before being packed and shipped to the United States of America for testing by the Federal Railroad Administration (FRA). In 1981 it was used between Concord, New Hampshire and Lowell in Massachusetts demonstrating the flexibility of railbus technology. Sadly during one of these runs the vehicle was in a collision with a road vehicle on a railroad crossing. Repairs were carried out in the US and the car subsequently saw testing with Amtrak. Between 1982-85 the vehicle was stored out of use and in 1986 it was sold into preservation at Steamtown, Pennsylvania, where it worked for more than 10 years. In 1996 it was sold for scrap only to be saved by the Durbin and Greenbrier Railroad, before going to the Connecticut Trolley Museum in 2000. Both:* CJM-C

Vehicle type:	Single DMS
Number range:	LEV2
Introduced:	1980
Built by:	D Wickham of Ware
Vehicle length (over body):	49ft 6in (15.3m)
Height:	12ft 9.5in (3.9m)
Width:	8ft 2.5in (2.5m)
Seating:	56S
Internal layout:	2+2
Gangway:	Not fitted
Toilets:	Not fitted
Weight:	25 tonnes
Brake type:	Air / cable
Power unit:	Leyland 690
Horsepower (total):	200hp (149kW)
Transmission:	Mechanical
Max speed:	75mph (121km/h)
Coupling type:	Emergency eye
Multiple restriction:	Not fitted
Door type:	Jack-knife folding
Body structure:	Steel (Leyland Bus2)
Owner/operator:	BR/Transmark

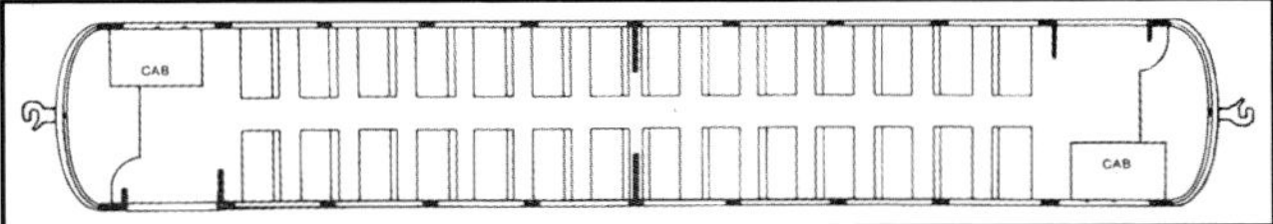

RB3 – 977020

Vehicle type:	Single DMS
Number:	(RB3) 977020
Introduced:	1981
Built by:	BREL Derby Litchurch Lane
Vehicle length (over body):	50ft 2¼in (15.3m)
Height:	12ft 9.5in (3.9m)
Width:	8ft 2.5in (2.5m)
Seating:	64S
Internal layout:	2+3
Gangway:	Not fitted
Toilets:	Not fitted
Weight:	19.5 tonnes
Brake type:	Air / cable
Power unit:	Leyland 690
Horsepower (total):	200hp (149kW)
Transmission:	Mechanical
Max speed:	75mph (121km/h)
Coupling type:	Emergency eye
Multiple restriction:	Not fitted
Door type:	Four section folding
Body structure:	Steel
Owner/operator:	BR Research

Below & Inset: *The second of the BR ordered railbuses was delivered from BREL Derby in 1981, and was formed of Leyland National 2 body sections and powered by a Leyland 690 200hp (149kW) engine. After a protracted test period involving minor trade union issues RB3, also numbered RDB977020, entered restricted passenger traffic on the Bristol to Severn Beach line from October 1981, remaining on the route for six months. In April 1982 the vehicle went to Laira to take part in an open day, before working north to South Yorkshire, being demonstrated in the Sheffield area. Testing and demonstrating in England was finished by summer 1982 when the vehicle was sold to Northern Ireland Railways, where after re-gauging to 5ft 3in (1600mm) it arrived on 5 August. When first introduced the set was painted in a green, white and orange livery, with BRE-Leyland Railbus branding on the bodyside. Originally for testing no yellow end was applied, but this was added before use on the Severn Beach line. The view below shows the vehicle as delivered at Old Dalby, while the inset image shows RDB977020 at Redlands on the Bristol to Severn Beach line on 10 November 1981.*
CJM / Alan Rimmer

Vehicle type:	Twin	Single DMS	Single DMS
Number range:	'Far East'	BREL 75 (RB002)	RB004
Introduced:	1984	1984	1984
Built by:	BREL Derby	BREL Derby	BREL Derby
Total length (over body):	100ft 1in (30.5m)	50ft 2¼in (15.29m)	50ft 2¼in (15.29m)
Height:	12ft 9.5in (3.9m)	12ft 9.5in (3.9m)	12ft 9.5in (3.9m)
Width:	8ft 2½in (2.5m)	8ft (2.44m)	8ft (2.44m)
Seating:	Total 120S	64S	58S
Internal layout:	Longitudinal	2+2	2+2
Gangway:	Between vehicles	Not fitted	Not fitted
Toilets:	Not fitted	Not fitted	Not fitted
Weight:	40 tonnes	20 tonnes	20 tonnes
Brake type:	Air	Air	Air
Power Unit:	One Leyland TL11	One Leyland TL11	One Leyland TL11
Horsepower (total):	200hp (149kW)	200hp (149kW)	200hp (149kW)
Transmission:	Mechanical	Mechanical	Mechanical
Max speed:	75mph (121km/h)	75mph (121km/h)	75mph (121km/h)
Coupling type:	Emergency	Emergency	Emergency
Multiple restriction:	Not fitted	Not fitted	Not fitted
Door type:	Four section folding	Four section folding	Four section folding
Body structure:	Steel	Steel	Steel
Owner/Operator:	Transmark	Transmark	Transmark

Below: ***Three further railbus demonstrators were built under the joint BREL/Leyland partnership, including a twin-car set seating 120 which was exported to Thailand in 1984, a single vehicle known as RB002 or BREL 75 and used in Canada, and RB004 which was shipped to the eastern side of the US for trials. BREL 75, illustrated below, was completed at BREL Derby Litchurch Lane in February 1984 and exported to Denmark, working south of Copenhagen; a year later it commenced German-Dutch cross-border workings, before returning to the UK and exported again to Sweden, returning to the UK in late 1985 before being reworked and exported to Canada for trials with VIA Rail. By 1986 these were complete and the vehicle returned to the UK and was used as a site office at BREL Derby. After this duty was completed it was sold to an Irish businessman in Dundalk. BREL 75 is seen at Thompson, Manitoba, on 30 May 1986.*** **David Othern**

Class 139

Vehicle type:	DMS
Number range:	39001-39002
Set numbers:	139001-139002
TOPS Classification:	139
Introduced:	2007-2008
Built by:	Main Road Sheet Metal, Leyland, for Parry People Movers
Vehicle length (over body):	28ft 6in (8.7m)
Height:	12ft 3in (3.77m)
Width:	7ft 10in (2.81m)
Seating:	20S
Internal layout:	1+1
Gangway:	Not fitted
Toilets:	Not fitted
Weight:	12.5 tonnes
Brake type:	Regen using flywheel & air
Primary power:	Ford MVH-420 engine
Horsepower (total):	86hp (64kW)
Flywheel (stored power):	500kg / 1m dia 1,000-1,500rpm wheel
Transmission:	Tandler bevel box with Linde hydrostatic transmission and spiral bevel gearbox
Max speed:	45mph (72km / h)
Coupling type:	Emergency
Multiple restriction:	Not fitted
Door type:	Double-leaf folding
Body structure:	Steel
Owner / operator:	London Midland
Notes:	Certified for main line use Stourbridge Junction to Stourbridge Town only

Below: *The short Stourbridge Town to Stourbridge Junction line became a case study for using alternative railcar technology in 2006 when Parry People Movers (PPM) introduced an experimental fly-wheel powered railcar on the route, replacing the previous heavy rail vehicles. A prototype vehicle numbered 999900 was used for a year before two purpose built PPM60 cars were introduced which became Network Rail Class 139, operated by London Midland and numbered 139001 and 139002. Some delay surrounded the delivery and full introduction of the '139s' but today the cars operate the regular shuttle service with excellent passenger feedback and few operating problems. Seats are provided for 20 passengers and power is collected either end of the line and operates a flywheel system below the car. The vehicles have a top speed of 45mph (not attained on the Stourbridge line). The Class 139s are captive to the Stourbridge shuttle service and have a small depot at Stourbridge Junction. Car No. 1390001 is illustrated.* **Jamie Squibbs**

Below: *The research and information gained from operating LEV 1 was such that the BRB could see major potential for using such trains in the future, but as a single car passenger capacity was very limited and a two or more vehicle option was put forward. From this emerged the Class 140 Leyland/BR Derby two-car railbus, basically two Leyland bus bodies coupled together with a gangway between and a more conventional driving cab at the outer ends. BR's then proposition for a replacement DMU was costly and many of the financially constrained local authorities were keen on low cost options. The Class 140 was fabricated at Leyland Workington and then transferred to BREL Derby for fitting out. The twin set had seating for 102 and room for nearly an equal amount standing. Two Leyland TL11 underfloor engines were fitted and the finished train was outshopped in what looked like BR blue and grey, but the blue was actually Barrow Corporation blue, paint left over from a bus production contract. In early June 1981 the set was demonstrated to the public in Leeds and Yorkshire before moving to the North East and then the Chester area. For the rest of 1981 and 1982 the set toured the country, being shown to councils and rail bodies and generating interest in the project. In 1984-85 No. 140001 took up operation from Plymouth Laira on the Liskeard to Looe and Plymouth to Gunnislake lines. By late 1985 the set was taken out of service, being stored at Laira and then Leeds Holbeck before it was finally officially withdrawn and sold for preservation, with the set currently under restoration on the Keith to Dufftown line. No. 140001 is seen at Leeds Holbeck on 21 April 1989.* CJM

Number range:	140001
Introduced:	1981
Built by:	Leyland bus body on BREL 4 wheel underframe, assembled at Derby
Formation:	DMS+DMSL
Vehicle numbers:	DMS - 55500 DMSL - 55501
Vehicle length:	57ft 5½in (15.98m)
Height:	11ft 5¾in (3.53m)
Width:	8ft 0½in (2.45m)
Seating:	Total - 102S DMS - 52S DMSL -50S
Internal layout:	2+2 bus
Gangway:	Within set only
Toilets:	DMSL - 1
Weight:	Total - 38 tonnes DMS - 19 tonnes DMSL - 19 tonnes
Brake type:	Air
Bogie type:	4-wheel chassis
Power unit:	1 x Leyland TL11 of 200hp (149kW) per vehicle
Transmission:	Mechanical
Transmission type:	SCGR500 4-speed
Horsepower (total):	400hp (298kW)
Max speed:	75mph (121km/h)
Coupling type:	Tightlock - outer Bar - inner
Multiple restriction:	Not authorised
Door type:	Folding
Special features:	-
Body structure:	Steel
Notes:	Development of LEV

Class 141

	As built (classified as 141/0)	Upgraded (classified as 141/1)
Number range:	141001-141020 (not originally carried)	141101-141120
Former number range:	-	141001-141020 (not in order)
Introduced:	1984	-
Refurbish/upgrade:	-	1988-89
Built by:	Leyland bus body on BREL frame, assembled at Derby	-
Refurbish/upgrade:	-	Upgrade - Hunslet-Barclay, Kilmarnock
Formation:	DMS+DMSL	DMS+DMSL
Vehicle numbers:	DMS - 55502-55521 DMSL - 55522-55541	DMS - 55502-55521 DMSL - 55522-55541
Vehicle length:	50ft 8¼in (15.45m)	50ft 8¼in (15.45m)
Height:	12ft 8¾in (3.88m)	12ft 8¾in (3.88m)
Width:	8ft 2½in (2.50m)	8ft 2½in (2.50m)
Seating:	Total - 94S DMS - 50S, DMSL - 44S	Total - 94S DMS - 50S, DMSL - 44S
Internal layout:	2+2 bus	2+2 bus
Gangway:	Within set only	Within set only
Toilets:	DMSL - 1	DMSL - 1
Weight:	Total - 42.5 tonnes DMS - 21 tonnes DMSL - 21.5 tonnes	Total - 42.5 tonnes DMS - 21 tonnes DMSL - 21.5 tonnes
Brake type:	Air	Air EP
Bogie type:	4-wheel chassis	4-wheel chassis
Power unit:	1 x Leyland TL11 of 205hp (153kW) per vehicle	1 x Leyland TL11 of 205hp (153kW) per vehicle§
Transmission:	Mechanical	Mechanical
Transmission type:	SCGR500 4-speed	SCGR500 4-speed
Horsepower (total):	410hp (306kW)	410hp (306kW)
Max speed:	75mph (121km/h)	75mph (121km/h)
Coupling type:	Tightlock - outer, Bar - inner Separate nose mounted jumpers	BSI - outer, Bar - inner
Multiple restriction:	Within class	Class 14x, 15x and 170
Door type:	Twin leaf folding pivot	Twin leaf folding pivot
Special features:	-	-
Body structure:	Steel	Steel
Notes:		§ Set 141113 fitted with Cummins LTA 10R of 230hp (171kW) and Voith T211r hydraulic transmission

Left: *After the detailed trials and testing of the Class 140 prototype, the BRB revised its low cost DMU or railbus plans to further reduce costs and from this emerged the Class 141, with a fleet of 20 two-car sets ordered in 1982 for South and West Yorkshire duties. Leyland again produced the bodies and BREL Derby manufactured the underframes with the two being married together in Derby. In original condition with nose end jumpers, set No. 141004 is seen when new in blue and grey livery at Leeds Neville Hill. Performance of this fleet was poor and soon a refurbishment project was launched.* CJM

Right Top: *Sets numbered higher than 141006 were introduced painted in light green and buttermilk, introduced at the time as the new MetroTrain colours. The livery soon became discoloured. Devoid of a set number, as the York operating authorities preferred to use vehicle numbers as identity, two sets are seen at Leeds. Such were the problems with the Class 141 fleet that a major technical upgrade and mini-refurbishment contract was let in 1988-89 to Hunslet-Barclay of Kilmarnock.* CJM

Right Middle: *The Kilmarnock upgrade project saw BSI auto-couplers installed which allowed the removal of the manual jumper connections on the front ends. Sets also received a major technical upgrade and a new coat of West Yorkshire PTE red and cream. Overhauled sets were reclassified as 141/1. Stored set No. 141116 is seen stored at the Fire Services Training School, Moreton-in-Marsh.* CJM

Below: *Viewed from its DMSL vehicle, set No. 141111 stands in the sun at Sheffield on 30 August 1990. All sets were withdrawn in 1997 and in 2000/01 12 sets were exported to Iran, and two to Holland. Others entered preservation in the UK and a couple were broken up for spares. Most of the exported sets were sold from Porterbrook via Cotswold Rail.* CJM

Class 142

Number range:	142001-142096
Introduced:	1985-87
Built by:	Leyland bus body on BREL underframe, assembled at BREL Derby
Formation:	DMS+DMSL
Vehicle numbers:	DMS - 55542-55591, 55701-55746 DMSL - 55592-55641, 55747-55792
Vehicle length:	51ft 0½in (15.55m)
Height:	12ft 8in (3.86m)
Width:	9ft 2¼in (2.80m)
Seating:	Total - 96-122S DMS - 46-62S (depending on layout) DMSL - 50-60S (depending on layout)
Internal layout:	2+3 or 2+2 (depending on operator)
Gangway:	Within set only
Toilets:	DMSL - 1
Weight:	Total - 49.5 tonnes DMS - 24.5 tonnes DMSL - 25 tonnes
Brake type:	Air EP
Bogie type:	4-wheel chassis
Power unit:	1 x Cummins LTA10-R of 225hp (165kW) per vehicle
Transmission:	Hydraulic
Transmission type:	Voith T211r
Horsepower (total):	450hp (330kW)
Max speed:	75mph (121km/h)
Coupling type:	Outer - BSI, Between cars - Bar
Multiple restriction:	Class 14x, 15x units
Door type:	Twin-leaf inward pivot
Body structure:	Aluminium alloy (bus body sections) on steel frame
Owner:	Angel Trains
Operator:	Northern Railways, Arriva Trains Wales

Below: *By far the largest fleet of production railbus sets were the Class 142s, using Leyland bus technology mounted on BREL Derby built chassis. A fleet of 96 two-car sets was introduced between 1985-87 and deployed originally in the Manchester and West Country areas before extending its operating range to the North East and North West. Originally seating was provided in the 2+3 style using traditional bus style seats, but over the years interior facelifts have seen many now with the more comfortable 2+2 seating using traditional seat styles. Originally owned by BR, under privatisation the Class 142s were transferred to Angel Trains ownership, who in 2013 leased the sets to just two operators, Northern Rail and Arriva Trains Wales. In the view below we see set No. 142091 painted in Regional Railways grey and two-tone blue in the bay platform at York. At the time this was a North Eastern unit; today it is still operating in the same area allocated to Heaton depot in Newcastle. At the time this image was recorded the set sported original four section folding doors; these have now been replaced with the two section doors.* CJM

Above: *The first 14 Class 142s off the Derby production line went to the Manchester area and were painted in Mancheter PTE orange and brown livery, with a black underframe and full yellow warning end; a joint BR and Manchester PTE logo was applied to the bodyside. Set No. 142008 is seen when brand new at Derby Litchurch Lane Works on 30 September 1985.* CJM

Below: *The second batch of '142s' to be delivered, Nos. 142015-142027, went to the Western Region for Devon and Cornwall branch line use, these were nicknamed 'Skipper' sets and painted in brown and cream livery, as shown on set No. 142021 pulling away from Aller Junction on 17 April 1987 forming the 10.30 Exeter St David's to Paignton service.* CJM

Class 142

Above: *A handful of Class 142s made a brief return to the former Western Region based at Exeter in the 2007-12 period covering for a shortage of suitable local stock. The sets came from and returned to the Northern franchise and while working on FGW were in Northern Spirit blue off-set by First Great Western branding. Two sets, with No. 142001 nearest the camera, depart from Dawlish Warren bound for Exmouth on 26 August 2008.* CJM

Left Middle: *The largest current user of the Class 142 or 'Pacer' stock is the Northern franchise with 79 sets based at either Newton Heath (Manchester) or Heaton (Newcastle). All are painted in the attractive blue, purple and grey Northern livery and all now have facelifted interiors. On 17 December 2007 set No. 142027 passes Pleasington with the 11.50 Colne to Blackpool South service. This example and the one illustrated above both have extra air vents on the front end.* Tom McAtee

Left Bottom: *In 2013 Arriva Trains Wales operated a fleet of 15 Class 142s, working alongside a fleet of Class 143s on Cardiff Valley local services. The Arriva Trains Wales sets have all been refurbished and now sport 2+2 high-back seats and much improved interiors. The exterior of sets is finished in turquoise and cream with full yellow ends and a grey roof. Set No. 142082 leads a Class 143 into Radyr station on 27 July 2011.* CJM

Below: *At the same time as the contracts were placed for the Class 142 railbus fleet, the BRB invited other companies to offer designs for further Railbus-based products. The established coach builder Walter Alexander in partnership with Andrew Barclay of Kilmarnock were awarded a contract to built 25 two-car sets later classified as 143. These were to a similar design specification as the Class 142s, but had a clean roof profile and more pleasing rounded cab front. The cab window area again used three glass screens, with the middle one housing a destination indicator at the top, rather than having this built into a cant rail panel as on the '142s'. The first 19 sets were finished in Provincial sector two-tone blue and white, while sets 143020-025 were finished in Tyne & Wear PTE yellow, reflecting that Tyne & Wear County Council funded their purchase. The first Class 143 was delivered in June 1985. The original SCG transmission was troublesome and all were eventually rebuilt with a Voith transmission; some renumbering took place at that time to identify which sets had which gearbox. Eventually all sets were renumbered into the 1436xx series. After privatisation the '143s' became the property of Porterbrook Leasing and today sets are operated by First Great Western and Arriva Trains Wales. Painted in Tyne & Wear 'Pacer' livery set No. 143024 is illustrated from its DMSL vehicle.* CJM

Number range:	143001-143025
Revised number range:	143601-143625
Introduced:	1985-86
Built by:	Walter Alexander body mounted on Andrew Barclay underframe, assembled by Andrew Barclay of Kilmarnock
Formation:	DMS+DMSL
Vehicle numbers:	DMS - 55642-55666 DMSL - 55667-55691
Vehicle length:	51ft0½ in (15.55m)
Height:	12ft 2¾in (3.73m)
Width:	8ft 10½ in (2.70m)
Seating:	Total - 92S + 12 tip up DMS - 48S + 6 tip up DMSL - 44S + 6 tip up
Internal layout:	2+2
Gangway:	Within set only
Toilets:	DMSL - 1
Weight:	Total - 48.5 tonnes DMS - 24 tonnes DMSL - 24.5 tonnes
Brake type:	Air EP
Bogie type:	4-wheel chassis
Power unit:	1 x Cummins LTA10-R of 225hp (165kW) per vehicle
Transmission:	Hydraulic
Transmission type:	Original - SCG, Modified - Voith T211r
Horsepower (total):	450hp (330kW)
Max speed:	75mph (121km/h)
Coupling type:	Outer - BSI, Between cars - Bar
Multiple restriction:	Class 14x, 15x
Door type:	Twin-leaf inward pivot
Body structure:	Aluminium alloy (bus body sections) on steel frame
Owner:	Porterbrook, Rail Assets Investments, Bridgend Council, Cardiff City Council
Operator:	Arriva Trains Wales, First Great Western

Class 143

Above: *After moving down from their original North Eastern operating area the Class 143s settled down well to working in the Cardiff and Bristol area; interiors were upgraded and 2+2 seating fitted, much improving the travelling experience. Carrying the short lived Valley Lines green, red and white livery, set No. 143605 arrives at Pontypridd with a service bound for Newport.* **CJM**

Left Middle: *In 2013 Arriva Trains Wales operated a fleet of 15 refurbished Class 143s on local Cardiff Valley services, being based at Cardiff Canton. These operated alongside Class 142s in a common pool. All are painted in Arriva Trains Wales turquoise livery. Set No. 143606 departs from Cardiff Central station.* **CJM**

Left Bottom: *First Great Western currently has a fleet of eight Class 143s based at Exeter for Devon branch line operations, taking the fleet to Exmouth, Barnstaple and Paignton, with an occasional trip to Plymouth. All sets are painted in FGW local lines branded livery and all interiors are facelifted with 2+2 seating. With its DMS coach seating 48 nearest the camera, set No. 143619 departs from its Dawlish Warren stop with an afternoon Exmouth to Paignton service on 9 August 2011.* **CJM**

Below: *In October 1985 the final order for railbus stock was placed when BR authorised funding for 23 units classified as 144. These were for use in the West Yorkshire PTE area. The bodies were produced by Walter Alexander and were thus almost identical to the earlier built Class 143s. The underframes for this contract were assembled by BREL and the trains were finished off at BREL Derby Litchurch Lane Works. With 3+2 bus style seating the new two car sets allocated to Leeds Neville Hill seated 122, but it was quickly found this was not high enough to cope with route demand. To cover part of this problem, West Yorkshire PTE ordered 10 intermediate motor seconds for inclusion in 10 units to make them three-car formations; the MS cars originally had 73 seats and thus a three-car '144' could seat 195. These MS vehicles were unique within the railbus build and were the only non-driving vehicles built. Originally built with Self Changing Gears equipment, after around two years this was replaced by a Voith transmission. On privatisation the Class 144 driving cars went to Porterbrook Leasing while the intermediate vehicles remained owned by WYPTE until 2012 when these too went to Porterbrook. In 2002 a major refresh of interiors was sanctioned when the 2+3 seating was replaced by 2+2, reducing the overall passenger accommodation, but improving the travelling environment. Originally in WYPTE red, the sets later carried Regional Railways livery and now all carry Northern Railway blue, purple and grey colours. On 16 April 2013 set No. 144006 is seen departing from Doncaster with a service bound for Lincoln, carrying Northern livery with Metro branding.* CJM

Number range:	144001-144013 – 2-car 144014-144023 – 3-car
Introduced:	1986-87
Built by:	Walter Alexander body on BREL underframe Assembled at BREL Derby Litchurch Lane
Formation:	144001-144013 - DMS+DMSL 144014-144023 - DMS+MS+DMSL
Vehicle numbers:	DMS - 55801-55823 MS - 55850-55859 DMS - 55824-55846
Vehicle length:	50ft 2in (15.29m)
Height:	12ft 2¾in (3.73m)
Width:	8ft 10½ in (2.70m)
Seating:	144001-144013 - Total - 87S + 6 tip up 144014-144023 - Total - 145S + 6 tip up DMS - 45S + 3 tip up MS - 58S DMSL - 42S + 3 tip up
Internal layout:	2+2
Gangway:	Within set only
Toilets:	DMSL - 1
Weight:	Total - 72 tonnes DMS - 24 tonnes MS - 23.5 tonnes DMSL - 24.5 tonnes
Brake type:	Air EP
Bogie type:	4-wheel chassis
Power unit:	1 x Cummins LTA10-R of 225hp (168kW) per vehicle
Transmission:	Hydraulic
Transmission type:	Original - SCG, Modified - Voith T211r
Horsepower (total):	144001-144013 - 450hp (330kW) 144014-144023 - 675hp (495kW)
Max speed:	75mph (121km/h)
Coupling type:	Outer - BSI, Between cars - Bar
Multiple restriction:	Class 14x, 15x
Door type:	Twin-leaf inward pivot
Body structure:	Aluminium alloy (bus body sections) on steel frame
Owner:	Porterbrook
Operator:	Northern Railways

Class 150

Class:	150/0	150/1 (2-car)	150/1 (3-car)
Number range:	150001-150002	150101-150150	150003-150019
Introduced:	1984	1985-86	Original - 1985-86 As 3-car - 1995-2011
Built by:	BREL York	BREL York	BREL York
Formation:	DMSL+MS+DMS	DMSL+DMS	DMSL+DMS(L)+DMS
Vehicle numbers:	DMSL - 55200-55201 MS - 55400-55401 DMS - 55300-55301	DMSL - 52101-52150 DMS - 57101-57150 -	DMSL - 52103-52119 DMS(L) - 522xx, 572xx DMS - 57103-57119
Vehicle lengths:	DMSL - 65ft 9¾ in (20.06m) MS - 66ft 2½ in (20.18m) DMSL - 65ft 9¾ in (20.06m)	DMSL - 65ft 9¾ in (20.06m) DMSL - 65ft 9¾ in (20.06m)	DMSL - 65ft 9¾ in (20.06m) DMSL - 65ft 9¾ in (20.06m)
Height:	12ft 4½ in (3.77m)	12ft 4½ in (3.77m)	12ft 4½ in (3.77m)
Width:	9ft 3¼ in (2.82m)	9ft 3¼ in (2.82m)	9ft 3¼ in (2.82m)
Seating:	Total - 240S DMSL - 72S MS - 92S DMS - 76S	Total - 124-144S DMSL - 59-71S DMS - 65-73S -	Total - 211 or 212S DMSL - 71S DMS(L) - 70/71S DMS - 70S
Internal layout:	2+3	2+3	2+3
Gangway:	Within set	Within set	Within set
Toilets:	DMSL - 1	DMSL - 1	DMSL - 1
Weight:	Total - 99.3 tonnes DMSL - 35.4 tonnes MS - 34.1 tonnes DMS - 29.8 tonnes	Total - 76.4 tonnes DMSL - 38.3 tonnes DMS - 38.1 tonnes	Total - 109-110.8 tonnes DMSL - 38.3 tonnes DMS(L) - 38.1/38.3 tonnes DMS - 38.1 tonnes
Brake type:	Air EP	Air EP	Air EP
Bogie type:	Powered - BX8P Trailer - BX8T	Powered - BP38 Trailer - BT38	Powered - BP38 Trailer - BT38
Power unit:	1 x Cummins NT855R4 of 285hp (213 kW) per vehicle	1 x Cummins NT855R5 of 285hp (213 kW) per vehicle	1 x Cummins NT855R5 of 285hp (213 kW) per vehicle
Transmission:	Hydraulic	Hydraulic	Hydraulic
Transmission type:	Voith T211r	Voith T211r	Voith T211r
Horsepower:	855hp (639kW)	570hp (426kW)	855hp (639kW)
Max speed:	75mph (121km/h)	75mph (121km/h)	75mph (121km/h)
Coupling type:	Outer - BSI Between cars - Bar	BSI	BSI
Multiple restriction:	Class 14x, 15x, 170, 172	Class 14x, 15x, 170, 172	Class 14x, 15x, 170, 172
Door type:	Bi-parting sliding (cab door slam)	Bi-parting sliding (cab door slam)	Bi-parting sliding (cab door slam, slide on 150/2 car)
Body structure:	Steel	Steel	Steel
Owner:	Angel Trains	Angel Trains	
Operator:	FGW	London Midland, FGW, Northern	
Notes:	Original prototype sets		Now disbanded

Right: *By the early 1980s the BRB needed urgent replacement for its 1950s fleets of first generation stock. Two builders, BREL and Metro-Cammell, were invited to design and build prototype three-car sets, which emerged as Class 150 and 151. The Class 150 design was selected as the new basis for the next generation DMU fleet and three different sub-classes were built. The two three-car prototypes became Class 150/0, the first two-car production sets became Class 150/1 and a follow-on order for sets with end gangways became Class 150/2. The two Class 150/0 sets were originally based in the Derby area and upon privatisation were allocated to Central Trains and then London Midland. In 2012 the two sets were transferred to First Great Western for Reading-Basingstoke duties. The first 50 production Class 150/1 sets without gangway ends emerged in 1985-86, followed by 85 two-car sets with end gangways in 1986-87, with sets allocated to all operating areas except the Southern. Originally sets had 2+3 seating and were finished in Provincial sector two-tone blue, white and grey. Today a huge diversity of liveries can be found. Although originally having a universal interior, today we see a wide variety of different interior*

150/2
150201-150285
1986-87

BREL York
DMSL+DMS
DMSL - 52201-52285
DMS - 57201-57285
-
DMSL - 65ft 9¾ in (20.06m)
DMSL - 65ft 9¾ in (20.06m)

12ft 4½ in (3.77m)
9ft 3¼ in (2.82m)
Total - 116-149S
DMSL - 60-73S
DMS - 56-76S
-
2+3 or 2+2
Throughout
DMSL - 1
Total - 74 tonnes
DMSL - 37.5 tonnes
DMS - 36.5 tonnes

Air EP
Powered - BP38
Trailer - BT38
1 x Cummins NT855R5 of
285hp (213 kW) per vehicle
Hydraulic
Voith T211r
570hp (426kW)
75mph (121km/h)
BSI

Class 14x, 15x, 170, 172
Bi-parting sliding
(cab door slide)

Steel
Angel Trains
Northern, London Midland,
FGW, Arriva Trains Wales

Above: *A pair of Class 150/1 units are seen departing from Shrewsbury displaying the original Provincial two-tone blue, grey and white livery. These sets had sliding passenger doors, but hinged doors on the driving cab.* CJM

Below: *One of the first major facelifts to the Class 150 fleet was undertaken by Centro, the West Midlands operator, who refurbished the passenger environment and repainted some sets in green and grey with white and blue body strips. Set No. 150116 displays this livery on 8 October 1990.* CJM

designs depending on operator. The set illustrated, No. 150123 at Gospel Oak, shows the Silverlink colours, applied to a handful of sets allocated to Bletchley for non-electrified branch line use. These sets were later transferred to First Great Western. No. 150123 shows revised Group Standard head and marker lights using LED technology CJM

Left Top: *Under the final years of the nationalised railway the Class 150s were operated by Regional Railways and most carried the sector's blue and grey colours. Upon privatisation operator branding was applied before full repaints could be undertaken. Set No. 150234 is seen at Weymouth on 8 October 2002 in Regional Railways colours but with Wessex Trains branding.* CJM

Left Middle: *Now sporting a fully refurbished interior, two-car set No. 150254 is seen from its DMS vehicle at Gloucester on 2 July 2009 painted in Arriva Trains turquoise and cream colours. To meet the Disabilities Discrimination Act, the passenger doors have to be in a contrasting colour, in this case light blue.* CJM

Left Below: *In 2002 a very distinctive Valley Lines livery was introduced for Class 150s based in Cardiff, with one coach painted red and the other green, both displaying pictogram branding. At the same time major interior refurbishment had been undertaken to include 2+2 high back seats and a better passenger environment. Set No. 150280 is seen at Pontypridd.* CJM

Below: *In October 2001 The Strategic Rail Authority split the Wales & West franchise with the formation of Valley Lines for the Cardiff area and Wessex Trains for the West Country. Wessex Trains developed their own deep purple livery in 2002 with pictogram branding of route scenes applied to the Class 150/2 fleet. The first to be re-liveried was No. 150244 in September 2002, which is viewed from its DTS carriage. Upon re-livery most Wessex sets were named, using stick-on plates applied under the innermost passenger window.* CJM

Above: *Under today's privatised railway, the Class 150 fleet operated by First Great Western, London Midland, Northern and Arriva Trains Wales. The FGW sets are painted in a mix of standard FGW blue and FGW Local Lines colours, off-set by pink passenger doors. Set No. 150244, the first to carry FGW Local Lines livery, is seen stabled at Exeter.* **CJM**

Right Middle: *Northern Rail is the operator of the largest number of Class 150s, forming the backbone of the operator's longer distance local services. All are painted in Northern colours, with a sizeable number having pictogram branding of points of interest on the Northern route applied. Passenger doors are in a contrasting grey to meet the Disabilities Discrimination Act requirements. Set No. 150228 is seen at Whaley Bridge on 7 August 2010.* **John Binch**

Right Below: *After being displaced from London Midland by Class 172s, the two original Class 150/0 sets were taken over by First Great Western for use on the Reading to Basingstoke line. Sets were repainted and internally re-fitted to FGW standards and set No. 150001 is seen at Basingstoke in summer 2012. These two sets have recently been brought into line with Class 150/1 stock.* **CJM**

Class 151

Number range:	151001-151002§
Introduced:	1984-85
Built by:	Metro-Cammell, Birmingham
Formation:	DMSL+MS+DMS
Vehicle numbers:	DMSL - 55202-55203 MS - 555402-55403 DMS - 55302-55303
Vehicle length:	DMS, DMSL - 65ft 6½in (19.98m) MS - 64ft 3½in (19.60m)
Height:	12ft 9¼in (3.85m)
Width:	9ft 2½in (2.81m)
Seating:	Total - 232S DMSL - 80S MS - 84S DMS - 68S
Internal layout:	2+2
Gangway:	Within set only
Toilets:	DMSL - 1
Weight:	Total - 96.9 tonnes DMSL - 32.4 tonnes MS - 32.1 tonnes DMS - 32.4 tonnes
Brake type:	Air EP
Bogie type:	Met-Camm
Power unit:	1 x Cummins NT855R4 of 285hp (213kW) per vehicle
Transmission:	Hydraulic
Transmission type:	Voith T211r
Horsepower (total):	855hp (638kW)
Max speed:	75mph (121km/h)
Coupling type:	BSI
Multiple restriction:	Class 14x, 15x
Door type:	Double leaf sliding
Special features:	-
Body structure:	Steel
Notes	§ Also numbered 151003-151004 for short period

Below: *In March 1983 the then Provincial Sector of the BRB agreed to order two prototype three-car DMU trains from two separate builders to evaluate design and operation prior to squadron orders being placed. The Class 150/0s were from BR's own workshops and the other comprised two Class 151 sets from Metro-Cammell of Birmingham. The builder with a huge history of constructing aluminium light rail vehicles decided to adopt aluminium technology to their product. Sadly, the Class 151 was late in delivery due to a number of design and trade union issues and by the time it did emerge in February 1985, squadron orders for Class 150s had already been place due to the speed that new trains were required. The Class 151 was thus delivered with no real prospect of further orders. It was allocated to Derby and performed well on local services such as the Derby-Matlock and Derby-Crewe routes. However, all was not lost for Metro-Cammell as the company became deeply involved in the main line Class 156 project. On the Class 151s passenger seating was in the 2+3 high-density layout with bi-parting sliding doors at the one third and two third positions; a separate sliding door was provided for the driving cab. One Cummins NT855R4 engine was attached under each vehicle with drive going to both wheelsets of one bogie. Externally the '151s' were finished in grey/silver with Provincial blue strips and yellow cab ends; the front ends were very striking and more futuristic than the BREL-built '150s'. The two Class 151s remained in limited service from Derby until March 1989 when they were withdrawn and stored at Derby. In 2000 the sets were sold to Endeavour Rail who planned to overhaul them for the main line; this never happened and both were broken up in 2004. Set No. 151001 is seen at Derby on 25 June 1987.* **CJM**

Above: *One of the regular routes on which to find the Class 151 was the Derby to Matlock line, with most of the Derby-based drivers trained on the fleet's unique operation. On 11 July 1986 set No. 151001 slows for the Matlock Bath stop forming the 17.48 Derby to Matlock service.* CJM

Below: *To avoid a numeric clash with the two BREL prototype Class 150 sets, for a time Derby renumbered the Class 151s as 151003 (151001) and 151004 (151002). No. 151003, together with a production Class 150/1 set, is seen inside Derby Etches Park depot on 22 April 1988.* CJM

Class 153

Number range:	153301-153385
Introduced:	As 153 - 1991-92 Originally as Class 155 2-car sets - 1987-88
Original build:	Leyland Bus, Workington
Rebuilt by:	Hunslet-Barclay, Kilmarnock
Formation:	DMSL
Vehicle numbers:	52301-52335, 57351-57387
Vehicle length:	76ft 5in (23.29m)
Height:	12ft 3⅜in (3.75m)
Width:	8ft 10in (2.69m)
Seating:	66 or 72S depending on operator
Internal layout:	2+2
Gangway:	Throughout
Toilets:	1
Weight:	41.2 tonnes
Brake type:	Air EP
Bogie type:	Powered - BREL P3-10 Trailer - BREL BT38
Power unit:	1 x Cummins NT855R5
Transmission:	Hydraulic
Transmission type:	Voith T211r
Horsepower (total):	285hp (213kW)
Max speed:	75mph (121km/h)
Coupling type:	BSI
Multiple restriction:	Class 14x, 15x, 170, 172 series
Door type:	Single-leaf sliding plug
Body structure:	Aluminium alloy on steel frame
Owner:	Angel Trains, Porterbrook
Operator:	Northern, East Midlands Trains, Arriva Trains Wales, Greater Anglia, London Midland, FGW
Notes:	Rebuilt from 35 Class 155 twin sets

Below: *In 1991-92 the then BR Provincial Sector saw a benefit from operating 70 single dual-cabbed power cars or 'Bubble cars' on local and lesser used routes, with the ability of running three-car sets if needed. This flexibility was seen as a boost to the ailing local travel market and a contract was drawn up to rebuilt the 35 relatively modern Class 155 Leyland two-car sets as 70 single car units, fitting a new compact driving cab at the original inner end. The conversion contract was awarded to Hunslet-Barclay of Kilmarnock, with the first vehicle complete on 18 July 1991. The rebuild work was major, with the original inner-end removed and a new cab end formed. Due to limited space between the vehicle end and the passenger door opening, the cab size was very limited and some difficulty was experienced with larger drivers getting into the cab area. Upon conversion seats were provided for 72 in the 2+2 low-density style, with hard wearing carpets provided and a single toilet compartment. No. 153317 is illustrated at the Hunslet-Barclay works from its new cab end. All Class 153s were originally painted in the then standard Regional Railways blue and grey colours with full yellow ends and black cab window surrounds. No. 153317 shows the original glazed door in the corridor end - now removed.* **CJM**

Right: *Under mid-1990s privatisation, the Class 153s became the property of Angel Trains and Porterbrook, and as of 2013 vehicles were leased to Northern Rail, East Midlands Trains, Arriva Trains Wales, Greater Anglia, London Midland and First Great Western. Prior to the formation of London Midland, sets were operated by the previous franchise holder Central Trains, whose green and yellow livery is seen on this pair of Class 153s, led by No. 153383 at Barrow on Soar in February 2008. This is the 'new' cab end, identifiable by the light clusters being mid-way up the body.* **CJM**

Left: *A total of 18 Class 153s are under the control of Northern Rail, based at Leeds Neville Hill. Eleven sets are owned by Angel Trains and seven by Porterbrook. Car No. 153304 is seen stabled in the south bay at Preston on 30 October 2008. The Northern '153s' seat 72 in the 2+2 style in a mix of airline and facing seats.* **CJM**

Right: *In the era of the Wales & West franchise three distinct liveries were adopted for the '153' fleet, with a deep pink/red adopted for the Wessex fleet operating on the Bristol-Southampton/ Weymouth route. However, as time came to prove, the sets could be found on any route. In pictogram Wessex route livery, two Class 153s, Nos. 153305 and 153318, depart from Dawlish on 5 August 2004 with the 16.24 Exmouth to Paignton service.* **CJM**

Left: *The Wales and West Class 153s dedicated to operations in Devon and Cornwall were repainted in an all black livery, off-set by gold branding and full yellow warning ends. If clean, this livery was very attractive. Viewed from its original Class 155 cab end, set No. 153377 is seen attached to a Class 150/2 at Bristol Temple Meads on 15 May 2004. The Class 153s are frequently used to strengthen Class 143, 150 and 158 stock to make three-car trains in peak periods.* **CJM**

Class 154

Class:	154
Number range:	154002
Former number:	150002
Introduced:	Originally 1984, rebuilt at EDU, RTC Derby 1987
Built by:	Originally BREL York , rebuilt at EDU, RTC Derby
Formation:	DMSL+MS+DMS
Vehicle numbers:	DMSL - 55201 MS - 55401 DMS - 55301
Vehicle length:	DMSL, DMS - 65ft 9¾in (23.62m) MS - 66ft 2½in (20.18m)
Height:	12ft 4½in (3.77m)
Width:	9ft 3¼in (2.82m)
Seating:	Total: 215S DMSL 58S, MS - 97S, DMS - 60S
Internal layout:	2+2 / 2+3
Gangway:	Within set
Toilets:	DMSL - 1
Weight:	Total - 110.2 tonnes DMSL - 37.9 tonnes MS - 34.4 tonnes DMS - 37.9 tonnes
Brake type:	Air EP
Bogie type:	Powered - BX8P, Trailer - BX8T
Power unit:	DMSL and DMS 1 x Cummins NT855R5 of 285hp (212.5kW) MS 1 x Rolls Royce 'Eagle' C6 305R of 350hp (261kW)
Transmission:	Hydraulic
Transmission type:	Voith T211r
Horsepower (total):	920hp (686kW)
Max speed:	90mph (140km/h)
Coupling type:	Outer end - BSI, Inner - bar
Multiple restriction:	Class 14x, 15x, 170
Door type:	Bi-parting sliding (cab door slam)
Special features:	DMSL / DMS fitted with air conditioning
Body structure:	Steel
Notes:	Original prototype 'Sprinter' returned to 150002

Below: *In 1987, the second of the original BREL prototype DMU pair, No. 150002, was selected for traction development tests in conjunction with the Class 158 project and was fitted with Cummins engines and a Voith transmission, being re-geared for 90mph (140km/h) operation and given a proposed Class 158 style interior. To identify the set from the conventional Class 150 breed, it was reclassified as Class 154 and based at Derby Etches Park. The conversion work was carried out by the Engineering Development Unit (EDU) at the Railway Technical Centre, Derby. The non-driving motor second was fitted with a twin-disc 'hot-shift' transmission for further development work. Later the Class 154 was used for ventilation and air conditioning tests, using the type of equipment to be installed on the Class 158s. These tests saw extra equipment installed on the roof on one driving car and changes to the interior panelling. Once fitted, the set was returned for test and service running and included a short period of time working in Scotland, the destination for the first Class 158s to be built. Once all test and research work was complete, No. 154002 was converted back to its standard configuration by the EDU, Derby, and reverted to its Class 150 identity. No. 154002 is seen in 'Sprinter' livery near Burton forming a Derby to Birmingham service on 23 May 1989.* **CJM**

Class	155/0	155/3
Number range:	155301-155335	155341-155347
Introduced:	1987-88	1988
Built by:	Leyland Bus, Workington	Leyland Bus, Workington
Formation:	DMSL+DMS	DMSL+DMS
Vehicle numbers:	DMSL - 52301-52335 DMS - 57301-57335	DMSL - 52341-52347 DMS - 57341-57347
Vehicle length:	76ft 5in (23.29m)	76ft 5in (23.29m)
Height:	12ft 3¾ in (3.75m)	12ft 3¾ in (3.75m)
Width:	8ft 10in (2.69m)	8ft 10in (2.69m)
Seating:	Total - 161S DMSL(A) - 81S DMSL(B) - 80S	Total - 156S DMSL - 76S DMS - 80S
Internal layout:	2+2	2+2
Gangway:	Throughout	Throughout
Toilets:	DMSL - 1	DMSL - 1
Weight::	Total - 78 tonnes DMSL - 39 tonnes DMS - 39 tonnes	Total - 77.8 tonnes DMSL - 39.2 tonnes DMS - 38.6 tonnes
Brake type:	Air EP	Air EP
Bogie type:	Powered BREL P3-10 Trailer - BREL BT38	Powered - BREL P3-10 Trailer - BREL BT38
Power unit:	1 x Cummins NT855R5 of 285hp (213kW) per vehicle	1 x Cummins NT855R5 of 285hp (213 kW) per vehicle
Transmission:	Hydraulic	Hydraulic
Transmission type:	Voith T211r	Voith T211r
Horsepower (total):	570hp (426kW)	570hp (426kW)
Max speed:	75mph (121km/h)	75mph (121km/h)
Coupling type:	BSI	BSI
Multiple restriction:	Class 14s, 15x	Class 14x, 15x, 170, 172 series
Door type:	Single-leaf sliding plug	Single-leaf sliding plug
Body structure:	Aluminium alloy on steel frame	Aluminium alloy on steel frame
Owner:	BRB	Porterbrook Leasing
Operator:	Regional Railways	Northern
Notes:	35 sets rebuilt to 70 single cars of Class 153	

Right: *On 15 January 1985 the BRB announced an order for 35 two-car 'Super Sprinter' sets had been awarded to Leyland. These vehicles would have 75ft long body shells and be allocated to Cardiff for long distance passenger services. Their interior was set out in the 2+2 low-density style, with carpeted floors and one toilet per train. The vehicle bodies used a riveted style bus structure. The first set, No. 155301, emerged from the Workington factory in spring 1987. A follow-on order for seven sets for West Yorkshire PTE followed in 1988; these sets are now operated by Northern Rail. The 35 original Class 155s were disbanded in 1991 to form 70 single car Class 153 vehicles. Set No. 155330 passes Sutton Bridge Junction bound for Cardiff in spring 1989. The set is carrying the Provincial 'Super Sprinter' livery.* **CJM**

Class 156

Number range:	156401-156514
Introduced:	1987-89
Built by:	Metro-Cammell, Birmingham
Formation:	DMSL+DMS
Vehicle numbers:	DMSL - 52401-52514 DMS - 57401-57514
Vehicle length:	75ft 6in (23.03m)
Height:	12ft 6in (3.81m)
Width:	8ft 11in (2.73m)
Seating:	As built Total - 163S DMSL - 79S DMS - 84S Modified Total - 140-152S DMSL - 68-74S DMS - 72-78S
Internal layout:	2+2
Gangway:	Throughout
Toilets:	DMSL - 1
Weight:	Total - 74.7 tonnes DMSL - 38.6 tonnes DMS - 36.1 tonnes
Brake type:	Air EP
Bogie type:	Powered - BREL P3-10 Trailer - BREL BT38
Power unit:	1 x Cummins NT855R5 of 285hp(213kW) per vehicle
Transmission:	Hydraulic
Transmission type:	Voith T211r
Horsepower (total):	570hp (426kW)
Max speed:	75mph (121km/h)
Coupling type:	BSI
Multiple restriction:	Class 14x, 15x, 170, 172 series
Door type:	Single-leaf sliding
Body structure:	Steel
Owner:	Porterbrook, Angel Trains
Operator:	East Midlands Trains, Greater Anglia, Northern, ScotRail

Below: *At the end of October 1985, the BRB announced a huge investment with Metro-Cammell for the design and construction of 114 two-car 'Super Sprinter' sets, classified as '156'. The body shells were supplied by Procor , W H Davis and Standard Wagon and the sets were fitted out at Washwood Heath, Birmingham. The first set emerged on 10 November 1987. The final 14 sets of the build were funded by Strathclyde PTE for Glasgow area use. The interiors were all set out in the low-density 2+2 style, with one toilet per train. On delivery the '156' fleet first went to East Anglia for Midlands and North West routes. Scotland received the next batch, before Leeds Neville Hill received an allocation for Trans-Pennine services. Due to problems with the Class 155s, some sets were drafted in to Cardiff for a short period. Originally all sets were finished in Provincial grey and blue. Set No. 156412 is seen passing Langley Mill on 17 February 1989 forming the 08.14 Blackpool North to Cambridge.* **CJM**

Left Top: *Many different liveries have been carried by the Class 156 fleet. Set No. 156416 shows the One livery adopted by the Anglia franchise holder in 2006. The set is seen at Ipswich.* CJM

Left Middle: *A livery which changed the entire image of the Class 156s was the Regional Railways scheme with black front window surrounds. It is shown here in set No. 156403 at Norwich complete with Central Trains branding on the side. On the right is an Anglia Railways-liveried Class 150/2.* CJM

Right Top: *After being delivered in Strathclyde orange livery, the Strathclyde Passenger Transport adopted a pleasing carmine and cream livery, shown here on Strathclyde sponsored set No. 156500. Since delivery a number of route specific upgrades have been carried out to the '156' fleet, but 2+2 seating has always been maintained. The '156s' benefited from a single sliding door at each end of each vehicle feeding a transverse walkway rather then going directly into the passenger saloon.* CJM

Right: *Today Northern Rail operates a fleet of 32 '156s' for longer-distance services. Set No. 156482 in standard Northern livery is seen at Preston.* CJM

Below: *Advertising liveries have been applied to some '156s', such as this one promoting the Chapelfield shopping centre in Norwich carried by No. 156402.* CJM

Class 158

Class:	158 (as built)
Number range:	158701-158872
Introduced:	1990-92
Built by:	BREL Derby
Formation:	DMSL(A) + DMSL(B) 158798-814 - DMSL(A)+MSL+DMCL DMSL+DMS
Vehicle numbers:	DMSL(A) - 57701-57872 DMSL(B) 52710-52872 MSL - 58701-58717
Vehicle length:	76ft 1¾in (23.21m)
Height:	12ft 6in (3.81m)
Width:	9ft 3¼in (2.82m)
Seating:	Total - (2-car) 138S, (3-Car) 208S DMSL(A), MS - 70S, DMSL(B) - 68S
Internal layout:	2+2S
Gangway:	Throughout
Toilets:	DMSL - 1, MSL - 1
Weight:	Total - 75.9 tonnes DMSL - 38.1 tonnes, DMSL - 37.8 tonnes, MSL - 38.5 tonnes
Brake type:	Air EP
Bogie type:	Powered - BREL P4, Trailer - BREL T4
Power unit:	158701-158814 1 x NT855R of 350hp (260kW) per vehicle 158815-158862 1 x Perkins 2006-TWH of 350hp (260kW) per vehicle 158863-158872 1 x NT855R of 400hp (300kW) per vehicle
Transmission:	Hydraulic
Transmission type:	Voith T211r
Horsepower (total):	158701-158862 - 700hp (522kW) 158863-158872 - 800hp (597kW) 158797-158814 - 1050hp (783kW)
Max speed:	90mph (145km/h)
Coupling type:	Outer - BSI, Inner - bar
Multiple restriction:	Class 14x, 15x
Door type:	Bi-parting sliding plug
Special features:	Some fitted with RETB wiring
Body structure:	Aluminium

Above: *The culture change in modern DMU technology came in 1989 when the first of 381 Class 158 vehicles emerged from Derby Works. These 'Express' units were destined for the longer distance main line routes, with the first sets taking up duty in Scotland; within a few years sets could be found throughout the country. Primarily formed as two-car sets a small batch of three-car units were introduced for busy routes. Three of the two-car sets, Nos. 158734, 158729 and 158733, are seen in the yard at BREL Derby Litchurch Lane before delivery to Scotland. The Class 158s had low-density 2+2 seating, with saloons fully carpeted. Air conditioning was provided throughout, with two emergency hopper windows fitted.* **CJM**

Left Below: *The three-car Class 158s were originally designed for the Trans-Pennine route, where the extra 70 seats were put to good use. The 158 fleet has seen use on many routes, being allocated to a wide number of depots including Haymarket, Neville Hill, Cardiff, Newton Heath, Heaton and Norwich. Three-car set No. 158806 is illustrated.* **CJM**

Below: *The final 10 Class 158s were built for the West Yorkshire PTE and were slightly different in their interior, not quite so plush as the Regional Railways version. Destined for longer distance metro services, the sets, Nos. 158901-158910, were allocated to Neville Hill. They are now operated by Northern Rail.* **CJM**

Class 158

Sub class:	158/0 (2-car)	158/0 (3-car)
Number range:	158701-158745/158763-158797/158799-158872	158752-158759/158798
Introduced:	1990-92	1990-92 (3-car) 2000
Built by:	BREL Derby	BREL Derby
Formation:	DMSL(A) + DMSL(B) or DMSL(A) + DMCL	DMSL(A)+MS+DMSL(B)
Vehicle numbers:	DMSL(A) - 57701-57745/57763-57797/57799-57872 DMSL(B) or DMCL 52701 - 52745/763-797/799-872	DMSL(A) - 52752-52759/52798 MSL - 58702-58716 DMSB(B) - 57752-57759/57798
Vehicle length:	76ft 1¾ in (23.20m)	76ft 1¾ in (23.20m)
Height:	12ft 6in (3.81m)	12ft 6in (3.81m)
Width:	9ft 3¼ in (2.82m)	9ft 3¼ in (2.82m)
Seating:	Total - 128S-146S - 15-32F/96S-127S* DMSL - 64-72S DMCL - 13-32F / 32-53S	Total - 204S DMSL(A) - 68S MS - 66S + 3 tip up DMSL(B) - 70S
Internal layout:	2+2S 2+2F	2+2
Gangway:	Throughout	Throughout
Toilets:	DMSL, DMCL, MSL - 1	DMSL - 1
Weight:	Total - 77 tonnes DMSL - 38.5 tonnes DMCL - 38.5 tonnes	Total - 115.5 tonnes DMSL - 38.5 tonnes MS - 38.5 tonnes DMSL - 38.5 tonnes
Brake type:	Air EP	Air EP
Bogie type:	Powered - BREL P4 Trailer - BREL T4	Powered - BREL P4 Trailer - BREL T4
Power unit:	158701-814 1 x NT855R of 350hp (260kW) per vehicle 158815-862 1 x Perkins 2006-TWH of 350hp (260kW) per vehicle 158863-872 1 x NT855R of 400hp (300kW) per vehicle	1 x NT855R of 350hp (260kW) per vehicle
Transmission:	Hydraulic	Hydraulic
Transmission type:	Voith T211r	Voith T211r
Horsepower (total):	158701-158862 - 700hp (522kW) 158863-158872 - 800hp (597kW)	1050hp (780kW)
Max speed:	90mph (145km/h)	90mph (145km/h)
Coupling type:	BSI	BSI
Multiple restriction:	Class 14x, 15x, 170, 172	Class 14x, 15x, 170, 172
Door type:	Bi-parting sliding plug	Bi-parting sliding plug
Special features:	RETB ready	RETB ready
Body structure:	Aluminium	Aluminium
Owner:	Porterbrook, Angel Trains	Porterbrook
Operator:	FSR, Northern, FGW, East Midlands Trains, Arriva	Northern, FGW
Notes:	* Depending on layout Northern 3-car sets fitted with chemical retention toilets	

Left: *From the mid-1990s InterCity and later Virgin West Coast obtained the services of five Class 158s for Birmingham, Liverpool and Manchester to Scotland services. Sets were fitted with quality first class seating, but otherwise were standard Class 158s, painted in Provincial livery. Still with 'Express' branding, sets 158748 and 158750 are seen at Carlisle on 18 February 1997 with an Angle-Scottish service. Note the revised shape of the frontal snowplough.* **CJM**

158/8	158/9	158/0
158880-158890	158901-158910	158950-158959
1991, as 158/8 - 2007	1991	1992 (as 3-car 2008)
BREL Derby, Wabtec Doncaster	BREL Derby	BREL Derby
DMCL+DMSL	DMSL(A)+DMSL(B)	DMSL+DMSL+DMSL
DMCL - 52737-52814 series	DMSL(A) - 52901-52910	DMSL - 527xx and 577xx series
DMSL - 57737-57814 series	DMSL(B) - 57901-57910	DMSL - 527xx and 577xx series
		DMSL - 527xx and 577xx series
76ft 1¾ in (23.20m)	76ft 1¾ in (23.20m)	76ft 1¾ in (23.20m)
12ft 6in (3.81m)	12ft 6in (3.81m)	12ft 6in (3.81m)
9ft 3¼ in (2.82m)	9ft 3¼ in (2.82m)	9ft 3¼ in (2.82m)
Total - 13F/114S	Total - 142S	Total - 200S - 202S
DMCL - 13F/44S	DMSL(A) - 70S	DMSL - 66
DMSL - 70S	DMSL(B) - 72S	DMSL - 68
		DMSL - 66 or 68
2+2S, 2+1F	2+2	2+2
Throughout	Throughout	Throughout
DMCL, DMSL - 1	DMSL - 1	DMSL - 1
Total - 77 tonnes	Total - 77 tonnes	Total - 115.5 tonnes
DMCL - 38.5 tonnes	DMSL(A) - 38.5 tonnes	DMSL - 38.5 tonnes
DMSL - 38.5 tonnes	DMSL(B) - 38.5 tonnes	DMSL - 38.5 tonnes
		DMSL - 38.5 tonnes
Air EP	Air EP	Air EP
Powered - BREL P4	Powered - BREL P4	Powered - BREL P4
Trailer - BREL T4	Trailer - BREL T4	Trailer - BREL T4
1 x NT855R of 350hp (260kW) per vehicle	1 x NT855R of 350hp (260kW) per vehicle	1 x NT855R of 350hp (260kW) per vehicle
Hydraulic	Hydraulic	Hydraulic
Voith T211r	Voith T211r	Voith T211r
700hp (522kW)	700hp (522kW)	1050hp (780kW)
90mph (145km/h)	90mph (145km/h)	90mph (145km/h)
BSI	BSI	BSI
Class 14x, 15x, 170, 172	Class 14x, 15x, 170, 172	Class 14x, 15x, 170, 172
Bi-parting sliding plug	Bi-parting sliding plug	Bi-parting sliding plug
RETB ready	RETB ready	RETB ready
Aluminium	Aluminium	Aluminium
Porterbrook	Eversholt	Porterbrook
South West Trains	West Yorkshire PTE	First Great Western

Right: *To meet the Disabilities Discrimination Act regulations the doors of modern trains must now be a different colour from the bulk of the bodywork, as demonstrated here on this Arriva Trains Class 158, which has cream doors to contrast against the turquoise of the body colour. Set No. 158818 is seen departing from Newport bound for Gloucester. All Arriva operated Class 158s now have better quality high-back seating.* **CJM**

Class 158

Right: *The changing of franchise operators, compounded by transfers of stock between different operators, has led to a huge number of different liveries and brandings over the years. This example, No 158845, fitted with Perkins engines, displays Arriva branding on Central Trains green and blue livery. The set is seen departing north from Crewe in July 2004. A total of 48 Class 158s were fitted with Perkins power units.* CJM

Left: *Another mix of liveries emerged after a number of the Trans-Pennine branded, Northern Spirit-liveried sets were transferred to First Great Western, as demonstrated by this image of three different operators' branding being applied to set No. 158778 at Gloucester in June 2008. When these sets operated the Trans-Pennine service they had some of the best first class area of any Class 158, down to traditional design table lamps by each seat. This set is now part of three-car set No. 158959.* CJM

Right: *This is another train that at first glance one might wonder who the official operator is. Three-car set No. 158773 is seen at Nottingham and still shows the basic body colour of Northern Spirit with the stylised 'N' on the bodyside. However, the set had been transferred to Central Trains when this illustration was captured on 12 November 2007. Two years later the middle car was removed and reformed in set 158755, and No. 158773 is now a two-car working for East Midlands Trains.* CJM

Left: *With a tell-tale ex-Scottish snowplough front, indicating a prior allocation, First Great Western Class 158 No. 158748 is seen at Gloucester. In 2013, FGW operated a fleet of 15 Class 158 two- and three-car sets; they are usually deployed on the longer distance services such as Cardiff/Bristol to Portsmouth as well as some services on the Weymouth to Worcester route. The sets are all refurbished and sport the FGW Local Lines livery. Set No. 158748 also sports a revised air conditioning system, recognisable by the large vent above the passenger doors.* CJM

Above: *Wessex Trains was one of the early users of pictogram image applications on the sides of trains, promoting routes, anniversaries or events. On 19 May 2004, set No. 158855, painted in Wessex silver and maroon, was named* **Exmoor Explorer** *in an event at Minehead on the West Somerset Railway, and for this high quality images of Exmoor and the locos on the West Somerset Railway were applied. This set was subsequently transferred to Northern Rail.* CJM

Right Middle: *Painted in Wales and Borders 'Alphaline' silver and blue and stylised 'A' on the bodyside, set No. 158835 arrives at Cardiff Central on 25 June 2002 with stock to form a north Wales service. Although with many changes, this set is still operated by Arriva Trains Wales and is one of the batch fitted for European Rail Traffic Management System (ERTMS).* CJM

Right Bottom: *South West Trains currently operates a small fleet of Class 158s which have been upgraded and refurbished in line with their Class 159 sets. Prior to having a specialised pool of modified units, SWT operated a handful on the Bristol-Salisbury-Waterloo route which were internally refurbished. One of these was set No. 158786 seen at Bristol Temple Meads on 6 July 2005* CJM

Class 159

Sub class:	159/0	159/1
Number range:	159001-159022	159101-159108
Former number range:	-	158800-158814 range
Introduced:	1992-93	As 158 - Originally 1991 As 159 - 2006 (rebuilt from Class 158)
Built by:	BREL Derby, fitted out by Rosyth Dockyard	Rebuilt: Wabtec, Doncaster
Formation:	DMCL+MSL+DMSL	DMCL+MSL+DMSL
Vehicle numbers:	DMCL - 52873-52894 MSL - 58718-58739 DMSL - 57873-57894	DMCL - 52800-52811 range MSL - 58701-58717 range DMSL - 57800-57811 range
Vehicle length:	76ft 1¾ in (23.20m)	76ft 1¾ in (23.20m)
Height:	12ft 6in (3.81m)	12ft 6in (3.81m)
Width:	9ft 3¼ in (2.82m)	9ft 3¼ in (2.82m)
Seating:	Total - 23F/170S DMCL - 23F/28S MSL - 70S DMSL - 72S	Total - 24F/170S DMCL - 24F/28S MSL - 70S DMSL - 72S
Internal layout:	2+1F/2+2S	2+1F/2+2S
Gangway:	Throughout	Throughout
Toilets:	DMCL, DMSL, MSL - 1	DMCL, DMSL, MSL - 1
Weight:	Total - 114.3 tonnes DMCL - 38.5 tonnes MSL - 38 tonnes DMSL - 37.8 tonnes	Total - 114.3 tonnes DMCL - 38.5 tonnes MSL - 38 tonnes DMSL - 37.8 tonnes
Brake type:	Air EP	Air EP
Bogie type:	Powered - BREL P4-4 Trailer - BREL T4-4	Powered - BREL P4-4 Trailer - BREL T4-4
Power unit:	1 x Cummins NTA855R of 400hp (300kW) per vehicle	1 x Cummins NTA855R of 350hp (260kW) per vehicle
Transmission:	Hydraulic	Hydraulic
Transmission type:	Voith T211r	Voith T211r
Horsepower (total):	1,200hp (900kW)	1,050hp (780kW)
Max speed:	90mph (145km/h)	90mph (145km/h)
Coupling type:	BSI	BSI
Multiple restriction:	14x, 15x, 170, 172	14x, 15x, 170, 172
Door type:	Bi-parting swing plug	Bi-parting swing plug
Body structure:	Aluminium	Aluminium
Owner:	Porterbrook	Porterbrook
Operator:	South West Trains	South West Trains

Left: *Chris Green, the Managing Director of Network SouthEast, was very keen to upgrade the Waterloo-Exeter route and obtained funding to buy 22 three-car Class 158s and modify them as Class 159s with revised interiors suitable for the route. Built at Derby, the sets then went to Rosyth for fitting out before delivery to Salisbury, a purpose built depot for the fleet. When delivered the fleet was painted in NSE colours. Seating is in the 2+2 (standard and 2+1 (first) low-density style. Set No. 159010 is seen inside the maintenance depot at Salisbury.* **CJM**

Above: *Under privatisation the 22 Class 159s passed to South West Trains, who refurbished the stock and applied their white main line livery. Many consider the Class 159s to be the finest of the DMUs in traffic; their ride and comfort is excellent and their failure rate very low. This is what can be achieved with a small dedicated fleet maintained by one depot. Set No. 159020 passes Surbiton on 10 August 2006 forming the 09.45 Salisbury to Waterloo.* CJM

Below: *As part of the South West Trains franchise commitment, extra trains were needed for the West of England route and for this extra units were required. Porterbrook leasing managed to obtain a further eight three-car Class 158 sets for the franchise and fully overhaul these to a Class 159 specification at Wabtec, Doncaster. Some slight detail differences exist between the two batches. Set No. 159102 is seen at Salisbury waiting to head to Exeter St David's on 5 December 2006.* CJM

Class 165 'Network Turbo'

Class:	165/0	165/1
Number range:	165001-165039	165101-165137
Introduced:	1990-92	1992-93
Built by:	BREL/ABB York	BREL/ABB York
Formation:	165001-165028 - DMSL+DMS 165029-165039 - DMSL+MS+DMS	165101-165117 - DMCL+MS+DMS 165118-165137 - DMCL+DMS
Vehicle numbers:	165001-165028: DMSL - 58801-58822, 58873-58878 DMS - 58834-58855, 58867-58872 165029-165039: DMSL - 58823-58833 MS - 55404-55414 DMS - 58856-58866	165101-165117: DMCL - 58953-58969 MS - 55415-55431 DMS - 58916-58932 165118-165137: DMCL - 58879-58898 DMS - 58933-58952
Vehicle length:	DMSL - 75ft 2½in (22.92m) MS - 74ft 6½in (22.72m) DMS - 75ft 2½ in (22.92m)	DMCL - 75ft 2½in (22.92m) MS - 74ft 6½in (22.72m) DMS - 75ft 2½ in (22.92m)
Height:	12ft 5¼ in (3.79m)	12ft 5¼ in (3.79m)
Width:	9ft 2½ in (2.81m)	9ft 2½ in (2.81m)
Seating:	165001-165028 - Total - 176S + 7 tip up DMSL - 82S + 7 tip up DMS - 94S 165029-165039 - Total - 282S + 7 tip up DMSL - 82S + 7 tip up MS - 106S DMS - 94S	165101-165117 - Total - 16F/270S DMCL - 16F/66S MS - 106S DMS - 98S 165118-165137 - Total - 16F/170S DMCL - 16F/72S DMS - 98S
Internal layout:	2+2/2+3	2+2F/2+3S
Gangway:	Within set	Within set
Toilets:	DMSL - 1	DMCL - 1
Weight:	165001-165028 - Total - 79.5 tonnes DMSL - 40.1 tonnes DMS - 39.4 tonnes 165029-165039 - Total - 116.5 tonnes DMSL - 40.1 tonnes MS - 37 tonnes DMS - 39.4 tonnes	165101-165117 - Total - 112 tonnes DMCL - 38 tonnes MS - 37 tonnes DMS - 37 tonnes 165118-165137 - Total - 75 tonnes DMCL - 38 tonnes DMS - 37 tonnes
Brake type:	Air EP	Air EP
Bogie type:	Powered - BREL P3-17 Trailer - BREL T3-17	Powered - BREL P3-17 Trailer - BREL T3-17
Power unit:	1 x Perkins 2006TWH of 350hp (260kW) per vehicle	1 x Perkins 2006TWH of 350hp (260kW) per vehicle
Transmission:	Hydraulic	Hydraulic
Transmission type:	Voith T211r	Voith T211r
Horsepower (total):	165001-165028 - 700hp (520kW) 165029-165039 - 1,050hp (780kW)	165101-165117 - 1,050hp (780kW) 165118-165137 - 700hp (520kW)
Max speed:	75mph (121km/h)	75mph (121km/h)
Coupling type:	BSI	BSI
Multiple restriction:	Class 165, 166, 168, 172 only	Class 165, 166, 168, 172 only
Door type:	Bi-parting swing plug	Bi-parting swing plug
Special features:	Chiltern sets fitted with ATP/trip-cocks, air conditioning	
Body structure:	Welded aluminium	Welded aluminium
Owner:	Angel Trains	Angel Trains
Operator:	Chiltern	First Great Western

Above: *In the 1990s the modernisation of the UK commuter and medium distance network was very important and again under the directorship of Chris Green the Thames and Chiltern routes were 'modernised'. For these lines a fleet of Class 165 'Turbo' sets in both two- and three-car formations was ordered from BREL/ABB York. The first sets in a stunning new body profile were 28 two-car sets and eleven three-car sets for Chiltern. These 23m long vehicles with underfloor power units were high-density with 2+2 and 2+3 seating. Bi-parting sliding plug doors were at the one third and two third points. Set No. 165003 above shows the as delivered condition in NSE livery with original design front lamp clusters.* **CJM**

Below: *The Chiltern line Class 165s were given a facelift under the privatised banner with air conditioning fitted and a slightly revised front end and internal layout. The original first class seating area to the rear of the driving cab in the DMCL cars was removed and the sets became all standard class. A new Chiltern Railways livery was also applied using white as the base body colour offset by a deep window band in mid blue and red lining. Set No. 165033 is seen at London Marylebone station on 2 September 2009.* **CJM**

Class 165 'Network Turbo'

Left Top: *For working on the Thames lines from Paddington and its associated branch lines a fleet of 20 two-car and 17 three-car Class 165/1 sets were built, entering service in 1992-93. Based at a new depot at Reading, the sets had seating in the 2+2 and 2+3 style with first class directly behind the cab in one driving car. Each three-car set could seat 270 standard and 16 first class passengers. Displaying the original NSE livery, three-car set No. 165103 is seen at Oxford with its DMS coach leading.* **CJM**

Left Middle: *Under privatisation and the formation of Thames Trains a new livery was devised using off-white as the core colour with a blue widow band and a green circle across the door positions to meet the requirements of door visibility. With First Group Link branding, two-car set No. 165129 is seen at Reading with its DMS vehicle nearest the camera.* **CJM**

Below: *Unlike the Chiltern-operated sets, the Thames line units were not modified with air conditioning and thus still retained their opening hopper windows. On the front ends the original style lamp clusters have also been retained. Three-car set No. 165102 is illustrated, departing from Reading bound for Oxford on 8 January 2007.* **CJM**

Above, Right and Below: *Today the Class 165/1 Thames fleet is operated by First Great Western with the operator's Dynamic Lines livery applied. These two and three-car sets are to remain on the Thames routes until the CrossRail service is launched, then it is proposed to cascade the sets to other routes; however, by then they will be around 28 years old! In the upper view is two-car set No. 165121 seen from its DMS end. On the right is intermediate MS No. 55431, while below is three-car set No. 165117 viewed from its DMC vehicle. All:* **CJM**

Class 166 'Network Turbo Express'

Number range:	166201-166221
Introduced:	1992-93
Built by:	BREL / ABB York
Formation:	DMCL(A)+MS+DMCL(B)
Vehicle numbers:	DMCL(A) - 58101-58121 MS - 58601-58621 DMCL(B) - 58122-58142
Vehicle length:	DMCL - 75ft 2½ in (22.92m) MS - 74ft 6½in (22.72m)
Height:	12ft 5¼in (3.79m)
Width:	9ft 2½in (2.81m)
Seating:	Total - 32F / 227S DMCL(A) - 16F / 68S MS - 91S DMCL(B) - 16F / 68S
Internal layout:	Standard - 2+2 / 2+3S, First - 2+1
Gangway:	Within set
Toilets:	DMCL - 1
Weight:	Total - 117.2 tonnes DMCL(A) - 39.6 tonnes MS - 38 tonnes DMCL(B) - 39.6 tonnes
Brake type:	Air EP
Bogie type:	Powered - BREL P3-17 Trailer - BREL T3-17
Power unit:	1 x Perkins 2006TWH of 350hp (260kW) per vehicle
Transmission:	Hydraulic
Transmission type:	Voith T211r
Horsepower (total):	1,050hp (780kW)
Max speed:	90mph (145km / h)
Coupling type:	BSI
Multiple restriction:	Class 165, 166 and 168 only
Door type:	Bi-parting swing plug
Special features:	Air conditioning
Body structure:	Welded aluminium
Owner:	Angel Trains
Operator:	First Great Western

Below: *Concurrent with the building of the Class 165s for Chiltern and Thames local services, NSE was authorised funding to build a fleet of 21 three-car main line sets, to replace loco-hauled services on the longer distance Thames routes between Paddington and Oxford and Newbury. The sets followed the same body profile as the Class 165s, but incorporated air conditioning and a more luxurious interior. First class seating was provided in both driving cars directly behind the cab position. The 2+3 and 2+2 seating also had a luggage stack. Toilets were provided in both driving cars, with a total train capacity of 32 first and 227 standard. All sets are based at Reading depot. As built sets were finished in standard Network SouthEast colours of red, white and blue, off-set by a yellow cab end and white roof, as shown on set No. 166202 at Oxford.* **CJM**

Right Top: *Under the Thames Trains privatised banner, the Class 166s were repainted by Ilford depot into the off-white and blue colours with a small bib yellow end. To meet the Disabilities Discrimination Act, a bright green swirl was applied over the door positions to aid position reference. Set No. 166215 is seen in this livery with First Group Link branding at Reading.* CJM

Right Middle: *The standard class seating on the Class 166s is a mix of 2+2 and 2+3, depending on vehicle and position. This shows the seating at the end of a Motor Standard coach, with seating in the 2+2 style, and seats grouped around good sized tables. Being longer distance outer-suburban units the '166s' are carpeted throughout.* CJM

Below: *Today, the 21 Class 166s are operated by First Great Western and all are painted in the company's Dynamic Lines livery, off-set with pink passenger doors. Cab doors are finished in the main body colour. Set No. 166211 is seen at Reading with a semi-fast service to London Paddington.* CJM

Class 168 'Clubman'

Sub class:	168/0	168/1	168/2
Design:	Networker outline	Turbostar outline	Turbostar outline
Number range:	168001-168005	168106-168113	168214-168219
Introduced:	1997-98	2000-02	2003-06
Built by:	Adtranz Derby	Adtranz/Bombardier Derby	Bombardier Derby
Formation:	DMSL(A)+MSL+MS+DMSL(B)	168106 - 168107 DMSL(A)+MSL+MS+DMSL(B) 168108 - 168113 DMSL(A)+MS+DMSL(B)	168214, 168218-168219 DMSL(A)+MS+DMSL(B) 168215 - 168217 DMSL(A)+MS+MS+DMSL(B)
Vehicle numbers:	DMSL(A) - 58151-58155 MSL - 58651-58655 MS - 58451-58455 DMSL(B) - 58251-58255	DMSL(A) - 58156-58163 MSL - 58756-58757 MS - 58456-58463 DMSL(B) - 58256-58263	DMSL(A) - 58164 - 58169 MS - 58365-58367 MS - 58464-58469 DMSL(B) - 58264 - 58269
Vehicle length:	77ft 6in (23.62m)	77ft 6in (23.62m)	77ft 6in (23.62m)
Height:	12ft 4½in (3.77m)	12ft 4½in (3.77m)	12ft 4½in (3.77m)
Width:	8ft 10in (2.69m)	8ft 10in (2.69m)	8ft 10in (2.69m)
Seating:	Total - 275S DMSL(A) - 57S MSL - 73S MS - 77S DMSL(B) - 68S	168106 - 168107 - Total - 275S 168108 - 168113 - Total - 202S DMSL(A) - 57S MSL - 73S MS - 76S DMSL(B) - 69S	168214/218/219 - Total 202S 168215 - 168217 - Total 278S DMSL(A) - 57S MS - 76S MS - 76S DMSL(B) - 69S
Internal layout:	2+2	2+2	2+2
Gangway:	Within set	Within set	Within set
Toilets:	DMSL, MSL - 1	DMSL, MSL - 1	DMSL, MSL - 1
Weight:	168.8 tonnes DMSL(A) - 43.7 tonnes MSL - 41 tonnes MS - 40.5 tonnes DMSL(B) - 43.6 tonnes	168106-107 - 175.1 tonnes 168108-113 - 132.2 tonnes DMSL(A) - 45.2 tonnes MSL - 42.9 tonnes MS - 41.8 tonnes DMSL(B) - 45.2 tonnes	168214/18/19 - 134.9 tonnes 168215-168217 - 178.2 tonnes DMSL(A) - 45.4 tonnes MSL - 43.3 tonnes MS - 44 tonnes DMSL(B) - 45.5 tonnes
Brake type:	Air EP	Air EP	Air EP
Bogie type:	Powered - P3-23 Trailer - T3-23	Powered - P3-23 Trailer - T3-23	Powered - P3-23 Trailer - T3-23
Power unit:	1 x MTU 6R183TD13H of 422hp (315kW) per car	1 x MTU 6R183TD13H of 422hp (315kW) per car	1 x MTU 6R183TD13H of 422hp (315kW) per car
Transmission:	Hydraulic	Hydraulic	Hydraulic
Transmission type:	Voith T211r	Voith T211r	Voith T211r
Horsepower (total):	1,688hp (1,260kW)	168106-107 - 1,688hp (1,260kW) 168108-113 - 1,266hp (945kW)	168214/18/19 - 1,266hp (945kW) 168215-217-1,688hp (1,260kW)
Max speed:	100mph (160km/h)	100mph (160km/h)	100mph (160km/h)
Coupling type:	Outer - BSI Inner - Bar	Outer - BSI Inner - Bar	Outer - BSI Inner - Bar
Multiple restriction:	Class 165, 166, 168, 172	Class 165, 166, 168, 172	Class 165, 166, 168, 172
Door type:	Bi-parting swing plug	Bi-parting swing plug	Bi-parting swing plug
Special features:	Chiltern ATP, trip cocks	Chiltern ATP, trip cocks	Chiltern ATP, trip cocks
Body structure:	Welded aluminium, bolt-on steel ends	Welded aluminium, bolt-on steel ends	Welded aluminium, bolt-on steel ends
Owner:	Porterbrook	Porterbrook, Eversholt	Porterbrook
Operator:	Chiltern Railways	Chiltern Railways	Chiltern Railways

Far Right: *Today the fleet of Class 168 stock comprises five first generation four car sets and five four car sets and nine three car sets of second generation 'Turbostar' design. All sets are based at Aylesbury depot with maintenance also carried out at Wembley. As the Chiltern line was one of the two routes used for automatic train protection (ATP) trials, the Class 168s are fitted with this equipment. The '168s' have a top speed of 100mph (160km/h) and are usually used on the fast and semi-fast services over the Chiltern Railways Marylebone to Birmingham corridor. Four car set No. 168217 and three-car set No. 168108 pass Acocks Green on 1 February 2013.* **John Binch**

Above: *The first new generation diesel units to be ordered under privatisation were five four-car Class 168 'Clubman' sets from Adtranz; these were the forerunner to the Class 170 'Turbostar' fleet. The new stock was needed to cover passenger growth on the Chiltern route. The sets were built as all one class with 2+2 seating in open saloons. Sliding plug doors were positioned at the one third and two third positions. Toilets were provided in three of the four vehicles. Following the success of these units, Adtranz and later Bombardier were contracted to build further Class 168s, but by this time the new standard 'Turbostar' body profile had been established, thus the '168' classification covers two different structural designs. The Class 168 fleet are equipped with 'trip cock' equipment to allow operation over the London Underground signalled Harrow-on-the-Hill to Amersham route. Sets are painted in standard Chiltern Railways livery. The first driving car of the build for set No. 168001 is seen inside Derby Works during commissioning.* CJM

Class 170 'Turbostar'

Class:	170/1	170/2	170/3
Number range:	170101-170117	170201-170208 and 170270-170273	170301-170309
Introduced:	1998-99 (2001 MC)	170201-170208 - 1999 170270-170273 - 2002	2000-01
Built by:	Adtranz Derby	170201-170208: Adtranz Derby 170270-170208: Bombardier Derby	Adtranz Derby
Formation:	170101-170110: DMSL+MS+DMCL 170111-170117: DMSL+DMCL	170201-170208: DMCL+MSL+DMSL 170270-170273: DMSL+DMCL	DMCL+DMSL
Vehicle Nos.:	170101-170110: DMSL - 50101-110 MS - 55101-55110 DMCL - 79101-110 170111-170117: DMSL - 50111-50117 DMCL - 79111-79117	170201-170208: DMCL - 50201-50208 MSL - 56201-56208 DMSL - 79201-79208 170270-170273: DMSL - 50270-50273 DMCL - 79270-79273	DMCL - 50301-50308/399 DMSL - 79301-79308/399
Vehicle length:	77ft 6in (23.62m)	77ft 6in (23.62m)	77ft 6in (23.62m)
Height:	12ft 4½ in (3.77m)	12ft 4½ in (3.77m)	12ft 4½ in (3.77m)
Width:	8ft 10in (2.69m)	8ft 10in (2.69m)	8ft 10in (2.69m)
Seating:	170101-170110: Total 9F/191S 170111-170117: Total - 9F/111S 170102-170110: DMSL - 59S MS - 80S DMCL - 9F/52S 170111-170117: DMSL - 59S DMCL - 9F/52S	170201-170208: Total - 7F/173S 170270-170273: Total - 9F/110S 170201-170208: DMCL - 7F/39S MSL - 68S DMSL - 66S 170270-170273: DMSL - 57S DMCL - 9F/53S	Total - 8F/108S DMCL - 8F/43S DMSL - 65S
Internal layout:	Standard 2+2 First 2+2	Standard 2+2 First 2+1	Standard 2+2 First 2+1
Gangway:	Within set	Within set	Within set
Toilets:	DMSL - 1, DMCL - 1	One per vehicle	One per vehicle

170/3	170/4	170/5	170/6
170393-170398,	170401-170434 170450-170478	170501-170523	170630-170639
2002-04	1999-2005	1999-2000	2000
Bombardier Derby	Adtranz Derby/ Bombardier Derby	Adtranz Derby	Adtranz Derby
170393-170396 DMCL+MSLRB+DMSL 170397-170398 DMSL+MS+DMCL	170401-170424: DMCL(A)+MS+DMCL(B) 170425-170434: DMCL(A)+MS+DMSL(B) 170450-170461: DMSL(A)+MS+DMSL(B) 170470-170478: DMSL(A)+MS+DMSL(B)	170501-170517: DMSL(A)+DMSL(B) 170518-170523: DMSL+DMCL	170630-170635: DMSL(A)+MS+DMSL(B) 170636-170639: DMSL+MS+DMCL
170393 - 170396: DMCL - 50393-50396 MSLRB - 56393-56396 DMSL - 79393-79396 170397-170398: DMSL - 50397-50398 MS - 56397-56398 DMCL - 79397-79398	170401-170424: DMCL(A) - 50401-50424 MS - 56401-56424 DMCL(B) - 79401-79424 170425-170434: DMCL(A) - 50425-50434 MS - 56425-56434 DMCL(B) - 79425-79434 170450-170478: DMSL(A) - 50450-50478 MS - 56450-56478 DMSL(B) - 79450-79478	170501-170517: DMSL(A) - 50501-50517 DMSL(B) - 79501-79517 170518-170523: DMSL - 50518-50523 DMCL - 79518-79523	170630-170635: DMSL(A) - 50630-50635 MS - 56630-56635 DMSL(B) - 79630-79635 170636-170639: DMSL - 50636-50639 MS - 56636-56639 DMCL - 79636-79639
77ft 6in (23.62m)	77ft 6in (23.62m)	77ft 6in (23.62m)	77ft 6in (23.62m)
12ft 4½ in (3.77m)	12ft 4½ in (3.77m)	12ft 4½ in (3.77m)	12ft 4½ in (3.77m)
8ft 10in (2.69m)	8ft 10in (2.69m)	8ft 10in (2.69m)	8ft 10in (2.69m)
170393-170396: Total: 7F/161S DMCL - 7F/41S MSLRB - 53S DMSL - 67S 170397-170398 Total: 9F/191S DMSL - 59S MS - 80S DMCL - 9F/52S	170401-170434: 18F/168S 170450-170461: Total - 198S 170470-170478: Total - 200S 170401-170434: DMC(A) - 9F/43S MS - 76S DMC(B) - 9F/49S 170450-170461: DMSL(A) - 55S MS - 76S DMSL(B) - 67S 170470-170478: DMS(A) - 57S MS - 76S DMSL(B) - 67S	170501-170517: Total - 122S DMSL(A) - 55S DMSL(B) - 67S 170518-170523: Total - 9F/111S DMSL - 59S DMCL - 9F/52S	170630-170635: Total - 196D DMSL(A) - 55S MS - 74S DMSL(B) - 67S 170636 - 170639: Total - 9F/191S DMSL - 55S MS - 80S DMCL - 9F/52S
Standard 2+2 First 2+1	Standard 2+2 First 2+1	Standard 2+2 First 2+1	Standard 2+2 First 2+1
Within set	Within set	Within set	Within set
One per vehicle	One per vehicle	One per vehicle	One per vehicle

Class 170 'Turbostar'

Class:	170/1	170/2	170/3
Weight:	170101-170110 Total - 132.8 tonnes 170111-170116 Total - 89.8 tonnes DMSL - 45 tonnes MS - 43.0 tonnes DMCL - 44.8 tonnes	170201-170208: Total - 133.7 tonnes 170270-170273 Total - 88.4 tonnes DMCL- 45 tonnes MSL - 45.3 tonnes DMSL – 43.4 tonnes	Total - 91.6 tonnes DMCL - 45.8 tonnes DMSL - 45.8 tonnes
Brake type:	Air	Air	Air
Bogie type:	One P3-23c and one T3-23c per car	One P3-23c and one T3-23c per car	One P3-23c and one T3-23c per car
Power unit:	1 x MTU 6R 183TD 13H of 422hp (315kW) per car	1 x MTU 6R 183TD 13H of 422hp (315kW) per car	1 x MTU 6R 183TD 13H of 422hp (315kW) per car
Transmission:	Hydraulic Voith T211r	Hydraulic Voith T211r	Hydraulic Voith T211r
Horsepower:	3-car - 1,266hp (945kW) 2-car - 844hp (630kW)	3-car - 1,266hp (945kW) 2-car - 844hp (630kW)	844hp (630kW)
Max speed:	100mph (161km/h)	100mph (161km/h)	100mph (161km/h)
Coupling type:	BSI	BSI	BSI
Multiple working:	Class 15x, 170-172	Class 15x, 170-172	Class 15x, 170-172
Door type:	Bi-parting slide plug	Bi-parting slide plug	Bi-parting slide plug
Special features:	Air conditioned	Air conditioned RETB	Air conditioned
Body structure:	Welded aluminium	Welded aluminium	Welded aluminium
Owner:	Porterbrook	Porterbrook	Porterbrook
Operator:	CrossCountry	Greater Anglia	First TransPennine

Left Top: *The most numerous of the new generation DMU designs is the Class 170 'Turbostar' built by Adtranz/Bombardier at Derby Litchurch Lane. Between 1998 and 2005 some 140 two- and three-car sets were built giving service with many privatised operators throughout the UK rail network. The first operator to use the stock was Midland Main Line with a fleet of Class 170/1s which are now in use with other operators. All vehicles are built to a common platform, with interiors of various designs to meet local needs installed. Each vehicle is powered by a single MTU 6R 183TD engine, driving a Voith hydraulic transmission, and sets have a top speed of 100mph (160km/h). Anglia Railway-liveried three-car set No. 170203 is illustrated at Colchester.* **CJM**

Left Below: *Introduced in 1999-2000, Birmingham-based Central Trains took delivery of 23 two-car Class 170/5 and 10 three-car Class 170/6s. The allocation following franchise changes is now split between London Midland and CrossCountry trains. In Central Trains days, two-car set no. 170511 pauses at Newport forming a Birmingham to Cardiff service. Note the careful use of green and yellow to provide the contrasting colour for the passenger doors.* **CJM**

170/3	170/4	170/5	170/6
Total - 137.5 tonnes DMCL - 46.5 tonnes MSLRB/MS - 44.7 tonnes DMSL - 46.3 tonnes	Total - 133.2 tonnes DMCL(A) - 45.8 tonnes DMSL - 46.3 tonnes MS - 41.4 tonnes	Total - 91.7 tonnes DMSL(A) - 45.8 tonnes DMSL(B) - 45.9 tonnes DMCL - 45.9 tonnes	Total - 134.1 tonnes DMSL(A) - 45.8 tonnes MS - 42.4 tonnes DMSL(B) - 45.9 tonnes DMCL - 45.9 tonnes
Air	Air	Air	Air
One P3-23c and one T3-23c per car	One P3-23c and one T3-23c per car	One P3-23c and one T3-23c per car	One P3-23c and one T3-23c per car
1 x MTU 6R 183TD 13H of 422hp (315kW) per car	1 x MTU 6R 183TD 13H of 422hp (315kW) per car	1 x MTU 6R 183TD 13H of 422hp (315kW) per car	1 x MTU 6R 183TD 13H of 422hp (315kW) per car
Hydraulic Voith T211r	Hydraulic Voith T211r	Hydraulic Voith T211r	Hydraulic Voith T211r
1,266hp (945kW)	1,266hp (945kW)	844hp (630kW)	1,266hp (945kW)
100mph (161km/h)	100mph (161km/h)	100mph (161km/h)	100mph (161km/h)
BSI	BSI	BSI	BSI
Class 15x, 170-172	Class 15x, 170-172	Class 15x, 170-172	
Bi-parting slide plug	Bi-parting slide plug	Bi-parting slide plug	Bi-parting slide plug
Air conditioned	Air conditioned	Air conditioned	Air conditioned
Some - RETB	RETB	Some - RETB	Some - RETB
Welded aluminium	Welded aluminium	Welded aluminium	Welded aluminium
Porterbrook	Porterbrook, Eversholt	Porterbrook	Porterbrook
ScotRail, CrossCountry	ScotRail	London Midland/ CrossCountry	London Midland/ CrossCountry

Right Top: *One of the original Class 170/1 sets built for Midland Main Line, No. 170114, is illustrated in its latest guise, carrying CrossCountry Trains livery. In more recent franchise changes the 17 original Class 170/1s were transferred to CrossCountry to operate on the Nottingham to Cardiff route as well as through services from the Midlands to East Anglia. This two-car set, fully refurbished and seen at Newport, seats nine first and 111 standard. The first class area is directly behind the driving cab of the DMCL vehicle.* **CJM**

Right Below: *The present Midlands train operator London Midland operates a fleet 17 Class 170/5 two car sets and six Class 170/6 three car sets, which are usually deployed on longer distance services. These units have been refurbished with standard class only accommodation, unlike the sets of the same sub-class operated by CrossCountry Trains which still have seating for first class passengers in the DMCL coach. Set No. 170508 is seen at Gloucester in the period when London Midland operated local services to Worcester.* **CJM**

Class 171 'Turbostar'

Sub class:	171/7	171/8
Number range:	171721 - 171730	171801 - 171806
Introduced:	2003-05	2004
Built by:	Bombardier Derby	Bombardier Derby
Formation:	DMCL+DMSL	DMCL(A)+MS+MS+DMCL(B)
Vehicle numbers:	DMCL - 50721-729/392 DMSL - 79721-729/392	DMCL(A) - 50801 - 50806 MS - 54801 - 54806 MS - 56801 - 56806 DMCL(B) - 79801 - 79806
Vehicle length:	77ft 6in (23.62m)	77ft 6in (23.62m)
Height:	12ft 4½ in (3.77m)	12ft 4½ in (3.77m)
Width:	8ft 10in (2.69m)	8ft 10in (2.69m)
Seating:	Total 9F/107S DMCL 9F/43S DMSL 64S	Total - 18F/241S DMCL(A) 9F/43S MS 74S MS 74S DMCL(B) 9F/50S
Internal layout:	Standard 2+2 First 2+1	Standard 2+2 First 2+1
Gangway:	Within set	Within set
Toilets:	DMCL, DMSL - 1	DMCL - 1
Weight:	Total - 95.4 tonnes DMCL - 47.6 tonnes DMSL - 47.8 tonnes	Total - 180.4 tonnes DMCL(A) - 46.5 tonnes MS - 43.7 tonnes MS - 43.7 tonnes DMCL(B) - 46.5 tonnes
Brake type:	Air	Air
Bogie type:	One P3-23c and one T3-23c per car	One P3-23c and one T3-23c per car
Power unit:	1 x MTU 6R 183TD of 422hp (315kW) per car	1 x MTU 6R 183TD of 422hp (315kW) per car
Transmission:	Hydraulic	Hydraulic
Transmission type:	Voith T211r to ZF final drive	Voith T211r to ZF final drive
Horsepower:	844hp (630kW)	Total 1,688hp (1,260kW)
Max speed:	100mph (161km/h)	100mph (161km/h)
Coupling type:	Dellner 12	Dellner 12
Multiple restriction:	Class 171	Class 171
Door type:	Bi-parting slide plug	Bi-parting slide plug
Special features:	Air conditioned	Air conditioned
Body structure:	Aluminium	Aluminium
Owner:	Porterbrook	Porterbrook
Operator:	Southern	Southern

Left: *When South Central, later Southern, modernised its DMU fleet, it purchased Bombardier 'Turbostar' stock, which were classified as Class 171. These sets come in both two- and four-car formations and are based at Selhurst for use on the London Bridge-Oxted-Uckfield and Ashford-Brighton routes. Sets are owned by Porterbrook and carry Southern livery. Intermediate Motor Standard No. 54803 from set No. 171803, seating 74, is shown.* **Antony Christie**

Above: *The Class 171/7 classification is given to the 10 two-car sets formed of a DMCL and a DMSL, providing seats for nine first and 107 standard class passengers, in keeping with prior 'Turbostar' designs; the first class is located directly behind the driving cab. The two-car sets are used on the Brighton-Hastings line as well as supplementing four-car sets on main line duties. Set No. 171726 is seen passing Honor Oak Park.* **Antony Christie**

Below: *The six four car sets are classified as 171/8 and provide accommodation for 18 first and 241 standard class passengers. Set No. 171806 is illustrated at Crowborough on 2 February 2008.* **Antony Christie**

Class 172 'Turbostar'

Sub class:	172/0	172/1	172/2
Number range:	172001-172008	172101-172104	172211-172222
Introduced:	2010	2011	2011
Built by:	Bombardier, Derby	Bombardier, Derby	Bombardier, Derby
Formation:	DMS+DMS	DMSL+DMS	DMSL+DMS
Vehicle numbers:	DMS - 59311-59318 DMS - 59411-59418 -	DMSL - 59111-59114 DMS - 59211-59214 -	DMSL - 50211-50222 DMS - 79211-79222 -
Vehicle lengths:	DMS - 76ft 3 in (23.27m) DMS - 76ft 3 in (23.27m)	DMSL - 76ft 3 in (23.27m) DMS - 76ft 3 in (23.27m)	DMSL - 76ft 3 in (23.27m) DMS - 76ft 3 in (23.27m)
Height:	12ft 4½in (3.77m)	12ft 4½in (3.77m)	12ft 4½in (3.77m)
Width:	8ft 8 in (2.69m)	8ft 8 in (2.69m)	8ft 8 in (2.69m)
Seating:	Total - 124S DMS - 60S DMS - 64S -	Total - 145S DMSL - 65S DMS - 80S -	Total - 121S + 7 tip up DMSL - 53S + 4 tip up DMS - 68S + 3 tip up -
Internal layout:	2+2	2+2	2+2
Gangway:	Within set	Within set	Throughout
Toilets:	None	DMSL - 1	DMSL - 1
Weight:	Total - 83.1 tonnes DMS - 36.5 tonnes DMS - 41.6 tonnes	Total - 82.2 tonnes DMSL - 41.4 tonnes DMS - 40.8 tonnes	Total - 83.2 tonnes DMSL - 41.9 tonnes DMS - 41.3 tonnes
Brake type:	Air EP	Air EP	Air EP
Bogie type:	B5006	B5006	B5006
Power unit:	1 x MTU 6H1800R83 of 484hp (360kW) per vehicle	1 x MTU 6H1800R83 of 484hp (360kW) per vehicle	1 x MTU 6H1800R83 of 484hp (360kW) per vehicle
Transmission:	Mechanical	Mechanical	Mechanical
Transmission type:	ZG	ZG	ZG
Horsepower:	968hp (720kW)	968hp (720kW)	968hp (720kW)
Max speed:	75mph (121km/h)	75mph (121km/h)	100mph (161km/h)
Coupling type:	BSI	BSI	BSI
Multiple restriction:	Class 14x, 15x, 170, 172	Class 14x, 15x, 170, 172	Class 14x, 15x, 170, 172
Door type:	Twin-leaf swing plug	Twin-leaf swing plug	Twin-leaf swing plug
Body structure:	Aluminium	Aluminium	Aluminium
Owner:	Angel Trains	Angel Trains	Porterbrook
Operator:	London Overground	Chiltern	London Midland

Left & Right: *In 2007-08 both Porterbrook and Angel Trains ordered new generation diesel-mechanical units for three operators, London Overground, Chiltern and London Midland. The first sets to emerge were eight two-cars for use on London Overground's non-electrified route between Gospel Oak and Barking. Painted in LO livery the sets have a basic interior with 2+2 seats and lots of standing room. These sets are likely to be phased out in the near future as trains with more capacity are required. Set No. 172006 is seen in the bay at Gospel Oak. The seating layout as used on the London Overground sets is shown right. Both:* **CJM**

172/3
172331-172345
2011
Bombardier, Derby
DMSL+MS+DMS
DMSL - 50331-50345
MS - 56331-56345
DMS - 79331-79345
DMSL - 76ft 3 in (23.27m)
MS - 76ft 6in (23.36m)
DMS - 76ft 3 in (23.27m)
12ft 4½in (3.77m)
8ft 8 in (2.69m)
Total - 193S + 7 tip up
DMSL - 53S + 4 tip up
MS - 72S
DMS - 68S + 3 tip up
2+2
Throughout
DMSL - 1
Total - 121.3 tonnes
DMSL - 41.9 tonnes
MS - 38.1 tonnes
DML - 41.3 tonnes
Air EP
B5006
1 x MTU 6H1800R83 of
484hp (360kW) per vehicle
Mechanical
ZG
1,449hp (1,080kW)
100mph (161km/h)
BSI
Class 14x, 15x, 170, 172
Twin-leaf swing plug
Aluminium
Porterbrook
London Midland

Above: *To provide extra stock for Chiltern services, four Class 172 diesel-hydraulic sets without end corridors were ordered and delivered in 2011. The sets look like the later Class 170s and are painted in standard Chiltern Railways livery. Set No. 172101 is seen departing from Marylebone on 10 May 2013.* **Antony Christie**

Above: *When London Midland ordered both two- and three-car Class 172s through Porterbrook Leasing, these sets included end gangways to allow trains to operate in multiple providing a through access for passengers and revenue protection staff. This inclusion required a full re-design of the front end and led to a protracted delivery. Two-car set No. 172222 is seen at Worcester. In the London Midland configuration these sets seat 121 standard class passengers in the 2+3 high-density style. The three-car sets seat an extra 72 passengers. The LM sets are painted in full LM livery and are allocated to Tyseley depot, being deployed in the Birmingham area.* **CJM**

Class 175 'Coradia 1000'

Class:	175/0	175/1
Number range:	175001-175011	175101-175116
Introduced:	1999-2001	1999-2001
Built by:	Alstom, Birmingham	Alstom, Birmingham
Formation:	DMSL(A)+DMSL(B)	DMSL(A)+MSL+DMSL(B)
Vehicle numbers:	DMSL(A) - 50701-50711 DMSL(B) - 79701-79711	DMSL(A) - 50751-50766 MSL - 56751-56766 DMSL(B) - 79751-79766
Vehicle length:	75ft 7in (23.03m)	DMSL - 75ft 7in (23.03m) MSL - 75ft 5in (22.98m)
Height:	12ft 4in (3.75m)	12ft 4in (3.75m)
Width:	9ft 2in (2.79m)	9ft 2in (2.79m)
Seating:	Total - 118S DMSL(A) - 54S DMSL(B) - 64S	Total - 186S DMSL(A) - 54S MSL - 68S DMSL(B) - 64S
Internal layout:	2+2	2+2
Gangway:	Within set	Within set
Toilets:	DMSL(A), DMSL(B) - 1	DMSL(A), MSL, DMSL(B) - 1
Weight:	Total - 99.5 tonnes DMSL(A) - 48.8 tonnes DMSL(B) - 50.7 tonnes	Total - 147.7 tonnes DMSL(A) - 50.7 tonnes MSL - 47.5 tonnes DMSL(B) - 49.5 tonnes
Brake type:	Air	Air
Bogie type:	Alstom FBO LTB-MBS1, TB-MB1, MBS1-LTB	Alstom FBO LTB-MBS1, TB-MB1, MBS1-LTB
Power unit:	One Cummins N14 of 450hp (335kW) per car	One Cummins N14 of 450hp (335kW) per car
Transmission:	Hydraulic	Hydraulic
Transmission type:	Voith T211rzze to ZF final drive	Voith T211rzze to ZF final drive
Horsepower (total):	900hp (670kW)	1,350hp (1,005kW)
Max speed:	100mph (161km/h)	100mph (161km/h)
Coupling type:	Outer - Scharfenberg, Inner - bar	Outer - Scharfenberg, Inner - bar
Multiple restriction:	Within type and Class 180	Within type and Class 180
Door type:	Single-leaf swing plug	Single-leaf swing plug
Special features:	Air conditioned	Air conditioned
Body structure:	Steel	Steel
Owner:	Angel Trains	Angel Trains
Operator:	Arriva Trains Wales	Arriva Trains Wales

Left: *The Alstom 'Coradia 1000' DMU was offered to the rail industry in 1998. The design platform was accepted by First Group who ordered trains for their then North Western and Great Western operations. On North Western a fleet of 27 two- and three-car low-density sets was ordered, based at Chester for medium-long distance operation. Painted in as delivered First 'Barbie Doll' livery, set No. 175001 is seen inside Chester depot. The '175s' are set out for standard class occupancy and have a toilet in each vehicle. Power is provided by a Cummins N14 engine under each vehicle.* CJM

Above: *With franchise changes in 2003 the North Western operation was absorbed into a Welsh franchise and the Class 175s became operated by Arriva Trains Wales, who soon applied their Arriva branding to the First Group livery. One of the longer three-car sets, No. 175107, is illustrated at Newport while working a Holyhead to Cardiff service on 27 June 2007. The three car Class 175s provide accommodation for 186 standard class passengers.* CJM

Right Middle: *Devoid of any operator branding, First North Western liveried two-car set No. 175008 is seen near Rhyl on 29 July 2004 bound for Holyhead. Perhaps not the most pleasing units to look at, the Class 175s have performed well and have a very low failure rate, with traincrew and passengers liking their operation.* CJM

Right Below: *Soon after Arriva Trains took over the Class 175 fleet, the operator's turquoise livery started to appear on the stock, broken up by a yellow band as solebar height and light blue passenger doors. Arriva branding in both English and Welsh was applied to the bodyside. The intermediate Motor Standard No. 56766 from set No. 175116 is shown.* CJM

Class 180 'Coradia 1000'

Number range:	180101-180114
Introduced:	2000-01
Built by:	Alstom, Birmingham
Formation:	DMSL(A)+MFL+MSL+MSLRB+DMSL(B)
Vehicle numbers:	DMSL(A) - 50901-50914, MFL - 54901-54914 MSL - 55901-55914, MSLRB - 56901-56914 DMSL(B) - 59901-59914
Vehicle length:	DMSL(A), DMSL(B) - 77ft 7in (23.71m) MFL, MSL, MSLRB - 75ft 5in (23.03m)
Height:	12ft 4in (3.75m)
Width:	9ft 2in (2.79m)
Seating:	Total - 42F/226S DMSL(A) - 46S, MFL - 42F MSL - 68S, MSLRB - 56S DMSL(B) - 56S
Internal layout:	Standard 2+2 First 2+1
Gangway:	Within set
Toilets:	One per vehicle
Weight:	Total - 252.5 tonnes DMSL(A) - 51.7 tonnes, MFL - 49.6 tonnes MSL - 49.5 tonnes, MSLRB - 50.3 tonnes DMSL(B) - 51.4 tonnes
Brake type:	Air
Bogie type:	Alstom MB2
Power unit:	One Cummins QSK19 of 750hp (560kW) per vehicle
Transmission:	Hydraulic
Transmission type:	Voith T312br to ZF final drive
Horsepower (total):	3,750hp (2,800kW)
Max speed:	125mph (201km/h)
Coupling type:	Outer - Scharfenberg, Inner - Bar
Multiple restriction:	Within type and Class 175
Door type:	Single-leaf swing plug
Body structure:	Steel
Special features:	Air conditioned
Owner:	Angel Trains
Operator:	First Great Western, First Hull Trains, Grand Central

Left Below: *The Alstom 'Coradia 1000' design platform also extended to a fleet of 14 five-car luxury 125mph (201km/h) Class 180s for First Great Western. These stunning sleek units were a bit of a disappointment to the operators with numerous faults and problems, and saw a protracted introduction into service. The five-car sets were low-density with standard class seating in the 2+2 and first class in the 2+1 style. One of the standard class intermediate vehicles had a small buffet, and a catering point was provided in the first class intermediate vehicle for the FGW at seat trolley service. To maintain the overall streamlined effect of the train, the end fully automatic Scharfenberg coupling was housed behind a sliding front panel, which was also the cause of many problems. After First Great Western completed their HST fleet refurbishment, the Class 180s were phased out of service and stored. After a short time First Group's Hull Trains operation took over four sets and refurbished them for use on the King's Cross to Hull route, while a further five sets were taken over by Open Access operator Grand Central for use on their East Coast services. For a period, several sets were used by North Western on Manchester area duties, while others were stored pending transfer to East Coast. By 2012 First Great Western funded the overhaul of five sets for use on the Paddington-Oxford-Worcester corridor; these sets were fully overhauled and brought up to modern specification by Wabtec and now sport the FGW Dynamic Lines livery. The first of the fleet, No. 180101, with its number stuck on the front, is seen arriving at Paddington when brand new.* **CJM**

Right: *With no coupling covers attached, First Hull Trains set No. 180113 is illustrated painted in Dynamic Lines livery at Doncaster on 16 April 2013. It is understood that no attempt will be made to refit the coupling covers and use the retractable function of the Scharfenberg coupling* **CJM**

Above: *FGW set No. 180106 is seen departing from Reading with a service for London on 10 August 2006. One of the operating problems with the '180s' was the first class carriage being an intermediate vehicle.* **CJM**

Right: *The five sets operated by Grand Central are painted in their black and orange house colours as seen on set No. 180105 at Doncaster on 16 April 2013. These sets are usually referred to as 'Zephyrs'. A number of interior changes were made to the GC sets, including tables with games inscribed on the surface.* **CJM**

Class 185 'Desiro'

Number range:	185101-185151
Introduced:	2005-07
Built by:	Siemens Transportation, Germany
Formation:	DMCL+MSL+DMS
Vehicle numbers:	DMCL - 51101-51151 MSL - 53101-53151 DMS - 54101-54151
Vehicle length:	DMCL, DMS - 77ft 11in (23.76m) MSL - 77ft 10in (23.75m)
Height:	12ft 4in (3.75m)
Width:	9ft 3in (2.84m)
Seating:	Total - 15F/156S + 12 tip up DMCL 15F/18S + 8 tip up MSL 72S DMS 64S + 4 tip up
Internal layout:	First 2+1 Standard 2+2
Gangway:	Within set
Toilets:	MSL - 1, DMCL - 1
Weight:	Total - 163.1 tonnes DMCL - 55.4 tonnes MSL - 52.7 tonnes DMS - 55 tonnes
Brake type:	Air
Bogie type:	Siemens
Power unit:	One Cummins OSK19 of 750hp (560kW) per car
Transmission:	Hydraulic
Transmission type:	Voith Turbopack T312 with SK-485 final drive
Horsepower (total):	2,250hp (1,680kW)
Max speed:	100mph (161km/h)
Coupling type:	Dellner 12
Multiple restriction:	Within class only
Door type:	Bi-parting sliding plug
Body structure:	Aluminium
Special features:	Air conditioned, power points, CCTV
Owner:	Eversholt
Operator:	First TransPennine

Below: *The contract for new trains to modernise the Trans-Pennine route was awarded to Siemens for 51 three-car diesel-hydraulic 'Desiro' sets. Based at Ardwick, Manchester, the sets are high quality low-density stock, painted in First Dynamic Lines livery. With its DMS vehicle nearest the camera, set No. 185130 departs from Preston bound for Manchester and the East Coast.* **CJM**

Above: *The Class 185s seat 15 first class passengers in the Driving Motor Composite Lavatory vehicle; this is recognisable from the outside by having no windows ahead of the first pair of passenger doors on the driver's side. First class seating is in the 2+1 style while all standard class seats are in the 2+2 format. The structural design of these sets is very similar to the 'Desiro' EMU products in use with various UK operators. Note the anti-climber teeth on the front end which should engage if the vehicle is in an impact with another like fitted vehicle. No. 185113 is illustrated at Doncaster.* CJM

Below: *The Class 185 intermediate vehicle is a Motor Standard Lavatory and seats 72 passengers. The coach also houses one standard design toilet compartment. Passenger access is by two pairs of bi-parting sliding plug doors feeding a cross walkway. On the roof of the vehicle is an air conditioning assembly. Vehicle No. 53113 from set No. 185113 is illustrated.* CJM

Class 210

Class:	210 (3-car)	210 (4-car)
Number:	210002	210001
Introduced:	1981	1981
Built by:	BREL Derby	BREL Derby
Formation:	DMS+TS+DTS	DMBS+TS+TC+DTS
Vehicle numbers:	DMS - 60200 (53000) TS - 60400 (57000) DTS - 60301 (54001)	DMBS - 60201 (53001) TS - 60401 (57001) TC - 60450 (58000) DTS - 60300 (54000)
Vehicle length:	DMS, DTS - 65ft 0½in (19.83m) TS - 65ft 4in (19.92m)	DMBS, DTS - 65ft 0½in (19.83m) TS, TC - 65ft 4in (19.92m)
Height:	12ft 3½ (3.75m)	12ft 3½ (3.75m)
Width:	9ft 3in (2.81m)	9ft 3in (2.81m)
Seating:	Total - 203S DMS - 45S TS - 84S DTS - 74S	Total - 22F/232S DMBS - 28S TS - 84S TC - 22F/46S DTS - 74S
Internal layout:	First 2+1 Standard 2+2S	First 2+1 Standard 2+2S
Gangway:	Throughout	Throughout
Toilets:	Not fitted	TC - 1
Weight:	Total - 117.7 tonnes DMS - 62 tonnes TS - 26.8 tonnes DTS - 28.9 tonnes	Total - 146.7 tonnes DMBS - 63 tonnes TS - 26.8 tonnes TC - 28 tonnes DTS - 28.9 tonnes
Brake type:	Air, EP	Air, EP
Bogie type:	Power - BREL - BP20 Trailer - BREL BT13	Power - BREL - BP20 Trailer - BREL BT13
Power unit:	1 x MTU 12V396 TC11 of 1,140hp (850kW) in DMS	1 x Paxman 6RP200L of 1,125hp (839kW) in DMBS
Transmission:	Electric	Electric
Transmission alternator:	GEC	Brush
Traction motor type:	GEC	Brush
Horsepower:	1,140hp (850kW)	1,125hp (839kW)
Max speed:	90mph (145km/h)	90mph (145km/h)
Coupling type:	Tightlock	Tightlock
Multiple restriction:	Class 210 only	Class 210 only
Door type:	Double leaf sliding	Double leaf sliding

Below: *Built as two test bed units as part of the project to design and built replacement DMU stock for medium and longer distance routes, BREL Derby was contracted in 1980 to build a three- and four-car Class 210 DEMU fitted with an above floor prime mover, with quality passenger interiors meeting a similar design specification to the Class 317 'Bed-Pan' and Class 455 dc EMUs, broadly based on Mk3 coach technology. The design specification was tough and demanded crew/passenger operated doors, a full length gangway, and low noise. The passenger environment had to be 'good' for the short haul traveller, or the long distance passenger. The three-car set No. 210002 was all standard class and powered by an MTU engine. The four-car set, No. 210001, had first class in one of the intermediate coaches and was powered by a Paxman engine. This view shows the intermediate Trailer Standard No. 57001 (later renumbered to 60401) from the four-car set No. 210001; this was basically a Class 317/455 vehicle seating 84 in the 2+3 style.* **CJM**

Above: *With its power car nearest the camera, the four-car set No. 210001 is seen on the Western Region during its period on main line trials in 1985. The Paxman 6RP200L engine was set to develop 1,125hp (839kW) and was quite capable of seeing the set travel at its maximum 90mph (145km/h) top speed. The TC (Trailer Composite) vehicle is third from the front and had its first class accommodation located between the two door positions, seating 22 passengers.* CJM

Below: *The MTU-powered three-car set No. 210002 is seen with its Driving Trailer Standard nearest the camera dozing on the buffer stops at Paddington on 1 November 1984. When the two '210s' were operated on the Western Region they were usually confined to the Paddington to Reading corridor where a number of drivers and guards were specially trained on their operation. The pair were often the subject of inspection by the BRB and other possible customers.* CJM

Class 220 'Voyager'

Number range:	220001-220034
Introduced:	2000-01
Built by:	Bombardier Transportation*
Formation:	DMSL+MS+MSL+DMFL
Vehicle numbers:	DMSL - 60301-60334, MS - 60701-60734 MSL - 60201-60234, DMFL - 60401-60434
Vehicle length:	77ft 6in (23.62m)
Height:	12ft 4in (3.76m)
Width:	8ft 11in (2.72m)
Seating:	Total - 26F/174S DMSL - 42S, MS - 66S MSL - 66S, DMFL - 26F
Internal layout:	First 2+1 Standard 2+2
Gangway:	Within set
Toilets:	DMSL, MSL, DMFL - 1
Weight:	Total - 194.7 tonnes DMSL - 51.2 tonnes, MS - 45.9 tonnes MSL - 46.7 tonnes, DMFL - 50.9 tonns
Brake type:	Air, EP rheostatic
Bogie type:	Bombardier B5005
Power unit:	1 x Cummins of 750hp (560kW) per car
Transmission:	Electric
Transmission package:	Onix
Traction motor type:	8 x Alstom Onix 800 per train
Horsepower:	3,000hp (2,240kW)
Max speed:	125mph (201km/h)
Operating range:	1,350 miles (2,173km)
Route availability:	2
Coupling type:	Outer: Dellner 12 Inner: Bar
Multiple restriction:	Class 220, 221 and Class 57/3
Door type:	Single-leaf swing plug
Body construction:	Steel
Special fittings:	Air conditioning, non tilt
Owner:	Halifax/Bank of Scotland
Operator:	Arriva CrossCountry

* Body shells assembled in Belgium, fitted out at Bombardier plants in Wakefield, UK, and Brugge, Belgium.

Below: *Some of the most controversial modern multiple unit style trains must be the Bombardier-built 'Voyager' sets built for Virgin Trains as a replacement for loco-hauled and HST stock used on its CrossCountry operation. The four-car sets offered only around half the accommodation of the trains they replaced and many found their ambience poor, seating cramped and poor onboard service, with frequently broken or defective toilets. The first 'Voyager' sets to emerge from factories in Brugge in Belgium and Wakefield in the UK were four-car non-tilt sets. These had three standard class carriages seating 174 and one first class coach seating 26. First class seating was in the 2+1 style, while standard seats were in the 2+2 configuration, principally using aircraft layout. The first set emerged from the Brugge factory for testing on 18 October 2000. Another problem with the 'Voyager' stock was the lack of luggage accommodation; in earlier days with loco-hauled and HST stock, passengers had lots of space, but with the Class 220s and 221s virtually all space was full of seats and only limited luggage stacks were provided. The Class 220 fleet operated with Virgin Trains on its CrossCountry business until the franchise was transferred to Arriva CrossCountry Trains in November 2007 and the company set about applying its livery to the stock. Painted in Virgin Trains silver and red livery, this is intermediate TS No. 60213 from set No. 220013.* CJM

Above: *Showing the very impressive Virgin Trains red and silver livery, set No. 220016 hurries past Dawlish and along the sea wall on 8 July 2006. The set's Driving Motor Standard Lavatory (DMSL) vehicle is nearest the camera. The non-tilt 'Voyager' stock in Virgin days carried a silvery background Virgin badge on the front.* CJM

Below: *Showing the latest CrossCountry silver and brown livery with the remains of a Virgin red roof, set No. 220003 heads past Langstone Rock in summer 2012. This set has its Driving Motor First Lavatory at the front, identifiable by the yellow cant rail band and the yellow cover on the drum of the coupling.* CJM

Class 221 'Super Voyager'

Class:	221 (5-car)	221 (5-car) (4-car)
Number range:	221101-221118, 221142-221143¶	221119-221140 221141
Introduced:	2001-02	2001-2002
Built by:	Bombardier Transportation*	Bombardier Transportation*
Formation:	DMSL+MSL(A)+MSL(B)+MSRMB+DMFL	DMSL+MS+MSL(A)+MSL(B)+DMFL
Vehicle numbers:	DMSL - 60351-60368 , 60392-60393 MSL(A) - 60951-60968, 60992-60993 MSL(B) - 60851-60868 , 60994, 60794 MSRMB - 60751-60768, 60792-60793 DMFL - 60451-60468, 60492-60493	DMSL - 60369-60390, 60391 MS - 60769-60790, 60791 MSL(A) - 60969-60990, 60991 MSL(B) - 60869-60890, - DMFL - 60469-60490, 60491
Vehicle length:	77ft 6in (23.67m)	77ft 6in (23.67m)
Height:	12ft 4in (3.75m)	12ft 4in (3.75m)
Width:	8ft 11in (2.73m)	8ft 11in (2.73m)
Seating:	5-car Total - 26F/222S, DMSL - 42S MSL(A) - 66S MSL(B) - 62S MSRMB - 52S DMFL - 26F	5-car Total - 26F/244S, 4-car Total - 26F/176S DMSL - 42S MS - 66S MSL(A) - 68S MSL(B) - 68S DMFL - 26F
Internal layout:	First 2+1 Standard 2+2	First 2+1 Standard 2+2
Gangway:	Within set	Within set
Toilets:	DMSL, MSL, DMFL - 1	DMSL, MSL, DMFL - 1
Weight:	Total - 278.3 tonnes DMSL - 58.9 tonnes MSRMB - 53.1 tonnes MSL(A) - 56.6 tonnes MSL(B) - 53.1 tonnes DMFL - 56.6 tonnes	Total - 5-car - 280.7 tonnes, 4-car - 226.3 tonnes DMSL - 58.5 tonnes MS - 54.1 tonnes MSL(A) - 54.8 tonnes MSL(B) - 54.4 tonnes DMFL - 58.9 tonnes
Brake type:	Air, EP rheostatic	Air, EP rheostatic
Bogie type:	Bombardier HVT	Bombardier HVT
Power unit:	1 x Cummins of 560kW (750hp) at 1800rpm per car	1 x Cummins of 560kW (750hp) at 1800rpm per car
Transmission:	Electric Onix	Electric Onix
Traction motor:	10 Alstom Onix 800 per train	10 or 8 Alstom Onix 800 per train
Horsepower:	3,750hp (2,796kW)	5-car 3,750hp (2,796kW) 4-car 3,000hp (2,237kW)
Max speed:	125mph (201km/h)	125mph (201km/h)
Operating range:	1,200 miles (1,931km)	1,200 miles (1,931km)
Route availability:	4	4
Coupling type:	Outer: Dellner 12, Inner: Bar	Outer: Dellner 12 Inner: Bar
Multiple restriction:	Class 220/221 only	Class 220/221 only
Door type:	Single-leaf swing plug	Single-leaf swing plug
Body construction:	Steel	Steel
Special fittings:	Air conditioning, tilt fitted	Air conditioning, tilt (isolated)
Owner:	Halifax/Bank of Scotland	Halifax/Bank of Scotland
Operator:	Virgin Trains	Arriva CrossCountry

* Body shells assembled in Belgium, fitted out at Bombardier plants in Wakefield, UK, and Brugge, Belgium.
¶ Originally sets 221142-221143 were four car units

Above: *One of the keys to the success of the introduction of the Virgin 'Super Voyager' sets fitted with a tilt facility was to be able to reduce journey times by taking curves at an increased speed, tilting the structure of the train to keep a perfect ride and stability. The system was complex and took a long time to commission and sadly today is isolated on all the sets operating on the CrossCountry corridor. 'Super Voyager' set No. 221133 heads towards Kennaway Tunnel, Dawlish, in June 2004.* **CJM**

Below: *Of the original fleet of 'Super Voyager' sets, 23 are operated by CrossCountry, with the balance of 20 sets operated by Virgin Trains for West Coast non-electrified use. On 17 April 2013 five-car CrossCountry set No. 221125, with its first class coach leading, passes Clay Cross junction, Chesterfield.* **CJM**

Class 222 'Meridian' and 'Pioneer'

Sub class:	222/0 'Meridian' (7-car)	222/4 'Meridian' (5-car)	222/1
Number range:	222001-222006	222007-222023	222101-222104
Introduced:	2004-05	2004-05	2005
Built by:	Bombardier Brugge	Bombardier Brugge	Bombardier Brugge
Formation:	DMF+MF+MF+ MSRMB MS+MS+DMS	DMF+MC+MSRMB+ MS+DMS	DMF+MC+MSRMB+DMS
Vehicle numbers:	DMF - 60241-60246 MF - 60345-47/60445-47 MF - 60341-44/60441-43 MSRMB - 60621-60626 MS - 60561-60566 MS - 60544-60556 DMS - 60161-60166	DMF - 60247-60263 MC - 60442/60918-60933 MSRMB - 60627-60643 MS - 60531-60567 DMS - 60167-60183	DMF - 60271-60274 MC - 60571-60574 MSRMB - 60681-60684 DMS - 60191-60194
Vehicle length:	Driving - 78ft 2in (23.85m) Int - 78ft 2in (23.00m)	Driving - 78ft 2in (23.85m) Int - 78ft 2in (23.00m)	Driving - 78ft 2in (23.85m) Int - 75ft 4in (23.00m)
Height:	12ft 4in (3.75m)	12ft 4in (3.75m)	12ft 4in (3.75m)
Width:	8ft 11in (2.73m)	8ft 11in (2.73m)	8ft 11in (2.73m)
Seating:	Total - 106F/236S DMF - 22F MF - 42F MF - 42F MSRMB - 62S MS - 68S DMS - 38S	Total - 50F/192S DMF - 22F MC - 28F/22S MSRMB - 62S MS - 68S DMS - 40S	Total - 33F/148S DMF - 22F MC - 11F/46S MSRMB - 62S DMSO - 40S
Internal layout:	First 2+1 Standard 2+2	First 2+1 Standard 2+2	First 2+1 Standard 2+2
Gangway:	Within set	Within set	Within set
Toilets:	DMF, MF, MS, DMS - 1	DMF, MC, MS, DMS - 1	DMF, MC, DMS - 1
Weight:	Total - 337.8 tonnes DMF -52.8 tonnes MF - 46.8 tonnes MF - 46.8 tonnes MSRMB - 48 tonnes MS - 47 tonnes DMSO - 49.4 tonnes	Total - 249 tonnes DMF - 52.8 tonnes MC - 48.6 tonnes MSRMB - 49.6 tonnes MS - 47 tonnes DMSO - 51 tonnes	Total - 197.3 tonnes DMF - 52.8 tonnes MC - 47.1 tonnes MSRMB - 48 tonnes DMSO - 49.4 tonnes
Brake type:	Air, EP regenerative	Air, EP regenerative	Air, EP regenerative
Bogie type:	Bombardier B5005	Bombardier B5005	Bombardier B5005
Power unit:	1 x Cummins QSK9R of 560kW (750hp) per car	1 x Cummins QSK9R of 560kW (750hp) per car	1 x Cummins QSK9R of 560kW (750hp) per car
Transmission:	Electric 16 x Alstom Onix 800 per train	Electric 10 x Alstom Onix 800 per train	Electric 8 x Alstom Onix 800 per train
Horsepower:	5,250hp (3,920kW)	3,750hp (2,800kW)	3,000hp (2,240kW)
Max speed:	125mph (201km/h)	125mph (201km/h)	125mph (201km/h)
Operating range:	1,350 miles (2,173km)	1,350 miles (2,173km)	1,350 miles (2,173km)
Route availability:	4	2	2
Coupling type:	Dellner 12	Dellner 12	Dellner 12
Multiple restriction:	Class 222	Class 222	Class 222
Door type:	Single-leaf swing plug	Single-leaf swing plug	Single-leaf swing plug
Body construction:	Steel	Steel	Steel
Owner:	Eversholt	Eversholt	Eversholt
Operator:	East Midlands Trains	East Midlands Trains	East Midlands Trains
Notes:			Previously 'Pioneer' sets Operated by Hull Trains

Far Right: *Following the transfer of the Midland Main Line operation to Stagecoach Rail and its relaunch as East Midlands Trains, a new Stagecoach-based livery was adopted, based on the red, white and blue, with an attractive swirl at the cab ends. Five car set No. 222017 is seen at Nottingham with the set's Driving Motor Standard Lavatory nearest the camera.* **CJM**

Above: *After delivery of the Class 220 and 221 stock to the UK, Bombardier offered its product to other operators and soon HSBC Rail placed an order for Midland Main Line and Hull Trains for what became the Class 222s; although similar, these were quite different from the Virgin fleets in terms of equipment and interior design. For Midland Main Line sets were formed into nine- and four-car rakes, but after operating experience this was changed to seven- and five-car formations. Four additional four car sets were built for Hull Trains, but after these were replaced by Class 180s, the Hull 222s were transferred to Derby to join the Midland fleet, which by that time was operated by Stagecoach East Midlands Trains. Painted in Midland Main Line livery, sets Nos. 222011 (right) and 222004 (left) are seen at Nottingham.* **CJM**

Right Middle: *The Class 222s use low-density seating throughout, with 2+2 in standard class and 2+1 in first class. First Class seats are of the reclining type, with angle headrests. Each seat has a table and East Midlands trains offer a complimentary at seat service. In the main the Class 222s operated by EMT work on the St Pancras to Derby-Sheffield route, while the HST fleet tends to operate on the St Pancras to Nottingham corridor. A first class interior is illustrated.* **Antony Christie**

Waterloo & City Stock

Classification:	Waterloo & City	Waterloo & City	Waterloo & City	Waterloo & City
Number range:	1-12	13-17	21-30, 31-32	33-36
Introduced:	1898	1899-1900	1898, 1904	1922
Built by:	Jackson Sharp	Dick Kerr	20-31 Jackson Sharp 31-32 Electric TW	L&SWR
Type:	Single ended Motor Car	Double ended Motor Car	Trailer	Trailer
Vehicle length:	51ft 3in (15.62m)	50ft 9in (15.47m)	49ft 9in (15.16m)	49ft 2in (14.99m)
Height:	9ft 8ft (2.95m)	9ft 8ft (2.95m)	9ft 8ft (2.95m)	9ft 8ft (2.95m)
Width:	8ft 6in (2.59m)	8ft 6in (2.59m)	8ft 6in (2.59m)	8ft 6in (2.59m)
Seating:	52	52	56	58
Internal layout:	2+2, Bench	2+2, Bench	2+2, Bench	2+2, Bench
Gangway:	Emergency	Emergency	Emergency	Emergency
Toilets:	Not fitted	Not fitted	Not fitted	Not fitted
Weight:	?	?	?	?
Brake type:	Air	Air	Air	Air
Bogie type:	Special	Special	Special	Special
Power collection:	600V dc third rail	600V dc third rail	600V dc third rail	600V dc third rail
Traction motor type:	Siemens	Siemens	-	-
Horsepower:	120hp (89kW)	120hp (89kW)	-	-
Max speed:	35mph (56km/h)	35mph (56km/h)	35mph (56km/h)	35mph (56km/h)
Coupling type:	Special	Special	Special	Special
Multiple restriction:	Orig WC Stock	Orig WC Stock	Orig WC Stock	Orig WC Stock
Door type:	Gate/Sliding	Gate/Sliding	Gate/Sliding	Gate/Sliding

Below: *The London & South Western Railway (L&SWR) predicted huge growth in passenger traffic requiring to go direct into the City of London as early as the mid 1840s, with authorisation given for the project as early as 1846. However, due to financial constraints this was abandoned in 1848. In the mid 1890s, with more knowledge of tunnelling, the L&SWR resurrected the project with the building of the Waterloo & City tube railway which opened in 1898 linking Waterloo with Bank station adjacent to the Bank of England. Stock for the line were formed as five four-car trains and later supplemented by other stock. The five-car trains (one of which is illustrated below) were built by Jackson & Sharp of Wilmington, Delaware, USA. Subsequent cars were built in the UK by Dick Kerr of Preston and even the L&SWR's own workshops. During off-peak periods, shorter trains operated and it was for this reason that the Dick Kerr double ended motor cars were built allowing trains of any length to operate. The line, equipped with a side contact third rail, was powered from the line's own power station until 1915 when main line electrification saw the line fed from the main system. These original vehicles with wooden seats continued in operation until 1940 when they were replaced by the Southern Railway.* CJM-C

L&SWR Motor Sets

Below: *The London & South Western Railway (L&SWR) commenced electrification of its main suburban lines from London Waterloo in 1913, opening the system to Wimbledon via East Putney, Kingston, Hampton Court, Shepperton, the Hounslow loop line and to Guildford in 1915. To operate the service a fleet of 84 three-car sets was built at Eastleigh Works, in many ways they were the forerunner to the 3-SUB stock. Each set, originally numbered E1-E84 and after the grouping in 1923 1201-1284, could seat between 170-185 passengers of which one third were first class; the first class accommodation was progressively reduced. The coaches used to form these 84 EMUs were rebuilt from 1904-built four-car steam hauled suburban stock. The vehicles selected for conversion to driving cars had a 'torpedo' shaped cab fitted; this was full width with the driving controls on the left in the direction of travel. Between the two front windows was a slot for a stencil train route indicator, which at the time used a single letter of the alphabet, but later two-character route indicators were installed. All vehicles were later augmented into four-car 4-SUB stock and renumbered in the 41xx and 42xx series. Set No. E40 is seen passing Cromer Road at the southern end of East Putney tunnel.* CJM-C

Classification:	LSWR SUB
L&SWR number range:	E1-E84
Grouping number range:	1201-1284
Former number range:	Former loco-hauled
Alpha code:	3-SUB
Introduced:	1914-17
Built by:	L&SWR Eastleigh
Formation:	DMBT+TC+DMBC
Vehicle numbers:	DMBT: 80xx and 81xx series TC: 93xx series DMBC:87xx series
Set length:	193ft 0¾in (58.85m)
Vehicle length:	64ft 4¼in (19.62m)
Height:	12ft 7in (3.83m)
Width:	9ft 1in (2.77m)
Seating:	170-185 (33% being first class)
Internal layout:	Compartment
Gangway:	Not fitted
Toilets:	Not fitted
Weight:	Total - 95 tons DMBT, DMBC - 33 tons TC - 29 tons
Brake type:	Air
Bogie type:	L&SWR
Power collection:	600-660V third rail
Traction motor type:	BTH
Horsepower:	1,000hp (746kW)
Max speed:	60mph (97km/h)
Coupling type:	Screw
Multiple restriction:	Within type
Door type:	Slam

LBSCR SL, CP and CW stock

Classification:	SL (South London)	CP (Crystal Palace)
Number range:	1E - 8E	-
Introduced:	1908-09	1911-13
Built by:	Metropolitan Amalgamated Carriage & Wagon	Metropolitan Amalgamated Carriage & Wagon - DMTB + DTC LBSCR Lancing - TC
Formation:	8 x DMTB+TF (C)+DMBT or 16 x DMTB+DMTB	DTC+DMBT+DTC (not fixed)
Vehicle numbers:	DMTB - (SR) 8601-8616 (LBSCR) 3201-3224 (series) TF - (SR) 7644-7651 (LBSCR) 3202-3223 (series) DTC - (SR) 9811-9824 (LBSCR) 3225-3230, 4057-4060, 4065-4068	DMTB - (SR) 8567-8600 (LBSCR) 3231-3264 DTC - (SR) 9825-9892 (LBSCR) 4001-4076
Set length:	NA	NA
Vehicle length:	63ft 7in (19.38m)	54ft (16.46m)
Height:	12ft 3in (3.73m)	12ft 1in (3.68m)
Width:	9ft 5in (2.87m)	8ft (2.44m)
Seating:	Total: 74F/144T	Total: 48F/170T
Internal layout:	Compartment	Compartment
Gangway:	No	No
Toilets:	No	No
Weight:	Total - 104 tons DMBT - 54 tons TF - 30 tons DTC - 20 tons	Total - 78¾ tons DMBT - 52¼ tons DTC - 24½ tons
Brake type:	Air	Air
Bogie type:	LBSCR	LBSCR
Power collection:	6,700V ac overhead Bow Collector	6,700V ac overhead Bow Collector
Traction motor type:	4 x 115hp (86kW) Winter Eichberg	4 x 150hp (112kW) Winter Eichberg
Horsepower:	460hp (343kW)	600hp (447kW)
Max speed:	75mph (121km/h)	75mph (121km/h)
Coupling type:	Screw	Screw
Multiple restriction:	Within type	Within type
Door type:	Slam	Slam
Notes:	Rebuilt to dc sets 1928-29	Rebuilt to dc sets 1928-29

CW (Coulsdon & Wallington)
-
1923-24
Metropolitan Carriage Wagon & Finance

DTT+DTC+MBV+TC+DTT

21 x MBV, 60 x DT, 20 x TC
DTT - 9169-9208
TC - 9655-9674
DTC - 9893-9914
MBV - 10101-10121

NA
MBV - 42ft 1in (12.83m)
12ft 1in (3.68m)
8ft (2.44m)
?
Compartment/Saloon
No
No
Total - ?
MBV - 62 tons

Air
LBSCR
6,700V ac overhead
Bow Collector
4 x 250hp (190kW) GEC
1,000hp (746kW)
75mph (121km/h)
Screw
Within type
Slam
Rebuilt to dc sets 1928-29
MBVs rebuilt as brake vans

Left & Above: *In 1903 the London, Brighton & South Coast Railway obtained authority to electrify its network using a German overhead power system operating at 6,700V ac. The company decided that the first line to electrify was the South London Line between London Bridge and Victoria via Denmark Hill. Trains for this were provided by eight three-car trains were privided, known as SL stock. SL Driving Motor Third Brake No. 3204 and Driving Trailer Composite No. 4057 are illustrated at Peckham Rye, clearly showing the design of the bow power collector. The next line to be electrified was the route to Crystal Palace, for which a fleet of vehicles identified as CP (Crystal Palace) was built. Due to gauging restrictions these were shorter and narrower than the SL stock and emerged between 1911 and 1913. The image at the top shows car No. 3236, a Driving Motor Third Brake when new at the Metropolitan Amalgamated Carriage & Wagon shops, Birmingham. The third and final route to be electrified was the Coulsdon and Wallingford for which another fleet of trains identified as CW was built, with the line being electrified from April 1925. Power for the CW stock came from a fleet of 21 Motor Luggage Vans numbered 10101-10121; these were built by the Metropolitan Carriage Wagon and Finance Co of Saltley, Birmingham, and were basically a locomotive with no passenger accommodation but with an intermediate guards van and luggage space. The views middle and above show vehicle No. 10101 when brand new. After the LBSCR overhead system was abandoned in 1926 in favour of third rail electrification, these luggage vans were rebuilt as bogie goods brake vans, some of which are still in use today. All:* CJM-C

North Eastern Tyneside Electrics

Classification:	NER Tyneside
Introduced:	1904-28
Built by:	NER York
Formation:	3-8 car formations 1904 stock - 56 Motor Cars, 44 Trailers, 2 MPVs 1905 -15 - 22 vehicles plus MPV 1920 - 20 fire replacement vehicles built 1938 - Sets refurbished to form 18 2-car sets
Vehicle numbers / seats:	DMLF - 3239-62 (44F) DMLC - 3239 / 40-59 / 60-62 (18F / 23 or 26T) DMT - 3212-36, 3268-69, 3792-93 (60-68T) TT - 3180-3206, 3781-91 (68-72T) DTT - 3185 / 88-93 / 95-99, 3200 / 06-11, 3507 / 18-24 (63-64T) DMBT then DMC - 3237 / 38 / 63-65 (42T) MPV - 3266-3267, 3525 CTC - 3694 (24F / 40T) CTT - 3731 / 33 / 44 / 45 / 47 (80T) DMBC - 3770-01, 3794 (20F / 28T)
Vehicle length:	56ft 6in (17.22m)
Height:	12ft 9in (3.89m)
Width:	8ft 8in (2.64m)
Internal layout:	Open saloon
Gangway:	No
Toilets:	No
Weight:	Driving cars - 29ton 15cwt - 30ton 1cwt Trailer cars - 21ton 3cwt - 22ton 4cwt Motor Luggage Van - 39ton 6cwt
Brake type:	Air
Bogie type:	North Eastern
Power collection:	600V dc third rail
Traction motor type:	1904-05 stock 2 x 125hp (93kW) BTH 1920 stock 2 x 140hp (104kW) BTH
Horsepower:	250hp (186kW)
Max speed:	60mph (97km / h)
Coupling type:	Cowhead
Multiple restriction:	Within class
Door type:	Slam

Below: *In 1902 it was seen that passenger figures were dropping in the Newcastle area due to the introduction of tramways. The North Eastern Railway answered this by agreeing an electrification scheme from Newcastle Central to South Shields, North Shields via Heaton and Benton as well as the Walker loop. British Thomson-Houston was awarded the electrical contract to supply train equipment, while the NER's York Works built the new trains. Several different types of vehicle were constructed to cope with the different passenger flows, including motor luggage vans. The original stock had clerestory roofs, and seating was a mix of longitudinal and transverse with hinged passenger doors; large luggage vans were provided. Between 1904 and the late 1920s a number of changes to formations and layouts took place, including the building of replacement stock in 1922 to cover for vehicles lost in a depot fire. These vehicles, of which No. NER3785 (LNER No. 23785) is illustrated below, had semi-elliptical roofs. Originally the stock was finished in NER livery, but later LNER colours were applied. Car 23785 is a driving trailer, attached to a modernished six car set.* CJM-C

Lancaster-Morecambe/Heysham Sets

Introduced:	1908
Built by:	Midland Railway, Derby (two DTs converted from hauled stock)
Formation:	Single, or multiple
Vehicle numbers:	3 x Driving Motor - 28610-28612 6 x Driving Trailers - 29290-29295
Set length:	110ft 6in (33.68m)
Vehicle length:	DMT - 60ft (18.29m) DTT - 59ft 6in (18.14m)
Height:	12ft 8in (3.86m)
Width:	9ft 0in (2.74m)
Seating:	DMT - 56T DTT - 64T
Internal layout:	Open
Gangway:	No
Toilets:	No
Weight:	DMT - 36ton 5cwt DTT - 26ton 3cwt
Brake type:	Vacuum
Bogie type:	MR
Power collection:	6.6kV ac overhead
Traction equipment:	2 x Siemens then 1 x Westinghouse
Horsepower:	220hp (164kW)
Max speed:	30mph (48km/h)
Coupling type:	Screw
Multiple restriction:	With design
Door type:	Slam

Below: *The Midland Railway branches from Lancaster to Morecambe and Heysham, which formed part of the so called 'Little North Western' Railway, were involved in a ground-breaking electrification project by the Midland Railway in 1908, operating what were arguably the world's first 'modern' electric multiple unit trains. Route electrification used a 6,600V ac overhead system, installed by Siemens and it opened between 13 April and 14 September 1908, using purpose built or converted rolling stock. The electrical equipment was provided jointly by Siemens and Westinghouse. Power for the system was generated by gas-powered Westinghouse dynamos. The route continued operation until the early 1950s, when it was selected for further power development trials, being electrified at 25kV ac using the overhead system and becoming the prototype for subsequent BR electrification. Two of the original three Driving Motor Third cars, Nos. LMS28610 and 28612, stand side by side at Morecambe Promenade. As can be seen, all power and control equipments were housed in underframe mounted boxes. Power collection on these vehicles was by means of a diamond shaped collector, mounted directly above the main driving cab at the motor end of the car. As these were some of the first ever electric railway vehicles, large signs were attached to the roof line of the coach adjacent to the collector, reading 'It is Dangerous to touch this Apparatus'. The vehicles were finished in LMS maroon livery, with gold LMS branding and numbers. The doors in the car coach ends were for emergency purposes only.* CJM-C

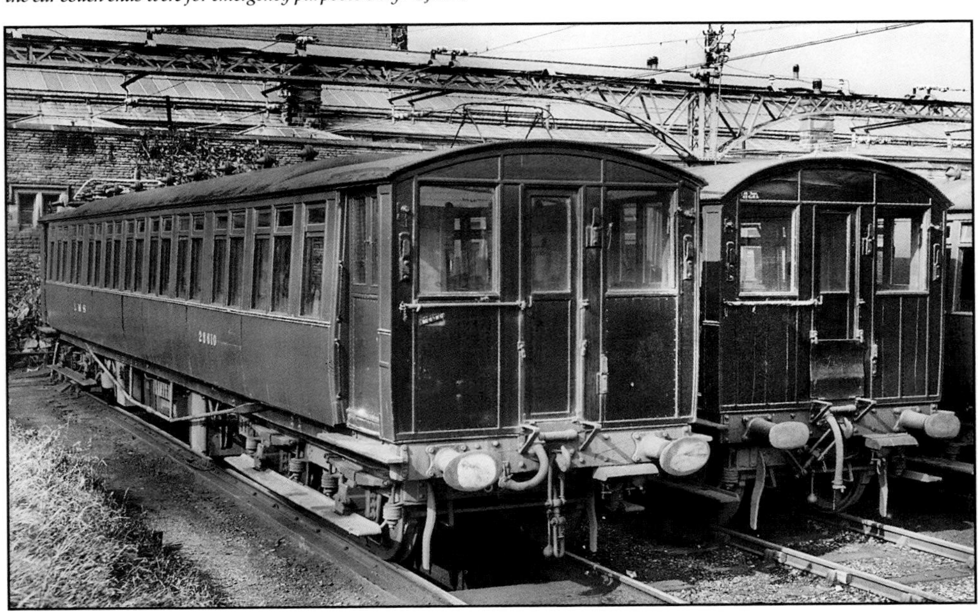

Manchester-Bury Sets

Introduced:	1915-21
Built by:	L&Y Railway, Newton Heath
Formation:	DMBT+CTT+DMBT+CTF+DMBT
Vehicle numbers:	DMBT - L&Y - 3502-3539 , LMS - 14572-14609 BR - M28500-M28537 CTT - L&Y - 3602-3615, LMS - 14669-14682 BR - M29200-M29213 CTF - L&Y 500-513, LMS - 10933-10946 BR - M28700-28713
Set length:	5-car - 326ft 3in (99.44m)
Vehicle length:	63ft 7in (19.38m)
Height:	12ft7in (3.84m)
Width:	9ft 4in (2.84m)
Seating:	Total - 72F/317T DMBT - 74T CTT - 93T CTF - 72F
Internal layout:	Open
Gangway:	No (emergency end doors)
Toilets:	No
Weight:	Total - 243 tons DMBT - 55 tons CTT/CTF - 39 tons
Brake type:	Air
Bogie type:	L&Y
Power collection:	1,200V dc side contact third rail
Traction motor type:	DMBT - 4x200hp (149.14kW) Dick Kerr
Horsepower:	5-car 2,400hp (1,790kW)
Max speed:	60mph (97km/h)
Coupling type:	Auto
Multiple restriction:	Within design
Door type:	Slam

Below: *The Newton Heath Works of the Lancashire & Yorkshire Railway built 66 vehicles for use on the electrified Manchester to Bury route between 1915 and 1921. The vehicles were of all metal construction. Each of the DMBT coaches had a driving position at each end, which occupied one third of the front end; a gangway door was provided in the centre and on the non-driving side an equipment case was located. In the DMBT cars a luggage area accessed by a roller shutter door was located behind the cab position at the No. 1 end. Passenger seating was in the 3+2 style, with entrance by means of hinged doors. The DMBT cars had a central push through door in the gangway to divide smoking and non-smoking sections. In the Control Trailer vehicles much the same layout was followed but no luggage space was provided. In the third class cars seating was 3+2, while in the first class vehicles seating used the 2+2 layout. On the front ends a roof mounted roller-blind destination indicator was provided, with power and control jumpers located below the driving cab front window; sockets were located on the non-driving side. Buffer beam air connections were provided. In the two views below we see five car sets, which was the norm for operation. The upper image in full LYR livery shows a glazed wooden door in the gangway position, while the image below shows a five-car set in LMS livery led by DMBT No. 28515, which has blinds missing from its destination indicator. Both:* CJM-C

Holcombe Brook Sets

Below: *The Holcombe Brook branch from Bury was electrified in 1913 using a 3,500V dc overhead system, which had been developed to test operating and trains systems for future electrification projects. The rolling stock used consisted of two motor coaches and two trailers. Two pantographs were fitted to the power cars, which were both raised when in operation. The cars had open saloon 3+2 seating for 75. The trailer cars seated 85 in a similar layout. Vacuum operated side steps were provided as some of the stations on the short route were ground level. As part of the electrification project, one car was fitted with a 150hp traction motor and the other a 250hp motor. After a few years of operation power supply problems emerged and from 1918 the line was energised at 1,200V dc. In 1927 the LMSR withdrew the four Holcombe Brook cars and authorised them for conversion to a trial diesel multiple unit set fitted with a Beardmore oil engine (see DMU section). Led by driving motor car No. 3501 a two-car set arrives at Holcombe Brook in 1915.* CJM-C

Introduced:	1913
Built by:	L&Y Newton Heath
Formation:	DMBT+DTT
Vehicle numbers:	DMBT - L&Y - 3500-01, LMS - 14570-71 DTT - L&Y 3600-01, LMS - 14667-68
Set length:	127ft 2in (37.8m)
Vehicle length:	63ft 7in (19.38m)
Height:	12ft 7in (3.84m)
Width:	9ft 4in (2.84m)
Seating:	DMBT - 75T, DTT - 85T
Internal layout:	Open, 3+2
Gangway:	No (emergency end doors)
Toilets:	No
Weight:	Total - 86 tons
Brake type:	Air
Bogie type:	L&Y
Power collection:	3,500V dc overhead *
Traction motor type:	Car 3500 - 4 x 150hp (112kW) D Kerr Car 3501 - 4 x 250hp (186kW) D Kerr
Horsepower:	Car 3500 - 600hp (447kW) Car 3501 - 1,000hp (746kW)
Max speed:	45mph (72km/h)
Coupling type:	Screw
Multiple restriction:	Within vehicle design
Door type:	Slam
Note:	* Also operated as three car From 1917 operated at 1,200V dc and converted to 1,200V third rail in 1918. Rebuilt in 1927 as diesel set.

LNWR Sets

Classification:	LNWR	LMS
Introduced:	1914, 1922	1926, 1932
Built by:	LNWR	Metropolitan Carriage, Clayton and Midland Railway
Formation:	DMBT+TT+DTT	DMBT+TT+DTT
Vehicle numbers:	DMBT - 28219-28222, 28000, 28223-28299 TC - ? DTT - ?	London sets DMBT - M28001M-M28025M TT - M29400M-M29409M / M29600M-M29621M DTT - M28800M-M28824M Liverpool sets DMBT - M28301M-M28310M TC - M29800M-M29811M DTT - M29100M-M29110M
Set length:	175ft 6in (53.49m)	175ft 6in (53.49m)
Vehicle length:	57ft 0in (17.37m)	57ft 0in (17.37m)
Height:	12ft 5in (3.78m)	12ft 5in (3.78m)
Width:	9ft 6in (2.90m)	9ft 3in (2.82m)
Seating:	1914 Siemens - 38F/138T 1914 & 1922 - Oerlikon - 33F/130T	London - Original - 40F/248T London - Revised - 288S Liverpool - 24F/252T DMBT - 84T TC - 24F/72T, DMBT - 96T
Internal layout:	Open	Compartment
Gangway:	No	No
Toilets:	No	No
Weight:	Total - ? DMBT - ? TC - ? DTT - ?	Total - 114 tons DMBT - 56 tons TT - 28 tons, DTT - 30 tons
Brake type:	Air	Air
Bogie type:	LNWR	Midland
Power collection:	630V dc third/fourth rail	630V dc third/fourth rail
Traction motor type:	1914 - 4-sets - 4 x 250hp (186kW) Siemens 1914 - 38-sets - 4 x 260hp (193kW) Oerlikon 1922 - 75-sets - 4 x 260hp (193kW) Oerlikon	4 x 265hp (198kW) Metro Vic
Horsepower:	1914 - Siemens - 1,000hp (746kW) 1914 & 1922 Oerlikon - 1,040hp (776kW)	1,060hp (790kW)
Max speed:	60mph (97km/h)	60mph (97km/h)
Coupling type:	Screw	Screw
Multiple restriction:	Within class	Within class
Door type:	Slam	Slam
Notes:		25 sets for London area 11 sets for Liverpool area. Plus spare cars. Some sets operated with spare vehicles to form 7-car sets

Left: *In 1914 the London & North Western Railway introduced electric stock on its London suburban lines from Euston to Watford and Richmond to Broad Street. The first sets had Siemens equipment with later builds using Oerlikon equipment. The three car units were dc powered using the third rail system. The 1914 and 1922 introduced sets were of an open layout, while 1926-32 introductions used compartments. Preserved DMBT No. 28249 in LMS livery is seen preserved at the National Railway Museum, York.* CJM

Mersey Electrics Sets

Classification:	1903 Stock	Follow-on stock
Stock:	24 DMs and 33 Trailers	1908 4 trailers, 1923 2 DMs, 1925 5-car set 1936 10 trailers
Introduced:	1903	1908-25
Built by:	Westinghouse	1908 - Westinghouse, 1923 - Cravens 1925/36 - Gloucester RC&W
Formation:	Various	Various
Vehicle numbers:	1-110	
Set length:	Depending on formation	Depending on formation
Vehicle length:	DMs - 59ft (17.98m) Trailers - 58ft (17.68m)	DMs - 59ft (17.98m) Trailers - 58ft (17.68m)
Height:	12ft 6in (3.84m)	12ft 6in (3.84m)
Width:	8ft 7in (2.62m)	8ft 7in (2.62m)
Seating:	?	?
Internal layout:	Saloon	Saloon
Gangway:	No, emergency end doors	No, emergency end doors
Toilets:	No	No
Weight:	DMs - 36.5 tons Trailers - 20 tons	DMs - 38.5 tons Trailers - 21 tons
Brake type:	Air	Air
Bogie type:	Special	Special
Power collection:	600V dc third rail	600V dc third rail
Traction motor type:	Westinghouse	Westinghouse
Horsepower:	4 x 115hp (86kW) Westinghouse	4 x 125hp (93kW) EE
Max speed:	60mph (97km/h)	60mph (97km/h)
Coupling type:	Knuckle	Knuckle
Multiple restriction:	With type	With type
Door type:	Slam	Slam
Special features:	-	-

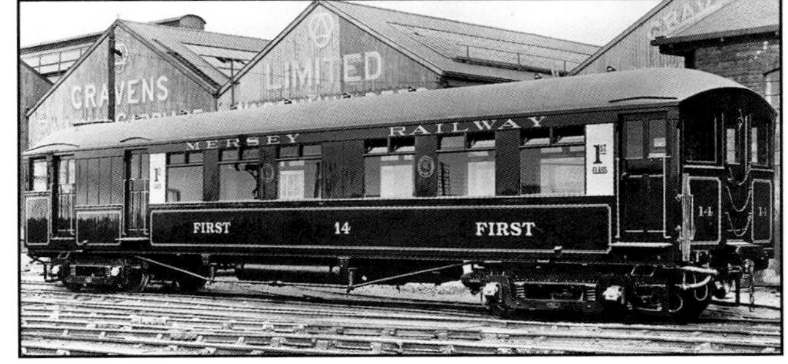

Right: *The Mersey Railway at the turn of the 1900s was virtually bankrupt, passenger returns were low and the railway dirty, with passengers preferring to travel by boat and road transport. The American Westinghouse Company was keen to enter the UK market and electrified the railway, introducing US outline passenger stock. In 1903 24 motor cars and 33 trailers were built in the UK complete with clerestory roofs and open gated ends. The vehicles were not heated. However, their introduction saw a turn around in Mersey rail passengers and between 1908 and 1925 many extra vehicles were built, this time to more traditional UK designs. The stock used terminal recharged air brake equipment (supplied by Westinghouse). The stock was painted in Mersey Railway maroon. After the railway grouping in 1923, the Mersey Railway became part of the LMS. In the right upper view we see one of the original US designed trains led by Driving Motor Car No. 2, while in the lower view we see later built first class driving car No. 14. Both:* CJM-C

Liverpool-Southport/Ormskirk Sets

Classification:	1904 & 1913 stock
Stock:	Originally 1904 - 56 vehicles Extra 1905 - 2DM, 12 TT Extra 1906 - 8 DM, 6 TF, 6 TT Baggage/Workmans - 2 1913 - 18DMs, 29TTs, 7TF. 4DTT
Introduced:	1904-13
Built by:	L&Y Newton Heath
Formation:	DMT+TF+TT+DMT
Vehicle numbers:	DMT - L&Y 3000-3066 LMS 28433-28498 TF - L&Y 400-440 LMS 29300-29340 TT - L&Y 3100-3150 LMS 29194-29199, 29500-29544
Vehicle length:	60ft 4¾in-63ft 7in (18.41-19.38m)
Height:	12ft 8in (3.81m)
Width:	10ft (3.04m), later 9ft 4in (2.84m)
Seating:	Total: 66F/218-222T DMT - 66-69T, TF - 66F, TT - 80-100T
Internal layout:	Saloon
Gangway:	Within set
Toilets:	No
Weight:	Total - 132 tons DMT - 46 tons TF/TT - 20 tons
Brake type:	Vacuum, later air
Bogie type:	L&Y
Power collection:	625V dc third rail
Traction motor type:	4 x 150hp (117kW) Dick Kerr Later 4 x 250hp (186kW) Baggage 2 x 150hp (117kW)
Horsepower:	600hp (447kW) Baggage: 300hp (223.5kW)
Max speed:	60mph (97km/h
Coupling type:	End - Screw, Inner - Automatic
Multiple restriction:	Within design
Door type:	Slam

Below: *The Lancashire & Yorkshire Railway were early pioneers of suburban electrification from Liverpool to Southport and Ormskirk as early as 1904 when the 23½-mile (38km) line to Southport was energised using a 625V third rail supply. The L&Y Newton Heath built trains were some of the widest ever to operate in the UK at 10ft (3.04m), they were some 60ft (18.41m) in length and had open saloon interiors. The sets had clerestory roofs, with a full width driving cab at the outer end. The original cab was tapered, but after a few years these were rebuilt to the box design. Roof roller destination blinds were fitted and vehicles had gangways fitted. No toilets were provided. Braking was provided by vacuum. Directly behind the driving cab was a luggage compartment, fed by a roller shutter door. Car No. 3002 leads a four-car formation in this 1905 view and clearly shows the tapered driving cab sides.* CJM-C

Above: *Modified in 1908-09 with the non-tapered driving cab, an original 1904 driving car leads a three-car train at Woodvale in 1922, carrying the circuit number 3 on the front end. This design of driving car seated 78 in the 2+3 style.* CJM-C

Right Middle: *A seven-car formation of 1907-08 built Liverpool-Southport stock is seen led by car No. 3051, one of six diagram 88 vehicles. These cars seated 80 third class passengers in the 2+3 style, with half the carriage set aside for smokers. A one third width driving cab was provided at either end.* CJM-C

Right Bottom: *With its roller blind destination indicator reading 'Stopping Train Liverpool' a seven-car set is seen in the car sheds with 1907-built Driving Motor Brake Third No. 3045 at the near end. This coach has an 'L' shaped luggage compartment to the rear and side of the driver's compartment. Passenger seating was for 66 with mainly reversible seats, enabling the guard to change the position of the backs to enable passengers to face the direction of travel. Half the vehicle was set aside for smokers.* CJM-C

Liverpool Overhead Stock

Introduced:	1892-99
Built by:	Electric Construction / Brown Marshall & Co
Stock:	Original 15 x two-car - DM+DM By 1895 an additional 8 three-car sets
Vehicle numbers:	1-46
Vehicle length:	1892 - 45ft 0in (13.71m) 1894 - 40ft 0in (12.19m)
Height:	11ft 9in (3.58m)
Width:	8ft 6in (2.59m) [10 cars increased to 9ft 4in (2.84m) in 1902 to increse capacity]
Seating:	18F/41S
Internal layout:	Open - transverse
Gangway:	No
Toilets:	No
Weight:	20-24 tons
Brake type:	Air
Bogie type:	LOR
Power collection:	500-630V dc third rail
Traction motor type:	2 x 60-70hp (45-52kW)
Horsepower:	120-140hp (90-104kW) Modified 1902 - 100hp (75kW)
Max speed:	40mph (72km/h)
Coupling type:	Special
Multiple restriction:	Within LOR stock
Door type:	Slam, Sliding
Notes:	1945-47 seven sets modernised with metal body and power operated sliding doors

Below: *The Liverpool Overhead Railway (LOR) or the* Dockers Umbrella *as it became known, was first suggested in the 1850s, but it was not until 1888 that authority to build the two-track line was given, running between Herculaneum Dock and Alexandra Dock on opening in 1893. Extensions were soon made to Dingle and Seaforth. Originally when proposed the line was to use steam traction, but in 1891 it was agreed to use electric power at 500V dc collected by a third rail originally mounted centrally between the running rails. The line opened on 4 February 1893, using single electric motor cars, any number of which could be coupled together and worked in multiple. The vehicles were built by Brown Marshall between 1892 and 1899. Originally 60hp motors were fitted but these were later upgraded to 70hp and even 100hp motors were fitted. The stock had air brakes, with air being topped up at terminating points. The sets had open style interiors with both first and third class seating. Trains mainly operated as either two or three power cars coupled together or with two driving power cars and a trailer between. Following an extension of the LOR over the L&Y tracks to Seaforth & Litherland, the third rail was moved from the centre of the tracks to the side. The Liverpool Overhead remained in operation as a private venture even after railway nationalisation in 1948. The line was forced to close due to the huge investment required to replace the wrought iron structures on which the railway ran. The final trains operated on 30 December 1956. Car No. 4 leads a three-car train at Seaforth.* CJM-C

Right Top: *The wooden bodied LOR driving cars had one powered and one trailer bogie; the powered bogie housed two traction motors. The interior of the cars was 'basic' with in third class vehicles wooden seats mainly in the transverse style; four hinged passenger doors were provided on each side of vehicles. The cab for the motorman occupied one third of the front, with a unique 'porch' style side window into which the driver could lean to see a good view of the train. Car No. 3 is seen at Gladstone Dock, with a charming sign on the platform advising 'Station for Canadian Pacific Steamers'.* CJM-C

Right Middle: *Running as a two-car set, driving car No. 9 arrives at James Street on 13 October 1956, just weeks before the final closure of the line.* CJM-C

Below: *By the late 1940s the LOR needed to either modernise or replace its stock as the trains were already some 50 years old. A scheme was adopted to replace the original all wooden body with a wooden frame and aluminium sheet panel structure incorporating guard controlled sliding doors. The cab ends became very box like and the overall appearance would not have won any design awards. The front end incorporated a destination indicator and a red rear marker light, and control jumpers were housed under the buffer beam. Overhauled cars also incorporated an externally mounted rear view mirror. A total of seven trains were refurbished, before it was deemed too expensive to progress. Refurbished cars Nos. 16, 12 and 15 are seen at Seaforth & Litherland.* CJM-C

Southern 3SUB

Classification:	3SUB
Number range:	1285-1801
Introduced:	1925-32
Built by:	Southern Railway
Formation:	DMBT+TC+DMBT or DMBT+TC+DMBC
Vehicle numbers:	DMBT - 8127-8749 (not in order) DMBC - 8793-8900 (not in order) TC - 9301-9749 (not in order) 97xx, 98xx and 99xx series also used
Set length:	181ft 8in (55.37m) - 193ft 0¾in (58.85m)
Vehicle length:	58ft 1in (17.70m) - 64ft 4¼in (19.62m)
Height:	12ft 7in (3.83m)
Width:	9ft 1in (2.77m)
Seating:	Various between 56F-180T - 50F-200T
Internal layout:	Compartment and open
Gangway:	No
Toilets:	No
Weight:	Total - 132-143 tons (depending on build)
Brake type:	Air
Bogie type:	SR
Power collection:	660V dc third rail
Traction motor type:	Early sets 4 x 275hp EE Later sets 4 x 250hp EE
Horsepower:	Early sets 1,100hp (820kW) Later sets 1,000hp (746kW)
Max speed:	75mph (121km/h)
Coupling type:	Screw
Multiple restriction:	Within class and 1936 design stock
Door type:	Slam
Notes:	Most sets augmented to four-car (4SUB)

Below: *Under the Southern Railway, electrification spread quickly and so did the introduction of new electric trains. The base unit for commuter operation were three-car suburban units, known as 3SUB stock. Large numbers of this type were introduced throughout the 1920s and 30s with sets numbered in the 1285-1801 series; many different designs and configurations were introduced depending on their intended area of operation and from which stock the vehicles had been rebuilt. Sets were all finished in Southern green livery with grey roofs and black underframes. All sets were equipped with full multiple control equipment, enabling up to four sets (12 cars) to operate together under the full power and brake control of the driver in the leading cab. All three of the Southern sections, Western, Central and Eastern, had an allocation of 3SUB stock. As passenger growth rapidly expanded, more and longer trains were required and thus most of the 3SUB sets were later augmented to four-car sets and reclassified. With a single 'T' route display meaning Tattenham Corner, 3 SUB No. 1618 is seen departing from Tadworth in early 1928.* CJM-C

Southern Trailer Sets

Classification:	Trailer sets
Number range:	989-1200
Introduced:	1920-37
Built by:	L&SWR, SECR, LBSCR, Southern Railway
Formation:	TT+TT some TT+TC
Vehicle numbers:	8901-9300 series
Set length:	105ft - 129ft 4in (32.0m - 39.42m) - various depending on origin
Vehicle length:	Various depending on origin
Height:	12ft 5in - 12ft 9in (3.78m - 3.89m)
Width:	9ft 1in - 9ft 3in (2.77m - 2.81m)
Seating:	Various between 168-204T
Internal layout:	Compartment, saloon
Gangway:	No
Toilets:	No
Weight:	Various between 19-29 tonnes
Brake type:	Air
Bogie type:	L&SWR, SECR, LBSCR
Power collection:	None
Traction motor type:	None
Horsepower:	None
Max speed:	75mph (121km/h)
Coupling type:	Screw
Multiple restriction:	Work with SUB stock
Door type:	Slam

Below: *By 1920 passenger levels were such on the London & South Western routes into Waterloo that extra capacity was required, either with extra trains or longer trains. As no additional trains were available, train lengthening was adopted and to achieve this a fleet of 24 two-coach trailer sets were formed; these were basically loco hauled stock fitted with EMU compatibility brake and waist height jumpers which could be coupled between two powered sets. The Trailer Set project was a great success and soon further sets were introduced, using a wide variety of vehicles and operating on all three Southern divisions after the 1923 grouping. Some of the later converted trailer cars were later used as the fourth vehicle when augmenting 3SUB to 4SUB stock. Trailer set No. 1176 is illustrated, with car No. 9272 nearest the camera. This vehicle was an original LBSCR Crystal Palace (CP) motor coach.* **CJM-C**

Southern 2SL, 2WIM

Classification:	2SL	2WIM
Number range:	1801-1808	1809-1812
Revised number range:	1901-1908	1909-1912
Alpha code:	2SL	2WIM
Introduced (rebuilt):	1929	1929
Built by:	Peckham Rye (conversion)	Peckham Rye (conversion)
Formation:	DMBT+DTC	DMBC+DTT
Vehicle numbers:	DMBT - 8723-8730 DTC - 9751-9758	DMBC - 9818-9821 DTT- 9951-9954
Set length:	127ft 2in (38.7m)	127ft 4in (38.81m)
Vehicle length:	DMBT - 63ft 7in (19.38m) DTC - 63ft 7in (19.38m)	DMBC - 63ft 8in (19.41m) DTT - 63ft 8in (19.41m)
Height:	12ft 4in (3.76m)	12ft 4in (3.76m)
Width:	9ft 6in (2.9m)	9ft 6in (2.9m)
Seating:	16F/108T	12F/90T
Internal layout:	Compartment	Compartment
Gangway:	No	No
Toilets:	No	No
Weight:	Total - 78 tons DMBT - 45 tons DTC - 33 tons	Total - 76 tons DMBC - 44 tons DTT - 32 tons
Brake type:	Air	Air
Bogie type:	SR Central/Suburban design	SR Central/Suburban design
Power collection:	660V dc third rail	660V dc third rail
Traction motor type:	2 x 225hp (205kW) MV339	2 x 225hp (205kW) MV339
Horsepower:	550hp (410kW)	550hp (410kW)
Max speed:	60mph (97km/h)	60mph (97km/h)
Coupling type:	Screw	Screw
Multiple restriction:	Within type	Within type
Door type:	Slam	Slam
Notes:	Former LBSCR SL stock	Former LBSCR SL stock

Left: *Introduced in May 1929 were eight two-car South London (SL) sets, converted from former LBSCR overhead stock. The compartment sets seated 18 first and 108 third class passengers and remained in traffic until 1954, being replaced by EPB stock. Painted in green livery, set No. 1805 is seen at Mitcham from its power car end while working on the Wimbledon-West Croydon line.* CJM-C

Right: *Four additional two-car sets were formed from spare LBSCR overhead stock, classified as 2WIM these sets; Nos. 1809-1812, were rebuilt from former first class trailer cars and brought up to dc operating standards with full width driving cabs for use on the electrified Wimbledon to West Croydon line. Painted in all over SR green livery, set No. 1810 is seen in the bay at West Croydon on 31 March 1951. In their modified form these sets seated 12 first and 90 third class passengers.* CJM-C

Below: *The 2NOL (two-carriage NO Lavatory) sets were converted from previous steam hauled vehicles at Eastleigh Works in 1934-36, to provide suburban stock for the Brighton to West Worthing, Horsted Keynes to Seaford/Ore route as well as on the Windsor lines out of London Waterloo. The sets seated 24 first and 135 third class passengers, with first class seating provided in three compartments in the DTC coach. An interesting point with these sets was that when the final eight sets were built, they were fitted with electro-pneumatic control equipment, the first on a Southern EMU. During World War 2 in 1942 a number of sets were de-motored and operated as trailer stock, usually with 4SUB units. In the usual Southern hand-me-down fashion, after the NOL sets were withdrawn in the mid 1950s a number gave their frames to the EPB/HAP stock then under construction. On 9 April 1959, set No. 1840 is seen at Sydenham Hill, viewed from its Driving Motor Brake Third end.*
Rodney Lissenden

Classification:	2NOL
Number range:	1813-1890
Origin:	Former LSWR coaches
Introduced:	1934-36
Built by:	Eastleigh Works
Formation:	DMBT+DTC
Vehicle numbers:	DMBT - 8596-8615, 9861-9910, 9781-9788 DTC - 9913-9950, 9961-9999 Not in order
Set length:	129ft 3in (39.39m)
Vehicle length:	DMBT - 64ft 9in (19.74m) DTC - 64ft 9in (19.74m)
Height:	12ft 4in (3.76m)
Width:	9ft 2in (2.79m)
Seating:	24F / 135T
Internal layout:	Compartment, saloon
Gangway:	No
Toilets:	No
Weight:	Total - 70 tons DMBT - 43 tons DTC - 27 tons
Brake type:	Air
Bogie type:	SR Central type
Power collection:	660-750V dc third rail
Traction motor type:	2 x 250hp (186.5kW) MV or EE
Horsepower:	500hp (373kW)
Max speed:	60mph (97km/h)
Coupling type:	Screw
Multiple restriction:	Within class and 1936 stock
Door type:	Slam

Southern 4LAV

Classification:	4LAV
Number range:	2921-2955
Former number range:	1921-1953
Introduced:	1931-32, 1940
Built by:	Eastleigh Works
Formation:	DMBT+TCL+TC+DMBT
Vehicle numbers:	DMBT - 10501-10565 odds, 10497-10499 TCL - 12001-12033, 11999-12000 TC - 11501-11535 DMBT - 10502-10566 (evens), 10498-10500
Set length:	257ft 2½in (78.40m)
Vehicle length:	64ft 3½in (19.60m)
Height:	12ft 8¾in (3.88m)
Width:	9ft 3in (2.82m)
Seating:	70F/204T
Internal layout:	Compartment, saloon
Gangway:	No
Toilets:	1
Weight:	Total - 139 tons
Brake type:	Air
Bogie type:	SR suburban
Power collection:	660-750V dc third rail
Traction motor type:	4 x 275hp (205kW) MV339
Horsepower:	1,100hp (820kW)
Max speed:	75mph (121km/h)
Coupling type:	Screw
Multiple restriction:	SR 1936 design
Door type:	Slam

Below: *The first Southern Railway main line electric multiple unit stock was a fleet of 33 four-coach LAVatory sets introduced in 1931 for use on the Brighton line electrification scheme, working semi-fast and stopping services. Sets were originally allocated numbers in the 19xx series, but these were changed to the 29xx series in 1937. These sets were non-gangwayed and non corridor fitted. Toilets were provided in the intermediate TCL coach, so those wishing to use the facilities, had to travel in the correct vehicle of the train. Electrical and control equipment conformed to the 1936 standard enabling sets to be coupled to both 1936-equipped main line and suburban stock for full multiple operation. Originally painted in all over Southern green, sets were later repainted into BR green with small yellow panels; some sets gained yellow panels and even full yellow ends, but none were repainted in rail blue. In early 1940 two additional LAV sets were built at Eastleigh, with their body profile similar to the HAL stock; internal fittings were the same as the earlier LAV stock. Set No. 2927 is illustrated at Haywards Heath.* **Colin Boocock**

Above: *In common with all Southern EMU stock of the period, screw couplings were fitted with buffer beam level main reservoir and brake pipes, and body mounted waist height power and control jumpers, meaning that attachment and detachment was a drawn out affair and required staff to go between vehicles in an area of danger close to the live rail. The front end equipment is seen on LAV set No. 2932 in immaculate condition.* **Ray Elsdon**

Below: *With the TCL coach as the second in the formation, containing five first and three third (second) class corridor accessed compartments, set No. 2939 departs from Brighton on 5 September 1968 with a semi-fast service to London Victoria. The TCL coach had one toilet compartment (of the same design) at each end, and a hinged door in the corridor between the two classes of travel. By reports of the period, these sets were very rough and uncomfortable, especially on indifferent track. By the time this view was taken, roof mounted air horns had been fitted in place of the original whistle.* **CJM-C**

Southern - PUL and CITY

Classification:	PUL	CITY
Number range:	3001-3020	3041-3043
Former number range:	2001-2020	2041-2043
Introduced:	1932	1932
Built by:	Metro-Cammell, BRCW, Eastleigh	Metro-Cammell, BRCW, Eastleigh
Formation:	DMBTO+TTK+TCK+TPCK+ TCK+DMBTO	DMBTO+TFK+TFK+TPCK+ TFK+DMBTO
Vehicle numbers:	DMBTO - 11003-11046 series TTK - 10001-10020 TCK - 11751-11789 (odds) TPCK - 256-278 (Pullman named) TCK - 11752-11790 (evens) DMBTO - 11004-11046	DMBTO - 11001, 11002, 11015 TFK - 12251, 12254, 12257 TFK - 12252, 12255, 12258 TPCK - 272, 273, 270 TFK - 12253, 12256, 12259 DMBTO - 11041, 11042, 11016
Set length:	399ft (121.6m)	386ft (117.7m)
Vehicle length:	DMBTO, TCK, TTK - 63ft 6in (19.36m) TPCK - 68ft 0in (20.73m)	DMBTO - 63ft 6in (19.36m) TFK - 59ft 0in (17.99m) TPCK - 68ft 0in (20.73m)
Height:	12ft 8½in (3.88m)	12ft 8½in (3.88m)
Width:	9ft 5in (2.87m)	9ft 5in (2.87m)
Seating:	60F/212T +12F/16T Pullman DMBTO - 52T, TTK - 68T TCK - 30F/24T	126F/104-108T + 12F/16T Pullman DMBTO - 52T, TFK - 42F TPCK - 12F/16T, TFKP - 30F
Internal layout:	2+2, Compartment, Pullman	2+2, Compartment, Pullman
Gangway:	Within set	Within set
Toilets:	DMBTO x 1, TTK, TCK x 2	DMBTO x 1, TFK x 2
Weight:	Total - DMBTO - 52-59 tons TTK, TCK - 35 tons	Total - DMBTO - 59 tons TFK - 34 tons, TPCK - 43 tons
Brake type:	Air	Air
Bogie type:	SR	SR
Power collection:	660V-0750V dc third rail	660V-0750V dc third rail
Traction motor type:	8 x 225hp (168kW) MV163	8 x 225hp (168kW) MV163
Horsepower:	1,800hp (1,342kW)	1,800hp (1,342kW)
Max speed:	75mph (121km/h)	75mph (121km/h)
Coupling type:	Screw	Screw
Multiple restriction:	1936 SR type	1936 SR type
Door type:	Slam	Slam

Left: *The Southern Railway ordered a pair of experimental Driving Motor Third main line cars in 1931, one each from BRCW and MCWF. The two were formed with ex steam stock intermediate trailers and a Pullman to undertake tests before squadron orders were placed. Car 11001 from BRCW is illustrated, showing set No. 2001. This weighed in at 57 tons and had seats for 56 third class passengers in the 2+2 style. Testing was carried out on all three Southern divisions in 1931-32 and the set was disbanded at the end of 1932. Its two test driving cars were later to be used in 6CITY sets 2041 and 2042. This vehicle is not PUL 2001 detailed above. Note the flat side including panelling over the solebar and the clean appearance of the front end when looked at alongside other stock.* **CJM-C**

Above & Below: *In 1932 the Southern Railway introduced 20 six-car express trains on the Victoria to Brighton line, and each contained one Pullman Car Co Pullman vehicle. The trains were jointly built by Eastleigh, Metro-Cammell and BRCW. These sets had corridors between vehicles with third class seating in 2+2 and first in compartments plus the Pullman vehicle with its high-quality interior. The sets were painted in Southern green except for the Pullman cars which were in umber and cream and all were named after women. These were some of the first trains to carry an underslung motor generator, providing a 70V supply for on train auxiliaries. Under the SR EMU code system, these sets became 6PUL. Three further Pullman formed sets were introduced, when three six-car CITY sets were introduced for the London Bridge to Brighton business service, linking Sussex with the City of London. These sets emerged in 1932. Originally the PUL and CITY sets were numbered in the 20xx series, butthis was later changed to the 30xx series. In the upper view is set No. 3043 from its non-Pullman end (Pullman car fourth from front), painted in later BR livery. In the view below we see the same set in early British Railways livery with the Pullman car at the leading end (third from front). Both:* **CJM-C**

Southern 6PAN

Classification:	PAN
Number range:	3021-3037
Former number range:	2021-2037
Introduced:	1935
Built by:	Metro-Cammell, BRCW, Eastleigh
Formation:	DMBTO+TTK+TFK+TFKP+ TTK+DMBTO
Vehicle numbers:	DMBTO - 11047-11079 (odds) TTK - 10021-10053 (odds) TFK - 12260-12276 TFKP - 12501-12517 TTK - 10022-10054 (evens) 11048-11080 (evens)
Set length:	392ft 2in (119.5m)
Vehicle length:	DMBTO, TFKP - 63ft 6in (19.36m) TFK - 59ft 0in (1.99m) TTK - 63ft 6in (19.36m)
Height:	12ft 8½in (3.88m)
Width:	9ft 3in (2.82m)
Seating:	72F/240T DMBTO - 52T TTK - 68TF TFK - 42F TFKP - 30F
Internal layout:	2+2, Compartment
Gangway:	Within set
Toilets:	DMBTO x 1, TFK, TTK x 2
Weight:	Total - DMBTO - 59 tons TFKP - 32 tons TTK, TFK - 35 tons
Brake type:	Air
Bogie type:	SR Suburban
Power collection:	660V-0750V dc third rail
Traction motor type:	8 x 225hp (168kW) EE163
Horsepower:	1,800hp (1,342kW)
Max speed:	75mph (121km/h)
Coupling type:	Screw
Multiple restriction:	1936 SR type
Door type:	Slam

Below: *The Southern Railway ordered 17 six-car PANtry (6PAN) units for the 1935 electrification of the lines to Eastbourne and Hastings, originally numbered 2021-2037, later amended to 3021-3037. The 34 driving motor cars were a split order: 17 came from the BRCW works and 17 from the Metropolitan Carriage Wagon & Finance works, both in Birmingham. Intermediate cars were built at the Southern's own works at Eastleigh. These sets were basically the same as the 6PUL sets, but with a first class trailer with a pantry in place of the Pullman car. Externally the driving cars were recognisable as they had fixed size windows with a single airstream ventilator above. Traction and control equipment came from British Thomson - Houston (BTH). The sets stayed on their intended London to Eastbourne, Hastings, Brighton and West Worthing routes, frequently working in multiple with a 6PUL or 6CITY set. From delivery the sets were painted in Southern, later BR green. The sets were withdrawn and reformed in the mid 1960s. As many of the vehicles were in good condition, in 1965 several were reformed to introduce a further batch of 6COR sets numbered 3041-3050, finally being withdrawn in 1969. Set No. 3021 is seen departing from Horsham on 10 October 1965 forming the 09.18 Victoria to Bognor Regis/Portsmouth service.* Ray Elsdon

AM1 - Lancaster-Morecambe/Heysham Prototype

Below: *Although the early BR classification AM1 is seldom used for these four sets, documents show this was their intended class. These sets were prototype ac EMUs converted from fourth-rail dc stock in 1952 for traction development work and used on the short Lancaster-Morecambe and Heysham line. This line had previously been electrified using a 6,600V ac system. These 1952 vehicles were rebuilt from original 1914-built LNWR stock built by Metropolitan Carriage, Wagon & Finance and used on the West London electrified system mainly between Willesden and Earls Court. After being taken out of service at the start of World War 2, the sets were stored and some 12 years later became the stock for these ac development test trains. A total of four sets were modified, each with slightly different equipment to gauge the best items to order for production 25kV EMUs. Much of the original overhead power equipment used with the 6,600V tests was reused, but some sections of new and proposed power supply equipment were erected. Set No. 022 with DMBS No. M28222M nearest the camera is seen below. Set numbers were not carried, but were referred to by the last two digits from the DMBS vehicle.* CJM-C

Classification:	AM1
Number range:	(Set 019 - Set 022)
Former number:	From 1914 LNWR Willesden-Earls Court stock stored in 1940
Introduced:	1952
Originallt built by:	Metropolitan Carriage Wagon & Finance
Formation:	DMBS+TSO+DTSO
Vehicle numbers:	DMBS - M28219M-M28222M TSO - M29721M-M29724M DTSO - M29021M-M29024M
Set length:	175ft 6in (53.49m)
Vehicle length:	57ft oin (17.37m)
Height:	12ft 5in (3.78m)
Width:	9ft 6in (2.90m)
Seating:	Total - 147S (sets 019-021), 157S (set 022) DMBS - 28 or 38S, TSO - 63S, DTSO - 56s
Internal layout:	Open
Gangway:	No
Toilets:	No
Weight:	Total - 111 tons DMBS - 57 tons, TSO - 26 tons, DTSO - 28 tons
Brake type:	Air
Bogie type:	LNWR
Power collection:	25kV ac overhead
Traction motor type:	4 x 215hp (160kW) EE
Horsepower:	860hp (641kW)
Max speed:	60mph (97km/h)
Coupling type:	Screw
Multiple restriction:	Within type
Door type:	Slam

Tyneside Sets

Classification:	Articulated Twin sets	Single
Number range:	29xxx	29xxx
Introduced:	1937	1937
Built by:	Metropolitan-Cammell	Metropolitan-Cammell
Formation:	12 x Type A - MBT+DTT 16 x Type B - MBLT+DTF 18 x Type C - MBT+TT 18 x Type D - MBLT+TF	MBT, DTT, MPV
Vehicle numbers:	Type A - MBT - E29101E-E29112E DTT - E29301E-E29312E Type B - MBLT - E29113E-E29128E DTF - E29313E-E29328E Type C - MBT - E29129E-E29146E TT - E29229E-E29246E Type D - MBLT - E29147-E29164E TF - E29247-E29264E	MBT - E29165E, E29166E DTT - E29376E-29390E MPV - E29467E, E29468E
Original LNER numbers:	Type A - 24145-24168 Type B - 24169-24200 Type C - 24201-24236 Type D - 24237-24272	MBT - 24273, 29274 MPV - 2424, 2425
Vehicle length:	55ft 9in (16.99m)	59ft 0in (17.98m)
Height:	12ft 2½in (3.72m)	12ft 2½in (3.72m)
Width:	9ft 0¾in (2.76m)	9ft 0¾in (2.76m)
Seating:	Type A - MBT - 52T, DTT - 76T Type B - MBLT - 48T, DTF - 28F/32U Type C - MBT - 52S, TT - 80T Type D - MBLT - 48T, DTF - 28F/36U	MBT - 52S, DTT - 68S MPV -
Internal layout:	2+2	2+2
Gangway:	Within set	-
Toilets:	No	No
Weight:	MBT-DTT - 54ton 19cwt-55ton 7cwt MBT-TT - 53ton 12cwt-54ton 6cwt	MBT - 47ton 5cwt DTT - 26ton 10cwt MPV - 38ton 15cwt
Brake type:	Air EP	Air EP
Bogie type:	LNER Articulated	LNER 2 axle
Power collection:	600V dc third rail	600V dc third rail
Traction motor type:	2 x 154hp (115kW) Crompton Parkinson	MBT - 2 x 154hp (115kW) Crompton Parkinson MPV - 4 x 154hp (115kW) Crompton Parkinson
Horsepower:	308hp (230kW)	MBS - 308hp (230kW) MPV - 616hp (460kW)
Max speed:	60mph (97km/h)	60mph (97km/h)
Coupling type:	Cowhead	Cowhead
Multiple restriction:	Within class only	Within class only
Door type:	Sliding	Sliding

Notes: From 4 May 1959 first class was removed and sets declassified to second class

Above: *Modernisation of the Tyneside electrified system took place in 1937 when a fleet of 64 articulated twin-sets was delivered from Metro-Cammell. The sets carried a stunning LNER red and cream livery and were a major improvement on the older stock. Four types of unit were formed, usually operating as four- or six-car formations. In addition to the twin sets, four single cars were built. Sets accommodated both first and third class passengers using bucket seats. Vehicles were produced from steel and carried the latest Westinghouse electro-pneumatic brake equipment. With just a small square opening for the driver to see the road ahead, a six-car formation of articulated stock arrives at Newcastle.* CJM-C

Right Middle: *Repaints of stock in the 1950s saw BR multiple unit green applied, changing its appearance. A six-car Tynemouth to Newcastle via Benton train is seen at Manors on 15 August 1959, showing standard BR green livery.* CJM-C

Right Bottom: *1937-built single Motor Luggage Van No. E29467E is seen at Manors in late 1959. As can be seen the standard front end design was used, with four pairs of bi-parting doors leading into the luggage van.* CJM-C

Manchester-Altrincham Sets

Introduced:	1931, 1939
Built by:	Metropolitan-Cammell
Formation:	DMBT+TC+DTT
Vehicle numbers:	DMBT - M28571M-M28594M (MSJAR 01-24) TC - M29390M-M29396M (MSJAR 151-158) M29650-M29671M (MSJAR - 100-122) DTT - M29231-M29252M (MSJAR - 51-74)
Set length:	174ft 0in (53m)
Vehicle length:	58ft (17.68m)
Height:	12ft 8in (3.86m)
Width:	9ft 5in (2.87m)
Seating:	Total - Original 40F/228T, Modified 24F/252T DMBT - 72T TC - Original 40F/48T, Modified 24F/72T DTT - 108T
Internal layout:	Compartment
Gangway:	No
Toilets:	No
Weight:	Total - 118 tons DMBT - 57 tons, TC - 30 tons, DTT - 31 tons
Brake type:	Air
Bogie type:	?
Power collection:	1,500V dc overhead
Traction motor type:	4 x 328hp (245kW) GEC
Horsepower:	1,312hp (978kW)
Max speed:	60mph (97km/h)
Coupling type:	Screw
Multiple restriction:	With class
Door type:	Slam
Notes:	Planned to become BR Class 505

Below: *The Manchester, South Junction and Altrincham Railway (MSJAR), was at the Grouping in 1923 owned jointly by the London Midland &Scottish and London &North Eastern Railways. In 1931 it was agreed to electrify the 8½mile (13.7km) route from Manchester London Road to Altrincham, using the 1,500v dc overhead system. To operate the service, 22 three-car EMUs were built by Metropolitan-Cammell, together with two spare power cars. The route opened for electric operation on 11 May 1931. The MSJAR stock was based at a depot at Altrincham and operated exclusively over the line for 40 years. In 1939 extra intermediate vehicles were taken into stock, these being rebuilds of older vehicles. In 1961 the MSJAR line was cut back to Manchester Oxford Road, as at the time the LMR Crewe to Manchester electrification included the section through Manchester Piccadilly to Oxford Road. The MSJAR EMUs, proposed to be given the TOPS classification 505, were withdrawn in April 1971 when the route was upgraded to 25kV ac operation. In the view below we see three of the MSJAR electric sets at Altrincham, from left to right Nos. 22, 12 and 20, all viewed from the power car end.* CJM-C

Right Top: *In the 1950s the three-car MSJAR sets were gradually repainted into BR green livery, complete with a red buffer beam and often white or silver buffer heads. The dc sets had a large cross-arm pantograph mounted above the drivers' cab, equipment bay and guards van of the DMBT vehicle. Seating on this vehicle was for 72, with a passenger door by each seating bay. Front end equipment consisted of a screw coupling, air pipes and a control cable. Car No. M28573M leads in this view at Altrincham in May 1958.* CJM-C

Right Middle: *Viewed from its Driving Trailer Third, which provided accommodation for 108 third class passengers, car No. M29237M leads a three-car set into Altrincham in 1956. These units did not operate in fixed sets, but were always referred to by coach numbers. It was possible to lengthen sets by inserting extra intermediate trailers. The DMBT vehicles had sufficient power to move an eight car train if needed.* CJM-C

Below: *Painted in BR green with a small yellow warning panel, DMBT No. M28585M leads a train out of one of the bay platforms at Manchester Oxford Road on 5 May 1963 after the main through platforms had been converted to 25kV ac overhead working. The first class seating on these sets was provided in the intermediate TC coach.* CJM-C

Pre-TOPS - 4DD

Classification:	4DD
Number range:	4901-4902
Former number range:	4001-4002
Alpha code:	4-DD (4car **D**ouble **D**ecker)
Introduced:	1949-50
Built by:	BR Eastleigh
Formation:	DMBS+TS+TS+DMBS
Vehicle numbers:	DMBS - 13001-13004 TS - 13501-13504
Set length:	257ft 5in (78.46m)
Vehicle length:	DMBS - 62ft 6in (19.05m) TS - 62ft 0in (18.90m)
Height:	12ft 8¾in (3.88m)
Width:	9ft 3in (2.82m)
Seating:	Total - 508S + 44 tip up DMBS - Lower deck - 55S, Upper deck - 55S + 10-tip up TS - Lower deck - 78S, Upper deck - 66S + 12 tip up TS - Lower deck - 78S, Upper deck - 66S + 12 tip up DMBS - Lower deck - 55S, Upper deck - 55S + 10-tip up
Internal layout:	2+3
Gangway:	No
Toilets:	Not fitted
Weight:	Total - 134 tons DMBS - 39 tons TSO - 28 tons TS - 28 tons DMBS - 39 tons
Brake type:	Air (Westinghouse)
Bogie type:	SR
Power collection:	660-750V dc third rail
Traction motor type:	4 x EE507
Horsepower:	1,000hp (746kW)
Max speed:	75mph (121km/h)
Coupling type:	Screw
Multiple restriction:	1936 design SR EMUs
Door type:	Slam

Below: *Just prior to railway nationalisation in 1948, the Southern Railway tabled a plan to design and build a double-deck train in an attempt to increase capacity in the already overcrowded South Eastern commuter corridor. Due to obvious height constraints, the vehicles could not be double-deck like a motor bus, but had staggered high-low seating, with a few shallow steps to the upper deck. Based on a 4SUB unit profile, the first of the 4DD (Double Deck) units emerged from Eastleigh Works in late 1949, quickly to be followed by a second set; their numbers were 4001 and 4002 and they were allocated to Slade Green. The public were less than impressed about the cramped conditions and difficulty in reaching the upper deck. People boarded the train and sat in the lower seats leaving the upper level nearly empty. The presence of the seat base also restricted standing room. Each four-coach DD set could accommodate 552 seated passengers and BTC publicity claimed a further 150 could stand, meaning that in the peak period with the two sets working together between Dartford and Charing Cross 1,404 passengers could be moved on just one train. The sets were painted in BR multiple unit green and incorporated a roller blind route display. In the late 1960s the pair were repainted into BR rail blue and given full yellow ends. In November 1970 the pair were renumbered to 4901 and 4902 to vacate the number space for the new PEP units. The double deck sets remained in operation until 1 October 1971 when they made their final journey between Charing Cross and Dartford via Bexley. Set No. 4001 is illustrated. Note the slight recess on the guards van and cab compared with the rest of the vehicle.* CJM-C

Below: *For many years the Southern Region had been keen to operate a Trailer Control (TC) system, and this first came to fruition in the summer of 1963 when a rake of seven redundant EMU vehicles were formed together as set No. 900 (later 701); it was formed of modified 2BIL driving cars and five former 4SUB trailers. In September 1963 the set commenced operation on a peak hour London Bridge to Tunbridge Wells West via Oxted service. In technical terms, although this set was called a TC in Southern documents, it was not possible to control the powering loco from the ex BIL cab cars and had to be hauled at all times. In 1965 another TC project was put forward, to convert redundant PUL and PAN stock and form them into 6TC sets. Only one set was actually formed, No. 601. This commenced operation on the Oxted line in 1966 before being transferred to the Western section at Clapham Junction for use on the Clapham Junction to Kensington Olympia peak hour service. The 6TC set seated 72 first and 264 second class passengers. Power for the train was a modified Class 33 No. D6580 which was the pioneer of push-pull traction power on the Southern. It was fitted with remote control equipment and could be driven from the cab of the attached TC set. This work paved the way for the subsequent Waterloo-Bournemouth-Weymouth push-pull operations. Set No. 701 is illustrated.* CJM-C

Classification:	6TC	7TC
Number range:	601	900 later 701
Introduced:	1965	1963
Built by:	Eastleigh	Eastleigh
Formation:	DTBS+TSK+TS+ TS+TS+DTBS COR/PAN/PUL stock	DTBS+TS+TC+TS TS+TS+DTS 2BIL DTS + SUB TSs
Vehicle numbers:	DTBS 11154 TSK - 10014, 10009 TCK - 11768 TSK - 10041 DTBS - 11229	DTBS - 10573 TS - 10346, 10349 TC - 11485 TS - 10353, 10351 DTC - 12107
Set length:	381ft 2in (116.2m)	448ft 10½in (136.8m)
Vehicle length:	63ft 6in (19.35m)	DTS - 62ft 6in (19.05m) TC/TS - 62ft (18.9m)
Height:	12ft 9½in (3.89m)	12ft 8¾in (3.88m)
Width:	9ft 3in (2.81m)	9ft 3in (2.81m)
Seating:	72F/264S	Total: - 48F/636S DTBS - 52S TS -120S, TC-30S/48F DTS - 56S
Internal layout:	Saloon/compartment	Saloon/compartment
Gangway:	No	No
Toilets:	TS x 2	No
Weight:	Total - ?	Total - 216 tons
Brake type:	Air	Air
Bogie type:	SR trailer	SR trailer
Power collection:	Unpowered	Unpowered
Traction motor type:	No	No
Horsepower:	No	No
Max speed:	75mph (121km/h)	75mph (121km/h)
Coupling type:	Screw	Screw
Multiple restriction:	Hauled	Hauled
Door type:	Slam	Slam

Pre-TOPS - Tyneside EPB

Introduced:	1955
Built by:	BR Eastleigh
Formation:	DMBS+DTS
Vehicle numbers:	DMBS - 65311-65325 DTS - 77100-77114
Set length:	132ft 8¼in (40.44m)
Vehicle length:	64ft (19.51m)
Height:	12ft 9½in (3.90m)
Width:	9ft 3in (2.82m)
Seating:	Total: 176S DMBS - 74S DTS - 102S
Internal layout:	2+3
Gangway:	No
Toilets:	No
Weight:	Total - 70 tons DMBS - 40 tons DTS - 30 tons
Brake type:	Air (EP/Auto)
Bogie type:	Mk3D
Power collection:	600-750V dc third rail
Traction motor type:	2 x EE507 at 250hp (186.4kW)
Horsepower:	500hp (373kW)
Max speed:	75mph (121km/h)
Coupling type:	Inner - Link Outer - Buck-eye
Multiple restriction:	Within class
Door type:	Slam
Notes:	Later formed part of Southern Region Class 416 fleet

Below: *Modernisation of the Tyneside electrified system took place in 1954-55, when a fleet of 15 two-car sets was built at Eastleigh Works, based on the then current 2EPB stock for the Southern, except these sets had a longer guards brake van in the DMBS vehicle. The DMBS vehicles seated 74 and the Driving Trailer Composite (DTC) seated 8 first and 82 second class passengers. Power was provided by two English Electric 250hp (186.4kW) traction motors mounted on the bogie below the brake van. Unlike the Southern Region, the Tyneside sets were fitted with two line destination indicators and four front and one rear marker lights located between the two cab windows. Sets were fitted with end drop-head buck-eye couplings and Pullman rubbing plates, waist height multiple control jumpers and air pipes. The Tyneside EPB stock was painted green throughout its life in the North East. The sets were transferred to the Southern Region to join the 2EPB fleet based on the South Western Division on 10 August 1963. Once on the SR, the sets were refurbished with the first class removed and standard two position route indicator boxes fitted. A pair of two-car sets with a DMBS vehicle nearest the camera is seen at Hebburn.* CJM-C

Pre-TOPS - Tyneside MLV

Below: *Concurrent with the Eastleigh EPB build for Tyneside, the North Eastern operator purchased a new Motor Luggage Van No. E68000, built to EPB profile. The double ended single car was for use on the South Shields line, and had four pairs of double opening doors on each side and a central guards office. The coach was 67ft 1in (20.44m) long over buffers and was fitted with two English Electric 507 traction motors giving a combined output of 500hp (373kW). In addition to its electro-pneumatic air brakes, the vehicle had a vacuum exhauster and was able to haul a training load of around 100 tons. As well as its own electric power, the MLV was fitted with traction batteries which enabled up to 20 minutes operation away from the live rail supply. Prior to delivery to the North East, the MLV operated trials on the Southern Region. In addition to having two open vans for the transport of light goods, the interior was fitted with a number of fold-down seats, enabling the vehicle to be used as a workmen's train if needed. When the EPB stock was transferred away from the Tyneside area on 10 August 1963, the MLV was transferred to the London Midland Region.* CJM-C

Classification:	MLV
Introduced:	1955
Built by:	BR Eastleigh
Formation:	Single car Motor Luggage Van
Vehicle number:	E68000
Vehicle length:	67ft 1in (20.44m)
Height:	12ft 9 ½in (3.90m)
Width:	9ft in (2.77m)
Seating:	None
Internal layout:	Open - 2 luggage compartments
Gangway:	No
Toilets:	No
Weight:	45 tons
Brake type:	Air (EP/Auto), also fitted with vacuum exhauster for hauling vacuum brake fitted van stock
Bogie type:	Mk 3B
Power collection:	660-750V dc third rail and traction battery (around 20min supply)
Traction motor type:	2 x EE507 of 250hp (186.4kW)
Horsepower:	500hp (373kW)
Max speed:	75mph (121km/h)
Coupling type:	Buck-eye
Multiple restriction:	With Tyneside EPB fleet
Door type:	Double leaf slam
Special features:	Authorised to haul vacuum or air brake trailing load of up to 100 tons

Class 302

	As built	Rebuilt condition
Number range:	302201-302312	302201-302312
Former number range:	201-312	-
Alpha code:	AM2	AM2
Introduced:	1958-60	Rebuilt 1981-82
Built by:	BR Doncaster/York	-
Rebuilt by:	-	BR Eastleigh
Formation:	BDTS+MBS+TC+DTS	BDTC+MBS+TS+DTS
Vehicle numbers:	BDTS - 75085-75100, 75190-75210, 75286-75360 MBS - 61060-61132, 61190-61228 TC - 70060-70132, 70190-70228 DTS - 75033-75044, 75060-75084, 75211-75285	BDTC - 75085-75100, 75190-75210, 75286-75360 MBS - 61060-61132, 61190-61228 TS - 70060-70132, 70190-70228 DTS - 75033-75044, 75060-75084, 75211-75285
Set length:	266ft 7in (81.26m)	266ft 7in (81.26m)
Vehicle length:	BDTS, DTS - 63ft 11½in (19.49m) MBS, TC - 63ft 6in (19.35m)	BDTC, DTS - 63ft 11 ½in (19.49m) MBS, TS - 63ft 6in (19.35m)
Height:	13ft 0½in (3.97m)	13ft 0½in (3.97m)
Width:	9ft 3in (2.82m)	9ft 3in 9ft 3in (2.82m)
Seating:	Total - 19F/344S BDTS - 80S MBS - 96S TC - 19F/60S DTS - 108S	Total - 24F/302S BDTC - 24F/52S MBS - 76S TS - 86S DTS - 88S
Internal layout:	First 2+1, Standard 2+3	First 2+2, Standard 2+3
Gangway:	Within set	Within set
Toilets:	Not fitted	Not fitted
Weight:	Total - 155ton 10cwt BDTS - 36 tons MBS - 56ton 10cwt TC -31 tons DTS - 32 tons	Total - 162.6 tonnes BDTC - 39.5 tonnes MBS - 55.3 tonnes TS - 34.4 tonnes DTS - 33.4 tonnes
Brake type:	Air (EP/Auto)	Air (EP/Auto)
Bogie type:	Gresley	Powered - Gresley TS - B4, Others - B5
Power collection:	6.25kV and 25kV ac overhead	25kV ac overhead
Traction motor type:	4 x EE536A	4 x EE536A
Horsepower:	768hp (573kW)	768hp (573kW)
Max speed:	75mph (121km/h)	75mph (121km/h)
Coupling type:	Buck-eye	Buck-eye
Multiple restriction:	Eastern Region EMU series	Eastern Region EMU series
Door type:	Slam	Slam
Special features:	-	-

Left: *Built by Doncaster and York Works, the 112 AM2 (Class 302) EMUs were introduced for use on the London, Tilbury & Southend route between 1958-60. The four-car sets were based on the Mk1 coach design and were high-density sets with an intermediate power car. First class seating was provided originally in a TC intermediate coach; later this was repositioned in one of the driving cars. Painted in as delivered green livery, set No. 205 is illustrated. Originally these sets were able to operate from both 6.25 and 25kV ac overhead.* CJM-C

Parcels
302990-302993
-
AM2
Rebuilt 92
-
BR Ilford
BDTPMV+MPMV+DTPMV
BDTPMV - 68100-68103
MPMV - 68020-68023
DTPMV - 68207-68210

199ft 5in (60.81m)
BDTPMV, DTPMV - 63ft 11½in (19.49m)
MPMV - 63ft 6in (19.35m)
13ft 0½in (3.97m)
9ft 3in 9ft 3in (2.82m)
Total - None
BDTPMV - 0
MPMV - 0
DTPMV - 0
-
Open
Within set
Not fitted
Total - 128.1 tonnes
BDTPMV - 39.1 tonnes
MPMV - 55.1 tonnes
DTPMV - 33.9 tonnes
-
Air (EP/Auto)
BDTPMV, DTPMV - B5
MPMV - GresLEy
25kV ac overhead
4 x EE536A
768hp (573kW)
75mph (121km/h)
Buck-eye
Eastern Region EMU series
Slam
Royal Mail use

Above: *After BR green, sets were painted in BR rail blue and then blue and grey colours. A major refurbishment in 1981-82 saw the sets opened out and the first class repositioned into one of the driving cars. Seating remained in the 2+3 high-density style. During refurbishment, the 6.25kV equipment was removed. Painted in blue and grey livery, set No. 302222 is seen at Fenchurch Street. These sets were based at East Ham depot.* CJM

Above: *In Network SouthEast days the 302s were operated on both the LT&S and Great Eastern routes, remaining in front line operation until 1999. Painted in NSE colours, devoid of its original headcode display and sporting a headlight, set No. 302221 is seen at Ilford from its Battery Driving Trailer Composite vehicle. The set's buck-eye coupling is in the lowered position.* CJM

Right: *In 1992 a need arouse for the conveyance of Royal Mail letter and parcel traffic on the Great Eastern route and four Class 302s were rebuilt into Royal Mail sets. This saw the removal of the TS vehicle, reducing the sets to three carriages and fitting roller shutter doors, two on each side of the driving cars and one on each side of the power car. The rebuild work was carried out at Ilford, the sets were renumbered in the 302/9 sub class and were painted in Royal Mail red. Set No. 302991 is illustrated. Note that the saloon passenger windows were retained.* CJM-C

Class 303 & 311

	As built		Rebuilt
Number range:	303001-303091	311092-311110	303001-303091
Former number range:	001-091	092-110	001-091
Alpha code:	AM3	AM11	AM3
Introduced:	1959-61	1967	1959-61
Built:	Pressed Steel	Cravens	Pressed Steel
Formation:	DTS+MBS+BDTS	DTS+MBS+BDTS	DTSO+MBSO+BDTSO
Vehicle numbers:	DTS - 75566-75600, 75746-75801 MBS - 61481-61515 61812-61867 BDTS - 75601-75635 75802-75857	DTS - 76130-76148, altered to 76403-76421 MBS - 76403-76421 BDTS - 76149-76167	DTSO - 75566-75600, 75746-75801 MBSO - 61481-61515 61812-61867 BDTS0 - 75601-75635 75802-75857
Set length:	199ft 6in (60.81m)	199ft 6in (60.81m)	199ft 6in (60.81m)
Vehicle length:	DTS , BDTS - 63ft 11½in (19.50m) MBS - 63ft 2¼in (19.36m)	DTS , BDTS - 63ft 11½in (19.50m) MBS - 63ft 2¼in (19.36m)	DTSO , BDTSO - 63ft 11½in (19.50m) MBSO - 63ft 2¼in (19.36m)
Height:	12ft 8in (3.86m)	12ft 8in (3.86m)	12ft 8in (3.86m)
Width:	9ft 3in (2.82m)	9ft 3in (2.82m)	9ft 3in (2.82m)
Seating:	Total - 236S DTS - 83S, MBS - 70S BDTS - 83S	Total - 236S DTS - 83S, MBS - 70S BDTS - 83S	Total - 160S DTSO - 56S, MBSO - 48S BDTSO - 56S
Internal layout:	2+3 high density	2+3 high density	2+2 low density
Gangway:	No	No	Within unit
Toilets:	Not fittted	Not fittted	Not fitted
Weight:	Total - 128 tons DTS - 34 tons MBS - 56 tons BDTS - 38 tons	Total - 129 tons DTS - 34 tons MBS - 57 tons BDTS - 38 tons	Total - 125.2 tonnes DTS0 - 34.4 tonnes MBSO - 56.4 tonnes BDTSO - 34.4 tonnes
Brake type:	Air (Auto/EP)	Air (Auto/EP)	Air (Auto/EP)
Bogie type:	Gresley	Gresley	Gresley
Power collection:	25kV ac overhead	25kV ac overhead	25kV ac overhead
Traction motor type:	4 x Metro Vic	4 x Metro Vic	4 x Metro Vic
Gear ratio:	70:17	70:17	70:17
Horsepower:	828hp (618kW)	828hp (618kW)	828hp (618kW)
Max speed:	75mph (121km/h)	75mph (121km/h)	75mph (121km/h)
Coupling type:	Buck-eye	Buck-eye	Buck-eye
Multiple restriction:	Within Class and Class 311	Within Class and Class 303	Within Class and Class 311
Door type:	Bi-parting sliding	Bi-parting sliding	Bi-parting sliding
Special features:	-	-	-

Left: *Known as the Glasgow Blue Trains, the AM3 and AM11 fleets built by Pressed Steel and Cravens were the mainstay of Glasgow electrification for many years being introduced between 1959-67. The original fleet consisted of 91 three-car sets with a middle power car and two driving trailers at each end. Fitted with crew-controlled sliding doors, these sets accommodated 236 second class passengers in the 2+3 style. The original 91 sets were used on the North Clyde and Cathcart Circle lines. Painted in Strathclyde PTE orange and with a headlight in place of a headcode panel, set No. 303077 is seen at Glasgow Central on 22 March 1994.* CJM

Right: *Following introduction of new stock in the Glasgow area and a decline in passenger numbers, several Class 303s were transferred to the North West in the 1980s, operating at first in the Liverpool area and later in Manchester especially on the Manchester to Hadfield/Glossop route. Retaining a headcode panel displaying two white dots, set No. 303053 in seen in Greater Manchester orange and brown livery at Ilford on 19 May 1989.* CJM

Below: *Following privatisation the remaining 303s were taken over by ScotRail and four sets were repainted in SPT's carmine and cream livery, as shown on set No. 303023 arriving at Glasgow Central.* CJM

Right: *In 1992 Class 303 No. 303049 was selected to take part in the Intelligent Train Project and renumbered to 303999, which was jointly funded by NSE, BR Research, CrossRail and the private sector. The train was fitted with 'databus' technology passing information about all train systems to a central 'brain'. As part of the project the between vehicle couplings were replaced with modified Tightlocks with electrical connections. The set was outbased at Clacton and operated both day and night test runs evaluating equipment in 1993. Other tests included high-quality station to train television images in conjunction with driver only operation. The set is seen at Clacton on 2 December 1992.* CJM

Class 304

	As built		
Sub class:	304/1	304/2	304/3
Number range:	001-015	016-035	036-045
Former number range:	-	-	-
Alpha code:	AM4	AM4	AM4
Introduced:	1960	1960	1961
Built by:	BR Wolverton	BR Wolverton	BR Wolverton
Formation:	BDTS+MBS+TC+DTBS	BDTS+MBS+TC+DTBS	BDTS+MBS+TC+DTBS
Vehicle numbers:	BDTS - 75045-75059 MBS - 61045-61059 TC - 70045-70059 DTBS - 75645-75659	BDTS - 75680-75699 MBSO - 61628-61647 TC - 70483-70502 DTBS - 75660-75679	BDTS - 75868-75877 75699, 75868-75877 MBSO - 61873-61882 61647, 61873-61882 TC - 70243-70252 75679, 75858-75867 DTBS - 75858-75867
Set length:	246ft 6½in (75.15m)	246ft 6½in (75.15m)	246ft 6½in (75.15m)
Vehicle length:	BDTS, DTBS - 64ft 0½in (19.52m) MBS, TC - 63ft 6½in (19.37m)	BDTS, DTBS - 64ft 0½in (19.52m) MBSO, TC - 63ft 6½in (19.37m)	BDTS, DTBS - 64ft 0½in (19.52m) MBSO, TC - 63ft 6½in (19.37m)
Height:	12ft 4½in (3.77m)	12ft 4½in (3.77m)	12ft 4½in (3.77m)
Width:	9ft 3in (2.82m)	9ft 3in (2.82m)	9ft 3in (2.82m)
Seating:	19F/318S BDTS - 80S MBS - 96S TC - 19F/60S DTBS - 82S	19F/294S BDTS - 80S MBS - 72S TC - 19F/60S DTBS - 82S	19F/294S BDTS - 80S MBS - 72S TC - 19F/60S DTBS - 82S
Internal layout:	First - compartments Standard - 2+3	First - compartments Standard - 2+3	First - compartments Standard - 2+3
Gangway:	Within set	Within set	Within set
Toilets:	BDTS - 1, TC - 2	BDTS - 1, TC - 2	BDTS - 1, TC - 2
Weight:	Total - 151ton 17cwt BDTS - 35ton 12cwt MBS - 53ton 12cwt TC - 31ton 5 cwt DTBS - 31ton 8 cwt	Total - 151ton 17cwt BDTS - 35ton 12cwt MBS - 53ton 12cwt TC - 31ton 5 cwt DTBS - 31ton 8 cwt	Total - 151ton 17cwt BDTS - 35ton 12cwt MBS - 53ton 12cwt TC - 31ton 5 cwt DTBS - 31ton 8 cwt
Brake type:	Air (EP/Auto)	Air (EP/Auto)	Air (EP/Auto)
Bogie type:	Gresley	Gresley	Gresley
Power collection:	6.25kV ac and 25kV ac overhead	6.25kV ac and 25kV ac overhead	6.25kV ac and 25kV ac overhead
Traction motor type:	4 x BTH	4 x BTH	4 x BTH
Horsepower:	828hp (617.4kW)	828hp (617.4kW)	828hp (617.4kW)
Max speed:	75mph (121km/h)	75mph (121km/h)	75mph (121km/h)
Coupling type:	Buck-eye	Buck-eye	Buck-eye
Multiple restriction:	Within type and Class 310	Within type and Class 310	Within type and Class 310
Door type:	Slam	Slam	Slam
Special features:			

Some sets also operated for a short period in 1985 as 4-car units with the TC vehicle declassified to TS

Right: *Originally built for use on the first phases of the West Coast electrification between Crewe and Manchester, Liverpool and Rugby, these BR-designed four-car sets were built at Wolverton to the standard ac EMU body style. The first 15 sets went new to Manchester Longsight from April 1957. A further 20 sets emerged in 1959, Nos. 016-035 for the Crewe-Liverpool service, and had slightly different body design. A third and final batch, Nos. 036-045, followed in 1961 for the Crewe-Rugby section. These were high-density sets with doors by each seating bay with second class seats in the 2+3 style, while first class seating was in compartments. Under the TOPS numeric classification*

Rebuilt/modified
304
304001-304045
001-045
AM4
Modified 1985
BR Wolverton
BDTS+MBS+DTBS
BDTS - 75045-75059, 75680

MBS - 61045-61059, 61628

DTBS - 75645-75659, 75660

-
184ft 8in (56.29m)
BDTS, DTBS - 64ft 0½in (19.52m)
MBS, - 63ft 6½in (19.37m)

12ft 4½in (3.77m)
9ft 3in (2.82m)
304001-304015 - 244S
304016-304045 - 234S
BDTS - 80S
MBS - 82S (304001-015), **
MBS - 72S (304016-045)
DTBS - 82S
-
Standard - 2+3

Within set
BDTS -1
Total - 123.5 tonnes
BDTS - 37 tonnes
MBS - 54.5 tonnes
DTBS - 32 tonnes
-
Air (EP/Auto)
Gresley
25kV ac overhead

4 x BTH
828hp (617.4kW)
75mph (121km/h)
Buck-eye
Within type and Class 310
Slam
** One compartment in MBS locked out of use

Above: *Displaying as built green livery with yellow body lining (the only EMUs so treated), the Battery Driving Trailer Second No. M75691 from set No. 027 is shown from its non-driving side, clearly displaying the door by each seating bay and the mid vehicle length toilet accessible from both seating bays. These sets were buck-eye fitted with all connections, pneumatic and jumpers body mounted.* CJM-C

Above: *After the era of BR green livery, all over rail blue with full yellow warning ends was applied from the late 1960s. With its headcode box out of use and seen from its BDTS end, set No. 304011, one of the original batch delivered, is seen departing from Stockport in summer 1980. The Class 304s were gradually displaced from West Coast work with some going to the NSE area. Other sets remained in operation in the Crewe/Manchester area until 1996, gaining Regional Railways livery.* CJM

these sets became Class 304. Painted in 1980s blue and grey livery, set No. 304015 is seen from its BDTS vehicle at Manchester Piccadilly. By this time the headcode box displayed just white dots. CJM

Class 305

	As built	As built	Modified
Sub class:	305/1	305/2	305/1
Number range:	401-452	501-519	401-452
Former number range:	-	-	-
Alpha code:	AM5	AM5	AM5
Introduced:	1960	1960	1960
Built by:	BR York	BR Doncaster	BR York
Formation:	BDTS+MBS+DTS	BDTS+MBS+TC+DTS	BDTC+MBS+DTS
Vehicle numbers:	BDTS - 75462-75513 MBS - 61429-61480 DTS - 75514-75565	BDTS - 75424-75442 MBS - 61410-61428 TC - 70356-70374 DTS - 75443-75461	BDTS - 75462-75513 MBS - 61429-61480 DTS - 75514-75565
Set length:	200ft 1in (60.98m)	266ft 8½in (81.29m)	200ft 1in (60.98m)
Vehicle length:	BDTS, DTS - 63ft 11½in (19.49m) MBS - 63ft 6in (19.66m)	BDTS, DTS - 63ft 11½in (19.49m) MBS, TC - 63ft 6in (19.66m)	BDTC, DTS - 63ft 11½in (19.49m) MBS - 63ft 6in (19.66m)
Height:	12ft 6½in (3.82m)	12ft 6½in (3.82m)	12ft 6½in (3.82m)
Width:	9ft 3in (2.82m)	9ft 3in (2.82m)	9ft 3in (2.82m)
Seating:	Total - 272S BDTS - 94S MBS - 84S DTS - 94S	Total - 19F/344S BDTS - 80S MBS - 96S TC - 19F/60S DTS - 108S	Total - 20 or 24F/180 or 204S BDTC - 24F/52S or 20F/40S MBS - 58 or 76S DTS - 70 or 88S
Internal layout:	Standard - 2+3	Standard - 2+3	Standard - 2+3 First - 2+2
Gangway:	No	No	Within set
Toilets:	Not fitted	DTS, TC - 1	Not fitted
Weight:	Total - 118 tons BDTS - 32 tons MBS - 54 tons DTS - 32 tons	Total - 149 tons BDTS - 32 tons MBS - 54 tons TC - 31 tons DTS - 32 tons	Total - 125.7 tonnes BDTC - 36.5 tonnes MBS - 56.5 tonnes DTS - 32.7 tonnes
Brake type:	Air (Auto/EP)	Air (Auto/EP)	Air (Auto/EP)
Bogie type:	Gresley	Gresley	Gresley
Power collection:	6.25kV ac and 25kV ac overhead	6.25kV ac and 25kV ac overhead	25kV ac overhead
Traction motor type:	4 x GEC WT380	4 x GEC WT380	4 x GEC WT380
Horsepower:	800hp (596.5kW)	800hp (596.5kW)	800hp (596.5kW)
Max speed:	75mph (121km/h)	75mph (121km/h)	75mph (121km/h)
Coupling type:	Buck-eye	Buck-eye	Buck-eye
Multiple restriction:	Within ER EMUs	Within ER EMUs	Within class only
Door type:	Slam	Slam	Slam
Special features:	-	-	-

Left: *Structurally using the standard ac EMU profile, 52 inner suburban and 19 outer suburban Lea Valley sets were introduced in 1960. These three and four-car sets formed the backbone of electrified services for many years through to the Network Southeast period. Set No. 508, one of the four-car sets, is seen at Bethnal Green painted in green livery with a yellow central vertical band on the front. These four-car sets seated 19 first and 344 second class passengers.* CJM-C

Modified
305/2
501-519
-
AM5
1960
BR Doncaster
BDTS+MBS+TS+DTS
BDTS - 75424-75442
MBS - 61410-61428
TS - 70356-70374
DTS - 75443-75461
266ft 8½in (81.29m)
BDTS, DTS - 63ft 11½in (19.49m)
MBS, TS - 63ft 6in (19.66m)

12ft 6½in (3.82m)
9ft 3in (2.82m)
Total - 32S
BDTS - 76S

MBS - 76S
TS - 86S
DTS - 88S
Standard - 2+3

Within set
DTS, TC - 1
Total - 157.2 tonnes
BDTC - 36.5 tonnes
MBS - 56.5 tonnes
TS - 31.5 tonnes
DTS - 32.7 tonnes
Air (Auto/EP)
Gresley
25kV ac overhead

4 x GEC WT380
800hp (596.5kW)
75mph (121km/h)
Buck-eye
Within class only
Slam
-

Above: *With Hertford East on its blind and painted in 1970s rail blue, three-car set No. 414 approaches Bethnal Green in 1979. The 52 three-car sets were all standard class and in the high-density style provided accommodation for 272 passengers. They were buck-eye/Pullman rubbing plate fitted and had all connections mounted on the body, not requiring shunting staff to go onto the track to do attachment/ detachment duties. The nose end equipment consisted on a brake and main reservoir pipe and a multiple working jumper cable. The intermediate Motor Standard has its pantograph at the far end.* CJM

Above: *With new replacement stock still awaited, a number of Class 305s remained in operation well into Network SouthEast days, receiving basic refurbishment over the years. Reduced to a three-car set by removal of the TC coach, set No. 305523 displays NSE livery at Ilford depot on 30 March 1992 and also shows the fitting of front marker lights and a sealed beam headlight.* CJM-C

Right: *Due to late and protracted deliveries of Class 323 stock a number of Class 305s were overhauled and repainted into Regional Railways livery operating in the Manchester area in 1992. After this work was over, the sets went north to Scotland, based at Glasgow Shields for Edinburgh-North Berwick duties. On 7 January 1992, ex works Regional Railways set No. 305507 poses in the carriage sidings at Stockport.* CJM

Class 306

	As built	Rebuilt
Number range:	001-092	306001-306092
Former number range:	01-92	001-092
Alpha code:	AM6	AM6
Introduced:	1949	Rebuilt 1960-61
Built by:	DMBTO/TTO - Metro-Cammell DTTO - Birmingham RCW	Rebuilt by - Stratford
Formation:	DMBTO+TTO+DTTO	DMSO+TBSO+DTSO
Vehicle numbers:	MBTO - 65201-65292 TTO - 64501-64592 DTTO - 65601-65692	DMSO - 65201-65292 TBSO - 64501-64592 DTSO - 65601-65692
Set length:	177ft 7in (54.13m)	177ft 7in (54.13m)
Vehicle length:	DMBTO - 60ft 4½in (18.4m) TTO - 55ft 0½in (16.77m) DTTO - 55ft 4in (16.86m)	DMSO - 60ft 4½in (18.4m) TBSO - 55ft 0½in (16.77m) DTSO - 55ft 4in (16.86m)
Height:	13ft 1in (3.98m)	13ft 1in (3.98m)
Width:	9ft 3in (2.81m)	9ft 3in (2.81m)
Seating:	Total - 176S DMBTO - 48T TTO - 68T DTTO - 60T	Total - 168S DMSO - 62S PTSB - 46S DTSO - 60S
Internal layout:	2+3	2+3
Gangway:	No	No
Toilets:	Not fitted	Not fitted
Weight:	Total - 105tons 9cwt DMBTO - 51tons 8cwt TTO - 26tons 11cwt DTTO - 27ton 10cwt	Total - 105tons 19 cwt DMSO - 51tons 19 cwt PTSB - 26tons 10 cwt DTSO - 27tons 10 cwt
Brake type:	Air (EP/Auto)	Air (EP/Auto)
Bogie type:	Thompson	Thompson
Power collection:	1,500V dc overhead	25kV ac overhead
Traction motor type:	4 x EE504	4 x EE504
Horsepower:	840hp (468kW)	840hp (468kW)
Max speed:	75mph (121km/h)	75mph (121km/h)
Coupling type:	Screw	Screw
Multiple restriction:	Within class	Within class
Door type:	Bi-parting sliding	Bi-parting sliding
Special features:		

Right: *The British Transport Commission introduced a fleet of 92 three-car trains for the Liverpool Street to Shenfield line in 1949, operating at 1,500V dc. The high-density sets with power operated sliding doors originally had their pantograph and guards brake van in the driving car. In 1960 when the sets were rebuilt for ac operation the pantograph and guards van were moved to the intermediate vehicle. In ex works as delivered condition set No. '46 is seen at Ilford in 1950. These sets were built with the steam era marker light route indicator system, changing in 1960 to a two character route display.* CJM-C

Below: *Viewed from its Driving Trailer Second Open end, set No. 043 is illustrated at Southend Victoria, alongside a Class 307 unit. The Class 306 is painted in 1970s rail blue with full yellow warning ends. The DTSO vehicles seated 60 third (later second) class passengers in the 2+3 style. These sets were fitted with straps for standing passengers to hold. The sets were non gangwayed and had a top speed of 75mph (121km/h).* Les Bertram

Right: *A broadside view of the original dc layout of DMBTO vehicle No. E65202, clearly showing the cab, guards and passenger doors and the pantograph position.* K. L. Cook

Below: *Approaching Bethnal Green on 3 November 1980, set No. 023 plus two others form the 09.03 Liverpool Street to Gidea Park all stations service. The power car is leading, which is coupled to the pantograph end of the PTSB.* CJM

Class 307

	Original dc design	dc-ac rebuild	Refurbishment
Number range:	01s-32s	101-132	307101-307132
Former number range:	-	01s-32s	101-132
Alpha code:	AM7	AM7	AM7
Introduced:	1956	1960-62	1983-84
Built/rebuilt by:	BR Eastleigh	BR Eastleigh	BR Eastleigh
Formation:	DTSO+MBS+TC+DTS	DTBS+MS+TC+DTS	DTBS+MS+TS+DTC
Vehicle numbers:	DTSO - 75001-75032 MBS - 61001-61032 TC - 70001-70032 DTS - 75101-75132	DTBS - 75001-75032 MS - 61001-61032 TC - 70001-70032 DTS - 75101-75132	DTBS - 75001-75032 MS - 61001-61032 TS - 70001-70032 DTC - 75101-75132
Set length:	265ft 8½in (80.99m)	265ft 8½in (80.99m)	265ft 8½in (80.99m)
Vehicle length:	DTSO, DTS - 63ft 11½n (19.5m) MBS, TC - 63ft 6in (19.35m)	DTBS, DTS - 63ft 11½n (19.5m) MS, TC - 63ft 6in (19.35m)	DTBS, DTS - 63ft 11½n (19.5m) MS, TS - 63ft 6in (19.35m)
Height:	13ft 0½in (3.97m)	13ft 0½in (3.97m)	13ft 0½in (3.97m)
Width:	9ft 3in (3.97m)	9ft 3in (3.97m)	9ft 3in (3.97m)
Seating:	Total - 19F/344S DTSO - 80S MBS - 96S TC - 19F/60 DTS - 108S	Total - 19F/344S DTBS - 84S MS - 120S TC - 19F/60S DTS - 80S	Total - 24F/302S DTBS - 66S MS - 98S TS - 86S DTC - 24F/52S
Internal layout:	Standard - 3+2, Compartments First - Compartments	Standard - 3+2, Compartments First - Compartments	Standard - 3+2 First 2+2
Gangway:	No	No	Within set
Toilets:	DTS - 2, TC - 2	DTS - 2, TC - 2	DTC - 2, TS - 2
Weight:	Total - 154tons 2cwt DTSO - 43tons 9cwt MBS - 50ton 13cwt TC - 30 tons DTS - 30 tons	Total - 153tons 14cwt DTBS - 43ton 12cwt MS - 49 ton 13cwt TC - 30 tons DTS - 30 ton 9cwt	Total - 154.5 tonnes DTBS - 43 tonnes MS - 47.5 tonnes TS - 31 tonnes DTC - 33 tonnes
Brake type:	Air (Auto/EP)	Air (Auto/EP)	Air (Auto/EP)
Bogie type:	ET, ED, Gresley	ET, ED, Gresley	ET, ED, Gresley
Power collection:	1,500 V dc overhead	6.25kV and 25kV ac overhead	25kV ac overhead
Traction motor type:	4 x EE	4 x EE	4 x EE
Horsepower:	696hp (519kW)	696hp (519kW)	696hp (519kW)
Max speed:	75mph (121km/h)	75mph (121km/h)	75mph (121km/h)
Coupling type:	Buck-eye	Buck-eye	Buck-eye
Multiple restriction:	Within ER fleet	Within ER fleet	Within ER fleet
Door type:	Slam	Slam	Slam

Notes: DTC vehicles rebuilt as PCVs for Rail Express Systems - as hauled stock

Left: *Showing its as delivered condition with lamp route indicator and dc power jumpers, set No. 04s passes Gidea Park on 6 June 1958 forming a Liverpool Street bound service. In original condition these sets seated 19 first and 344 third class passengers. In common with the electric multiple unit policy of the day, these Eastleigh products were fitted with drop-head buck-eye couplers with a Pullman rubbing plate above and retractable saddle side buffers.*
K. L. Cook

Right: *In 1956 a fleet 32 four-car EMUs were built at Eastleigh Works for the Great Eastern main line, working between Liverpool Street and Southend Victoria. The sets operated from the then 1,500V dc overhead system and originally had their pantograph and guards brake van in one of the intermediate vehicles. When the Great Eastern route was upgraded to 25kV ac operation the sets were rebuilt, moving the power collection and brake compartment into one of the driving cars. When built the sets were finished in BR green and the front ends sported a light route indication system and nose mounted power jumpers. Upon conversion to ac, standard four character headcode boxes were fitted and standard air and multiple unit control jumpers were installed. Seating was a mix of 3+2 and compartment with first class seating originally and after the 1960 rebuild placed in an intermediate vehicle. In 1983-84 sets were fully refurbished with a revised open seating plan; this saw the first class accommodation move to a driving car. Painted in 1970s BR rail blue, set No. 115 is seen at Liverpool Street on 3 November 1980.* CJM

Right Middle: *In 1990, after being made redundant in the London area, a significant number of Class 307s were transferred to Neville Hill for Leeds area electrification prior to delivery of new rolling stock. Most sets retained blue/grey or NSE colours but five sets emerged repainted in West Yorkshire PTE red and cream. Showing this livery, set No. 307120 stands beside set No. 307119 at Leeds City on 27 July 1990.* CJM

Right Bottom: *The Class 307 vehicles seemed to be always being rebuilt and in 1994-96 43 driving cars were rebuilt by Hunslet-Barclay of Kilmarnock into Propelling Control Vehicles (PCVs) to operate at the remote end of diesel or electric powered Royal Mail trains. In the PCV cab a 'power demand' switch was installed which when operated would indicate to the driver of the propelling locomotive the power requirement. The driver in the PCV had control of the brake. The PCVs were used mainly in the London area to get trains in and out of the Princess Royal Distribution Centre at Wembley. PCV No. 94315 is illustrated during test running, rebuilt from car No. 75132.* CJM

Class 308

	As built		
Class:	308/1	308/2	308/3
Number range:	133-165	313-321	453-455
Former number range:	-	-	-
Alpha code:	AM8	AM8	AM8
Introduced:	1961-62	1961	1961
Rebuilt:	-	-	-
Built by:	BR York	BR York	BR York
Refurbished by:	-	-	-
Formation:	BDTS+MBS+TC+DTS	BDTS+MLV+TC+DTS	BDTS+MBS+DTS
Vehicle numbers:	BDTS - 75878-75886, 75896-75919 MBS - 61883-61915 TC - 70611-70643 DTS - 75887-75895, 75929-75952	BDTS - 75920-75928 MLV - 68011-68019 TC - 70644-70652 DTS - 75953-75961	BDTS - 75741-75743 MBS - 61689-61691 DTS - 75992-75994
Set length:	268ft 8½in (81.90m)	268ft 8½in (81.90m)	189ft 9½in (56.93m)
Vehicle length:	BDTS, DTS - 64ft 0½in (19.52m) MBS, TC - 63ft 6in (19.35m)	BDTS, DTS - 64ft 0½in (19.52m) MLV, TC - 63ft 6in (19.35m)	BDTS, DTS - 64ft 0½in (19.52m) MBS - 63ft 6in (19.35m)
Height:	13ft 0½in (3.97m)	13ft 0½in (3.97m)	13ft 0½in (3.97m)
Width:	9ft 3in (2.81m)	9ft 3in (2.81m)	9ft 3in (2.81m)
Seating:	Total - 19F/344S BDTS - 80S MBS - 96S TC - 19F/60S, DTS - 108S	Total - 19F/248S BDTS - 80S MLV - 0 TC - 19F/60S, DTS - 108S	Total - 272S BDTS - 94S MBS - 84S DTS - 94S
Internal layout:	3+2	3+2	3+2
Gangway:	Within set	Within set	Within set
Toilets:	TC, BDTS - 2	TC, BDTS - 2	Not fitted
Weight:	Total - 153 tons BDTS - 36 tons MBS - 54 tons TC - 31 tons DTS - 32 tons	Total - 150tons 12cwt BDTS - 36 tons MBS - 51tons 12cwt TC - 31 tons DTS - 32 tons	Total: 121.4 tonnes BDTS - 35 tonnes MBS - 54.9 tonnes DTS - 31.5 tonnes
Brake type:	Air (Auto/EP)	Air (Auto/EP)	Air (Auto/EP)
Bogie type:	Gresley	Gresley	Gresley
Power collection:	6.25kV and 25kV ac overhead	6.25kV and 25kV ac overhead	6.25kV and 25kV ac
Traction motor type:	EE	EE	EE
Horsepower:	800hp (596kW)	800hp (596kW)	800hp (596kW)
Max speed:	75mph (121km/h)	75mph (121km/h)	75mph (121km/h)
Coupling type:	Buck-eye	Buck-eye	Buck-eye
Multiple restriction:	Within ER EMU stock	Within ER EMU stock	Within ER EMU stock
Door type:	Slam	Slam	Slam

Left: *The nine AM8 four-car sets numbered 313-321 each contained a Motor Luggage Van. These were arranged with a standard guards office and van at the pantograph end, with a large luggage compartment fed by two pairs of hinged doors on either side taking up the rest of the vehicle. The sets were deployed on the London, Tilbury & Southend route and were introduced in 1961, a product of Eastleigh Works. Car No. E68011 is shown, which was later rebuilt as MBS No. E62431.* CJM-C

Refurbished			
308/1	308/2	308/3	WYPTE
308133-308165	308993-308995	308453-308455	308133-308165
133-165	314/19/20	453-455	133-165
AM8	AM8	AM8	AM8
-	-	1961	
1981-1983	1983	1981	1994
BR York	BR York	BR York	BR York
BREL Wolverton	BR Ilford	BREL Wolverton	BREL Doncaster
BDTC+MBS+TS+DTS	BDTS+MLV+DTLV	BDTS+MBS+DTS	BDTC+MBS+DTS
BDTC - 75878-75886, 75896-75919 MBS - 61883-61915 TS - 70611-70643 DTS - 75887-75895, 75929-75952	BDTS - 75926-75928 MLV - 68012-68018 DTLV - 75959-75961	BDTS - 75741-75743 MBS - 61689-61691 DTS - 75992-75994	BDTC - 75878-75886, 75896-75919 MBS - 61883-61915 DTS - 75887-75895, 75929-75952
268ft 8½in (81.90m)	189ft 9½in (56.93m)	189ft 9½in (56.93m)	189ft 9½in (56.93m)
BDTC, DTS - 64ft 0½in (19.52m) MBS, TS - 63ft 6in (19.35m)	BDTS, DTLV - 64ft 0½in (19.52m) MLV - 63ft 6in (19.35m)	BDTS, DTS - 64ft 0½in (19.52m) MBS - 63ft 6in (19.35m)	BDTC, DTS - 64ft 0½in (19.52m) MBS - 63ft 6in (19.35m)
13ft 0½in (3.97m)	13ft 0½in (3.97m)	13ft 0½in (3.97m)	13ft 0½in (3.97m)
9ft 3in (2.81m)	9ft 3in (2.81m)	9ft 3in (2.81m)	9ft 3in (2.81m)
Total - 24F/302S BDTC - 24F/52S MBS - 76S TS - 86S, DTS - 88S	Total - 0 BDTS - 0 MLV - 0 DTLV - 0	Total - 272S BDTS - 94S MBS - 84S DTS - 94S	Total - 24F/214 or 216S BDTC - 24F/50 or 52S MBS - 76S DTS - 88S
3+2	3+2	3+2	3+2
Within set	Within set	Within set	Within set
TC, BDTS - 2	Not fitted	TC, BDTS - 2	BDTS - 2
Total - 153 tonnes BDTC - 36 tonnes MBS - 54 tonnes TS - 31 tonnes DTS - 32 tonnes	Total: 120.5 tonnes BDTS - 36.5 tonnes MLV - 52 tonnes DTLV - 32 tonnes	Total: 119 tons BDTS - 35 tonnes MBS - 54.9 tonnes DTS - 31.5 tonnes	Total - 124.3 tonnes BDTC - 36.3 tonnes MBS - 55 tonnes DTS - 33 tonnes
Air (Auto/EP)	Air (Auto/EP)	Air (Auto/EP)	Air (Auto/EP)
Gresley	Gresley	Gresley	Gresley
25kV ac overhead	25kV ac overhead	6.25kV and 25kV ac overhead	25kV ac overhead
EE	EE	EE	EE
800hp (596kW)	800hp (596kW)	800hp (596kW)	800hp (596kW)
75mph (121km/h)	75mph (121km/h)	75mph (121km/h)	75mph (121km/h)
Buck-eye	Buck-eye	Buck-eye	Buck-eye
Within ER EMU stock	Within ER EMU stock	Within ER EMU stock	Within Class
Slam	Slam	Slam	Slam

Right: *A reduction in the amount of parcels and Royal Mail traffic saw four of the MLVs rebuilt as passenger vehicles at Wolverton Works. The rebuilding work saw some slightly unusual body styling especially at the non brake van end as some of the original electrical equipment was retained. This resulted in 6½ bays of second class seating served by a door in alternate bays. MBS No. E62432 is illustrated from its brake end; this was previously MLV No. E68014.* CJM-C

Class 308

Above: *Built to the standard EMU design, three batches of AM8s, later Class 308, were built at York Works in 1961-62. Built for 25kV ac operation, the first 33 four-car sets were destined for the Great Eastern routes from Liverpool Street to Shenfield, Colchester, Walton and Clacton. The sets seated 19 first and 344 second class passengers in the high-density style. On delivery all sets were painted green. The second batch to emerge was nine sets for the LT&S line; these were four-car sets but included a Motor Luggage Van. The third batch consisted of three three-car sets for Liverpool Street-Chingford/ Enfield services. The sets remained on their intended routes until displaced by modern stock; this allowed 21 sets to be transferred to Leeds for use on the Leeds to Skipton newly electrified route. Between 1981-83 all sets were internally refurbished with a number of seating changes. Set No. 317 with an MLV is seen when new .* CJM-C

Left Middle: *By the mid 1960s small yellow warning ends were applied and after 1967 full yellow ends were made standard. Four-car set No. 144 is seen near Colchester in August 1964 with its BDTS leading.* J. C. Beckett

Left Bottom: *Following 1980s refurbishment with marker lights on the front end, blue and grey liveried set No. 308156 approaches Dagenham Dock on 19 September 1984.* CJM

Above: *During the 1980s refurbishment project, undertaken at Wolverton Works, the first class seating was moved from the intermediate Trailer Composite vehicle to the driving coach attached to the power/pantograph vehicle. All vehicles were opened out and the interior was very pleasing, while still retaining the high-density 2+3 layout. Set No. 308153 is seen from its DTS vehicle at Tilbury Riverside.* Michael J. Collins

Below: *A total of 21 Class 308s were overhauled at BREL Doncaster in 1994 for use on the Leeds-Skipton and Leeds-Doncaster local services, prior to new stock being introduced. The three-car sets were finished in West Yorkshire PTE red and cream as shown on set No. 308152 at Doncaster on 5 April 1995.* CJM

Class 309

As built			
Class:	309/1	309/2	309/3
Number range:	601-608	611-618	621-627
Former number range:	-	-	-
Alpha code:	AM9	AM9	AM9
Introduced:	1962	1962	1962
Built by:	BR York	BR York	BR York
Formation:	DMBSK+BDTS	BDTC+MBSK+TRB+DTC	BDTC+MBSK+TSO+DTC
Vehicle numbers:	DMBSK - 61940-61947 BDTS - 75984-75991	BDTC - 75637-75644 MBSK - 61932-61939 TRB - 69100-69107 DTC - 75976-75983	BDTC - 75962-75968 MBSK - 61925-61931 TSO - 70253-70259 DTC - 75969-75975
Set length:	132ft 9¼in (40.48m)	265ft 8½in (80.99m)	265ft 8½in (80.99m)
Vehicle length:	64ft 6in (19.66m)	64ft 6in (19.66m)	64ft 6in (19.66m)
Height:	13ft 0½in (3.97m)	13ft 0½in (3.97m)	13ft 0½in (3.97m)
Width:	9ft 3in (2.82m)	9ft 3in (2.82m)	9ft 3in (2.82m)
Seating:	Total - 108S DMBSK - 48S BDTS - 60S	Total - 36F/112S/32U BDTC - 18F/32S MBSK - 48S TRB - 32U DTC - 18F/32S	Total - 36F/176S BDTC - 18F/32S MBSK - 48S TSO - 64S DTC - 18F/32S
Internal layout:	Standard - 2+2, Compartment	Standard - 2+2, Compartment First - 2+1	Standard - 2+2, Compartment, First - 2+1
Gangway:	Throughout	Throughout	Throughout
Toilets:	BDTS - 1	BDTC, DTC - 1	BDTC, DTC - 1
Weight:	Total - 99 tons DMBSK - 59 tons BDTS - 40 tons	Total - 168 tons BDTC - 39 tons MBSK - 57 tons TRB - 36 tons DTC - 36 tons	Total - 167 tons BDTC - 39 tons MBSK - 57 tons TSO - 34 tons DTC - 37 tons
Brake type:	Air (EP/Auto)	Air (EP/Auto)	Air (EP/Auto)
Bogie type:	Commonwealth	Commonwealth	Commonwealth
Power collection:	6.25kV ac and 25kV ac overhead	6.25kV ac and 25kV ac overhead	6.25kV ac and 25kV ac overhead
Traction motor type:	4 x EE	4 x EE	4 x EE
Horsepower:	1,128hp (841kW)	1,128hp (841kW)	1,128hp (841kW)
Max speed:	100mph (161km/h)	100mph (161km/h)	100mph (161km/h)
Coupling type:	Buck-eye	Buck-eye	Buck-eye
Multiple restriction:	Within class	Within class	Within class
Door type:	Slam	Slam	Slam
Special features:	-	-	-

Left: *The 1962-introduced Great Eastern main line electric units, finished in a stunning lined maroon livery, brought new dimensions of luxury travel to the Liverpool Street-Clacton/Walton route, and were based on Mk1 coach designs. A mix of two- and four-car sets were built, the four-car formations included a Motor Brake Standard Corridor, housing the pantograph, traction equipment and guards brake van together with six compartments seating 48. Car GE61931 is illustrated from set No. 627.* CJM-C

Modified formations

Class:	309/1	309/3
Number range:	309601-309608	309611-309627
Former number range:	601-608	611-627
Alpha code:	AM9	AM9
Introduced:	1962	1962
Built by:	BR York	BR York
Formation:	DMBS+TS+TC+BDTS	BDTC+MBS+TS+DTS
Vehicle numbers:	DMBS - 61940-61947 TS - 71569-71572, 71108-71110 TC - 71573-71576, 71111-71114 BDTS - 75984-75991	BDTC - 75637-75644, 75962-75968 MBS - 61925-61939 (not in order) TS - 70253-70259, 71754-71761 (not in order) DTS - 75969-75983 (not in order)
Set length:	265ft 8½in (80.99m)	265ft 8½in (80.99m)
Vehicle length:	64ft 6in (19.66m)	64ft 6in (19.66m)
Height:	13ft 0½in (3.97m)	13ft 0½in (3.97m)
Width:	9ft 3in (2.82m)	9ft 3in (2.82m)
Seating:	Total - 24F/196S DMBS - 48S TS - 64S TC - 24F/24S BDTS - 60S	Total - 18F/194S BDTC - 18F/32S MBS - 48S TS - 64S DTS - 50S
Internal layout:	2+1F/2+2S	2+1F/2+2S
Gangway:	Throughout	Throughout
Toilets:	TS, BDTS - 1	BDTC, TS, DTS - 1
Weight:	Total - 167.5 or 170 tonnes DMBS - 60 tonnes TS - 32 or 34.5 tonnes TC - 35.5 tonnes BDTS - 40 tonnes	Total - 169 tonnes BDTC - 40 tonnes MBS - 57 tonnes TS - 35 tonnes DTS - 37 tonnes
Brake type:	Air (EP/Auto)	Air (EP/Auto)
Bogie type:	Commonwealth	Commonwealth
Power collection:	25kV ac overhead	25kV ac overhead
Traction motor type:	4 x EE	4 x EE
Horsepower:	1,128hp (841kW)	1,128hp (841kW)
Max speed:	100mph (161km/h)	100mph (161km/h)
Coupling type:	Buck-eye	Buck-eye
Multiple restriction:	Class 302-312	Class 302-312
Door type:	Slam	Slam
Special features:	Originally 2-car sets	

Right: *Eight of the Liverpool Street-Clacton/Walton sets included buffet cars, again based on the then standard Mk1 hauled design. Mounted on Commonwealth bogies these vehicles accommodated 32 in officially unclassified seats, allowing both first and second class passengers equal access to the refreshment vehicle. By the mid-1980s the need for the refreshment service on this route disappeared and the buffet cars were removed and broken up with replacement Mk1 hauled stock modified and inserted. GE 69103 from set 614 is illustrated. This vehicle was broken up by Vic Berry in 1984 .* CJM-C

Class 309

Left Top: *The stylish design of the 1962 Clacton/Walton electrics, especially when in lined maroon livery with a yellow corridor connecting door, was always impressive. The original rounded cab windows also improved the styling of these sets, but were later sadly replaced by flat units due to replacement costs. Four-car set No. 618 is illustrated from its Battery Driving Trailer Composite end.* CJM-C

Left Middle: *The Clacton sets were later repainted into main line blue and grey livery complete with a full yellow warning end. One of the original two-car sets, No. 607, is identifiable by having the pantograph on the roof of the driving car, but now strengthened to three-car status with an additional Trailer Composite. This set also sports the revised flat front windows.* CJM

Below: *Under the Network SouthEast banner, the Class 309s remained in operation over their intended route until replaced by newer stock. As the sets were of main line standards new homes were quickly found working in the North West, mainly in the Manchester area. In full NSE livery, set No. 309627, a fully refurbished set with hopper top windows, slows for the Colchester stop on 9 April 1992 with a Clacton to Liverpool Street service.* Michael J. Collins

Class 310

	As built	Modified condition	
Class:	310	310/0	310/1
Number range:	046-095	310046-310095	310101-310113
Former number range:	-	046-095	From 310/0 fleet
Alpha code:	AM10	AM10	AM10
Introduced:	1965-67	1965-67	1965-67
Built/rebuilt by:	BR Derby	BR Derby	BR Derby
Formation:	BDTS+MBS+ TS+BDTC	BDTSOL+MBSO+ TSO+DTCOL	BDTSOL+MBSO+DTCOL
Vehicle numbers:	BDTS - 76130-76179 MBS - 62071-62120 TS - 70731-70780 BDTC - 76180-76229	BDTSOL - 76130-76179/ 228/998 MBSO - 62071-62120 TSO - 70731-70780 DTCOL - 76180-76229 *	BDTSOL - from main series MBSO - from main series DTOCL - from main series
Set length:	265ft 8½in (80.99m)	265ft 8½in (80.99m)	199ft 3¼in (60.74m)
Vehicle length:	BDTS/BDTC - 65ft 1¾in (19.86m) MBS/TS - 65ft 4½in (19.93m)	BDTSOL/DTCOL - 65ft 1¾in (19.86m) MBSO/TSO - 65ft 4½in (19.93m)	BDTSOL/DTCOL - 65ft 1¾in (19.86m) MBSO - 65ft 4½in (19.93m)
Height:	13ft 0½in (3.97m)	13ft 0½in (3.97m)	13ft 0½in (3.97m)
Width:	9ft 3in (2.82m)	9ft 3in (2.82m)	9ft 3in (2.82m)
Seating	Total - 26F/293S BDTS - 80S MBS - 70S TS - 100S BDTC - 26F/43S	Total -24F/289S (*313S) BDTSOL - 60S¶ MBSO - 68S TSO - 98S DTCOL - 24F/43S or 67S	310101-310111 Total - 321S BDTSOL - 80S MBSO - 68S DTSOL - 75S 310112-310113 Total - 24F/191S BDTSOL - 80S MBSO - 68S DTCOL - 24F/43S
Internal layout:	First - 2+2 Standard - 2+3	First - 2+2 Standard - 2+3	First - 2+2 Standard - 2+3
Gangway:	Within set (except between MBS/TS)	Within set	Within set
Toilets:	BDTS - 2, BDTC - 2	BDTSOL - 2, DTCOL - 2	BDTSOL - 2, DTCOL - 2
Weight:	Total - 158 tonnes BDTS - 36.8 tonnes MBS - 56.9 tonnes TS - 30.3 tonnes BDTC - 34.0 tonnes	Total - 160.6 tonnes BDTSOL - 37.3 tonnes MBSO - 57.2 tonnes TSO - 31.7 tonnes DTCOL - 34.4 tonnes	Total - 128.9 tonnes BDTSOL - 37.3 tonnes MBSO - 57.2 tonnes DTCOL - 34.4 tonnes
Brake type:	Air (auto/EP)	Air (auto/EP)	Air (auto/EP)
Bogie type:	B4	B4	B4
Power collection:	25kV ac overhead	25kV ac overhead	25kV ac overhead
Traction motor type:	4 x EE546	4 x EE546	4 x EE546
Horsepower:	1,080hp (806kW)	1,080hp (806kW)	1,080hp (806kW)
Max speed:	75mph (121km/h)	75mph (121km/h)	75mph (121km/h)
Coupling type:	Buck-eye	Buck-eye	Buck-eye
Multiple restriction:	Class 304, 310	Class 310/312 series	Class 310/312 series
Door type:	Slam	Slam	Slam
Special features:		* Standard class only	

In later years many vehicles operated with first class declassified
¶Seating alterations: Car 76228 seats 68S and 76998 75S

Class 310

Above: *Introduced between 1965 and 1967 for use on the West Coast electrified route from London Euston to Birmingham, and built at Derby, the sets sported a pleasing rounded front end originally using curved windows. They were based at Bletchley and originally painted in BR rail blue. The sets were high-density and had an intermediate power car, with one of the two driving trailers housing limited first class. The sets were part through corridor fitted, but due to technical equipment people could not walk between the MBS and TS coach. Six new Class AM10s, later Class 310s, stand on shed at Bletchley displaying 1960s BR rail blue.* CJM-C

Left Middle: *Viewed from its BDTC end, rail blue-liveried No. 070 is seen near Wembley in 1980. The composite vehicles seated 26 first and 43 second class passengers. The '310s' were fitted with drop-head buck-eye couplings and Pullman rubbing plates with high level air and jumper connections. The Class 310s were able to operate with the Class 304s.* CJM

Left Below: *In later BR days standard blue and grey livery was applied to the Class 310 fleet, with white dots being installed in the out of use four-character route indicator. Set No. 049 passes Carpenders Park on 14 May 1984 forming the 10.02 Euston to Birmingham semi-fast service.* CJM

Above: *After replacement on West Coast services, the Class 310s were transferred to the LT&S line as well as to the Great Eastern, operating for Network SouthEast. Painted in NSE colours and sporting the 1980s applied flat front windscreens, set No. 310094 with BDTC car No. 76193 leading is seen at Clacton depot in April 1990.* CJM

Below: *A total of 13 Class 310s were reduced to three-car formation for operation in the Birmingham area and later by Regional Railways in the Liverpool, Manchester and Crewe area. The modified sets were classified 310/1 and emerged in the grey and blue of Regional Railways off-set by a white and blue bodyside band. Set No. 310108 arrives at Crewe with a service from Liverpool.* CJM

Class 311 See Class 303

Class 312

	As built		
Class:	312/0	312/1	312/2
Number range:	312001-312026	312101-312119	312201-312204
Former number range:	-	-	312001-312004
Alpha code:	AM12	AM12	AM12
Introduced:	1976-78	1975-76	1976
Built/rebuilt by:	BREL York	BREL York	BREL York
Formation:	BDTSOL+MBSO+ TSO+DTCOL	BDTSOL+MBSO+ TSO+DTCOL	BDTSOL+MBSO+ TSO+DTCOL
Vehicle numbers:	BDTSOL - 76949-76974 MBSO - 62484-62509 TSO - 71168-71193 DTCOL - 78000-78025	BDTSOL - 76975-76993 MBSO - 62510-62528 TSO - 71194-71212 DTCOL - 78026-78044	BDTSOL - 76994-76997 MBSO - 62657-62660 TSO - 71277-71280 DTCOL - 78045-78048
Set length:	256ft 8½in (78.24m)	256ft 8½in (78.24m)	256ft 8½in (78.24m)
Vehicle length:	BDTSOL, DTCOL - 65ft 1¾in (19.86m) MBSO, TSO - 65ft 4½in (19.93m)	BDTSOL, DTCOL - 65ft 1¾in (19.86m) MBSO, TSO - 65ft 4½in (19.93m)	BDTSOL, DTCOL - 65ft 1¾in (19.86m) MBSO, TSO - 65ft 4½in (19.93m)
Height:	12ft 9¼in (3.89m)	12ft 9¼in (3.89m)	12ft 9¼in (3.89m)
Width:	9ft 3in (2.82m)	9ft 3in (2.82m)	9ft 3in (2.82m)
Seating:	Total - 25F/297S BDTSOL - 84S MBSO - 68S TSO - 98S DTCOL 25F/47S	Total - 25F/297S BDTSOL - 84S MBSO - 68S TSO - 98S DTCOL 25F/47S	Total - 25F/297S BDTSOL - 84S MBSO - 68S TSO - 98S DTCOL 25F/47S
Internal layout:	Standard - 2+3 First - 2+1	Standard - 2+3 First - 2+1	Standard - 2+3 First - 2+1
Gangway:	Within set	Within set	Within set
Toilets:	BDTSOL - 1, DTCOL - 2	BDTSOL - 1, DTCOL - 2	BDTSOL - 1, DTCOL - 2
Weight:	Total - 156.6 tonnes BDTSOL - 34.9 tonnes MBSO - 56 tonnes TSO - 30.5 tonnes DTCOL - 35.2 tonnes	Total - 156.6 tonnes BDTSOL - 34.9 tonnes MBSO - 56 tonnes TSO - 30.5 tonnes DTCOL - 35.2 tonnes	Total - 156.6 tonnes BDTSOL - 34.9 tonnes MBSO - 56 tonnes TSO - 30.5 tonnes DTCOL - 35.2 tonnes
Brake type:	Air (EP/Auto)	Air (EP/Auto)	Air (EP/Auto)
Bogie type:	BDTSOL, TSO, DTCOL - BREL BT8 MBSO - BREL BP14	BDTSOL, TSO, DTCOL - BREL BT8 MBSO - BREL BP14	BDTSOL, TSO, DTCOL - BREL BT8 MBSO - BREL BP14
Power collection:	25kV ac overhead	6.25kV & 25kV ac overhead	25kV ac overhead
Traction motor type:	4 x EE546	4 x EE546	4 x EE546
Gear ratio:	61:19	61:19	63:17
Horsepower:	1,080hp (806kW)	1,080hp (806kW)	1,080hp (806kW)
Max speed:	90mph (145km/h)	90mph (145km/h)	75mph (121km/h)
Coupling type:	Buck-eye	Buck-eye	Buck-eye
Multiple restriction:	With Class and Class 310	With Class and Class 310	With Class and Class 310
Door type:	Slam	Slam	Slam
Notes:			Modified to 312/1s Nos. 312727-312730

Right Above: *When new outer suburban EMUS were ordered in the mid-1970s, the basic body structure of the Class 310 was used to form this fleet of Class 312s built by BREL York. Three batches were constructed: 312/0 consisted of 26 sets for Great Northern line use from King's Cross to Royston, which were painted in blue and grey and numbered 312001-026; 19 sets for Great Eastern numbered 312101-312119, which were painted in blue and grey; and four Class 312/2s Nos. 312201-312204 for West Midlands, also painted in rail blue. Soon after introduction the sets were renumbered into the 312/7 series. When new, set No. 312015 is seen arriving at London King's Cross with a semi-fast service from Royston. The set's Driving Trailer Composite Open Lavatory coach is leading. In original condition these vehicles seated 25 first and 47 standard class passengers. Seating was in the 2+2 in first and 2+3 in standard.* CJM

Below: *The 19 Class 312/1 sets, originally numbered 312101-312119, were based at Ilford depot and were delivered in all over rail blue with grey roofs and a full yellow warning end. To avoid a number clash with other Great Eastern electric stock a renumbering policy was quickly introduced with the sets taking the numbers 312781-312799; renumbering was done in order. On GE metals the new sets were deployed on longer distance services such as Colchester, Clacton and Walton. With a sticky number '781' in the front window, set No. 312101 passes Stratford bound for Liverpool Street in December 1979. As can be seen the front ends of this class were very similar to the Class 310s with just some minor changes to the cab window surrounds and a more open design around the air pipes. The four members of the Birmingham-based Class 312/2 fleet were later absorbed into the Class 312/0 fleet.* CJM

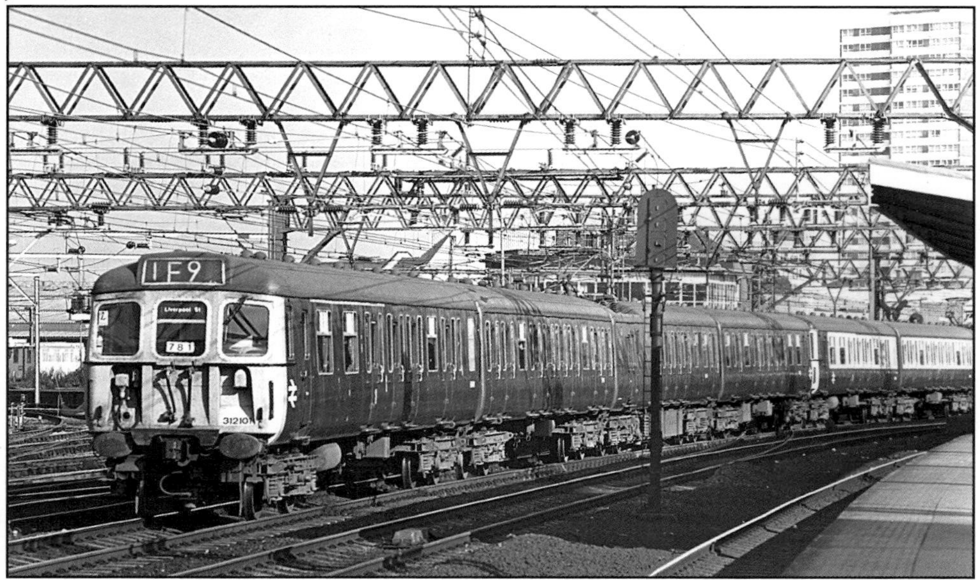

Class 312

	Rebuilt condition	
Sub class:	312/0	312/1
Number range:	312701-312730	312781-312799
Former number range:	312001-312026, 312201-312204	312101-312119
Alpha code:	AM12	AM12
Introduced:	1976-78	1975-76
Built/rebuilt by:	BREL York	BREL York
Formation:	BDTSOL+MBSO+TSO+DTCOL@	BDTSOL+MBSO+ TSO+DTCOL
Vehicle numbers:	BDTSOL - 76949-76974, 76994-76997 MBSO - 62484-62509, 62657-62660 TSO - 71168-71193, 71277-71280 DTCOL - 78000-78025, 78045-78048	BDTSOL - 76975-76993 MBSO - 62510-62528 TSO - 71194-71212 DTCOL - 78026-78044
Set length:	256ft 8½in (78.24m)	256ft 8½in (78.24m)
Vehicle length:	BDTSOL, DTCOL / DTSOL@- 65ft 1¾in (19.86m) MBSO, TSO - 65ft 4½in (19.93m)	BDTSOL, DTCOL - 65ft 1¾in (19.86m) MBSO, TSO - 65ft ½in (19.93m)
Height:	12ft 9¼in (3.89m)	12ft 9¼in (3.89m)
Width:	9ft 3in (2.82m)	9ft 3in (2.82m)
Seating:	Total - 25F/297S or 322S@ BDTSOL - 84S MBSO - 68S TSO - 98S DTCOL (DTSOL) 25F/47S or 72S	Total - 25F/297S BDTSOL - 84S MBSO - 68S TSO - 98S DTCOL 25F/47S
Internal layout:	Standard - 2+3 First - 2+1	Standard - 2+3 First - 2+1
Gangway:	Within set	Within set
Toilets:	BDTSOL - 1, DTCOL/DTSOL - 2	BDTSOL - 1, DTCOL - 2
Weight:	Total - 156.6 tonnes BDTSOL - 34.9 tonnes MBSO - 56 tonnes TSO - 30.5 tonnes DTCOL (DTSOL) - 35.2 tonnes	Total - 156.6 tonnes BDTSOL - 34.9 tonnes MBSO - 56 tonnes TSO - 30.5 tonnes DTCOL - 35.2 tonnes
Brake type:	Air (EP/Auto)	Air (EP/Auto)
Bogie type:	BDTSOL, TSO, DTCOL - BREL BT8 MBSO - BREL BP14	BDTSOL, TSO, DTCOL BREL BT8 MBSO - BREL BP14
Power collection:	25kV ac overhead	25kV ac overhead
Traction motor type:	4 x EE546	4 x EE546
Gear ratio:	61:19	61:19
Horsepower:	1,080hp (806kW)	1,080hp (806kW)
Max speed:	90mph (145km/h)	90mph (145km/h)
Coupling type:	Buck-eye	Buck-eye
Multiple restriction:	With Class and Class 310	With Class and Class 310
Door type:	Slam	Slam
Notes:	@ 312725-312730 have the DTCOL declassified to DTSOL	

Above: *The final four sets of the Class 312 order (312/2s) went to the West Midlands for the Birmingham New Street to Birmingham International shuttle; after this use ended the sets were transferred to Ilford to operate alongside the 317/0 sets, which had then moved from the Great Northern to the Great Eastern. In NSE livery and with an early headlight, set No. 312730 (ex 312204) is seen at Ilford from its BDTSOL end. Class 312s also spent a period operating on the LT&S lines out of Fenchurch Street.* CJM

Below: *As time progressed and the Class 312 entered the privatised railway, the sets remained on the Great Eastern section, operated by First Great Eastern operating longer distance outer suburban services such as Harwich, Clacton and Walton. Looking very smart in the Great Eastern colours, set No. 312707 is seen at Harwich Town, with its Driving Trailer Composite Open Lavatory nearest the camera. In later days during one of several facelift make-overs some of the passenger doors were sealed up to improve the travelling experience. All sets were withdrawn in 2003-04, and two vehicles have been preserved.* CJM

Class 313

Sub class:	313/0 & 313/1	313/2
Number range:	313018-313064, 313122-313134	313201-313220
Former number range:	-	313101-313120 (ex 313001-313020)
Introduced:	1976-1977	As 313/2 - 2010
Built/rebuilt by:	BREL York	As 313/2 - Wolverton
Formation:	DMSO+PTSO+BDMSO	DMSO+PTSO+BDMSO
Vehicle numbers:	DMSO - 62546-62592 PTSO - 71230-71276 BDMSO - 62610-62656	DMSO - 62529-62548 PTSO - 71213-71232 BDMSO - 62593-61612
Set length:	199ft 6in (60.83m)	199ft 6in (60.83m)
Vehicle length:	DMSO/BDMSO - 64ft 11½in (19.80m) PTSO - 65ft 4¼in (19.92m)	DMSO/BDMSO - 64ft 11½in (19.80m) PTSO - 65ft 4¼in (19.92m)
Height:	11ft 9in (3.58m)	11ft 9in (3.58m)
Width:	9ft 3in (2.82m)	9ft 3in (2.82m)
Seating:	Total: 231S DMSO - 74S, PTSO - 83S, BDMSO - 74S	Total: 196S DMSO - 64S, PTSO - 68S, BDMSO - 64S
Internal layout:	2+2/2+3 high density	2+2/2+3 high density
Gangway:	Within set, emergency end doors	Within set, emergency end doors
Toilets:	Not fitted	Not fitted
Weight:	Total - 104.5 tonnes DMSO - 36 tonnes PTSO - 31 tonnes BDMSO - 37.5 tonnes	Total - 104.5 tonnes DMSO - 36 tonnes PTSO - 31 tonnes BDMSO - 37.5 tonnes
Brake type:	Air (Westcode), rheostatic	Air (Westcode), rheostatic
Bogie type:	BX1	BX1
Power collection:	25kV ac overhead & 750V dc third rail	25kV ac overhead & 750V dc third rail
Traction motor type:	8 x GEC G310AZ	8 x GEC G310AZ
Horsepower:	880hp (657kW)	880hp (657kW)
Max speed:	75mph (121km/h)	75mph (121km/h)
Coupling type:	Outer - Tightlock Inner - Bar	Outer - Tightlock Inner - Bar
Multiple restriction:	Within class only	Within class only
Door type:	Bi-parting sliding	Bi-parting sliding
Special features:		CCTV
Construction:	Steel frame, aluminium alloy body	Steel frame, aluminium alloy body
Owner:	Eversholt	HSBC
Sub-class detail:	As built units (refurbished), originally for Great Northern electrification	Fitted with extra shoegear

Left: *The first production 1972-design high-density suburban EMUs to be introduced following trials with the PEP stock was this fleet of 64 three-car sets for the Great Northern electrification project in 1976-77 to operate between Moorgate and Welwyn Garden City/Hertford North. To enable operation over the sub-surface 'widened lines' the sets were fitted for both third rail power collection (750V dc) and overhead power collection at 25kV ac. Painted in blue/grey livery, the sets were allocated to new depot facilities at Hornsey. With a high-density layout and two pairs of bi-parting sliding doors on each carriage, the sets seated 231 in 2+3 open style. Soon after delivery set No. 313001 is seen with a four-character route display above the non-driving front window.* CJM

Above: *The 313/0s have remained on their intended route throughout their lives, passing to Network SouthEast and later privatised control. Displaying standard NSE colours set No. 313048 is seen with its Battery Driving Motor Standard Open (BDMSO) end leading at Hornsey depot.* CJM

Right Middle: *With improved use of resources, capacity was found in the Class 313 diagrams to allocate some units for a time to Great Eastern, but these soon returned to the core fleet. However, during modernisation of the Euston-Watford and Stratford-Richmond lines Class 313s were transferred to these routes, along with the later added Willesden to Clapham Junction service. This deployment continued under privatisation, with the sets operating for Silverlink. Changes to the third rail power collection shoes were required for this route due to longer gaps in the third rail. Painted in Silverlink colours set No. 313117 is seen at Kensington Olympia on a Willesden to Clapham service.* CJM

Right Bottom: *Today Southern operates a fleet of 19 Class 313/2s on its Coastway routes radiating from Brighton. Southern sets were all refurbished at Wolverton and now seat just 196 passengers. Sets carry a pictogram version of Southern livery with images of the Coastway route, and are allocated to Brighton. No. 313210 is seen at Bognor Regis on 30 January 2013.* John Binch

Class 314

Number range:	314201-314216
Introduced:	1979-80
Built/rebuilt by:	BREL York
Formation:	DMSO+PTSO+DMSO
Vehicle numbers:	DMSO - 64583-64614 PTSO - 71450-71465
Set length:	199ft 6in (60.83m)
Vehicle length:	DMSO - 64ft 11½in (19.80m) PTSO - 65ft 4¼in (19.92m)
Height:	11ft 6½in (3.58m)
Width:	9ft 3in (2.82m)
Seating:	Total - 212S DMSO - 68S PTSO - 76S DMSO - 68S*
Internal layout:	2+3 high density *
Gangway:	Within set (emergency end doors)
Toilets:	Not fitted
Weight:	Total - 102 tonnes DMSO - 34.5 tonnes PTSO - 33 tonnes DMSO - 34.5 tonnes
Brake type:	Air (Westcode), rheostatic
Bogie type:	BX1
Power collection:	25kV ac overhead
Traction motor type:	314201-314206 - 8 x Brush TM61-53 314207-314216 - 8 x GEC G310AZ
Horsepower:	880hp (657kW)
Max speed:	75mph (121km/h)
Coupling type:	Outer - Tightlock, Inner - Bar
Multiple restriction:	Within class only
Door type:	Bi-parting sliding
Construction:	Steel frame, aluminium alloy body
Owner:	Angel Trains

Note: * Set 314203 has an ex-Class 507 DMSO (64426) seating 74S

Below: *This is another of the 1972-design EMUs based of the PEP prototype. These 16 three-car sets were built for Strathclyde use in 1979-80 to operate on the then recently opened Argyle line as well as on the North Clyde route. The sets remained on their original routes until 2002 when stock cascading saw them transfer to the Cathcart Circle and some Inverclyde services to Gourock and Wemyss Bay. The sets are high-density with seats for 212 passengers in the 2+3 style. Two pairs of bi-parting sliding doors are provided on each side of each coach. To conform with tunnel evacuation, emergency end doors are provided. When originally built sets were painted in blue and grey livery with the GG Trans-Clyde bodyside branding. Set No. 314202 is illustrated when brand new.* CJM

Above: *The livery in which most people will remember the '314s' is the bright Strathclyde orange and black, as shown on set No. 314216 at Whifflet with a service bound for Coatbridge on 4 June 1996; by this time the passenger operations in Scotland had been taken over by ScotRail and their branding is seen applied to the bodyside just behind he driving cab. This set shows signs of impact with a set of buffer stops, with the footholds bent on the front end. This was a common problem with all the 1972-design units, which could easily roll backwards during the driver's preparation duties.* CJM

Below: *In 2011 the Class 314 fleet started to receive a life extension overhaul at Railcare Glasgow with the plan to retain the sets until after 2016. This work included bogie exchanges, electrical modifications, cab enhancements, passenger saloon upgrade including new seat covers, and new lino, and an overhaul of the couplers. The work saw at least five sets emerge in the new Scottish Railways Saltire livery, as shown on set No. 314212 at Cathcart on 7 August 2012 forming the 18.50 Glasgow Central-Glasgow Central via Cathcart service.* Robin Ralston

Class 315

Number range:	315801-315861
Introduced:	1980-81
Built/rebuilt by:	BREL York
Formation:	DMSO+TSO+PTSO+DMSO
Vehicle numbers:	DMSO - 64461-64582 TSO - 71281-71341 PTSO - 71389-71449
Set length:	264ft 10in (80.72m)
Vehicle length:	DMSO - 64ft 11½in (19.80m) TSO/PTSO - 65ft 4¼in (19.93m)
Height:	11ft 9in (3.58m)
Width:	9ft 3in (2.82m)
Seating:	Total: 318S DMSO - 74S TSO - 86S PTSO - 84S DMSO - 74S
Internal layout:	2+2/2+3 high density
Gangway:	Within set, end emergency door
Toilets:	Not fitted
Weight:	Total: 127.5 tonnes DMSO - 35 tonnes TSO - 25.5 tonnes PTSO - 32 tonnes DMSO - 35 tonnes
Brake type:	Air (Westcode), rheostatic
Bogie type:	BX1
Power collection:	25kV ac overhead
Traction motor type:	315801-315841 - 8 x Brush TM61-53 315842-315861 - 8 x GEC G310AZ
Horsepower:	880hp (657kW)
Max speed:	75mph (121km/h)
Coupling type:	Outer - Tightlock, Inner - Bar
Multiple restriction:	Within class
Door type:	Bi-parting sliding
Construction:	Steel frame, aluminium alloy body
Owner:	Eversholt

Below: *A further 61 1972-design four-car EMUs emerged from York Works in 1980-81 for use on Great Eastern suburban routes, to replace older slam door stock which was life expired. The sets classified as '315' seated 318 in the high-density mode. Each set had two driving power cars, with a Pantograph Trailer Second and a normal Trailer Second between; no provision was made for first class. The sets were allocated to Ilford depot. Originally painted in blue/grey livery, the sets were later finished in NSE colours before becoming the operating property of First Great Eastern and West Anglia Great Northern; franchise changes then saw the fleet operated by Anglia and now the Greater Anglia franchise. The Class 315s have always operated on their intended route. At present there is little prospect of any replacement for the '315' fleet; the new CrossRail stock will operate a number of the services in the east of London and in 2013 it was announced that when this happens the fleet is likely to be overhauled and sent to South Wales for Cardiff Valley electrification. In blue and grey livery, set No. 315801, the pioneer of the fleet, is seen at Stamford Hill forming the 16.42 Cheshunt to Liverpool Street service on 15 October 1984.* CJM

Top: *It's amazing what a coat of paint can do. The train looks totally different when decorated in the stunning First Great Eastern blue and green swirl colours. The first to carry the new livery, No. 315809 is seen at Shenfield on 15 April 1997.* CJM

Above: *In the One Railway livery, '315s' looked a little bland. Set No. 315857 shows this colour with the addition of National Express branding at Stratford in March 2008.* CJM

Right: *Under the Greater Anglia franchise a number of '315s' have emerged in all over base white with bodyside branding, off-set by red passenger doors. With modified front lamp clusters, set No. 315806 is seen at Pudding Mill.* Antony Christie

Class 316

Class:	316	316
Number:	316999	316998 and 316997
Former Number	210001/210002, 457001	307118
Introduced:	As Class 210: 1981 As Class 316: 1990	As Class 307: 1956 As Class 316: 1992
Built by:	As 210 - BREL Derby	As Class 307 - BR Eastleigh
Rebuilt by:	As 316 - RTC Derby	As Class 316 - RTC Derby
Formation:	DMS+TS+TS+DMS	DTBS+MS+DTC
Vehicle numbers:	DMS - 67300 (60300/54000) PTSO - 71246 TS - 67401 (60401/57001) DMS - 67301 (60301/54001)	DTBS - 75018 (977708) MS - 61018 (977709) DTC - 75118 (977710)
Vehicle length:	DMS 65ft 0½in (19.83m) PTSO - 65ft 4¼in (19.93m) TS - 65ft 4in (19.92m)	DTBS / DTC - 63ft 11½in (19.5m) MS - 63ft 6in (19.35m)
Height:	12ft 3½ (3.75m)	13ft 0½in (3.97m)
Width:	9ft 3in (2.82m)	9ft 3in (2.82m)
Seating:	Not fitted - development train	Not fitted - development train
Internal layout:	-	-
Gangway:	Throughout	Within set
Toilets:	Not fitted	Not fitted
Weight:	Total - 124.9 tonnes DMS - 32 tonnes PTSO - 32 tonnes TS - 28.9 tonnes DMS - 32 tonnes	Total - 123.5 tonnes DTBS - 43 tonnes MS - 47.5 tonnes DTC - 33 tonnes
Brake type:	Air, EP	Air, EP
Bogie type:	Power - BREL - BP20 Trailer - BREL BT13 PTSO - BX1	??
Traction package:	Networker development	Class 323 development
Horsepower:	1,140hp (850kW)	
Max speed:	90 mph (145km/h)	75mph (121km/h)
Coupling type:	Tightlock	Buck-eye
Multiple restriction:	Not fitted	Not fitted
Door type:	Double leaf sliding	Slam
Special features:	Development train, converted from Class 457 No. 457001 for ac traction development	Development train for Networker modified from Class 307 stock for Class 323 Holec traction development

Left: *The Class 316 number has been used for two different traction propulsion test trains. The first came in 1990 when as part of the Networker development project three redundant Class 210 vehicles and a PTSO from a Class 313 were formed together to establish the operational reliability of ac three-phase control and traction systems. The ex-Class 210 driving cars were fitted out with traction equipment with the usual contents of the underslung boxes placed inside the original passenger saloons to observe performance. While working on ac traction development the set was based at Clacton depot, where this view of the train was recorded. Standard NSE livery was applied plus the body legend 'Traction Development for the 1990s'.* CJM

Above & Right: *After withdrawal in 1992, the two driving trailers and the motor coach from Class 307 set No. 307118 went into departmental service as a development unit for Holec traction equipment. The set was rebuilt at the Engineering Development Unit (EDU) Derby for ac development work and renumbered as 316998, entering test running in 1993. The pantograph coach had its traction package mounted inside the former passenger saloon to enable observation and attention to be given. The set is illustrated (above) inside the EDU on 9 August 1993. After ac traction work was completed, the set was again modified at the EDU in Derby into a dc traction development set, the intermediate MSO having third rail collector shoes mounted on both bogies. In this state the set operated several main line trips over the South Western main line and is seen (right) passing Pirbright Junction on 23 March 1995 in multiple with Class 411 test set No. 1620, which at the time was being used for central door locking tests.*
CJM / Brian Stephenson

Class 317

Class:	317/1	317/5	317/6
Number range:	317337-317348	317501-317515	317649-317672
Previous numbers:	317301-317348	317301-317320	317349-317372
Introduced:	1981-82	1981-82	1985-86
Refurbished:	-	from 2005	1999-2000
Built by:	DTSO, MSO - BREL York TCO - BREL Derby	DTSO, MSO - BREL York TCO - BREL Derby	BREL York
Refurbished by:	-	Ilford	Railcare Wolverton
Formation:	DTSO(A)+MSO+ TCO+DTSO(B)	DTSO(A)+MSO+ TCO+DTSO(B)	DTS+MSO+ TSO+DTCO
Vehicle numbers:	DTSO(A) - 77036-77047 MSO - 62671-62708 TCO - 71613-71624 DTSO(B) - 77084-77095	DTSO(A) - 77001-77024 MSO - 62661-62680 TCO - 71577-71596 DTO(B) - 77048-77067	DTSO - 77200-19, 280-283 MSO - 62846-65, 886-889 TSO - 71734-53, 762-765 DTCO- 77220-39, 285-287
Set length:	265ft 6in (80.94m)	265ft 6in (80.94m)	265ft 6in (80.94m)
Vehicle length:	DTSO(A) - 65ft ¾in (19.83m) MSO - 65ft 4¼in (19.92m) TCO - 65ft 4¼in (19.92m) DTSO(B) - 65ft ¾in (19.83m)	DTSO(A) - 65ft ¾in (19.83m) MSO - 65ft 4¼in (19.92m) TCO - 65ft 4¼in (19.92m) DTSO(B) - 65ft ¾in (19.83m)	DTSO(A) - 65ft ¾in (19.83m) MSO - 65ft 4¼in (19.92m) TCO - 65ft 4¼in (19.92m) DTSO(B) - 65ft ¾in (19.83m)
Height:	12ft 1½in (3.70m)	12ft 1½in (3.70m)	12ft 1½in (3.70m)
Width:	9ft 3in (2.82m)	9ft 3in (2.82m)	9ft 3in (2.82m)
Seating:	Total - 22F/270S DTSO(A) - 74S MSO - 79S TCO - 22F/46S DTSO(B) - 71S	Total - 22F/270S DTSO(A) - 74S MSO - 79S TCO - 22F/46S DTSO(B) - 70S	Total - 24F/244S DTSO - 64S MSO - 70S TSO - 62S DTCO - 24F/48S
Internal layout:	2+2F/2+3S	2+2/2+3	2+2F/2+2S
Gangway:	Throughout	Throughout	Throughout
Toilets:	TCO - 2	TCO - 2	TSO - 2
Weight:	Total - 137 tonnes DTSO(A) - 29.5 tonnes MSO - 49 tonnes TCO - 29 tonnes DTSO(B) - 29.5 tonnes	Total - 137 tonnes DTSO(A) - 29.5 tonnes MSO - 49 tonnes TCO - 29 tonnes DTSO(B) - 29.5 tonnes	Total - 137 tonnes DTSO - 29.5 tonnes MSO - 49 tonnes TSO - 29 tonnes DTCO - 29.5 tonnes
Brake type:	Air	Air	Air
Bogie type:	Powered - BREL BP20 Trailer - BREL BT13	Powered - BREL BP20 Trailer - BREL BT13	Powered - BREL BP20 Trailer - BREL BT13
Power collection:	25kV ac overhead	25kV ac overhead	25kV ac overhead
Traction motor type:	4 x GEC G315BZ	4 x GEC G315BZ	4 x GEC G315BZ
Horsepower:	1,328hp (990kW)	1,328hp (990kW)	1,328hp (990kW)
Max speed:	100mph (161km/h)	100mph (161km/h)	100mph (161km/h)
Coupling type:	Outer - Tightlock Inner – Bar	Outer - Tightlock Inner – Bar	Outer - Tightlock Inner – Bar
Multiple restriction:	Within class	Within class	Within class
Door type:	Bi-parting sliding	Bi-parting sliding	Bi-parting sliding
Special fittings:	Pressure ventilated	Pressure ventilated	Convection heating
Total sets in traffic:	12	15	24
Construction:	Steel	Steel	Steel
Owner:	Angel Trains	Angel Trains	Angel Trains
Operator:	First Capital Connect	Greater Anglia	Greater Anglia
Sub-class detail:	Phase 1 sets	Phase 1 sets	Phase 2 refurbished

317/7	317/8
317708-317732 (nine units)	317881-317892
317308-317332 (random)	317321-317336
1981-82	1981-82
2000	2006-2007
BREL York	DTSO, MSO - BREL York TCO - BREL Derby
Railcare Wolverton	Ilford
DTSO+MSO+TSO+DTCO	DTSO+MSO+TCO+DTSO
DTSO - 77007-77031 series MSO - 62668-62692 series TSO - 71584-71608 series DTCO - 77055-77079 series	DTSO - 77020-77035 MSO - 62681-62696 TCO - 71597-71612 DTSO - 77068-77083
265ft 6in (80.94m)	265ft 6in (80.94m)
DTSO(A) - 65ft ¾in (19.83m) MSO - 65ft 4¼in (19.92m) TSO - 65ft 4¼in (19.92m) DTCO - 65ft ¾in (19.83m)	DTSO(A) - 65ft ¾in (19.83m) MSO - 65ft 4¼in (19.92m) TCO - 65ft 4¼in (19.92m) DTSO(B) - 65ft ¾in (19.83m)
12ft 1½in (3.70m)	12ft 1½in (3.70m)
9ft 3in (2.82m)	9ft 3in (2.82m)
Total - 22F/172S DTS0(A) - 52S MSO - 62S TSO - 42S DTCO - 22F/16S	Total - 20F/245S DTSO(A) - 66S MSO - 71S TCO - 20F/42S DTSO(B) - 66S
2+1F/2+2S	2+2F/2+3S
Throughout	Throughout
TSO- 2	TCO - 2
Total - 144.5 tonnes DTS - 31.4 tonnes MSO - 51.3 tonnes TSO - 30.2 tonnes DTC - 31.6 tonnes	Total - 137 tonnes DTSO(A) - 29.5 tonnes MSO - 49 tonnes TCO - 29 tonnes DTSO(B) - 29.5 tonnes
Air	Air
Powered - BREL BP20 Trailer - BREL BT13	Powered - BREL BP20 Trailer - BREL BT13
25kV ac overhead	25kV ac overhead
4 x GEC G315BZ	4 x GEC G315BZ
1,328hp (990kW)	1,328hp (990kW)
100mph (161km/h)	100mph (161km/h)
Outer - Tightlock Inner – Bar	Outer - Tightlock Inner – Bar
Within class	Within class
Bi-parting sliding	Bi-parting sliding
Pressure ventilated	Pressure ventilated
9	12
Steel	Steel
Angel Trains	Angel Trains
Greater Anglia	Greater Anglia
Stansted Express units	Stansted Express general

Above: *A batch of 48 series 1 and 20 series 2 Class 317s were built by BREL York and Derby between 1981-1986. The first 48 sets numbered 317301-348 were introduced for the St Pancras-Bedford electrification 'BedPan' line. Introduction was protracted due to industrial and technical issues. The use on this route was short lived as from 1987 dual-voltage Class 319s were introduced and the '317s' went to the West Coast route for a few years, moving again in 1989 to the Great Northern and West Anglia lines. The front end used a new standard MU style with a central gangway door, Tightlock couplers and marker/tail lights on the bodywork. The front end of 317510, the original 317310 is shown.* CJM

Right: *When the Class 317s emerged, new standards of driver comfort and equipment were found, with an electronic brake controller on the left and an easy to operate four position power controller on the right side. This cab is from set No. 317336, fitted with TPWS (below the clip board), cab radio above the clip board and driver's reminder appliance to the right of the telephone.* CJM

Class 317

Above: *The first tranche of Class 317s, Nos. 371301-317348, had a box shape top to the front end, with exposed warning horns. Lights were installed separately on the front end. The windows in the passenger saloons had small bottom hinged opening lights which were solid metal and not glazed. In as built condition, No. 317318 is seen on 20 January 1984 approaching Radlett with the 10.50 Bedford to St Pancras.* CJM

Right: *The second batch of 20 Class 317s, Nos. 371349-317368, were delivered with a more pleasing rounded top front end and Group Standard light clusters, as shown on set No. 317366 painted in NSE livery. These sets had larger opening lights to their saloon windows* CJM

Left: *The Class 317s were displaced from their intended 'BedPan' line by the introduction of Class 319 Thameslink stock, operating through Bedford to South London and South Coast trains. The '317s' found new employment on the West Coast working local services from Euston to Birmingham via Northampton. Further displacement saw sets transferred to Great Northern routes. In 1996 Prism Rail took over the franchise of the LT&S route and hired Class 317s to operate some services; initially just two sets but soon a total of 18 operated from East Ham depot. These sets, in NSE colours, had their NSE stripes revised to green to reflect the house colours of Prism. Set No. 317301 is seen at Fenchurch Street.* CJM

Right: *In 2013, the First Capital Connect franchise operated a fleet of 12 Class 317/3s (317337-317348) allocated to Hornsey for outer suburban services. All were painted in First livery, but when the franchise was first taken over from WAGN, a number of sets operated in WAGN dark purple with First branding, as shown on set No. 317342.* CJM

Below: *National Express upgraded nine Class 317/0s to 317/7s with smooth front end roof lines in 2000 for Stansted Express use; the interiors were also revised with extra luggage space. Set No. 317729 shows this modification. In 2013 all nine sets were stored out of use pending a new operator.* CJM

Right: *Class 317/2 standard class interior, showing the 2+3 seat layout, NSE blue moquette, opening hopper windows (of this design only fitted to the 317/2) and the wide passenger vestibule.* CJM

Class 318

Number range:	318250-318270
Introduced:	1985-86
Built/rebuilt by:	BREL York
Formation:	DTSOL+MSOP+DTSO
Vehicle numbers:	DTSOL - 77240-77259/77288 MSO - 62866-62885/62890 DTSO - 77260-77279/77289
Vehicle length:	DTSOL/DTSO - 65ft 0¾in (19.83m) MSO - 65ft 4¼in (19.92m)
Height:	12ft 1½in (3.70m)
Width:	9ft 3in (2.82m)
Seating:	Total - 213S DTSOL - 64S MSO - 77S DTSO - 72S
Internal layout:	2+2/2+3 high density
Gangway:	Within set
Toilets:	DTSOL - 1
Weight:	Total: 107.5 tonnes DTSOL - 30 tonnes MSO - 50.9 tonnes DTSO - 26.6 tonnes
Brake type:	Air (Westcode)
Bogie type:	DTSOL/DTSO - BREL BT13 MSO - BREL BP20
Power collection:	25kV ac overhead
Traction motor type:	4 x Brush TM2141
Horsepower:	1,438hp (1,072kW)
Max speed:	90mph (145km/h)
Coupling type:	Outer - Tightlock Within set - Bar
Multiple restriction:	Within type only
Door type:	Bi-parting sliding
Special features:	PA, CCTV, PIS
Total sets in traffic:	21
Construction:	Steel
Owner:	Eversholt
Operator:	First ScotRail

Below: *The 21 Class 318s, built for and used exclusively on Strathclyde services, were basically a three-car version of the final design of Class 317, except they were for standard class occupancy only with seating for 213 passengers. The sets were gangwayed throughout and were formed of two driving trailers flanking a central power car. Built at York, the sets emerged in Strathclyde orange and black in 1985-86 for use on the Ayrshire Coast line. One toilet was provided in one of the driving cars. In recent times the entire Class 318 fleet has been refurbished, andas part of that work the original front end gangway has been removed and an additional window formed in the original gangway door. This work has allowed an improved driving cab for these sets. Painted in Strathclyde orange and black livery, set No. 318261 is seen adjacent to a Class 303 at Glasgow Central on 22 March 1994.* CJM

Above and Right Middle: *In the later part of the 1990s, after the take over of Scottish services by ScotRail under privatisation, the fleet received some interior enhancements, as well as an application of the then new Strathclyde Passenger Transport carmine and cream livery, a traditional livery which looked very smart on these sets. In the upper view three-car ex-works carmine and cream liveried set No 318257 departs from Glasgow Central, while the view right shows the intermediate power car, with its pantograph at the near end. The Motor Standard Open (MSO) of the Class 318s has two Brush-supplied TM2141 traction motors on each bogie developing 1,438hp (1,072kW) per three-car set. Both:* CJM

Right Bottom: *The removal of the front gangway, to bring these sets in line with the Classes 320 and 334, has permitted a major improvement to the driving cab, which hitherto was cramped. The work was undertaken by Hunslet-Barclay of Kilmarnock, with modified sets carrying the carmine and cream colours. It is planned to apply the new Scottish Railways Saltire and blue livery to sets as they become due for repainting. Set Nos. 318252 and 318258 are seen near Lanark on 8 August 2012 forming the 17.34 service from Anderston.* Robert Ralston

Class 319

Sub class:	319/0	319/2	319/3
Number range:	319001-319013	319214-319220	319361-319386
Former number range:	-	319014-319020	319161-319186 (as 319/1)
Introduced:	1987	1987-88	1990
Rebuilt:	-	1996-97	1997-99
Built by:	BREL York	-	-
Rebuilt by:	-	Railcare Wolverton	Alstom Eastleigh
Formation:	DTSO(A)+MSO+ TSOL+DTSO(B)	DTSO+MSO+ TSOL+DTCO	DTSO(A)+MSO+ TSOL+DTSO(B)
Vehicle numbers:	DTSO(A) - 77291-77315(odd) MSO - 62891-62903 TSOL - 71772-71784 DTSO(B) - 77290-77314(even)	DTSO - 77317-77329 (odd) MSOL - 62904-62910 TSOL - 71785-71791 DTCO - 77316-77328 (even)	DTSO - 77459-77497, 77973-77983 (odd) MSO - 63043-63062, 63092-63098 TSOL - 71929-71948 71979-71984 DTSO(B) - 77458-77496, 77974-77984 (even)
Vehicle length:	DTSO(A) - 65ft ¾in (19.83m) DTSO(B) - 65ft ¾4in (19.83m) MSO - 65ft 4¼in (19.93m) TSOL - 65ft 4¼in (19.93m)	DTSO - 65ft ¾in (19.83m) DTCO - 65ft ¾in (19.83m) MSOL - 65ft 4¼in (19.93m) TSOL - 65ft 4¼in (19.93m)	DTSO(A) - 65ft ¾in (19.83m DTSO(B) - 65ft ¾in (19.83m) MSO - 65ft 4¼in (19.93m) TSOL - 65ft 4¼in (19.93m)
Height:	11ft 9in (3.58m)	11ft 9in (3.58m)	11ft 9in (3.58m)
Width:	9ft 3in (2.82m)	9ft 3in (2.82m)	9ft 3in (2.82m)
Seating:	Total - 319S DTSO(A) - 82S MSO - 82S TSOL - 77S DTSO(B) - 78S	Total - 18F/212S DTSO - 64S MSOL - 60S TSOL - 52S DTCO - 18F/36S	Total - 297S DTSO(A) - 70S MSO - 78S TSOL - 74S DTSO(B) - 75S
Internal layout:	Standard - 2+2, 2+3	Standard - 2+2 First - 2+1	Standard - 2+2, 2+3
Gangway:	Within set, emergency end doors	Within set, emergency end doors	Within set, emergency end doors
Toilets:	TSOL - 2	MSOL - 2, TSOL - 1	TSOL - 2
Weight:	Total - 136.5 tonnes DTSO(A) - 28.2 tonnes MSO - 49.2 tonnes TSOL - 31 tonnes DTSO(B) - 28.1 tonnes	Total - 136.5 tonnes DTSO - 28.2 tonnes MSOL - 49.2 tonnes TSOL - 31 tonnes DTCO - 28.1 tonnes	Total - 140.3 tonnes DTSO(A) - 29 tonnes MSO - 50.6 tonnes TSOL - 31 tonnes DTSO(B) - 29.7 tonnes
Brake type:	Air (Westcode)	Air (Westcode)	Air (Westcode)
Bogie type:	DTSO, TSOL - T3-7 MSO - P7-4	DTSO, DTCO, TSOL - T3-7 MSO - BREL P7-4	DTSO, TSOL - T3-7 MSO - P7-4
Power collection:	25kV ac overhead and 750V dc third rail	25kV ac overhead and 750V dc third rail	25kV ac overhead and 750V dc third rail
Traction motor type:	4 x GEC G315BZ	4 x GEC G315BZ	4 x GEC G315BZ
Horsepower:	1,438hp (1,072kW)	1,438hp (1,072kW)	1,438hp (1,072kW)
Max speed:	100 mph (161km/h)	100 mph (161km/h)	100 mph (161km/h)
Coupling type:	Outer - Tightlock Inner - Bar	Outer - Tightlock Inner - Bar	Outer - Tightlock Inner - Bar
Multiple restriction:	Within Class 319 series	Within Class 319 series	Within Class 319 series
Door type:	Bi-parting sliding	Bi-parting sliding	Bi-parting sliding
Total sets in traffic:	13	7	26
Owner:	Porterbrook	Porterbrook	Porterbrook
Operator:	First Capital Connect	First Capital Connect	First Capital Connect
Sub-class differences:	Original phase 1 units		'Metro' units

319/4
319421-319460
319021-319060
1988-89
1997-99
-
Railcare Wolverton
DTCO+MSO+
TSOL+DTSO
DTCO - 77331-77381,
77431-77457 (odd)
MSO - 62911-62974
TSOL - 71792-71879
DTSO - 77330-77380,
77470-77456 (even)

DTCO - 65ft ¾in (19.83m)
DTSO - 65ft ¾in (19.83m)
MSO - 65ft 4¼in (19.93m)
TSOL - 65ft 4¼in (19.93m)
11ft 9in (3.58m)
9ft 3in (2.82m)
Total: 12F/263S
DTCO - 12F/51S
MSO - 74S
TSOL - 67S
DTSO - 71S
Standard 2+2, 2+3
First 2+1
Within set,
emergency end doors
TSOL - 2
Total - 136.5 tonnes
DTSO(A) - 28.2 tonnes
MSO - 49.2 tonnes
TSOL - 31 tonnes
DTSO(B) - 28.1 tonnes
Air (Westcode)
DTSO, DTCO, TSOL - T3-7
MSO - P7-4
25kV ac overhead and
750V dc third rail
4 x GEC G315BZ
1,438hp (1,072kW)
100 mph (161km/h)
Outer - Tightlock
Inner - Bar
Within Class 319 series
Bi-parting sliding
40
Porterbrook
First Capital Connect
'CityFlier' units

Above: *Designed and built specifically to operate Thameslink services from the North of London to the South of London via Clerkenwell Tunnel, Network SouthEast took delivery of 60 four-car Class 319/0s in 1987-88. These sets incorporated a new design of front end with an emergency end door for tunnel evacuation if needed. The passenger saloons were all of the open type with seating in the 2+3 high-density style. The sets were corridor fitted throughout and were fitted with fully automatic Tightlock couplers. When first delivered sets were for all standard class occupancy, with accommodation for 319. The sets were dual voltage; tracks in the north and as far south as Farringdon and the Moorgate branch were energised using the overhead system at 25kV ac, while the tracks in the south and as far north as Farringdon were energised using the Southern third rail system at 750V dc. All sets were painted in NSE livery from new and the first 60 sets sported mid-grey around the front end. Set No. 319009 is seen at London Bridge.* CJM

Below: *A second batch of 26 Class 319s were introduced in 1990 classified as 319/1; these had a very slight variation to equipment and front end styling, with less moulding work around the coupling area. Their livery used a lighter shade of grey on the front end. In terms of internal layout these sets again used the high-density 2+3 layout, but incorporated first class seating in one of the driving cars, making it a Driving Trailer Composite Open seating 16 first and 54 standard class passengers. A unique feature to all Class 319s when introduced was the area directly behind the driving cab in the DTSO vehicle, which had fold down longitudinal seating which could be raised and the area converted into a Royal Mail area. A lockable door was located by the first pair of passenger doors. This feature was later removed on refurbishment and the end of transporting mail by rail. When brand new, the first of the follow-on order, No. 319161, is seen in the yard at BREL York awaiting commissioning and delivery to Selhurst.* CJM

Class 319

Above and Below: *Upon privatisation in the mid-1990s the first 20 Class 319 sets went to Connex South Central. Nos. 319001-319013 were dedicated to suburban operations, while Nos. 319014-319020 were modified at Wolverton Works as Brighton Express sets renumbered as 319214-220; these had low-density 2+2 interiors, a lounge, buffet counter and a disabled access toilet. Sets were repainted in Connex grey and yellow livery as shown above on set No. 319217 at Selhurst depot. The suburban batch retained their all second class seating in 2+3 and were later taken over by Southern, being repainted in their distinctive green and white livery; set No. 319011 is seen at Clapham Junction. Today, all Class 319s are deployed on the First Capital Connect Thameslink service. Both:* CJM

Above & Right: *In 2013 the Class 319 fleet was operated by First Capital Connect on its Thameslink corridor from Bedford/Luton in the north to Brighton, Sevenoaks and Wimbledon/ Sutton in the south. Today two main sub classes exist: 319/3 consists of 26 members which are all standard class sets seating 300 and are allocated to Bedford, and 319/4 consists of 40 units, which have first class accommodation in one driving trailer and seat 12 first and 277 standard. Most sets are finished in First Group corporate livery, and a few sets sport advertising colours. Set No. 319453 is illustrated above near Wimbledon, while set No. 319372 is seen right at Farringdon station.*
Both: Antony Christie

Right Below: *Class 319 interior, showing the use of 3+2 high-back seating with edge grab handles. Above seat luggage racks are provided for light items, while luggage stacks are provided for heavier items such as cases. The 319s are not air conditioned and thus have opening hopper windows. Lighting is by a central fluorescent gondola. In the future, following the introduction of new Thameslink stock and route modernisation, the Class 319s are expected to be cascaded to the Paddington-Reading-Newbury/Oxford route and Manchester to Liverpool following electrification work.* CJM

Class 320

Number range:	320301-320322
Introduced:	1990
Built by:	BREL York
Formation:	DTSO(A)+MSO+DTSO(B)
Vehicle numbers:	DTSO(A) - 77899-77920 MSO - 63021-63042 DTSO(B) - 77921-77942
Vehicle length:	DTSO(A) - 65ft ¾in (19.83m) MSO - 65ft 4¼in (19.92m) DTSO(B) - 65ft ¾in (19.83m)
Height:	12ft 4¾in (3.78m)
Width:	9ft 3in (2.82m)
Seating:	Total - 227S DTSO(A) - 76S MSO - 76S DTSO(B) - 75S
Internal layout:	Standard - 2+3
Gangway:	Within set
Toilets:	One to be installed
Weight:	Total - 111 tonnes DTSO (A) - 29.1 tonnes MSO - 51.9 tonnes DTSO(B) - 30.0 tonnes
Brake type:	Air (Westcode)
Bogie type:	DTSO(A), DTSO(B) - BREL T3-7 MSO - BREL P7-4
Power collection:	25kV ac overhead
Traction motor type:	4 x Brush TM2141B
Horsepower:	1,438hp (1,072kW)
Max speed:	75mph (121km/h) increased to 90mph (145km/h) in 2011-12
Coupling type:	Outer - Tightlock, Inner - Bar
Multiple restriction:	Within class
Door type:	Bi-parting sliding
Total sets in traffic:	22
Construction:	Steel
Owner:	Eversholt
Operator:	First ScotRail

Below: *In 1990 a batch of 33 three-car suburban sets, based on the previous 321 design, entered service in Scotland, funded by Strathclyde PTE to replace the ageing Class 303 and 311 stock. The sets were built at BREL York and consist of two Driving Trailer Standard Opens (DTSOs) flanking a Motor Standard Open (MSO) which also houses the power collection pantograph. Each set seats 227 in high-density 2+3 seating. The sets are corridor fitted within each set but do not have end gangways. Tightlock automatic couplers are fitted. When constructed these sets emerged in the Strathclyde orange and black livery, as depicted on sets Nos. 320321 and 320322 at BREL York awaiting delivery to Scotland.* CJM

Above: *The Strathclyde orange and black livery was progressively replaced in the late 1990s by the carmine and cream colours, as displayed on set No. 320306 at Glasgow Central on an Ayrshire line service. In more recent times, as sets have been overhauled and refurbished the latest Scottish Railways Saltire blue livery scheme has been applied.* CJM

Below: *The interior of the Class 320 sets is quite basic, with two transverse walkways by the door position feeding open seating saloons. In the main seating is in the 2+3 high-density style, with above seat luggage racks. Doors are passenger operated under the control of the train staff. As no air conditioning is provided opening hopper windows are fitted.* CJM

Class 321

Class:	321/3	321/4	321/9
Number range:	321301-321366	321401-321448	321901-321903
Introduced:	1988-90	1989-90	1991
Built by:	BREL York	BREL York	BREL York
Facelifted by:	Ilford	Ilford	Ilford
Formation:	DTCO+MSO+ TSOL+DTSO	DTCO+MSO+ TSOL+DTSO	DTSO(A)+MSO+ TSOL+DTSO(B)
Vehicle numbers:	DTCO - 78049-78094, 78131-78150 MSO - 62975-63020, 63105-63124 TSOL - 71880-71925, 71991-72010 DTSO - 77853-77898, 78280-78299	DTCO - 78095-78130, 78151-78162 MSO - 63063-63092, 62099-63104, 63125-63136 TSOL - 71949-71978, 71985-71990, 72011-72022 DTSO - 77943-77972, 78274-78279, 78300-78310	DTSO(A) - 77990-77992 MSO - 63153-63155 TSOL - 72128-72130 DTSO(B) - 77993-77995
Vehicle length:	DTCO - 65ft ¾in (19.83m) MSO - 65ft 4¼in (19.92m) TSOL - 65ft 4¼in (19.92m) DTSO - 65ft ¾in (19.83m)	DTCO - 65ft ¾in (19.83m) MSO - 65ft 4¼in (19.92m) TSOL - 65ft 4¼in (19.92m) DTSO - 65ft ¾in (19.83m)	DTSO(A) - 65ft ¾in (19.83m) MSO - 65ft 4¼in (19.92m) TSOL - 65ft 4¼in (19.92m) DTSO(B) - 65ft ¾in (19.83m)
Height:	12ft 4¾in (3.78m)	12ft 4¾in (3.78m)	12ft 4¾in (3.78m)
Width:	9ft 3in (2.82m)	9ft 3in (2.82m)	9ft 3in (2.82m)
Seating:	Total - 16F/292S DTCO - 16F/57S MSO - 82S TSOL - 75S DTSO - 78S	321401-321420 Total - 28F/271S DTCO - 28F/40S MSO - 79S TSOL - 74S DTSO - 78S 321421-321448 Total - 16F/283S DTCO - 16F/52S MSO - 79S TSOL - 74S DTSO - 78S	Total - 293S + 15 tip up DTSO(A) - 70S + 8 tip up MSO - 79S TSOL - 74S DTSO(B)- 70S + 7 tip up
Internal layout:	2+2F/2+3S	2+2F/2+3S	2+3S
Gangway:	Within unit only	Within unit only	Within unit only
Toilets:	TSOL - 2	TSOL - 2	TSOL - 2
Weight:	Total - 140 tonnes DTCO - 29.7 tonnes MSO - 51.5 tonnes TSOL - 29.1 tonnes DTSO - 29.7 tonnes	Total - 140.4 tonnes DTCO - 29.8 tonnes MSO - 51.6 tonnes TSOL - 29.2 tonnes DTSO - 29.8 tonnes	Total - 138.5 tonnes DTCO - 29.2 tonnes MSO - 51.1 tonnes TSOL - 29.0 tonnes DTSO - 29.2 tonnes
Brake type:	Air (Westcode)	Air (Westcode)	Air (Westcode)
Bogie type:	MSO - BREL P7-4 DTCO, DTSO, TSOL - BREL T3-7	MSO - BREL P7-4 DTCO, DTSO, TSOL - BREL T3-7	MSO - BREL P7-4 DTSO, TSOL - BREL T3-7
Power collection:	25kV ac overhead	25kV ac overhead	25kV ac overhead
Traction motor:	4 x Brush TM2141C	4 x Brush TM2141C	4 x Brush TM2141C
Horsepower:	1,438hp (1,072kW)	1,438hp (1,072kW)	1,438hp (1,072kW)
Max speed:	100mph (161km/h)	100mph (161km/h)	100mph (161km/h)
Coupling type:	Outer - Tightlock Inner - Bar	Outer - Tightlock Inner – Bar	Outer - Tightlock Inner - Bar
Multiple working:	Classes 317-323	Classes 317-323	Classes 317-323
Door type:	Bi-parting sliding	Bi-parting sliding	Bi-parting sliding
Total sets in traffic:	66	48	3
Construction:	Steel	Steel	Steel
Owner:	Eversholt	Eversholt	Eversholt
Operator:	Greater Anglia	London Midland Greater Anglia, FCC	Northern

Above: *One of the major Network SouthEast investments was the Class 321 fleet of four-car units introduced in 1988-90. The first 66 sets went to the Great Eastern lines based at Ilford and were numbered 321301-321366. The second tranche, classified as 321/4s and numbered 321401-321448, were for the West Coast for outer suburban use on the Euston-Birmingham corridor. Very slightly different interior design existed between the two sub classes. Originally the Class 321/3s seated 16 first and 292 standard, while the Class 321/4s seated 28 first and 371 standard. Set No. 321343 is seen when brand new at Ilford depot.* CJM

Below: *A final batch of three Class 321s were built at York in 1991 when West Yorkshire PTE funded sets Nos. 321901-321903 for use on the Doncaster to Leeds suburban services, replacing ageing Class 308s. The sets, at the time referred to as 'MetroTrains', were four-car all standard class high-density sets, with a total seating capacity of 309. Body structure was the same as the NSE units, except these were finished in the red and cream of the WYPTE. Sets were allocated to Leeds Neville Hill. These sets were later taken over by Northern Spirit, Arriva Trains Northern and presently Northern Rail. The three units were refurbished in 2006-07 by Hunslet-Barclay of Kilmarnock with revised interiors, reliability modifications and finished in the latest Northern livery. Set No. 321901 is seen at BREL York during its handover to WYPTE on 27 July 1991.* CJM

Class 321

Above: *National Express, the parent company operating the North London Railway franchise, renamed the operation to Silverlink from March 1997 and introduced a rather bright and quite stunning mauve, green and yellow livery. The Bletchley-allocated Class 321s were soon given these colours as demonstrated by sets Nos. 321418 and 321425 outside Bletchley depot on 7 February 2007. In November 2007 the franchise map was redrawn and Silverlink was disbanded with London area services taken over by Transport for London and Midlands services operated by London Midland.* CJM

Left Middle: *Full length train advertising in the UK has never been common and one of the first trains to support such a venture was Class 321 No. 321308, which Network SouthEast agreed to brand in full 3M advertising livery in July 1995. The application of pictogram vinyls was done by a private company at Ilford depot and the train is seen passing Manningtree on 25 July 1995 forming the 11.00 Liverpool Street to Ipswich.* CJM

Left Bottom: *The Class 321 intermediate TSO was fitted with two lavatory compartments at the end coupled to the Motor Standard Open (MSO) vehicle and thus has a slightly different window arrangement. The TSOL from Class 321/9 No. 321901, No. 72128, is illustrated. These vehicles seat 74 standard class passengers.* CJM

Above: *Under the original privatisation the Anglia franchise was awarded to First Group, who named the lines from Liverpool Street First Great Eastern. The company soon applied its corporate 'swirl' style livery to trains and structures. Class 312 No. 321438, one of the original West Coast batch, heads past Stratford on 12 July 2006 with its DTCO coach leading.* CJM

Below: *From 2004 National Express took over the Anglia franchise and quickly applied its corporate image to rolling stock. The pioneer of the Class 321 fleet set, No. 321301, passes Stratford on 28 April 2010. The set's DTCO is leading. In 2013 all the Anglia Class 321s were allocated to and maintained by Ilford depot.* CJM

Class 322

Number range:	322481-332485
Introduced:	1990
Refurbished:	2006
Built by:	BREL York
Refurbished by:	Hunslet-Barclay, Kilmarnock
Formation:	As built - DTCO+MSO+TSOL+DTSO, Modified - DTSO(A)+MSO+TSOL+DTSO(B)
Vehicle numbers:	DTCO/DTSO(A) - 78163-78167, MSO - 63137-63141 TSOL - 72023-72027, DTSO(B) - 77985-77989
Vehicle length:	DTCO/DTSO - 65ft ¾in (19.83m) MSO/TSOL - 65ft 4¼in (19.92m)
Height:	12ft 4 ¾in (3.78m)
Width:	9ft 3in (2.82m)
Seating:	As built: Total: 36F/217S - DTCO - 35F/22S, MSO - 70S, TSOL - 60S. DTSO - 65S Modified: Total: 291S + 2 tip up - DTSO - 58S, MSO -83S, TSOL - 76S, DTSO -74S
Internal layout:	2+3
Gangway:	Within unit
Toilets:	TSOL - 2
Weight:	Total - 138.7 tonnes DTCO/DTSO(A) - 29.3 tonnes, MSO - 51.5 tonnes, TSOL - 28.8 tonnes, DTSO(B) - 29.1 tonnes
Brake type:	Air (Westcode)
Bogie type:	MSO - BREL P7-4 DTCL/DTSO, TSOL - BREL T3-7
Power collection:	25kV ac overhead
Traction motor:	4 x Brush TM2141C
Horsepower:	1,438hp (1,072kW)
Max speed:	100mph (161km/h)
Coupling type:	Outer - Tightlock, Inner - Bar
Multiple restriction:	Within class, Classes 317-323
Door type:	Bi-parting, sliding
Total sets in traffic:	5
Construction:	Steel
Owner:	Eversholt
Current operator:	Northern Rail

Left: *Part of Network SouthEast's operation to modernise London's railways, launched by Chris Green, was the introduction of new state-of-the-art stock on the Great Eastern line, electrification to Cambridge and Stansted Airport, and the introduction of a dedicated fleet of trains to work Liverpool Street to Stansted Airport. To save huge extra design costs the basic outline of the Class 321 was used, into which a revised interior was fitted, with low-density 2+2 seating and extra luggage stowage areas for airline passengers. The sets were finished in a special Airport Express livery of light grey and green with Stansted Express bodyside branding. The sets remained on the Stansted Airport route until after privatisation and in 1997 they became common user with the rest of the West Anglia fleet. Soon afterwards four of the five sets were hired to North Western Trains for working a new Manchester Airport to London Euston service; two of them were then repainted in North Western blue and gold star livery. By 1999 with the Manchester Airport-Euston service abandoned the sets returned to West Anglia. In 2001 the non-standard sets went to First ScotRail for North Berwick line services. In 2004 the sets were returned to Ilford but lay dormant. In 2006 they again returned to Scotland for North Berwick duties, this time via a major refurbishment at Hunslet-Barclay to install a standard interior. In 2011 the sets were made redundant when 'Desiro' sets were introduced and the '322s' were transferred to Northern Rail at Leeds to work alongside the like bodied Class 321/9s. The original Stansted Express first class interior is shown.* CJM

Above: *After Chris Green took delivery of the first Class 322 Stansted Express unit No. 322481 at BREL York on 20 July 1990, the set operated a press special to London King's Cross, showing the sleek new trains in action. In Stansted grey and green livery, with just a NSE badge on the front end, set no. 322481 is seen at King's Cross.* CJM

Below: *Following introduction of Class 380 'Desiro' stock in Scotland, the five Class 322s were again shifted south, this time going to Northern Rail and based at Leeds Neville Hill where they joined the three Class 321/9s which were almost identical. The sets are usually deployed on the Doncaster to Leeds stopping service. Set No. 322482 is seen in the north facing bay at Doncaster showing Northern Rail blue livery with grey contrasting passenger doors.* Nathan Williamson

Class 323

Number range:	323201-323243
Introduced:	1992-93
Built/rebuilt by:	Hunslet TPL Leeds
Formation:	DMSO(A)+PTSOL+DMSO(B)
Vehicle numbers:	DMSO(A) - 64001-64043 PTSOL - 72201-72243 DMSO(B) - 65001-65043
Vehicle length:	DMSO - 76ft 8¾in (23.37m) PTSOL - 76ft 10¾in (23.44m)
Height:	12ft 4¾in (3.78m)
Width:	9ft 2 ¼in (2.80m)
Seating:	All except 323223-323225 - Total - 284S DMSO(A) - 98S PTSOL - 88S + 5 tip up DMSO(B) - 98S Sets 323223-323225 - Total - 244S DMSO(A) - 82S PTSOL - 80S DMSO(B) - 82S
Internal layout:	2+3 high density Sets – 323223-225 - 2+2
Gangway:	Within unit only
Toilets:	PTSOL - 1
Weight:	Total - 121.4 tonnes DMSO(A) - 41 tonnes PTSOL - 39.4 tonnes DMSO(B) - 41.0 tonnes
Brake type:	Air (Westcode)
Bogie type:	Powered - RFS BP62 Trailer - RFS BT52
Power collection:	25kV ac overhead
Traction motor type:	4 x Holec DMKT 52/24
Horsepower:	1,566hp (1,168kW)
Max speed:	90mph (145km/h)
Coupling type:	Outer - Tightlock, Inner - Bar
Multiple restriction:	Class 317-323
Door type:	Bi-parting sliding plug
Total sets in traffic:	43
Construction:	Welded aluminium alloy
Owner:	Porterbrook
Operator:	London Midland, Northern

Below: *The Regional Railways arm of British Railways ordered 43 high-density three-car EMUs from Hunslet Transportation Projects Ltd in 1990, initially to replace ageing DMU stock on the Birmingham Cross-City line. Regional Railways invested in the new company Hunslet-TPL who had recently been formed by engineers and staff who had departed from Birmingham-based Metro-Cammell. The bodyshells were assembled from welded aluminium in the Hunslet Leeds factory. The sets had major technical and operational issues and saw a protracted delivery. The original allocation was for the Birmingham area to operate sets 323201-323222 and 323240-323243 and the North Western area based in Manchester to operate sets 323223-323239; of this batch Nos. 323223-323225 had a revised interior with extra luggage stacks to cope with luggage demands on the Manchester to Manchester Airport corridor. These sets were formed of some of the longest EMU coaches in traffic measuring 76ft 10¾in (23.44m) in length. The conventional sets seated 284 passengers and the three modified Manchester Airport sets seated 244. When delivered, the Birmingham area sets were painted in Centro grey and green off-set with a blue and white body stripe, while the Regional Railways North West sets were in grey and brown. After the 1996 privatisation, the Birmingham area sets were taken over by Central Trains, which later became London Midland, while the North Western sets were taken over by First North Western, seeing an application of 'Barbie' livery. The present operator of these sets is Northern Rail. Below we see set No. 323203 displaying Centro livery at Birmingham New Street on a Cross-City duty.* CJM

Above: *Displaying First North Western livery, set No. 323233 is seen at Manchester Piccadilly on 24 July 2003. In the Manchester area the sets are deployed on Manchester-Glossop/Hadfield, Alderley Edge, Wilmslow, Stockport, Manchester Airport and Stoke services. In recent years refurbishing has been done at Manchester Traincare Centre with equipment, brake and bogie attention and upgraded interiors.* CJM

Below: *The Birmingham Cross-City fleet is now operated by London Midland and its green, grey and black livery has now been applied. With revised front group Standard lamp clusters, set No. 323215 is seen at Wylde Green on 23 November 2009.* Stacey Thew

Class 325

Number range:	325001-325016
Introduced:	1995-96
Built by:	Adtranz Derby
Formation:	DTPMV(A)+MPMV+TPMV+DTPMV(B)
Vehicle numbers:	DTPMV(A) - 68300-68330 (even numbers) MPMV - 68340-68355 TPMV - 68360-68375 DTPMV(B) - 68301-68331 (odd numbers)
Vehicle length:	DTPMV - 65ft 0¾in (19.83m) MPMV/TPMV - 65ft 4¼in (19.92m)
Height:	12ft 4¼in (3.77m)
Width:	9ft 3in (2.82m)
Seating:	None - Parcel/Mail space
Internal layout:	Open
Gangway:	Not fitted
Toilets:	Not fitted
Weight:	Total - 138.4 tonnes DTPMV(A) - 29.1 tonnes MPMV - 49.5 tonnes TPMV - 30.7 tonnes DTPMV(B) - 29.1 tonnes
Brake type:	Air (EP/auto)
Bogie type:	Powered - Adtranz P7-4 Trailer - Adtranz T3-7
Power collection:	25kV ac overhead and 750V dc third rail
Traction motor type:	4 x GEC G315BZ
Horsepower:	1,438hp (1,072kW)
Max speed:	100mph (161km/h)
Coupling type:	Drop-head buck-eye/screw
Multiple restriction:	Within type, TDM wired
Door type:	Roller shutter
Construction:	Steel
Special features:	Retractable buffers, intruder alarm
Owner:	Royal Mail
Operator:	Royal Mail/DBS

Below: *In 1995-96 a fleet of 16 four-car Royal Mail units was built by Adtranz Derby for the movement of Royal Mail postal traffic over the UK rail system. The sets were broadly based on the Class 319 and were fitted for dual electric operation, able to collect power from the overhead at 25kV ac or from the third rail at 750V dc. The end connections also allowed coupling of locomotives either electric or diesel to haul sets to virtually any destination, and they were fitted with TDM multiple control equipment. Each of the four vehicles, which were not gangwayed, comprised a large open stowage space, with brackets to hold the latest type of Royal Mail letter carriers. Access was by two wide roller shutter doors on either side of each coach. The sets had one power car coupled in an intermediate position generating 1,438hp (1,072kW). The sets were owned by Royal Mail and painted in Post Office red livery. Until privatisation the sets were operated by the Parcels arm, but after 1996 EWS took over their operation until Royal Mail withdrew from using rail as a method of transport. In 2004-10 GBRf operated the sets on limited duties and in 2010 DB-Schenker won a new Royal Mail contract to use the sets over the West Coast main line. Set No. 325006 is seen looking rather grubby at Crewe.* CJM

Above: *The driving cab of the Class 325 was a separate module, with no access to the train for security reasons. It is interesting that these ultra modern EMUs were fitted with older style drop-head buck-eye couplers and buffer beam mounted air pipes; this was required as the loco classes with which they were to operate were fitted with this type of equipment. Set No. 325008 is seen clearly showing the front end and underframe equipment of the DTPMV.* CJM

Right Middle and Below: *The intermediate power car, fitted with a pantograph at one end, was the heaviest vehicle in the formation, weighing in at 49.5 tonnes, and is illustrated right middle. The vehicle was mounted on Adtranz P7-4 motor bogies. The roller shutter doors were of the hand operated type for which only the Post Office staff had the key; the train crew did not have access to the train. A full intruder alarm system was fitted, with side warning lights, notification to the train crew and advice to the emergency services. The view right bottom shows intermediate TPMV car No. 68364. Both:* CJM

Class 332

Number range:	332001-332004, 332010-332014	332005-332009
Introduced:	1997-98, 2002	1997-98, 2002
Built by:	Siemens Germany, CAF Spain	Siemens Germany, CAF Spain
Formation:	332001-332004, DMFO+TSO+PTSOL+DMSO 332010-332014 DMSO+TSO+PTSOL+DMFLO	332005-333007 DMFO+TSO+PTSOL+TSO+DMSO 332008-333009 DMSO+TSO+PTSOL+TSO+DMFLO
Vehicle numbers:	332001-332004 DMFO - 78400-78406 (even numbers) TSO - 72405-72412 (random) PTSO - 63400-63403 DMSO - 78401-78407 (odd numbers) 332010-332014 DMSO - 78418-78426 (even numbers) TSO - 72402-72408 (random) PTSO - 63409-63413 DMFLO - 78419-78427 (odd numbers)	DMFO - 78408-78417 (even numbers) TSO - 72400-72413 (random) PTSO - 63404-63408 TSO - 72414-72418 DMFLO - 78409-78417 (odd numbers)
Vehicle length:	Driving cars - 77ft 10¾in (23.74m) Intermediate cars - 75ft 11in (23.14m)	Driving cars - 77ft 10¾in (23.74m) Intermediate cars - 75ft 11in (23.14m)
Height:	12ft 1½in (3.70m)	12ft 1½in (3.70m)
Width:	9ft 1in (2.75m)	9ft 1in (2.75m)
Seating:	332001-332004 - Total - 26F/148S DMFO - 26F TSO - 56S PTSOL - 44S DMSO - 48S 332010-332014 - Total - 14F/148S DMSO - 48S TSO - 56S PTSOL - 44S DMFLO - 14F	332005-332007 - Total - 26F/204S DMFO - 26F TSO - 56S PTSOL - 44S TSO - 56S DMSO - 48S 332008-332009 - Total - 14F/204S DMSO - 48S TSO - 56S PTSOL - 44S TSO - 56S DMFLO - 14F
Internal layout:	2+1F/2+2S	2+1F/2+2S
Gangway:	Within set	Within set
Toilets:	PTSOL + DMFLO - 1	PTSOL + DMFLO- 1
Weight:	Total - 179 tonnes (all types) DMFO - 48.8 tonnes TSO - 35.8 tonnes PTSO - 45.6 tonnes DMSO - 48.8 tonnes DMFLO - 48.8 tonnes	Total - 214.8 tonnes DMSO - 48.8 tonnes TSO - 35.8 tonnes PTSO - 45.6 tonnes TSO - 35.8 tonnes DMFLO - 48.8 tonnes
Brake type:	Air (regenerative)	Air (regenerative)
Bogie type:	CAF	CAF
Power collection:	25kV ac overhead	25kV ac overhead
Traction motor type:	4 x Siemens	4 x Siemens
Horsepower:	1,877hp (1,400kW)	1,877hp (1,400kW)
Max speed:	100mph (161km/h)	100mph (161km/h)
Coupling type:	Outer - Scharfenberg, Inner - Semi-auto	Outer - Scharfenberg, Inner - Semi-auto
Multiple restriction:	Within class and 333	Within class and 333
Door type:	Bi-parting sliding plug	Bi-parting sliding plug
Owner:	BAA	BAA
Operator:	Heathrow Express	Heathrow Express

Right Top: *The opening of a new electrified railway linking central London with Heathrow Airport in 1997 saw British Airports Authority operate a new Airport Express service, for which a fleet of 14 Siemens/CAF units were ordered. Originally they were delivered to the new depot facility at Old Oak Common as three-car sets, with a service starting between Paddington and Airport Junction using the three-car trains. Soon extra vehicles were delivered and currently nine four-car and five five-car trains are operated. Passenger seating is in the 2+2 mode for standard and 2+1 for first. Extra luggage stacks are provided to cope with high levels of luggage on the Airport route. Formed as a three-car set, No. 332008 is seen at the temporary Airport Junction station in January 1998.* CJM

Right Middle: *Class 332 standard (or express) class interior showing the original design of moquette; recently sets have been fully refurbished by Railcare at their Wolverton Works.* CJM

Below: *Due to the high profile of the Heathrow route, the operators usually have a full train length advertising campaign in operation, seeing most of the fleet given pictogram vinyl branding to the core Heathrow livery. In 2013 the contract was with Vodafone, whose livery is seen completely covering the first class driving car of set No. 332001 at Paddington, with smaller Vodafone branding applied to the rest of the set.* Antony Christie

Class 333

Number range:	333001-333016
Introduced:	2000, TSO added 2002-03
Built by:	Siemens Germany and CAF Spain
Formation:	DMSO(A)+PTSO+TSO+DMSO(B)
Vehicle numbers:	DMSO(A) - 78451-78481 (odd numbers) PTSO - 74461-74476 TSO - 74477-74492 DMSO(B) - 78452-78482 (even numbers)
Vehicle length:	DMSO - 77ft 10¾in (23.74m) PTSO/TSO - 75ft 11in (23.14m)
Height:	12ft 1½in (3.70m)
Width:	9ft 0¼in (2.75m)
Seating:	Total - 353S + 6 tip up DMSO(A) - 90S PTSO - 73S + 6 tip up TSO - 100S DMSO(B) - 90S
Internal layout:	2+3
Gangway:	Within set
Toilets:	PTSO - 1
Weight:	Total - 182.2 tonnes DMS(A) - 50.0 tonnes PTS - 46.7 tonnes TS - 38.5 tonnes DMS(B) - 50.0 tonnes
Brake type:	Air
Bogie type:	CAF
Power collection:	25kV ac overhead
Traction motor type:	4 x Siemens
Horsepower:	1,877hp (1,400kW)
Max speed:	100mph (161km/h)
Coupling type:	Outer - Scharfenberg, Inner - Bar
Multiple restriction:	Within class and 332
Door type:	Bi-parting sliding plug
Construction:	Steel
Owner:	Angel Trains

Below: *In 1999 authorisation was given for the purchase of new electric multiple units to operate West Yorkshire PTE services in the Leeds-Skipton area. Various builders were invited to tender with the winning bid coming from Siemens Transportation in Germany to build a fleet of 16 three-car sets based on the Heathrow Express Class 332s. Classified as 333 these sets were high-density 3+2 seating and did not have a first class area. Soon after introduction, passenger growth on the Aire Valley route increased and soon a fleet of 16 Trailer Standard Open vehicles was ordered to insert one in each set, thus increasing passenger carrying to 353 per four-car set. When originally delivered sets were painted in West Yorkshire PTE dark red, but today with the service operated by Northern Rail their branding is now applied to a modified version of WYPTE red. Set No. 333007 is seen at Ilkley with its DMSO(A) nearest the camera on 27 October 2012. All 64 Class 333 vehicles are based at Leeds Neville Hill depot. In addition to operating the Aire Valley services, the '333s' can occasionally be seen on the Leeds-Doncaster route.* Antony Christie

Class 334

Number range:	334001-334040
Introduced:	1999-2002
Built by:	Alstom, Washwood Heath
Formation:	DMSO(A)+PTSO+DMSO(B)
Vehicle numbers:	DMSO(A) - 64101-64140 PTSO - 74301-74340 DMSO(B) - 65101-65140
Vehicle length:	DMSO(A) - 69ft 0¾in (21.05m) PTSO - 65ft 4¼in (19.92m) DMSO(B) - 69ft 0¾in (21.05m)
Height:	12ft 3in (3.73m)
Width:	9ft 2¾in (2.81m)
Seating:	Total - 183S DMSO(A) - 64S PTSO - 55S DMSO(B) - 64S
Internal layout:	DMSO 2+2, PTSO 2+3
Gangway:	Within set
Toilets:	PTSO - 1
Weight:	Total - 124.6 tonnes DMSO(A) - 42.6 tonnes PTSO - 39.4 tonnes DMSO(B) - 42.6 tonnes
Brake type:	Air (regenerative)
Bogie type:	Alstom DMSO - LTB3, PTSO - TBP3
Power collection:	25kV ac overhead
Traction motor type:	4 x Alstom Onix
Horsepower:	1,448hp (1,080kW)
Max speed:	90mph (145km/h)
Coupling type:	Outer - Tightlock, Inner - Bar
Multiple restriction:	Within class only
Door type:	Bi-parting sliding plug
Construction:	Steel
Owner:	Eversholt

Below: *The first fleet of electric multiple units ordered by ScotRail under privatisation was awarded to Alstom, being a fleet of 40 three-car 'Juniper' platform sets, using the Alstom 'Onix' traction system. Built at the Alstom Washwood Heath plant in Birmingham the sets were delivered between 1999-2002 and saw a very protracted delivery time scale due to many technical issues. The sets are allocated to the main Scottish electric shed at Shields near Glasgow and were originally deployed on the Ayrshire route but by 2013 were more usually used on the North Clyde and Argyle lines. As delivered sets were painted in carmine and cream, but following refurbishment in recent times the new standard Scottish Railway livery of blue off-set by white Saltire branding has been applied. Each Class 334 seats 183 passengers in a mix of 2+2 and 2+3 styles. No first class is provided. Set No. 334006 is seen in the bay platform at Ayr.* CJM

Class 350 'Desiro'

Class	350/1	350/2
Number range:	350101 - 350130	350231-3502673
Introduced:	2004-05	2008-09
Built by:	Siemens - Vienna, Austria and Duewag, Germany	Siemens - Duewag, Germany
Formation:	DMSO(A)+TCO+PTSO+DMSO(B)	DMSO(A)+TCO+PTSO+DMSO(B)
Vehicle numbers:	DMSO(A) - 63761-63790 TCO - 66811-66840 PTSO - 66861-66890 DMSO(B) - 63711-63740	DMSO(A) - 61431-61467 TCO - 65231-65267 PTSO - 67531-67567 DMSO(B) - 61531-61567
Vehicle length:	66ft 9in (20.34m)	66ft 9in (20.34m)
Height:	12ft 1½in (3.69m)	12ft 1½in (3.69m)
Width:	9ft 2in (2.79m)	9ft 2in (2.79m)
Seating:	Total - 24F/200S + 9 tip up DMSO(A) - 60S TCO - 24F/32S PTSO - 48S + 9 tip up DMSO(B) - 60S	Total - 24F/243S + 9 tip up DMSO(A) - 70S TCO - 24F/42S PTSO - 61S + 9 tip up DMSO(B) - 70S
Internal layout:	2+2	2+3
Gangway:	Throughout	Throughout
Toilets:	TCO, PTSO - 1	TCO, PTSO - 1
Weight:	Total - 179.3 tonnes DMSO(A) - 48.7 tonnes TCO -36.2 tonnes PTSO - 45.2 tonnes DMSO(B) - 49.2 tonnes	Total - 166.1 tonnes DMSO(A) - 43.7 tonnes TCO - 35.3 tonnes PTSO - 42.9 tonnes DMSO(B) - 44.2 tonnes
Brake type:	Air (regenerative)	Air (regenerative)
Bogie type:	SGP SF5000	SGB SF5000
Power collection:	25kV ac overhead & 750V dc third rail	25kV ac overhead & 750V dc third rail
Traction motor type:	4 x Siemens 1TB2016-0GB02	4 x Siemens 1TB2016-0GB02
Horsepower:	1,341hp (1,000kW)	1,341hp (1,000kW)
Max speed:	110mph (177km/h)	110mph (177km/h)
Coupling type:	Outer - Dellner 12, Inner - Bar	Outer - Dellner 12, Inner - Bar
Multiple restriction:	Within class	Within class
Door type:	Bi-parting sliding plug	Bi-parting sliding plug
Construction:	Aluminium	Aluminium
Owner:	Angel Trains	Porterbrook
Operator:	London Midland	London Midland
Special features:	Air conditioned, CCTV, PIS	Air conditioned, CCTV, PIS

Left: *The Siemens 'Desiro' platform for EMUs has become a modern standard of reliability and quality. The original fleet of 30 sets (350/1) was intended for South West Trains as Class 450/2s, but were cancelled and built for a joint Silverlink/Central Trains operation on the West Coast route. The fully gangwayed four-car sets, now with a top speed of 110mph (177km/h), are operated by London Midland, based at purpose-built maintenance facilities at Northampton. Set No. 350110 in as delivered grey and blue is seen on the Siemens test track at Wildenrath in Germany.* CJM

350/3	350/4
350301-350310	350401-350410
2013-14	2013-14
Siemens - Duewag, Germany	Siemens - Duewag, Germany
DMSO(A)+TCO+PTSO+DMSO(B)	DMSO(A)+TCO+PTSO+DMSO(B)
DMSO(A) - 60141-60150	DMSO(A) - 60691-60700
TCO - 60511-60520	TCO - 60901-60910
PTSO - 60651-60660	PTSO - 60941-60950
DMSO(B) - 60151-60160	DMSO(B) - 60671-60674
66ft 9in (20.34m)	66ft 9in (20.34m)
12ft 1½in (3.69m)	12ft 1½in (3.69m)
9ft 2in (2.79m)	9ft 2in (2.79m)
Total - 19F/191S	Total - 19F/179S
DMSO(A) -	DMSO(A)
TCO -	TCO -
PTSO -	PTSO -
DMSO(B) -	DMSO(B)
2+2	2+2
Throughout	Throughout
TCO, PTSO - 1	TCO, PTSO - 1
Total - ?	Total - ?
DMSO(A) - ?	DMSO(A) - ?
TCO - ?	TCO - ?
PTSO - ?	PTSO - ?
DMSO(B) - ?	DMSO(B) - ?
Air (regenerative)	Air (regenerative)
SGB SF5000	SGB SF5000
25kV ac overhead	25kV ac overhead
4 x Siemens 1TB2016-0GB02	4 x Siemens 1TB2016-0GB02
1,341hp (1,000kW)	1,341hp (1,000kW)
100mph (161km/h)	100mph (161km/h)
Outer - Dellner 12,	Outer - Dellner 12,
Inner - Bar	Inner - Bar
Within class	Within class
Bi-parting sliding plug	Bi-parting sliding plug
Aluminium	Aluminium
Angel	Angel
First TransPennine	London Midland
Air conditioned, CCTV, PIS	Air conditioned, CCTV, PIS
On order	On order

Right: *A batch of 37 Class 350/2s soon followed off the German production line but with slightly revised interior seating. These sets are recognisable from the earlier Class 350/1 sets by having the top half of the gangway door painted black. Members of Class 350/1 and 350/2 are designed for dual power collection, either 750V dc third rail or 25kV ac overhead. All sets are now painted in London Midland livery. At the time of going to press two new sub classes of '350' were under construction, 10 sets for London Midland (350301-310) and 10 sets for First TransPennine Express (350401-410).* CJM

Class 357 'Electrostar'

Class:	357/0	357/2
Number range:	357001-357046	357201-357228
Introduced:	1999-2001	2001-02
Built by:	Adtranz Derby	Adtranz/Bombardier Derby
Formation:	DMSO(A)+MSO+PTSO+DMSO(B)	DMSO(A)+MSO+PTSO+DMSO(B)
Vehicle numbers:	DMSO(A) - 67651-67696 MSO - 74151-74196 PTSO - 74051-74096 DMSO(B) - 67751-67796	DMSO(A) - 68601-68628 MSO - 74701-74728 PTSO - 74601-74628 DMSO(B) - 68701-68728
Vehicle length:	DMSO(A), DMSO(B) - 68ft 1in (20.75m) PTSO, MSO - 65ft 11½in (20.10m)	DMSO(A), DMSO(B) - 68ft 1in (20.75m) PTSO, MSO - 65ft 11½in (20.10m)
Height:	12ft 4½in (3.77m)	12ft 4½in (3.78m)
Width:	9ft 2¼in (2.80m)	9ft 2¼in (2.80m)
Seating:	Total - 278S + 4 tip up DMSO(A) - 71S MSO - 78S PTSO - 58S + 4 tip up DMSO(B) - 71S	Total - 278S + 4 tip up DMSO(A) - 71S MSO - 78S PTSO - 58S + 4 tip up DMSO(B) - 71S
Internal layout:	2+3	2+3
Gangway:	Within set	Within set
Toilets:	PTSOL - 1	PTSOL - 1
Weight:	Total - 157.6 tonnes DMSO(A) - 40.7 tonnes MSO - 36.7 tonnes PTSO - 39.5 tonnes DMSO(B) - 40.7 tonnes	Total - 157.6 tonnes DMSO(A) - 40.7 tonnes MSO - 36.7 tonnes PTSO - 39.5 tonnes DMSO(B) - 40.7 tonnes
Brake type:	Air (rheostatic/regenerative)	Air (rheostatic/regenerative)
Bogie type:	Power - Adtranz P3-25 Trailer - Adtranz T3-25	Power - Adtranz P3-25 Trailer - Adtranz T3-25
Power collection:	25kV ac overhead (750v dc equipped)	25kV ac overhead (750v dc equipped)
Traction motor type:	6 x Adtranz (250kW)	6 x Adtranz (250kW)
Output:	2,010hp (1,500kW)	2,010hp (1,500kW)
Max speed:	100mph (161km/h)	100mph (161km/h)
Coupling type:	Outer - Tightlock, Inner - Bar	Outer - Tightlock, Inner - Bar
Total sets in service:	46	28
Multiple restriction:	Within class only	Within class only
Door type:	Bi-parting sliding plug	Bi-parting sliding plug
Owner:	Porterbrook	Angel Trains
Operator:	c2c	c2c

Below: *Under privatisation, the modernisation of the London, Tilbury &Southend (LT&S) line radiating from Fenchurch Street saw two fleets of Class 357 'Electrostar' built by Adtranz/Bombardier at their Derby plant. The sets had the then standard front end styling the company adopted for all EMU and DMU non-gangwayed stock. The first 46 sets, owned by Porterbrook, were introduced in 1999-2001, with a follow-on order for 28 near identical sets emerging in 2001-02 and owned by Angel Trains. The all standard class sets seat 278 in the 2+3 style and all sets are based at East Ham depot. When delivered the sets were painted in Prism Rail mauve with c2c branding; Prism Rail was later purchased by National Express. Set No. 357044 is seen from its DMSO(A) end at Stratford.* CJM

Above: *At present the LT&S route is operated under the c2c name by National Express, but this franchise is due to expire in September 2014 with major changes to route and service provision. Today all sets carry the National Express white livery with deep grey/blue doors. All '357s' are fitted with Tightlock couplers and members of both sub classes can operate together. On 8 December 2010, set No. 357203, one of the Angel Trains owned sets, arrives at Barking.* CJM

Below: *Bombardier, c2c and the Class 357 lease owners made huge investment in summer 2007 when full regenerative braking was introduced on the Class 357 fleet, returning power to the overhead power line during deceleration. To mark the achievement, set No. 357010 was painted in 'Green Train' livery and is seen at Fenchurch Street on 4 June 2007.* CJM

Class 360 'Desiro'

Class:	360/0	360/2
Number range:	360101-360121	360201-360205
Introduced:	2002-03	2004-06
Built by:	Siemens Transportation - Vienna, Austria and Duewag, Germany	Siemens Transportation - Duewag, Germany
Formation:	DMCO(A)+PTSO+TSO+DMCO(B)	DMSO(A)+PTSO+TSO(A)+TSO(B)+DMSO(B)
Vehicle numbers:	DMCO(A) - 65551-65571 PTSO - 72551-72571 TSO - 74551-74571 DMCO(A) - 68551-68571	DMSO(A) - 78431-78435 PTSO - 63421-63425 TSO(A) - 72431-72435 TSO(B) - 72421-72425 DMSO(B) - 78441-78445
Vehicle length:	66ft 9in (20.34m)	66ft 9in (20.34m)
Height:	12ft 1½in (3.95m)	12ft 1½in (3.95m)
Width:	9ft 2in (2.79m)	9ft 2in (2.79m)
Seating:	Total - 16F/256S + 9 tip up DMCO(A) - 8F/59S PTSO - 60S + 9 tip up TSO - 78S DMCO(A) - 8F/59S	Total - 333S + 9 tip up DMSO(A) - 63S PTSO - 59S + 9 tip up TSO(A) - 74S TSO(B) - 74S DMSO(B) - 63S
Internal layout:	2+2F/2+2 & 2+3S	2+3
Gangway:	Within set only	Within set only
Toilets:	PTOS - 1	PTOS - 1
Weight:	Total - 168 tonnes DMCO(A) - 45 tonnes PTSO - 43 tonnes TSO - 35 tonnes DMCO(B) - 45 tonnes	Total - 202.9 tonnes DMSO(A) - 44.8 tonnes PTSO - 44.2 tonnes TSO(A) - 35.4 tonnes TSO(B) - 34.1 tonnes DMSO(B) - 44.4 tonnes
Brake type:	Air regenerative	Air regenerative
Bogie type:	SGP SF5000	SGP SF5000
Power collection:	25kV ac overhead	25kV ac overhead
Traction motor type:	1TB2016 - 0GB02 three phase	1TB2016 - 0GB02 three phase
Output:	1,341hp (1,000kW)	1,341hp (1,000kW)
Max speed:	100mph (161km/h)	100mph (161km/h)
Coupling type:	Outer - Dellner 12, Inner - Semi-auto	Outer - Dellner 12, Inner - Semi-auto
Multiple restriction:	Within sub class	Within sub class
Door type:	Bi-parting sliding plug	Bi-parting sliding plug
Construction:	Aluminium	Aluminium
Owner:	Angel Trains	British Airports Authority
Special features:	Air conditioning, PIS	Air conditioning, PIS, GW ATP
Notes:		360201-204 were original demonstrator 'Desiro' sets 360001-004. Rebuilt without end gangways for Heathrow Connect. Additional TSO(B) cars added in 2006-07, 360205 delivered as 5-car

Left: *The first of the true Siemens 'Desiro' sets emerged in 2002 for First Great Eastern, when a fleet of 21 four-car outer suburban sets emerged, allocated to Ilford. These non-gangway fitted sets seated 16 first and 256 standard class passengers in a mix of 2+2 and 2+3 seating. The sets are fully air conditioned with a top speed of 100mph (161km/h). Assembled in aluminium, the sets use a Siemens three-phase traction package which has proved very reliable. Set No. 360105 is seen on the Siemens test track in Wildenrath, Germany, prior to delivery.* CJM

Right Top: *In addition to the first production 'Desiro' units, Angel Trains ordered four four-car test sets fitted with end gangways for development use. All sets operated on the Wildenrath test track and a couple were delivered to the UK for training purposes. After their development use was over the four sets were totally gutted and rebuilt by Siemens into the first four of the Class 360/2 Heathrow Connect sets, with new aluminium front ends changing the shape of the original train. Painted in Siemens white and turquoise livery, set 360003 is seen stabled next to a NSE 4VEP unit at the Wildenrath test track in April 2002.* CJM

Right Middle: *By November 2004 the four original Class 360/0 sets had been rebuilt, originally operating as four-car sets until a fifth intermediate TSO was constructed new. Four-car set No. 360203 is seen under test at Wildenrath painted in the original Heathrow Connect livery. The set is seen from its DMSO(B) end.* CJM

Below: *Soon after delivery, passenger numbers demanded an extra vehicle be added to the sets, giving a passenger total of 333 per train. In addition a new five-car set (360205) was built, illustrated at Southall painted in Heathrow Express Terminal 4 'shuttle' livery. All 360/2s are based at Old Oak Common Heathrow Express depot.* Antony Christie

Class 365 'Networker Express'

Number range:	365501-365541
Introduced:	1994-1995
Built by:	ABB/Adtranz York
Formation:	DMCO(A)+TSO+PTSO+DMSO(B)
Vehicle numbers:	DMCO(A) - 65894-65934 TSOL - 72241-72321 (odd numbers) PTSOL - 72240-72320 (even numbers) DMCO(B) - 65935-65975
Vehicle length:	DMCO - 68ft 6½in (20.89m) TSO/PTSO - 65ft 9¾in (20.06m)
Height:	12ft 4½in (3.77m)
Width:	9ft 2½in (2.81m)
Seating:	Total: 24F/244S (245S on sets 365517-365541) DMCO(A) - 12F/56S TSO - 64S (65S on sets 365517-365541) PTSO - 68S DMCO - 12F/56S
Internal layout:	2+2F, 2+2S
Gangway:	Within unit only
Toilets:	TSO, PTSO - 1
Weight:	Total: 150.9 tonnes DMCO(A) - 41.7 tonnes TSOL - 32.9 tonnes PTSOL - 34.6 tonnes DMCO(B) - 41.7 tonnes
Brake type:	Air (rheostatic/regenerative)
Bogie type:	Powered: Adtranz P3-16 Trailer: Adtranz T3-16
Power collection:	Originally: 365501-365516 750V dc third rail 365517-365541 25Kv ac overhead Modified: 25kV ac overhead
Traction motor type:	4 x GEC G354CX of 210hp (157kW)
Horsepower:	1,680hp (1,256kW)
Max speed:	100mph (161km/h)
Coupling type:	Outer - Tightlock, Inner - Semi auto
Multiple restriction:	Within class only
Door type:	Bi-parting sliding plug
Construction:	Aluminium alloy
Owner:	Eversholt

Below: *Following on from the Network Southeast 'Networker' project came 41 main line 'Networker Express' sets, to the same body profile as the standard 'Networker' but fitted with an outer suburban interior including first class seating in the driving cars. Under the original order the first 16 sets (365501-365516) were built for NSE SouthEastern use and were later used by Connex Southeast, and were fitted for dc only operation, no pantograph being installed. The remainder of the fleet (365517-365541) were built for Great Northern line use, which under privatisation became West Anglia Great Northern, and were fitted for only 25kV ac overhead operation. As built the sets had a standard 'Networker' front end profile, but in later years this was replaced with a new design, giving the appearance of a 'happy train'. With original front profile, dc set No. 365505 is seen at Borough Green during traction testing. Note the first class seating area directly behind the driving cab; this was found on both end vehicles.* CJM

Above: *One of the former dc sets, No. 365514, now sporting a new 'happy' front end and First Capital Connect NSE livery, is seen at Peterborough working a King's Cross-Peterborough service.* CJM

Right: *Designed for outer-suburban use, the Class 365s were built with low-density 2+2 seating in both standard and first class areas. This view shows the standard class seating arrangement.* CJM

Below: *All the '365s' are based at Hornsey and now all sport First Capital Connect livery, as shown on set No. 365529 at the depot in 2009.* CJM

Class 370 - APT

Details for half train formation

Number range:	370001-370006 + spare vehicles
Alpha code:	APT
Introduced:	1978-79
Built by:	BREL Derby
Formation:	DTS+TS+TRSB+TU+TF+TBF+M
Vehicle numbers:	DTS - 48101-48107 TS - 48201-48206 TRSB - 48401-48406 TU - 48301 -48306 TF - 48501-48506 TBF - 48601-48607 M - 49001-49007
Set length:	482ft 0½in (137.78m)
Vehicle length:	DTS - 70ft 4in (21.44m) M - 66ft 9in (20.4m) TS, TRSB, TU, TF, TBF - 70ft 4in (21.44m)
Height:	11ft 6in (3.51m)
Width:	8ft 11in (2.72m)
Seating:	Total - 72F/152S/43U DTS - 52S TS - 72S TRSB - 28S TU - 43U (unclassified) TF - 47F TBF - 25F M - 0
Internal layout:	First 2+1, Standard 2+2
Gangway:	Throughout from DTS inner end
Weight:	Total - 232.3 tons DTS - 33.7 tonnes TS - 24 tonnes TRSB - 26.75 tonnes TU - 24.15 tonnes TF - 24.3 tonnes TBF - 31.9 tonnes M -67.5 tonnes
Brake type:	Air/hydrokinetic
Bogie type:	Trailer self standing - BT12 Trailer articulated - BT11 Power - BP17a
Power collection:	25kV ac overhead
Traction motor type:	4 x Asea LJMA410F
Horsepower:	4,000hp (2,983kW)
Max speed:	125mph (201km/h)
Coupling type:	Inner - bar Outer - drop head buck-eye, schackle
Multiple restriction:	Within class, no multiple provision
Door type:	Sliding plug
Special features:	Tilting

Above: *The design and early specification for the passenger carrying Advanced Passenger Train (APT) started in 1973 under the control of the Derby based Chief Mechanical & Electrical Engineering Department. The electrically powered APT or Class 370 project was designed for use on the West Coast Main Line. Although separate from the APT-E gas turbine project, a huge amount of association between the two teams prevailed, including testing equipment and assisting in design principles. Authorised for assembly in 1974, three APT train sets were built at Derby, formed of six half train sets. Each half train was formed of a driving trailer, five intermediate trailers and a motor car. The motor cars were built with a steel body at Derby Locomotive Works, while the aluminium passenger cars were built at Derby Litchurch Lane. The testing of the train was conducted from the Railway Technical Centre, also in Derby. To allow greater speeds on the twisting West Coast route a full tilt system was installed. Although construction started in 1974 it was not until 1979 that powered main line testing commenced, following a long period of industrial action. Passenger testing commenced in April 1980, but was then further delayed by technical issues, not resuming passenger operation until December 1981. The train continued to operate on an on-off basis until December 1984 when it was withdrawn from test service, with most vehicles sadly broken up. One set is preserved at Crewe. The first half train, painted in its original InterCity livery, formed with just three passenger coaches and motor car, is seen in the yard at the Railway Technical Centre, Derby.* CJM

Right Middle: *Once authorised for passenger carrying, the Class 370, marshalled in various formations, operated 'shadow' services on the Euston-Preston-Carlisle-Glasgow corridor and was well liked by the passengers who chose to travel on it. Painted in the later InterCity APT livery, set No. 370006, with its power car as the third vehicle from the end, awaits departure from Preston on 23 March 1984 forming the 16.35 Euston to Glasgow Central. The leading DTS seated 52 standard class passengers in the 2+2 style.* Steve Carter

Right Below: *In test and passenger service the Class 370 set some outstanding time and speed records. During testing in December 1979 a speed of 162.2mph (261km/h) was recorded, while in passenger service on 7 December 1981 a set covered the 401 miles between Glasgow and Euston in just 4hr 13min, an average of 95.1mph. Towards the end of its operating days two shorter half sets were formed to test tilt systems, mainly operating over the twisting and undulating northern end of the West Coast route. Here, half set No. 390003 leads another half set down Shap incline on 14 October 1984 on a Carlisle to Crewe test run. Note the full tilt of the leading section.* Steve Carter

Class 373 'Eurostar'

Class:	373/0	373/2
Number range:	373001-022/373101-108/373201-232+ 3999 (spare PC)	373301-373314
Introduced:	1992-96	1996
Built by:	GEC Alstom	GEC Alstom
Formation:	DM+MS+TS+TS+TS+TS+TBK+TF+TF+TBF	DM+MS+TS+TS+TS+TBK+TF+TBF
Set length:	1,291ft 8in (393.72m)	1,046ft 4in (318.92m)
Vehicle length:	DM - 72ft 8in (22.15m) MS - 71ft 8in (21.84m) TS, TBK, TF, TBF - 61ft 4in (18.69m)	DM - 72ft 8in (22.15m) MS - 71ft 8in (21.84m) TS, TBK, TF, TBF - 61ft 4in (18.69m)
Height:	12ft 4½in (3.77m)	12ft 4½in (3.77m)
Width:	9ft 3in (2.82m)	9ft 3in (2.82m)
Seating:	Total - 103F/280S (half train) DM - 0, MS - 48S, TS - 58S, TS - 58S TS - 58S, TS - 58S, TBK - 0, TF - 39F TF - 39F, TBF - 25F	Total - 57F/232S DM - 0, MS - 48S, MS - 48S, TS - 58S TS - 58S, TS - 58S, TBK - 0, TF - 39F, TBF - 18F
Internal layout:	2+1F, 2+2S	2+1F, 2+2S
Gangway:	Within set and at half set end	Within set and at half set end
Toilets:	MS - 2, TBF - 1, TF - 1, TS - 1 or 2	MS - 1, TBF - 1, TF - 1, TS - 1 or 2
Weight:	Total - 816.1 tonnes DM - 68.5 tonnes MS - 44.6 tonnes TS - 28.1-29.7 tonnes TBK - 31.1 tonnes TF - 29.6 tonnes TBF - 39.4 tonnes	Total - 682.2 tonnes DM - 68.5 tonnes MS - 44.6 tonnes TS - 28.1-29.7 tonnes TBK - 31.1 tonnes TF - 29.6 tonnes TBF - 39.4 tonnes
Brake type:	Air	Air
Power collection:	25kV ac overhead, 3kV dc overhead¤ *	25kV ac overhead
Horsepower:	25kV ac operation - 16,400hp (12,240kW) 3kV dc operation - 7,368hp (5,000kW)	25kV ac operation - 16,400hp (12,240kW)
Max speed:	25kV ac operation 186mph (300km/h)	25kV ac operation 186mph (300km/h)
Coupling type:	Outer - Scharfenberg, Inner - Bar	Outer - Scharfenberg, Inner - Bar
Multiple restriction:	Not permitted	Not permitted
Door type:	Single-leaf sliding plug	Single-leaf sliding plug
Special features:	TVM430, CT equipment	TVM430, CT equipment
Total sets in traffic:	24 half sets	14 half sets used in mainland Europe
Construction:	Steel	Steel
Owner:	Eurostar UK, SNCF, SNCB	Eurostar UK
Operator:	Eurostar UK, SNCF, SNCB	SNCF
Notes:	¤ isolated	

* Sets 3201-04/07-10/15/16/23-30 are fitted with French 1,500V overhead equipment to allow South of France running.

\+ Sets 373203/04/25/26/27/28 modified for domestic French operation only and are now not part of Eurostar fleet.

Left: *With the authorisation to build the Channel Tunnel came orders for specialist trains to operate from London to mainland Europe. Trains based on the French TGV were constructed in both France and the UK, which emerged between 1992-96 as 'Eurostar' sets. Two types of train were built: those for London-Paris/Brussels operations were 20-car sets and those intended for North of London (NoL) to Europe services were formed of 16 cars. The NoL sets are now operated in mainland Europe as are some of the original 'Eurostar' sets due to smaller than expected passenger growth. The first of the Belgium sets, No. (37)3101, is seen outside North Pole depot in West London.* CJM

Above: *When originally launched in 1993 the 'Eurostar' sets used London Waterloo as their London terminal, requiring third rail power systems to be installed, further complicating these otherwise already complex trains. Third rail power was used from North Pole depot to Waterloo and as far as the Channel Tunnel. After opening of High Speed One in the UK and the building of new purpose built facilities at St Pancras, the sets were upgraded for overhead power collection only. New depot facilities were also built at Temple Mills. In the days of third rail dc operation, set No. (37)3009 passes Kensington Olympia en route from North Pole to Waterloo.* CJM

Below: *In 2000 five of the spare North of London (Class 373/3) sets were hired to Great North Eastern Railway for operation between London King's Cross and Leeds/York. Three of the sets were repainted into full GNER livery, while the other two retained unbranded 'Eurostar' white and yellow. A number of operating restrictions were imposed by Network Rail; limitation in power supply allowed only one set to operate at a time over the Hertford Loop. They could not operate north of York due to gauging issues, and in places their top speed was restricted to 110mph (177km/h). Their lease to GNER ended in December 2005 when all returned to Eurostar and stored; they are now operating in mainland Europe.* CJM

Class 375 'Electrostar'

Class:	375/3	375/6	375/7
Number range:	375301-375310	375601-375630	375701-375715
Introduced:	2001-02	1999-2001	2001-02
Built by:	Bombardier Derby	Adtranz/Bombardier Derby	Bombardier Derby
Formation:	DMCO (A)+TSO+DMCO(B)	DMCO(A)+MSO+ PTSO+DMCO(B)	DMCO(A)+MSO+ TSO+DMCO(B)
Vehicle numbers:	DMCO(A) - 67921-67930 TSO - 74351-74360 DMCO(B) - 67931-67940	DMCO(A) - 67801-67830 MSO - 74251-74280 PTSO - 74201-74230 DMCO(B) - 67851-67880	DMCO(A) - 67831-67845 MSO - 74281-74295 TSO - 74231-74245 DMCO(B) - 67881-67895
Vehicle length:	DMCO - 66ft 11in (20.40m) TSO - 65ft 6in (19.99m)	DMCO - 66ft 11in (20.40m) MSO, PTSO - 65ft 6in (19.99m)	DMCO - 66ft 11in (20.40m) MSO, TSO - 65ft 6in (19.99m)
Height:	12ft 4in (3.78m)	12ft 4in (3.78m)	12ft 4in (3.78m)
Width:	9ft 2in (2.80m)	9ft 2in (2.80m)	9ft 2in (2.80m)
Seating:	Total - 24F/152S DMCO(A) - 12F/48S TSO - 56S DMS(B) - 12F/48S	Total - 24F/218S DMCO(A) - 12F/48S MSO - 66S PTSO - 56S DMCO(B) - 12F/48S	Total - 24F/218S DMCO(A) - 12F/48S MSO - 66S TSO - 56S DMCO(B) - 12F/48S
Internal layout:	2+2	2+2	2+2
Gangway:	Throughout	Throughout	Throughout
Toilets:	TSO - 1	PTSO, MSO - 1	TSO, MSO - 1
Weight:	Total - 124.1 tonnes DMCO(A) - 43.8 tonnes TSO - 36.5 tonnes DMCO(B) - 43.8 tonnes	Total - 173.6 tonnes DMCO(A) - 46.2 tonnes MSO - 40.5 tonnes PTSO - 40.7 tonnes DMCO(B) - 46.2 tonnes	Total - 158.1 tonnes DMCO(A) - 43.8 tonnes MSO - 36.4 tonnes TSO - 34.1 tonnes DMCO(B) - 43.8 tonnes
Brake type:	Air, regenerative	Air, regenerative	Air, regenerative
Bogie type:	Power - Adtranz P3-25 Trailer - Adtranz T3-25	Power - Adtranz P3-25 Trailer - Adtranz T3-25	Power - Adtranz P3-25 Trailer - Adtranz T3-25
Power collection:	750V dc third rail	750V dc third rail, and 25kV ac overhead	750V dc third rail
Traction motor type:	4 x Adtranz	6 x Adtranz	6 x Adtranz
Output:	1,341hp (1,000kW)	2,012hp (1,500kW)	2,012hp (1,500kW)
Max speed:	100mph (161km/h)	100mph (161km/h)	100mph (161km/h)
Coupling type:	Originally: Tightlock Modified: Dellner 12, Inner - Bar	Originally: Tightlock Outer - Dellner 12, Inner - Bar	Originally: Tightlock Outer - Dellner 12, Inner - Bar
Multiple restriction:	Class 375 - 377	Class 375 - 377	Class 375 - 377
Door type:	Bi-parting sliding plug	Bi-parting sliding plug	Bi-parting sliding plug
Total sets in traffic:	10	30	15
Construction:	Aluminium, steel cabs	Aluminium, steel cabs	Aluminium, steel cabs
Owner:	Eversholt	Eversholt	Eversholt
Operator:	SouthEastern	SouthEastern	SouthEastern

Left: *All Class 375s were constructed at the Adtranz/Bombardier plant at Derby Litchurch Lane, with construction running from 1999 to 2004. In unbranded white livery, Class 375/3 No. 375304, one of the 10 three-car sets, is seen in the works yard awaiting commissioning. These three-car sets seat 24 first and 152 standard class passengers. When built the Class 375s were fitted with Tightlock couplings, but these were later changed to the more universal Dellner type. This illustration shows the Tightlock type.* CJM

375/8	375/9
375801-375830	375901-375927
2003-04	2003-04
Bombardier Derby	Bombardier Derby
DMCO(A)+MSO+ TSO+DMCO(B)	DMCO(A)+MSO+ TSO+DMCO(B)
DMCO(A) - 73301-73330 MSO - 79001-79030 TSO - 78201-78230 DMCO(B) - 73701-73730	DMCO(A) - 73331-73357 MSO - 79031-79057 TSO - 79061-79087 DMCO(B) - 73731-73757
DMCO - 66ft 11in (20.40m) MSO, TSO - 65ft 6in (19.99m)	DMCO - 66ft 11in (20.40m) MSO, TSO - 65ft 6in (19.99m)
12ft 4in (3.78m)	12ft 4in (3.78m)
9ft 2in (2.80m)	9ft 2in (2.80m)
Total - 24F/218S DMCO(A) - 12F/48S MSO - 66S TSO - 52S DMCO(B) - 12F/52S	Total - 24F/250S DMCO(A) - 12F/59S MSO - 73S TSO - 59S DMCO(B) - 12F/59S
2+2	2+2, 2+3
Throughout	Throughout
TSO, MSO - 1	TSO, MSO - 1
Total - 162.3 tonnes DMCO(A) - 43.3 tonnes MSO - 39.8 tonnes TSO - 35.9 tonnes DMCO(B) - 43.3 tonnes	Total - 161.9 tonnes DMCO(A) - 43.4 tonnes MSO - 39.3 tonnes TSO - 35.8 tonnes DMCO(B) - 43.4 tonnes
Air, regenerative	Air, regenerative
Power - Bombardier P3-25 Trailer - Bombardier T3-25	Power - Bombardier P3-25 Trailer - Bombardier T3-25
750V dc third rail	750V dc third rail
6 x Adtranz	6 x Adtranz
2,012hp (1,500kW)	2,012hp (1,500kW)
100mph (161km/h)	100mph (161km/h)
Originally: Tightlock Outer - Dellner 12, Inner - Bar	Originally: Tightlock Outer - Dellner 12, Inner - Bar
Class 375 - 377	Class 375 - 377
Bi-parting sliding plug	Bi-parting sliding plug
30	27
Aluminium, steel cabs	Aluminium, steel cabs
Eversholt	Eversholt
SouthEastern	SouthEastern

Below: *The huge post-privatisation modernisation of the former Southern Region rail systems started in 1999 with the ordering of the first on what has become the standard Adtranz/Bombardier UK EMU, the 'Electrostar'. Both the South Eastern and South Central franchises were operated by Connex and a massive order for 'Electrostar' sets was placed in various batches as funding was authorised. The stock destined for South Eastern, which eventually numbered 112 sets in three- and four-car formation, was classified as 375. Today five sub-classes exist all with slight technical detail differences. All sub classes except the Class 375/9 use 2+2 seating throughout, while the 375/9s have a limited number of 3+2 seats to increase capacity on the most heavily loaded routes. All sets are gangwayed throughout and are owned by Eversholt Leasing. The 30 members of Class 375/6 are fitted for dual power collection, 25kV ac overhead and 750V dc third rail. Commissioning of the 'Electrostar' fleet was a protracted affair. In this view we see all white liveried set No. 375603, one of the dual power collection sets, on display at London Victoria.* CJM

Class 375 'Electrostar'

Left: *All Class 375 'Electrostar' sets are based at Ramsgate depot and can be found operating the vast majority of main line services. The sets have a very high availability, are comfortable and well liked by the public and train crew. The base SouthEastern livery of white and grey is off-set by either yellow or blue doors, depending on the time of repaint. Most sets carry dual numbers either side of the front gangway. With later design light clusters, a large headlight and a combined marker/tail light, outer-suburban Class 375/9 set No. 375924 is seen near Arundel while on hire to SouthCentral in 2009.* Chris Wilson

Right: *Each of the four-car sets has one Motor Standard Open (MSO) and one Trailer Standard Open (TSO); the TSO also has housing on the roof for a pantograph. This view shows the TSO vehicle No. 78208 from Class 375/8 No. 375808. It is seen from the pantograph well end. These TSO vehicles house one toilet, the only one on the entire train. Sliding plug doors are fitted which can be controlled by the passenger with crew release and closing.* CJM

Below: *Four-car outer-suburban set No. 375918 is viewed from its DMCO(B) vehicle at Waterloo East. These sets, with a mix of 2+2 and 2+3 seating, accommodate 24 first and 250 standard class passengers.* CJM

Class 376 'Electrostar'

Below Right: *To cater for the high passenger volume of the inner suburban SouthEastern network from London to Kent, 36 high-capacity five-car non-gangwayed 'Electrostar' sets classified as 376 were introduced between 2004-05. These sets have 2+2 seating for 216 with large standing areas, and 116 'perch' seats per train, giving a seating/perch figure of 344; however, standing room exists for over 500. The sets are compatible with Class 375s, but usually only operate with other class members, and are restricted to the South Eastern suburban routes to Dartford. Set No. 376002 is seen approaching London Bridge. Without having the front gangway, room exists for an extra window which improves the all round visibility of these sets. Owned by Eversholt Rail, gangways could be retro-fitted if required for another operator.* CJM

Number range:	376001-376036
Introduced:	2004-05
Built by:	Bombardier Derby
Formation:	DMSO(A)+MSO+TSO+MSO+DMSO(B)
Vehicle numbers:	DMSO(A) - 61101-61136 MSO - 63301-63336 TSO - 64301-64336 MSO - 63501-63536 DMS)(B) - 61601-61636
Vehicle length:	DMSO - 66ft 11in (20.40m) TSO, MSO - 65ft 6in (19.99m)
Height:	12ft 4in (3.78m)
Width:	9ft 2in (2.80m)
Seating:	Total - 344S (216 seat, 12 tip, 116 perch) DMSO(A) - 36S, 6 Tip, 22 Perch MSO - 48S, 24 Perch TSO - 48S, 24 Perch MSO - 48S, 24 Perch DMSO(B) - 36S, 6 Tip, 22 Perch
Internal layout:	2+2 low-density with standing room
Gangway:	Within set
Toilets:	Not fitted
Weight:	Total - 192.9 tonnes DMSO(A) - 42.1 tonnes MSO - 36.2 tonnes TSO - 36.3 tonnes MSO - 36.2 tonnes DMSO(B) - 42.1 tonnes
Brake type:	Air rheostatic
Bogie type:	Power - Bombardier P3-25 Trailer - Bombardier T3-25
Power collection:	750V dc third rail
Traction motor type:	8 x Bombardier
Output:	2,682hp (2,000kW)
Max speed:	75mph (121km/h)
Coupling type:	Outer - Dellner 12, Inner - Bar
Multiple restriction:	Class 375-377
Door type:	Bi-parting sliding
Total sets in traffic:	36
Construction:	Aluminium with steel cabs
Owner:	Eversholt Rail
Operator:	SouthEastern

Class 377 'Electrostar'

Class:	377/1	377/2	377/3
Number range:	377101-377164	377201-377215	377301-377328
Original numbers:	-	-	375311-375338
Introduced:	2002-04	2002-03	2001-02
Built by:	Bombardier Derby	Bombardier Derby	Bombardier Derby
Formation:	DMCO(A)+MSO+ TSO+DMCO(B)	DMCO(A)+MSO+ TSO+DMCO(B)	DMCO(A)+TSO+ DMCO(B)
Vehicle numbers:	DMCO(A) - 78501-78564 MSO - 77101-77164 TSO - 78901-78964 DMCO(B) - 78701-78764	DMCO(A) - 78571-78585 MSO - 77171-77185 PTSO - 78971-78985 DMCO(B) - 78771-78785	DMCO(A) - 68201-68228 TSO - 74801-74828 DMCO(B) - 68401-68428
Vehicle length:	DMCO(A) - 66ft 11in (20.40m) MSO, TSO - 65ft 6in (19.99m)	DMCO(A) - 66ft 11in (20.40m) MSO, TSO - 65ft 6in (19.99m)	DMCO - 66ft 11in (20.40m) TSO - 65ft 6in (19.99m)
Height:	12ft 4in (3.78m)	12ft 4in (3.78m)	12ft 4in (3.78m)
Width:	9ft 2in (2.80m)	9ft 2in (2.80m)	9ft 2in (2.80m)
Seating:	Total - 24F/244S DMCO(A) - 12F/48S - 56S MSO - 62S - 70S TSO - 52S - 62S DMCO(B) - 12F/48S - 56S	Total - 24F/222S DMCO(A) - 12F/48S MSO - 69S PTSO - 57S DMCO(B) - 12F/48S	Total - 24F/152S DMCO(A) - 12F/48S TSO - 56S DMCO(B) - 12F/48S
Internal layout:	2+2, and 2+3 various	2+2, and 2+3	2+2, and 2+3
Gangway:	Throughout	Throughout	Throughout
Toilets:	MSO, TSO - 1	MSO, PTSO - 1	TSO - 1
Weight:	Total - 162.6 tonnes DMCO(A) - 44.8 tonnes MSO - 39 tonnes TSO - 35.4 tonnes DMCO(B) - 43.4 tonnes	Total - 168.3 tonnes DMCO(A) - 44.2 tonnes MSO - 39.8 tonnes PTSO - 40.1 tonnes DMCO(B) - 44.2 tonnes	Total - 122.4 tonnes DMCO(A) - 43.5 tonnes TSO - 35.4 tonnes DMCO(B) - 43.5 tonnes
Brake type:	Air regenerative	Air regenerative	Air regenerative
Bogie type:	Power - Bombardier P3-25 Trailer - Bombardier T3-25	Power - Bombardier P3-25 Trailer - Bombardier T3-25	Power - Bombardier P3-25 Trailer - Bombardier T3-25
Power collection:	750V dc third rail	750V dc third rail, and 25kV ac overhead	750V dc third rail
Traction motor type:	6 x Bombardier	6 x Bombardier	4 x Bombardier
Output:	2,012hp (1,500kW)	2,012hp (1,500kW)	1,341HP (1,000kW)
Max speed:	100mph (161km/h)	100mph (161km/h)	100mph (161km/h)
Coupling type:	Outer - Dellner 12, Inner - Bar	Outer - Dellner 12, Inner - Bar	Outer - Dellner 12, Inner - Bar
Multiple restriction:	Class 375 - 377	Class 375 - 377	Class 375 - 377
Door type:	Bi-parting sliding plug	Bi-parting sliding plug	Bi-parting sliding plug
Body structure:	Aluminium, steel ends	Aluminium, steel ends	Aluminium, steel ends
Special features:	PIS Provision for ac fitting	PIS Dual voltage sets	PIS Provision for ac fitting
Owner:	Porterbrook	Porterbrook	Porterbrook
Operator:	Southern	Southern	Southern
Note:	When delivered, early sets were classified as Class 375 and fitted with Tightlock couplers		

377/4	377/5	377/6
377401-377475	377501-377523	377601-377630
-	-	-
2004-05	2008-09	2013
Bombardier Derby	Bombardier Derby	Bombardier Derby
DMCO(A)+MSO+ TSO+DMCO(B)	DMCO(A)+MSO+ TSO+DMCO(B)	DMSO(A)+MSO+ TSO+MSO+DMSO(B)
DMCO(A) - 73401-73475 MSO - 78801-78875 TSO - 78601-78675 DMCO(B) - 73801-73875	DMCO(A) - 73501-73523 MSO - 75901-75923 TSO - 74901-74923 DMCO(B) - 73601-73623	DMSO(A) - 70101-70130 MSO(A) - 70201-70230 TSO - 70301-70330 MSO(B) - 70401-70430 DMSO(B) - 70501-70530
DMCO(A) - 66ft 11in (20.40m) MSO, TSO - 65ft 6in (19.99m)	DMCO(A) - 66ft 11in (20.40m) MSO, TSO - 65ft 6in (19.99m)	DMSO - 66ft 11in (20.40m) MSO, TSO - 65ft 6in (19.99m)
12ft 4in (3.78m)	12ft 4in (3.78m)	12ft 4in (3.78m)
9ft 2in (2.80m)	9ft 2in (2.80m)	9ft 2in (2.80m)
Total - 20F/221S DMCO(A) - 10F/48S MSO - 69S TSO - 56S DMCO(B) - 10F/48S	Total - 20F/218S DMCO(A) - 10F/48S MSO - 69S TSO - 53S DMSO(B) - 10F/48S	Total - 298S DMSO(A) - 60S MSO(A) - 64S TSO - 46S MSO(B) - 66S DMSO(B) - 62S
2+2, and 2+3	2+2, and 2+3	2+2, and 2+3
Throughout	Throughout	Throughout
MSO, TSO - 1	MSO, TSO - 1	MSO, TSO - 1
Total - 160.8 tonnes DMCO(A) - 43.1 tonnes MSO - 39.3 tonnes TSO - 35.3 tonnes DMCO(B) - 43.1 tonnes	Total - 160.8 tonnes DMCO(A) - 43.1 tonnes MSO - 39.3 tonnes TSO - 35.3 tonnes DMCO(B) - 43.1 tonnes	Total - ? tonnes DMSO(A) - ? tonnes MSO(A) - ? tonnes TSO - ? tonnes MSO(B) - ? tonnes DMSO(B) - ? tonnes
Air	Air	Air
Power - Bombardier P3-25 Trailer - Bombardier T3-25	Power - Bombardier P3-25 Trailer - Bombardier T3-25	Power - Bombardier P3-25 Trailer - Bombardier T3-25
750V dc third rail	750V dc third rail 25kV ac overhead	750V dc third rail 25kV ac overhead
6 x Bombardier	6 x Bombardier	6 x Bombardier
2,012hp (1,500kW)	2,012hp (1,500kW)	2,012hp (1,500kW)
100mph (161km/h)	100mph (161km/h)	100mph (161km/h)
Outer - Dellner 12, Inner - Bar	Outer - Dellner 12, Inner - Bar	Outer - Dellner 12, Inner - Bar
Class 375 - 377	Class 375 - 377	Class 375 - 377
Bi-parting sliding plug	Bi-parting sliding plug	Bi-parting sliding plug
Aluminium, steel ends	Aluminium, steel ends	Aluminium, steel ends
PIS	PIS	PIS
Provision for ac fitting	Dual voltage sets	Dual voltage sets
Porterbrook	Porterbrook	Porterbrook
Southern	First Capital Connect	Southern

Class 377 'Electrostar'

Left Top: *At the same time as Connex South Eastern through Eversholt procured the 'Electrostar' fleet, Connex SouthCentral ordered the Class 377s (originally 375s) via Porterbrook Leasing to replace the operator's slam door stock. All '377s' were built to the same basic design, although the various sub classes represent slightly different layouts, formations and technical alterations. Some external design differences can be found on some batches mainly involving headlights. A total of 64 Class 377/1s were introduced in 2002-03. During the course of this build the original three light lamp cluster was replaced with a two section unit.* CJM

Left Middle: *The largest sub class within the Class 377 order was for 74 four-car sets classified as 377/4. In these sets seating is 2+2 in both standard and first class except in the intermediate TSO which has 2+3 seating. Showing the revised two section head/marker light cluster, set No. 377470 is seen at Bombardier Derby.* CJM

Below: *To cater for routes with a lighter traffic flow, a fleet of 28 three-car sets was built; these were first off the Derby production line in 2001-02 and were orginally classified as Class 375/3 and fitted with Tightlock couplings. The sets were later fitted with Dellner couplings and reclassified as '377'. Set No. 377322 is seen at Brighton. When delivered these sets were numbered in the series 375311-375338; upon renumbering to the 377 series they became Nos. 377301-377328.* CJM

Above: Filteen of the Class 377/2 sets in traffic are dual voltage, able to collect power at 25kV ac from the overhead and from 750V dc via the third rail. These sets are usually deployed on the cross-London route from Croydon to Milton Keynes via Kensington Olympia, doing a voltage change near North Pole. When not needed for bi-voltage operation the sets operate domestic '377' rosters. No. 377211 is seen at Clapham Junction. CJM

Below: The 23 members of Class 377/5, which were originally built for SouthCentral operation, were diverted to First Capital Connect to assist with a major shortfall in units suitable for operation of Thameslink services between Bedford and Brighton. The sets are now on life-long lease to First Group and are painted in FCC 'Urban Lights' livery. The sets are based at Bedford Cauldwell Walk depot. Set No. 377517 is illustrated at East Croydon forming a Bedford to Brighton service in September 2011. CJM

Class 378 'Capitalstar'

Sub class:	378/1	378/2 (378/0)
Number range:	378135-378154	378201-378234, 378255-378257
Introduced:	2009-10	2009-11
Built by:	Bombardier Derby	Bombardier Derby
Formation:	DMSO(A)+MSO+TSO+DMSO(B)	DMSO(A)+MSO+TSO+DMSO(B)
Vehicle numbers:	DMSO(A) - 38035-38054 MSO - 38235-38254 TSO - 38335-38354 DMSO(B) - 38135-38154	DMSO(A) - 38001-38034, 38055-38057 MSO - 38201-38234, 38255-38257 TSO - 38301-38334, 38355-38357 DMSO(B) - 38101-38134, 38155-38157
Vehicle length:	DMSO - 67ft 2in (20.46m) MSO/TSO - 66ft 1in (20.14m)	DMSO - 67ft 2in (20.46m) MSO/TSO - 66ft 1in (20.14m)
Height:	12ft 4½in (3.77m)	12ft 4½in (3.77m)
Width:	9ft 2in (2.80m)	9ft 2in (2.80m)
Seating:	Total - 146S + 6 tip up DMSO(A) - 36S MSO - 40S TSO - 34S + 6 tip up DMSO(B) - 36S	Total - 146S + 6 tip up DMSO(A) - 36S MSO - 40S TSO - 34S + 6 tip up DMSO(B) - 36S
Internal layout:	Longitudinal	Longitudinal
Gangway:	Within set	Within set
Toilets:	None	None
Weight:	Total - 160.3 tonnes DMSO(A) - 43.5 tonnes MSO - 39.4 tonnes TSO - 34.3 tonnes DMSO(B) - 43.1 tonnes	Total - 160.3 tonnes DMSO(A) - 43.5 tonnes MSO - 39.4 tonnes TSO - 34.3 tonnes DMSO(B) - 43.1 tonnes
Brake type:	Air	Air
Power collection:	750V dc third rail	25kV ac overhead, 750V dc third rail
Traction motor type:	6 x Bombardier	6 x Bombardier
Output:	2,012hp (1,500kW)	2,012hp (1,500kW)
Max speed:	75mph (121km/h)	75mph (121km/h)
Coupling type:	Outer - Dellner 12, Inner - Bar	Outer - Dellner 12, Inner - Bar
Multiple restriction:	Class 375-378	Class 375-378
Door type:	Bi-parting sliding	Bi-parting sliding
Total sets in traffic:	20	37
Construction:	Aluminium	Aluminium
Owner:	QW Rail Leasing	QW Rail Leasing
Operator:	London Overground (TfL)	London Overground (TfL)
Notes:		378201-378234 built as 3-car sets and numbered 378001-378034

One additional Trailer Standard Open (TSO) has been ordered for each set for delivery in 2014-15

Left: *When originally delivered in 2009-10, the first 34 sets were formed as three-car sets and numbered 378001-378034. These were soon augmented to four-car status by adding an extra TSO vehicle, built as a follow-on order by Bombardier Derby, sets returning to Derby Works for the extra car to be inserted. When converted to four-car formation the sets were renumbered into the 378/2 series, retaining the last two digits of their original number. Three-car set No. 378007 is seen at Clapham Junction on a Willesden Junction bound service.* CJM

Right: *As part of the massive modernisation of the Transport for London system and the formation of the London Overground network came a fleet of 57 Class 378 'Electrostar' sets which operate on the Euston-Watford, Richmond-Stratford, Highbury-West Croydon/Crystal Palace and London orbital route. When delivered the first 34 sets were formed as three-car sets with an extra TS vehicle soon being added. The sets are based on the 'Electrostar' platform but have full width inter-vehicle gangways, longitudinal seating and lots of standing room. The non-gangwayed front end houses an emergency door for tunnel working. The Class 378/1 sets operate from the 750v dc third rail supply, while the Class 378/2 fleet are dual voltage and can operate from 750V dc third rail or from 25kV ac overhead. Dual voltage set No. 378229 is seen approaching Willesden Junction on a Watford-Euston service on 2 September 2010.* CJM

Below: *Class 378 interior showing the longitudinal seating layout, wide gangway connections between carriages and wide/spacious door vestibules, much in keeping with a London Underground train. Train doors are unlocked/closed by a conductor, while passengers have control over opening local doors.* CJM

Class 379 'Electrostar'

Number range:	379001-379030
Introduced:	2011
Built by:	Bombardier Derby
Formation:	DMOS+MOSL+PTOSL+DMOC
Vehicle numbers:	DMOS - 61201-61230 MOSL - 61701-61730 PTOSL - 61901-61930 DMOC - 62101-62130
Vehicle length:	DMOS/DMOC - 66ft 9in (20.4m) PTOSL, MOSL - 65ft 6in (19.99m)
Height:	12ft 4in (3.78m)
Width:	9ft 2in (2.80m)
Seating:	Total - 20F/189S DMOS - 60S MOSL - 62S PTOSL - 43S DMOC - 20F/24S
Internal layout:	First - 2+1 Standard - 2+2
Gangway:	Throughout
Toilets:	MOSL, PTOSL - 1
Weight:	Total - 161.97 tonnes DMOS - 42.1 tonnes MOSL - 36.65 tonnes PTOSL - 40.92 tonnes DMOC - 42.3 tonnes
Brake type:	Air rheostatic
Bogie type:	Power - Bombardier FlexxP3-25 Trailer - Bombardier Flexx T3-25
Power collection:	25kV ac overhead
Traction motor type:	6 x Bombardier 200kW
Output:	1,609hp (1,200kW)
Max speed:	100mph (161km/h)
Coupling type:	Outer - Dellner 12, Inner - Bar
Multiple restriction:	Class 375-379
Door type:	Bi-parting sliding plug
Construction:	Aluminium with steel cabs
Owner:	Lloyds-TSB Group

Above: *In 2009 Lloyds-TSB Group funded the purchase of 30 four-car 'Electrostar' sets for use on National Express East Anglia for operation between London Liverpool Street and Stansted Airport/Cambridge. The sets were delivered in 2011. The sets are in the low-density style with 2+2 seating and 2+1 in first class with spacious luggage stacks as they operate on the airport route. The fleet was delivered at the time of major franchise changes and thus appeared in all white livery onto which National Express and Stansted Express branding was applied. The sets are now operated by the Greater Anglia franchise. Set No. 379006 is illustrated at Cambridge.* CJM

Far Left: *Coupled between the two driving motor cars is a Motor Open Standard and Trailer Open Standard which also houses the pantograph. This view shows the Motor Open Standard vehicle, with its trailer bogie end nearest the camera. This vehicle shows the Stansted Express branding applied in the National Express style.* CJM

Right: *The Class 379s can be described as the luxury end of the 'Electrostar' product range, with comfortable 2+2 seats, with either fixed or fold down tables, carpeted floors and large luggage racks in each vehicle. Digital passenger information screens are provided throughout.* CJM

Class 380 'Desiro'

Class	380/0	380/1
Number range:	380001-380022	380101-380116
Introduced:	2010-11	2010-11
Built by:	Siemens Transportation - Duewag, Germany	Siemens Transportation - Duewag, Germany
Formation:	DMSO(A)+PTSO+DMSO(B)	DMSO(A)+PTSO+TSO+DMSO(B)
Vehicle numbers:	DMSO(A) - 38501-38522 PTSO - 38601-38622 DMSO(B) - 38701-38722	DMSO(A) - 38551-38566 PTSO - 38651-38666 TSO - 38551-38866 DMSO(B) - 38751-38766
Vehicle length:	75ft 5in (23.00m)	75ft 5in (23.00m)
Height:	12ft 4in (3.78m)	12ft 4in (3.78m)
Width:	9ft 2in (2.80m)	9ft 2in (2.80m)
Seating:	Total - 191S + 17 tip up DMSO(A) - 70S + 12 tip up PTSO - 57S DMSO(B) - 64S + 5 tip up	Total - 265S + 17 tip up DMSO(A) - 70S + 12 tip up PTSO - 57S TSO - 74S DMSO(B) - 64S + 5 tip up
Internal layout:	2+2	2+2
Gangway:	Throughout	Throughout
Toilets:	PTSO - 1	PTSO - 1, TSO - 1
Weight:	Total - 132.8 tonnes DMSO(A) - 45.1 tonnes PTSO - 42.4 tonnes DMSO(B) - 45.3 tonnes	Total - 167.5 tonnes DMSO(A) - 45.1 tonnes PTSO - 42.4 tonnes TSO - 34.7 tonnes DMSO(B) - 45.3 tonnes
Brake type:	Air rheostatic	Air rheostatic
Bogie type:	SGB5000	SGB5000
Power collection:	25kV ac overhead	25kV ac overhead
Traction motor type:	4 x Siemens 1TB2016-0GB02	4 x Siemens 1TB2016-0GB02
Output:	1,341hp (1,000kW)	1,341hp (1,000kW)
Max speed:	100mph (161km/h)	100mph (161km/h)
Coupling type:	Outer - Dellner 12, Inner - Bar	Outer - Dellner 12, Inner - Bar
Multiple restriction:	Within class only	Within class only
Door type:	Bi-parting sliding plug	Bi-parting sliding plug
Construction:	Aluminium with steel ends	Aluminium with steel ends
Owner:	Eversholt	Eversholt

Left: *The intermediate vehicles of the Class 380 fleet are both Trailers. On three-car sets a Pantograph Trailer Standard Open (PTSO) seats 57, while on the four-car sets a PTSO and a Trailer Standard Open (TSO) seating 74 are provided. In this view we see a PTSO vehicle, with its pantograph at the far end. Each vehicle of Class 380 design has two pairs of bi-parting sliding plug doors on each side. Passenger seating is in the low-density 2+2 style throughout.* CJM

Above & Below: *In July 2008, Scottish Railways ordered a fleet of 'Desiro' trains from Siemens to replace older stock on the Ayrshire routes. The order consisted of 22 three-car sets classified as 380/0 and 16 four-car sets classified as 380/1. Although part of the 'Desiro' family, these sets were fitted with a different rather ugly gangway door connection, rather than the more pleasing profile of the 444 and 450 designs. The sets are standard class only and each three-car Class 380 seats 191 and a four-car set 265 passengers. From new the units were painted in the distinctive Scottish Railways blue and Saltire livery, with ScotRail bodyside branding. In the above view we see Class 380/0 three-car set No. 380019 at Gourock on 23 May 2012 forming the 16.06 to Glasgow Central. In the view below, Class 380/1 four-car set No. 380113 is seen at Greenock West with a service from Glasgow Central to Gourock. Both:* Murdoch Currie

Class 390 'Pendolino'

Number range:	Class 390/0 - 390001-390052 (9-car sets) Class 390/1 - 390107-390157 (11-car sets§)
Introduced:	2001-05, 2010-13§
Built by:	Alstom, Washwood Heath, body shells from Italy Alstom, Savigliano, Italy§
Formation:	9-car - DMRF+MF+PTF+MF+TS+MS+PTSRMB+MS+DMSO 11-car - DMRF+MF+PTF+MF+TS§+MS§+TS+MS+PTSRMB+MS+DMSO DMRF - 69101-69157 MF - 69401-69457 PTF - 69501-69557 MF - 69601-69657 TS§ - 65303-65357 MS§ - 68903-68957 TS - 68801-68857 MS - 69701-69757 PTSRMB - 69801-69857 MS - 69901-69957 DMSO - 69201-69257
Vehicle length:	DMRF, DMSO - 81ft 3in (24.80m) MF, PTF, TS, MS, PTSRMB - 78ft 4in (23.90m)
Height:	11ft 6in (3.56m)
Width:	8ft 9in (2.73m)
Seating:	Total - 145F/294S or 145F/418S DMRF - 18F, MF - 37F, PTF - 44F, MF - 46F, TS - 76S, MS - 62S, PTSRMB - 48S, MS - 62S, MS - 62S§, MS - 62S§, DMSO - 46S
Internal layout:	2+1F/2+2S
Gangway:	Within set
Toilets:	MF, PTF, TS, MF, MSO, TS, MF(D) - 1
Weight:	Total - 459.7 tonnes DMRF - 55.6 tonnes MF - 52 tonnes PTF - 50.1 tonnes MF - 51.8 tonnes TS§ - 45.5 tonnes MS§ - 50 tonnes TS - 45.8 tonnes MS - 50 tonnes PTSRMB - 52 tonnes MS - 51.7 tonnes DMSO - 51 tonnes
Brake type:	Air (regenerative)
Bogie type:	Fiat/SIG tilting
Power collection:	25kV ac overhead
Traction motor type:	12 x Alstom Onix 800
Output:	6,839hp (5,100 kW) 8,793hp (6,557kW)§
Max speed:	140mph (225km/h) (Restricted to 125mph 200km/h)
Coupling type:	Outer - Dellner, Inner - Bar
Multiple restriction:	No multiple facility, operable with Dellner fitted Class 57/3
Door type:	Single-leaf sliding plug
Construction:	Aluminium
Special features:	Tilt
Owner:	Angel Trains

Left: *In common with Virgin policy, all the 'Pendolino' train sets carry cast nameplates, and over the years some of these have been changed to reflect events and people. The cast plate from No. 390010 is shown.* CJM

Above & Right: *The Virgin Trains modernisation of the West Coast Main Line saw the introduction of 53 'Pendolino' tilting train sets in 2001-05, supplimented by a further four in 2011-12. Originally these sets were formed of eight coaches; a ninth vehicle was later added and in 2011-12 31 sets were expanded to 11 coaches by adding two extra vehicles. The 'Pendolino' sets are based at Alstom Manchester, but receive daily manitenance at Alstom sites in Wembley (London), Oxley (Wolverhampton), Edge Hill (Liverpool) and Polmadie (Glasgow). The sets have a design speed of 140mph (225km/h) but in the UK are restricted to 125mph (200km/h). In the above view set No. 390019 departs from Preston on 30 October 2008 with the 13.47 to London Euston. It is usual for the first class seating of these sets to be at the London end. In the view right set No. 390017 passes South Kenton with a northbound service on 7 May 2010, with its DMSO vehicle nearest the camera. Both:* CJM

Class 395 'Javelin'

Number range:	395001 - 395029
Introduced:	2007-09
Built by:	Hitachi Industries, Kasado, Japan
Formation:	PDTSO1+MS1+MS2+MS3+MS4+PDTSO2
Vehicle numbers:	PDTSO1 - 39011-39291 MS1 - 39012-39292 MS2 - 39013-39293 MS3 - 39014-39294 MS4 - 39015-39295 PDTSO2 - 39016-39296
Vehicle length:	PDTSO - 68ft 5in (20.88m) MS - 65ft 6in (20m)
Height:	12ft 6in (3.81m)
Width:	9ft 2in (2.81m)
Seating:	Total: 340S + 12 tip up PDTSO1 - 28S + 12 tip up MS1 - 66S MS2 - 66S MS3 - 66S MS4 - 66S PDTSO2 - 48S
Internal layout:	2+2
Gangway:	Within unit only
Toilets:	PDTSO - 1
Weight:	Total: 276.2 tonnes PDTSO - 46.7 tonnes MS - 45.7 tonnes
Brake type:	Air (Rheostatic/regenerative)
Bogie type:	Hitachi
Power collection:	25kV ac overhead & 750V dc third rail
Traction motor type:	IGBT Converter, three-phase
Output:	2,253hp (1,680 kW)
Max speed:	HS1 - 140mph (225km/h) Normal - 100mph (161km/h)
Coupling type:	Outer - Scharfenburg, Inner - Bar
Multiple restriction:	Within class only (2-unit max)
Door type:	Single-leaf sliding
Total number in traffic:	29
Construction:	Aluminium
Owner:	Eversholt
Operator:	SouthEastern Trains
Special features:	PIS, CCTV, TVM430/KVB, GPS Air conditioned, SDO

Left: *With the construction of High Speed 1 (HS1) between London and the Channel Tunnel came the chance to use extra line capacity and operate domestic SouthEastern services over the line offering huge reduction in journey times between some Kent towns and London St Pancras. To operate these services a fleet of 29 six-car streamlined trains WAS built in Japan by Hitachi Industries. The sets are based at purpose-built facilities at Ashford (Kent) and provide a 140mph (225km/h) travelling experience. The sets have 2+3 seating with each train accommodating 340 passengers in one class. The sets can operate in multiple, using a Scharfenburg coupler hidden behind a hinged front fairing. Set No. 395002 is seen at St Pancras International station alongside a 'Eurostar' train set.* CJM

Above: *For the duration of the Olympic Games held in London in summer 2012, the Class 395 fleet was branded as 'Javelin' sets and operated special high speed services from St Pancras International to Stratford for competitors and spectators. 'Javelin' branded set No. 395009 is seen at Ramsgate in July 2012. In the background is Ramsgate SouthEastern depot with various Class 375 units.* Antony Christie

Right: *The interior of the Class 395s is somewhat basic, but this has to be viewed against the short journey times for travellers using the high speed service between Kent and London, with most journeys being less than one hour in duration. Seating is in the low density 2+2 style with a mix of airline and group seats. Moquette is in SouthEastern blue and mauve.* CJM

Class 401 – 2BIL

Number range:	2001-2152
Former number range:	1891-1900
Alpha code:	2-BIL
Introduced:	1935-38
Built by:	SR Eastleigh, frames from Lancing+
Formation:	MBSL+DTCL
Vehicle numbers:	MBSL - 10567-10718 DTCL - 12034-12110
Set length:	129ft 6in (39.47m)
Vehicle length:	62ft 6in (19.05m)
Height:	12ft 8¾in (3.88m)
Width:	9ft 3in (2.82m)
Seating:	Total: 24F/84S MBSL - 52S DTCL - 24F/32S
Internal layout:	First - compartment Standard - 2+3
Gangway:	No
Toilets:	MBSL, DTCL - 1
Weight:	Total - 74 tons 15cwt MBSL - 43 tons 10cwt DTCL - 31 tons 5cwt
Brake type:	Air (westinghouse)
Bogie type:	Surburban
Power collection:	660-750v dc third rail
Traction motor type:	2 x EE
Horsepower:	550hp (410kW)
Max speed:	75mph (121km/h)
Coupling type:	Screw
Multiple restriction:	SR types up to 1936 series (Group 1)
Door type:	Slam
Special features:	2001-10 fitted with electro-pneumatic control equipment

+ MBSL of sets 1891-1900 (2001-2010) built by Metro-Cammell/BRCW

Below: *The first batch of 10 semi-fast main line units classified as 2BIL emerged in 1935 for the Eastbourne line, formed of a Motor Brake Third and a Driving Trailer Composite; building of these was divided between Metropolitan-Cammell Carriage Wagon & Finance Co and Birmingham Railway Carriage & Wagon Co. The internal layout was all compartment, with one toilet located in the Driving Trailer Composite vehicle. A further batch of sets to the same general design was built at Eastleigh Works in 1936 for use on the Waterloo to Portsmouth and Alton lines; these were allocated the numbers 2011-2048. A further batch followed in 1937 when Nos. 2049-2116 emerged from Eastleigh for use on the Central section to Portsmouth and Bognor Regis. The final batch of units emerged in 1938 when sets Nos. 2117-2152 were delivered for the Waterloo to Reading line. Originally sets were painted in Southern green, but this later gave way to BR green and eventually yellow panels and ends were applied. A handful of sets remained in traffic long enough to receive BR rail blue livery. Set No. 2053 is viewed from its Motor Brake end at Christs Hospital.* CJM-C

Class 402 – 2HAL

Number range:	2601-2700		
Former number range:	-		
Alpha code:	2HAL		
Introduced:	1939-1948		
Built/rebuilt by:	SR/BR Eastleigh Works, frames from Lancing		
Formation:	DMBS+DTCL		
Vehicle numbers:	DMBS - 10719-10817 DTCL - 12186-12231, 12810-12853		
Set length:	129ft 6in (39.47m)		
Vehicle length:	62ft 6in (19.05m)		
Height:	12ft 8¾in (3.88m)		
Width:	9ft 3in (2.82m)		
Seating:	Sets 2601-2692 Total - 18F/110S or 24F/102S DMBS - 70S DTCL - 18 or 24F/40 or 32S	Sets 2693-2699 Total - 18F/124S DMBS - 84S DTCL - 18F/40S	Set 2700 Total - 24F/114S DMBS - 82S DTCL - 24F/32S
Internal layout:	Compartment		
Gangway:	No		
Toilets:	DTCL - 1		
Weight:	Sets 2601-2692 Total - 76 tons DMBS - 44 tons DTCL - 32 tons	Sets 2693-2699 Total - 73 tons DMBS - 42 tons DTCL - 31 tons	Set 2700 Total - 70 tons DMBS - 39 tons DTCL - 31 tons
Brake type:	Air Westinghouse		
Bogie type:	Surburban		
Power collection:	660-750V dc third rail		
Traction motor type:	2 x EE		
Horsepower:	550hp (410kW)		
Max speed:	75mph (121km/h)		
Coupling type:	Screw		
Multiple restriction:	SR EMU up to 1936 sesign (Group 1)		
Door type:	Slam		

Below: *The 2HAL or two-car HAlf Lavatory sets first emerged in 1939 for the London to Maidstone and Gillingham electrification, a product of Eastleigh Works. The sets numbered 2601-2676, were painted in Southern green and formed of a Driving Motor third and a Driving Trailer Composite, all passenger accommodation was in compartments and one lavatory was provided in the Composite coach. Total seating was provided for 18 first and 110 third class passengers. In 1939 Eastleigh built a further batch of 16 sets numbered 2677-2692 (with revised seating). Due to war losses, right at the start of the BR era a further six sets were authorised to be built at Eastleigh numbered 2693-2699; these differed in external appearance and looked more like the suburban stock then under construction. The final HAL emerged in 1955, when No. 2700 entered traffic. The sets remained in service until 1971. Set No. 2682, one of the 1939, batch is illustrated with its Driving Trailer Composite on the left.* CJM-C

Class 403 – 5BEL

Number range:	3051-3053		
Former number range:	2051-2053		
Alpha code:	5-BEL		
Introduced:	1932		
Built/rebuilt by:	Metropolitan-Cammell Carriage, Wagon & Finance Company		
Formation:	DMBPS+TKRK+TKRK+TPS+DMBPS		
Vehicle numbers:	3051	3052	3053
	DMPBS -288	DMPBS -291	DMPBS -292
	TKRK - 279 *Hazel*	TKRK - 280 *Audrey*	TKRK - 281 *Gwen*
	TKRK - 282 *Doris*	TKRK - 284 *Vera*	TKRK - 283 *Mona*
	TPS - 286	TPS - 287	TPS - 285
	DMPBS - 289	DMPBS - 290	DMPBS - 293
Set length:	345ft 0in (105.16m)		
Vehicle length:	69ft 0in (21.03m)		
Height:	12ft 8½in (3.87m)		
Width:	8ft 11½in		
Seating:	Total - 40F/152S DMPBS - 48S, TKRK - 20F TKRK - 20F, TPS - 56S DMPBS - 48S		
Internal layout:	First - 1+1 Standard - 2+2		
Gangway:	Within set		
Toilets:	DMPBS - 1, TKRK - 1, TPS - 1		
Weight:	Total - 249 tons DMPBS - 62 tons, TKRK - 43 tons TKRK - 43 tons, TPS - 39 tons DMPBS - 62 tonnes		
Brake type:	Air Westinghouse		
Bogie type:	Express		
Power collection:	660-750Vdc third rail		
Traction motor type:	8 x BTH		
Horsepower:	1,800hp (1,342kW)		
Max speed:	75mph (121km/h)		
Coupling type:	Screw		
Multiple restriction:	Within SR types up to 1936 stock		
Door type:	Slam		

Left, Above & Right: *The Southern Railway introduced three luxury five-car Pullman (5PUL) sets in 1932 for use on the London Victoria to Brighton route. They were the first all electric Pullman trains in the world and operated the new 'Southern Belle' service from 1933. The sets finished in Pullman umber and cream were most attractive and soon became well used. In 1934 the name was changed to 'Brighton Belle'. The sets were withdrawn and stored during the high war years of 1941-45 and returned to traffic in 1946/47. The sets continued to operate the fast Pullman service linking London with Brighton until 30 April 1972 when all three sets were withdrawn. In 1969 the three sets were passed through Eastleigh Works to emerge in the then new blue/grey Pullman livery. In the view left we see set No. 2053 in original 'Southern Belle' condition soon after introduction. The image above shows set No. 3051 leading a 10-car formation in 'Brighton Belle' days, while the view right shows the final blue/grey livery applied to set No. 3051 passing Clapham Junction.* **All:** CJM-C

Class 404 – 4COR, 4COR(N), 6COR, 4BUF, 4RES, 4GRI

Type:	4COR	4COR(N)	6COR
Number range:	3101-3168	3065-3071	3041-3050
Alpha code:	4COR	4COR(N)	6COR
Introduced:	1937-38 & 1965-66 reforms	1964 reforms	1965 reforms
Built by:	SR Eastleigh Works	SR Eastleigh Works	SR Eastleigh Works
Formation:	MBSO+TCK+TSK+MBSO	MBSO+TSK+TFK+MBSO	MBSO+TSK+TCK+ TFK+TSK+ MBSO
Vehicle numbers:	MBSO - 11081-11138, 11177-11228, TCK - 11791-11845 TSK - 10055-10109	MBSO - From Res fleet TSK - From Res fleet TFK - From Res fleet	MBSO - From PUL/PAN fleet TSK - From PUL/PAN fleet TCK - From PUL/PAN fleet TFK - From PUL/PAN fleet TSK - From PUL/PAN fleet
Set length:	265ft 2in (80.82m)	265ft 2in (80.82m)	399ft 6in (121.77m)
Vehicle length:	63ft 6in (19.35m)	63ft 6in (19.35m)	63ft 6in (19.35m)
Height:	12ft 8½in (3.87m)	12ft 8½in (3.87m)	12ft 8½in (3.87m)
Width:	9ft 3in (2.82m)	9ft 3in (2.82m)	9ft 3in (2.82m)
Seating:	Total - 30F/196S MBSO - 52S TCK - 30F/24S TSK - 68S MBSO - 52S	Total - 42F/172S MBSO - 52S TSK - 68S TFK - 42F MBSO - 52S	Total - 72F/264S MBSO - 52S TSK - 68S TCK - 30F/24S TFK - 42F TSK - 68S MBSO - 52S
Internal layout:	Standard - 2+2/compartment First - Compartment	Standard - 2+2/compartment First - Compartment	Standard - 2+2/compartment First - Compartment
Gangway:	Throughout	Throughout	Within set only
Toilets:	TCK, TSK - 2	TCK, TSK - 2	TCK, TSK, TFK- 2
Weight:	Total - 158ton 5cwt MBSO - 46ton 10cwt TCK - 32ton 12cwt TSK - 32ton 13cwt MBSO - 46ton 10cwt	Total - 157ton 10cwt MBSO - 46ton 10cwt TSK - 31ton 10cwt TFK - 33tons MBSO - 46ton 10cwt	Total - 254 tons MBSO - 59 tons TSK - 35 tons TCK - 35 tons TFK - 31 tons TSK - 35 tons MBSO - 59 tons
Brake type:	Air	Air	Air
Bogie type:	Express	Express	Express
Power collection:	660-750V dc third rail	660-750V dc third rail	660-750V dc third rail
Traction motor type:	4 x MV	4 x EE	4 x MV or 4 x EE
Horsepower:	900hp (671kW)	900hp (671kW)	900hp (671kW)
Max speed:	75mph (121km/h)	75mph (121km/h)	75mph (121km/h)
Coupling type:	Screw	Screw	Screw
Multiple restriction:	SR Multiple Unit 1936 design	SR Multiple Unit 1936 design	SR Multiple Unit 1936 design
Door type:	Slam	Slam	Slam
Notes:	3159-69 1965 RES/PUL/ PAN reforms	Rebuilt from 6 x 4RES and 1 x 4PUL units	Ex PUL/PAN vehicles

4BUF	4RES	4GRI
3073-3085 (3072)	3054-3072	3086-3088
4BUF	4RES	4GRI
1938	1937-38	1962 rebuild
SR Eastleigh Works	MBSO - SR Eastleigh Works TFK- Metro-Cammell TRKB - Birmingham RCW	SR Eastleigh Works
MBSO+TCK+TRB+MBSO	MBSO+TFK+TRKB+MBSO	MBSO+TFK+TRKG+MBSO
MBSO - 11229-11254 TCK - 11846-11858 TRB - 12518-12530	MBSO - 11139-11176 TFK - 12232-12250 TRKB - 12601-12619	From RES fleet 3056/65/68 From RES fleet 3056/65/68 From RES fleet 3056/65/68
265ft 2in (80.82m)	265ft 2in (80.82m)	265ft 2in (80.82m)
63ft 6in (19.35m)	63ft 6in (19.35m)	63ft 6in (19.35m)
12ft 8½in (3.87m)	12ft 8½in (3.87m)	12ft 8½in (3.87m)
9ft 3in (2.82m)	9ft 3in (2.82m)	9ft 3in (2.82m)
Total - 30F/128S/26U MBSO - 52S TCK - 30F/24S TRB - 26U MBSO - 52S	Total - 30F/104S/48Dining MBSO - 52S TFK - 30F/12Dining TRKB - 36Dining MBSO - 52S	Total - 30F/104S/48Dining MBSO - 52S TFK - 30F/12Dining TRKG - 36Dining MBSO - 52S
Standard - 2+2 / compartment First - Compartment	Standard - 2+2 / compartment First - Compartment	Standard - 2+2 / compartment First - Compartment
Throughout	Throughout	Throughout
TCK - 2	TFK - 1	TFK - 1
Total - 162ton 12cwt MBSO - 46ton 10cwt TCK - 32ton 12cwt TRB - 37tons MBSO - 46ton 10cwt	Total - 161 tons MBSO - 46ton 10cwt TFK - 33 tons TRKB - 35 tons MBSO - 46ton 10cwt	Total - 160 tons MBSO - 46ton 10cwt TFK - 33 tons TRKG - 34 tons MBSO - 46ton 10cwt
Air	Air	Air
Express	Express	Express
660-750V dc third rail	660-750V dc third rail	660-750V dc third rail
4 x MV	4 x MV	4 x MV
900hp (671kW)	900hp (671kW)	900hp (671kW)
75mph (121km/h)	75mph (121km/h)	75mph (121km/h)
Screw	Screw	Screw
SR Multiple Unit 1936 design	SR Multiple Unit 1936 design	SR Multiple Unit 1936 design
Slam	Slam	Slam
	3072 rebuilt after fire damage as prototype vehicle, classified as BUF	Rebuilt from RES stock

Class 404 – 4COR, 4COR(N), 6COR, 4BUF, 4RES, 4GRI

Left & Below: *The Southern four-car corridor sets classified as 4COR were first introduced in 1937 when Eastleigh built 29 sets for the Waterloo-Portsmouth route. The sets were gangwayed throughout enabling passengers/staff through access of up to three sets in multiple. To provide catering services on the route a fleet of 13 buffet car sets of the same design was introduced from 1938. A further batch of COR sets, Nos. 3130-55, was built in 1938 for the mid-Sussex electrification. Further sets numbered up to 3168 were added, some formed of new stock and others from rebuilt vehicles. Set No. 3123 is illustrated left at Guildford, while BUF set No. 3083 is seen below at Croydon. Both:* CJM-C

Left: *First class accommodation on the 4COR/BUF sets was provided in an intermediate Trailer Composite Corridor (TCK). This compartment vehicle has five first class compartments and three third (second) class compartments and two small toilet compartments, one at each end. On the compartment side a passenger door was provided by each compartment, while on the corridor side five passenger doors were provided. When built all sets were finished in Southern and later BR green.* CJM-C

Above: *In having the stencil headcode position taking the place on the non-driving window and with a flexible gangway and just one front driving window, these sets soon became knows as 'Nelson' stock. One of the driving cars from set No. 3131 is now part of the National Collection in York, where it is restored to original Southern green livery.* CJM

Below: *Although withdrawn in September 1972, most of the 4COR sets were repainted into BR rail blue livery with full yellow warning ends. Also, roller blind headcode boxes were fitted in place of the stencil type. Showing a revised headcode box and blue livery, set No. 3143 leads a 12-car formation through West Byfleet with a Portsmouth to Waterloo train in 1971.* CJM

Class 405 – 4SUB

Number range:	4101-4754 series
Former number range:	-
Alpha code:	4-SUB (4-car SUBurban)
Introduced:	1940-1951
Built by:	BR Eastleigh
Formation:	DMBS+TSO+TS+DMBS originlly DMBT+TTO+TT+DMBT
Vehicle numbers:	DMBS - 10829-11000, 11301-11392, 12650-12800 TSO - 10121-10143, 10439-10448, 12351-12406 TS - 10144-10438, 10449-10481, 11448-11500
Set length:	257ft 5in (78.46m)
Vehicle length:	DMBS - 62ft 6in (19.05m) TS/TSO - 62ft 0in (18.9m)
Height:	12ft 8¾in (388m)
Width:	9ft 3in (2.82m)
Seating:	Total - Various due to formation* DMBS - Between 82-102S*, TSO - 108-132S* TS - 102-120S*, DMBS - 82-102S*
Internal layout:	2+3, Compartment
Gangway:	No
Toilets:	Not fitted
Weight:	Total - Various due to formation* DMBS - 39-43 tons, TSO - 27-29 tons, TS - 26-29 tons, DMBS - 39-43 tons
Brake type:	Air (Westinghouse)
Bogie type:	SR
Power collection:	660-750V dc third rail
Traction motor type:	4 x EE507
Horsepower:	1,000hp (746kW)
Max speed:	75mph (121km/h)
Coupling type:	Screw
Multiple restriction:	1936 design SR EMUs
Door type:	Slam

* Some variation on seating/weight found on various builds

Left: *The four-car SUBurban units, 4SUB, started to emerge in 1940 when the Southern carriage works at Eastleigh released set No. 4101, formed originally of a DMBT, TC, TT and a DMBT. The sets entered traffic on the Eastern section in 1941, withseating for 60 first and 396 third class passengers. First class was dispensed with on suburban trains at the end of 1941 and the TC vehicles soon became TTs. It was not until 1944 that the second SUB No. 4102, entered traffic, after which numerous batches were delivered numbered in the 41xx, 42xx, 43xx, 46xx and 47xx series. Many different interior designs were included, culminating in many sets having three open design vehicles per set. The SUB design was delivered through until 1951 when the BTC opted for the more modern EPB stock. Painted in Southern green livery, set No. 4111 is illustrated. Note the warning whistle to the left of the driver's window.* CJM-C

Above: *After original allocation to the Eastern section, all three Southern divisions operated SUB stock. This view shows one of the first to have three open vehicles, set No. S4289 introduced in 1948.* CJM-C

Right: *One of the final SUB sets to be delivered, No. 4720, introduced in 1951, is seen at New Cross. Some of these sets were built at 3SUBs taking their fourth car from withdrawn augmented 3SUB stock.* CJM-C

Below: *Repaints from the late 1960s saw BR rail blue applied with full yellow warning ends, as shown on set No. 4660 passing Wimbledon in 1978. This is one of the sets fitted with roller blind route indicators. The SUB design remained in service until 1983.* CJM

Class 410 / 412 – 4BEP

Class	410	412
	As built	Refurbished
Number range:	7001-7022	(41)2301-(41)2307
Former number range:	-	70xx series
Alpha code:	4BEP (4 Buffet Electro Pneumatic)	4BEP (4 Buffet Electro Pneumatic)
Introduced originally:	1957	-
Introduced refurbished:	-	1983-84
Built by:	BR Eastleigh	-
Rebuilt by:	-	BREL Swindon
Formation:	DMBS+TC+TRB+DMBS	DMSO(A)+TBC+TRSB+DMSO(B)
Vehicle numbers:	DMBS - 61041-61044, 61390-61409, 61792-61811 series TC - 70041-70042, 70346-70355, 70601-70610 TRB - 69000-69021 DMBS - 61041-61044, 61390-61409, 61792-61811 series	DMSO(A) - 61736-61955 series TBC - 70354-70656 series TRSB - 69341-69347 DMSO(B) - 61736-61955 series
Set length:	265ft 8½in (80.99m)	265ft 8½in (80.99m)
Vehicle length:	64ft 9½in (19.75m)	64ft 9½in (19.75m)
Height:	12ft 6in (3.81m)	12ft 6in (3.81m)
Width:	9ft 3in (2.81m)	9ft 3in (2.81m)
Seating:	Total - 24F/136S/21Unclassified DMBS - 56S TC - 24F/24S TRB - 21Unclassified DMBS - 56S	Total - 24F/158S/9Unclassified DMSO(A) - 64S TBC - 24F/6S TRSB - 24S/9Unclassied DMSO(B) - 64S
Internal layout:	First - Compartment Standard - Compartment and 2+2	First - Compartment Standard - 2+2
Gangway:	Throughout	Throughout
Toilets:	TC - 2	TRSB - 1, TBC - 2
Weight:	Total - 7001-02 - 146 tons 7003-7022 - 151 tons DMBS - 7001-02 - 40 tons 7003-7022 - 41 tons TC - 7001-02 - 31 tons 7003-7022 - 33 tons TRB - 7001-02 - 35 tons 7003-7022 - 36 tons DMBS - 7001-02 - 40 tons 7003-7022 - 41 tons	Total - 159.4 tonnes DMSO(A) - 44.1 tonnes TBC - 36.2 tonnes TRSB - 35.5 tonnes DMSO(B) - 43.3 tonnes DMSO(B) - 43.6 tonnes
Brake type:	Air (EP/Auto)	Air (EP/Auto)
Bogie type:	Mk4/Commonwealth Powered - Mk6	Trailer - BR (SR) Powered - Mk3B, or Mk4
Power collection:	750V dc third rail	750V dc third rail
Traction motor type:	4 x EE507	4 x EE507
Horsepower:	1,000hp (746kW)	1,000hp (746kW)
Max speed:	90mph (145km/h)	90mph (145km/h)
Coupling type:	Buck-eye	Buck-eye
Multiple restriction:	1951-66 stock	1951-66 stock
Door type:	Slam	Slam
Special features:	7022 fitted with air conditioning	

Right Top: *Between 1957-63 a total of 133 four-car Buffet Electro Pneumatic or Corridor Electro Pneumatic sets were introduced. This included 22 buffet car sets. Which operated with the CEP stock to provide catering facilities on the Central and Eastern sections. The sets were formed of a Driving Motor Brake Second, Trailer Composite, Trailer Buffet and another Driving Motor Brake Second. Seating was for 24 first, 136 second and 21 unclassified in the buffet car. When originally built sets were painted in BR multiple unit green, this then changed to blue and grey. Set No. 7012 is seen near Paddock Wood; the buffet car is the second from front.* CJM

Right Middle: *In 1983 with no new stock in the pipeline a massive refurbishment project for the CEP/BEP fleet was undertaken at BREL Swindon. This saw a total rebuild of the BEP sets; the original DMBS cars were rebuilt as Driving Motor Standard Open vehicles, while the brake compartment was placed in the Trailer Composite coach. The original buffet cars were totally rebuilt with modern cooking facilities and new passenger areas, and the sets were also reclassified as 412. Set No. (41)2302 is seen on the Western section forming a Portsmouth to Waterloo service near Walton-on-Thames; the redesigned TBC is second from the front and the buffet vehicle third from the front. Seven modified buffet sets were introduced; the rest of the cars went into forming additional CEP stock.* CJM

Below: *The seven buffet-car rebuilds were a major undertaking, with new window positions and equipment. With its buffet end on the right, car No. 69343 is illustrated. The upgrade work saw a toilet compartment fitted and extra standard class seating.* CJM

Class 411 – 4CEP

	As built	Refurbished
Sub Class	-	411/5
Number range:	7101-7211	(41)1501-(41)1617 (41)1697-(41)1699
Former number range:	-	7101-7211
Alpha code:	4CEP (4 Corridor Electro Pneumatic)	4CEP (4 Corridor Electro Pneumatic)
Introduced originally:	1956-63	-
Introduced refurbished:	-	1983-84
Built by:	BR Eastleigh	-
Rebuilt by:	-	BREL Swindon
Formation:	DMBS+TC+TS+DMBS DMBS - 61033-61040, 61229-240/304-389/694-791, 61868-61871/948-961 TC - 70037-70040, 70043-70044/235-240/303-345, 70552-70600/653-659 TS - 70033-70036, 70229-70234/241-242/260-302, 70503-70551/660-666 DMBS - 61033-61040, 61229-61240/304-389/694-791, 61868-61871, 61948-61961	DMSO(A)+TBC+TSOL+DMSO(B) DMSO - From DMBS series on left (not in order) TBC - From TC series on left (not in order) TSOL - From TS series on left (not in order) DMSO - From DMBS series on left (not in order)
Set length:	265ft 8½in (80.99m)	265ft 8½in (80.99m)
Vehicle length:	64ft 9½in (19.75m)	64ft 9½in (19.75m)
Height:	12ft 6in (3.81m)	12ft 6in (3.81m)
Width:	9ft 3in (2.81m)	9ft 3in (2.81m)
Seating:	Total - 24F/200S DMBS - 56S TC - 24F/24S TS - 64S DMBS - 56S	Total - 24F/198S DMSO(A) - 64S TBC - 24F/6S TSOL - 64S DMSO(B) - 64S
Internal layout:	First - Compartment Standard - Compartment and 2+2 - Second	First - Compartment Standard - Compartment and 2+2
Gangway:	Throughout	Throughout
Toilets:	TS - 2, TC - 2	TSOl - 2, TBC - 2
Weight:	Total - 7101-7104 - 142 tons 7105-7211 - 147 tons DMBS - 7101-7104 - 40 tons 7105-7211 - 41 tons TC - 7101-7104 - 31 tons TS - 7101-7104 - 31 tons 7105-7211 - 32 tons	Total - 157.4 tonnes DMSO(A) - 44.1 tonnes TBC - 36.2 tonnes TSOL - 33.8 tonnes
Brake type:	Air (EP/Auto)	Air (EP/Auto)
Bogie type:	Powered - Mk3B, or Mk4 Trailer - Commonwealth	Powered - Mk3B, or Mk4 Trailer - Commonwealth
Power collection:	750V dc third rail	750V dc third rail
Traction motor type:	4 x EE507	4 x EE507
Horsepower:	1,000hp (746kW)	1,000hp (746kW)
Max speed:	90mph (145km/h)	90mph (145km/h)
Coupling type:	Buck-eye	Buck-eye
Multiple restriction:	1951-66 stock	1951-66 stock
Door type:	Slam	Slam
Special features:		1697-99 Mk 6 bogies

411/9 & 411/4
(41)1101-(41)1118 (1999)
(41)1401-(41)1406 (1993)
15xx and 16xx series
3CEP (3 Corridor Electro Pneumatic)
-
1993-99
-
Connex Ramsgate
DMSO(A)+TBC+DMSO(B)
DMSO - From DMBS series on left (not in order)

TBC - From TC series on left (not in order)

TSOL - From TS series on left (not in order)

DMSO - From DMBS series on left (not in order)

199ft 3in (60.73m)
64ft 9½in (19.75m)
12ft 6in (3.81m)
9ft 3in (2.81m)
Total - 24F/134S
DMSO(A) - 64S
TBC - 24F/6S
DMSO(B) - 64S

First - Compartment
Standard - Compartment and 2+2
Throughout
TBC - 2
Total - 123.6 tonnes

DMSO(A) - 44.1 tonnes

TBC - 36.2 tonnes

DMSO(B) - 43.3 tonnes
Air (Auto/EP)
Powered - Mk3B, or Mk4
Trailer - Commonwealth
750V dc third rail
4 x EE507
1,000hp (746kW)
90mph (145km/h)
Buck-eye
1951-66
Slam

Above & Below: *The 110 Eastleigh Works built 4-car Corridor Electro Pneumatic (4CEP) sets were the first main line electric multiple units built to the Mk1 coach design, mounted on an EMU underframe and fitted with electro-pneumatic brake equipment. Gangways were fitted throughout and drop-head buck-eye couplers were installed with Pullman rubbing plates. Sets Nos. 7101-7104 were built in 1956 as prototype sets and allocated to Brighton. Each set seated 24 first and 200 second class passengers. The two driving cars were of open layout, while the two intermediate vehicles were compartment. The driving cab was full width with the central gangway door; access was via the guards brake van. Traction equipment was mounted on the bogie directly below the driving cab/guards van in both driving cars. These sets had high level air and jumper connections and used a 70V control system rather than line volts; for this reason a motor generator set was provided. Following the prototype units, sets Nos. 7105-7153 were ordered in 1957/58 for phase one of the Kent Coast electrification; these incorporated a number of modifications including camshaft control equipment. Continued running of these sets showed a problem of rough ride and when a third batch was ordered for the 2nd phase of the Kent Coast electrification (Nos. 7154-7204) Commonwealth bogies were fitted. The final batch of CEP units entered service in 1963 when Nos. 7205-7211 were delivered for Western section use. In 1983 the CEP stock was the subject of a major refurbishment programme at BREL Swindon which saw the sets totally changed. In common with the BEP stock, the driving cars became Driving Motor Standards with the brake position transferred to the Trailer Composite coach. The windows were changed to include a top opening hopper rather than sliding quarter lights. The driving cars and the TS were open layout, with the Trailer Composite Brake vehicle still retaining side fed compartments. Between 1979-99 some 19 sets were reduced to three-car formation with the removal of the TSO vehicle for use on lower patronage branch lines. The Class 411 fleet was expanded during the Swindon refurbishment period when all but seven of the BEP units were modified as CEP stock, the buffet cars being replaced by Mk1 loco-hauled conversions to CEP TSOs, this work was undertaken at BREL Swindon. In the above view set No. 7105, the first of the production sets is seen when brand new in BR green livery. The view below shows set No. 7170, one of the Kent Coast phase two sets passing Ashford. Both:* CJM-C

Class 411 – 4CEP

Above: *By the late 1960s the CEP/BEP fleet started to emerge in all-over rail blue, but this was quickly superseded by standard blue and grey colours. Unrefurbished set No 7115 leads a 12-car formation of CEP stock through New Malden with a charter for Kent. The set's TC vehicle is second from the front.* CJM

Below: *As part of the BREL Swindon refurbishment, sets were renumbered into the 15xx and 16xx TOPS class series. Set No. (41)1519 is illustrated painted in London and SouthEast 'Jaffa cake' colours passing Petts Wood Junction on 5 June 1989.* CJM

Above: *After Network SouthEast was formed in the mid-1980s, the CEP/BEP stock was repainted into the corporate red, white and blue livery, as displayed on set (41)1545 at Rainham.* CJM

Below: *In 1993 the sub class 411/4 was formed when six three-car sets were marshalled under the NSE banner for Kent branch line use and renumbered in the 1401-1406 series. The sets were missing their TSO vehicle. One of the lines on which these shortened sets operated was the Sheerness branch, where set No. 1402 is illustrated. Also note the Group Standard headlight.* CJM

Class 413, 414, 418 – 2HAP, 2SAP, 4CAP

	SR HAP	SR SAP	BR HAP
Class:	414/1	414/1	414/2 - 6001-6042 414/3 - 6043-6173
Number range:	5601-5636	5601-5636	414/2 - 42xx series 414/3 - 43xx series
Former number range:	-	-	6001-6173
Alpha code:	2HAP	2SAP	2HAP
Introduced:	1957	1969 (modified)	1957-1959
Built by:	BR Eastleigh	BR Eastleigh	BR Eastleigh
Formation:	DMBS+DTC	DMBS+DTS	DMBS+DTC
Vehicle numbers:	DMBS - 14521-14556 DTC - 16001-16036	DMBS - 14521-14556 DTS - 16001-16036	DMBS - 65393-65434, 61241-61303, 61648-61688, 61962-61988 DTC - 77115-77156, 75361-75423, 75700-75740, 75995-76021
Set length:	129ft 6in (39.47m)	129ft 6in (39.47m)	132ft 8½in (40.45m)
Vehicle length:	62ft 6in (19.05m)	62ft 6in (19.05m)	63ft 11½in (19.49m)
Height:	12ft 9½n (3.90m)	12ft 9½n (3.90m)	12ft 9¼in (3.89m)
Width:	9ft 3in (2.82m)	9ft 3in (2.82m)	9ft 3in (2.82m)
Seating:	Total - 18F/122S DMBS - 84S DTC - 18F/38S - -	Total - 146S DMBS - 84S DTS - 62S - -	Total - 19F/134S DMBS - 84S DTC - 19F/50S - -
Internal layout:	First - Compartment Standard - 2+3	2+3, Compartment	First - Compartment Standard - 2+3
Gangway:	No	No	No
Toilets:	Not fitted	Not fitted	DTC - 2
Weight:	Total - 72 tons DMBS - 40 tons DTC - 32 tons - -	Total - 72 tons DMBS - 40 tons DTS - 32 tons - -	Total - 70 tons DMBS - 40 tons DTC - 30 tons - -
Brake type:	Air (EP/Auto)	Air (EP/Auto)	Air (EP/Auto)
Bogie type:	SR 40ft	SR 40ft	Mk4/Mk3B, Commonwealth
Power collection:	660-750V dc third rail	660-750V dc third rail	660-750V dc third rail
Traction motor type:	2 x EE507	2 x EE507	2 x EE507
Horsepower:	500hp (373kW)	500hp (373kW)	500hp (373kW)
Max speed:	75mph (121km/h)	75mph (121km/h)	90mph (145km/h)
Coupling type:	Inner - Link Outer - Buck-eye	Inner - Link Outer - Buck-eye	Inner - Link Outer - Buck-eye
Multiple restriction:	1951, 1957, 1963, 1966 SR EMUs	1951, 1957, 1963, 1966 SR EMUs	1951, 1957, 1963, 1966 SR EMUs
Door type:	Slam	Slam	Slam
Special features:	-	-	-
Notes:	SR design	SR design	BR design 6001-6042 fitted with contactor equipment, 6043-6173 fitted with camshaft control equipment

BR SAP	BR CAP
418/1 - 5901-5941 418/2 - 5942	413/2 - 3201-3213 413/3 - 3301-3311
5901-5942	3201-3213 3301- 3311
6001-6021, 6024-6044	From Class 414 fleet
2SAP	4CAP
1974 (modified)	As CAP - 1982
BR Eastleigh	BR Eastleigh
DMBS+DTS	DTC+DMBS+DMLS+DTC
DMBS - 65393-65434 DTC - 77115-77156	DMBS -From Class 414 fleet DTC - From Class 414 fleet
132ft 8½in (40.45m)	265ft 5in (80.90m)
63ft 11½in (19.49m)	63ft 11½in (19.49m)
12ft 9¼in (3.89m)	12ft 9¼in (3.89m)
9ft 3in (2.82m)	9ft 3in (2.82m)
Total - 153S DMBS - 84S DTC - 69S - -	Total - 38F/268S DTC - 19F/50S DMBS - 84S DMLS - 84S DTC - 19F/50S
2+3, Compartment	2+3, Compartment
No	No
DTS - 2	DTS - 2
Total - 70 tons DMBS - 40 tons DTS - 30 tons - -	Total 140 tons DTC - 30 tons DMBS - 40 tons DMLS - 40 tons DTC - 30 tons
Air (EP/Auto)	Air (EP/Auto)
Mk4/Mk3B, Commonwealth	Mk4/Mk3B, Commonwealth
660-750V dc third rail	660-750V dc third rail
2 x EE507	4 x EE507
500hp (373kW)	1,000hp (746kW)
90mph (145km/h)	90mph (145km/h)
Inner - Link Outer - Buck-eye	Inner - Link Outer - Buck-eye
1951, 1957, 1963, 1966 SR EMUs	1951, 1957, 1963, 1966 SR EMUs
Slam	Slam
-	-
BR design Most sets were returned to first/standard class in early 1970s, only to be downgraded again in 1974	BR design Driving controls from motor cars isolated, uncoupling chains removed and guards equipment removed from DMLS cars

Class 413, 414, 418 – 2HAP, 2SAP, 4CAP

Above: *Two distinct batches of HAP stock were built at Eastleigh Works from 1958, 36 two-car sets to Southern design and eventually a total of 173 to the later BR design. These two-car sets were formed of a Driving Motor Brake Third (second) and a Driving Trailer Composite. The Southern or Bulleid sets were ordered for the Thanet electrification, where they worked until 1969, when the sets were transferred to the Western section and declassified to all second class as SAP units. The BR designed HAP sets were destined for the Gillingham and Maidstone lines in Kent; the first 42 sets emerged in 1957-58, to be followed by a further 63 (6043-6105) for the Thanet lines. A further batch numbered 6106-6146 emerged for phase two of the Kent Coast electrification, with a further 27 sets (6147-73) emerging for the Central and Western sections. In this view we see Bulleid-design HAP No. 5608 from its DMBS vehicle showing all-over BR blue with a small yellow warning panel.* CJM

Left Middle: *Bulleid two-car set No. 5607 is seen from its DTC coach when new in 1958; note the large headcode numerals.* CJM

Left Bottom: *BR-design HAP unit No. 6007 is viewed from its DTC car. Note the warning whistle above the driver's front window. As delivered sets were in BR green, yellow ends were later added.* CJM

Right: *Repaints after 1968 saw BR rail blue applied with full yellow warning ends. A black triangle was applied at the DMBS end. After blue livery came the standard blue-grey colour scheme. Viewed from its DMBS end, set No. 6022 is seen at Fratton.* CJM

Below: *Displaying blue-grey livery, set No. 4312 (renumbered in the TOPS system) passes Clapham Junction with its DTC vehicle leading, coupled to two VEP units on a Bournemouth stopping service.* CJM

Right: *The BR design HAP fleet saw several changes over the years. In 1973 a batch was downgraded to standard class only and classified as SAPs, being renumbered in the 59xx series mainly for Waterloo-Windsor line work. Later a batch of Coastway HAP (CAP) sets was formed by semi permanently coupling two 2HAPs together to operate on the Portsmouth-Brighton route; these sets were reclassified as Class 413. Painted in NSE colours CAP No. 3301 is seen inside Stewarts Lane EMU shed. The intermediate cabs were isolated out of use.* CJM

Class 415 – 4EPB

	SR design	BR design	Rebuilt condition
Sub class:	415/1	415/2	415/4
Number range:	5001-5260	5301-5370	5401-5497
Former number range:	-	-	50xx, 51xx series
Alpha code:	4EPB (4-car Electro Pneumatic Brake)	4EPB (4-car Electro Pneumatic Brake)	4EPB (4-car Electro Pneumatic Brake)
Introduced:	1951-55	1957-59	-
Refurbished:			1979-1981
Built by:	BR Eastleigh	BR Eastleigh	-
Refurbished by:	-	-	BREL Eastleigh and BREL Horwich Works
Formation:	DMBS+TS+TSO+DMBS	DMBS+TS+TSO+DMBS	DMBSO+TSO+TSO+DMBSO
Vehicle numbers:	DMBS - 14001-14106, 14201-14520 TS - 15001-15078, 15159-15233, 15284-15393 TSO - 15101-15158, 15234-15283, 15334-15448	DMBS - 61516-61627 TS/TSO - 70375-70482	DMBSO - From 415/1 fleet TSO - From 415/1 fleet
Set length:	275ft 5in (83.95m)	263ft 11¼in (71.30m)	275ft 5in (83.95m)
Vehicle length:			
Height:	12ft 9½in (3.90m)	12ft 9½in (3.90m)	12ft 9½in (3.90m)
Width:	9ft 3in (2.82m)	9ft 3in (2.82m)	9ft 3in (2.82m)
Seating:	Total - 386S* DMBS - 82S TS - 120S* TSO - 102S* DMBS - 82S	Total - 392S DMBS - 84S TS - 112S TSO - 112S DMBS - 84S	Total - 268S DMBSO - 82S TSO - 102S TSO - 102S DMBSO - 82S
Internal layout:	2+3, Compartment	2+3, Compartment	2+3
Gangway:	No	No	No
Toilets:	Not fitted	Not fitted	Not fitted
Weight:	Total - 135 tons DMBS - 40 tons TS - 28 tons TSO - 27 tons	Total - 138 tons DMBS - 39-40 tons TS - 29 tons	Total - 139 tons DMBSO - 41 tons TSO - 29 tons TSO - 28 tons
Brake type:	Air (EP/Auto)	Air (EP/Auto)	Air (EP/Auto)
Bogie type:	SR 40ft type	Mk3D	SR 40ft type
Power collection:	660-750V dc third rail	660-750V dc third rail	660-750V dc third rail
Traction motor type:	4 x EE507	4 x EE507	4 x EE507
Horsepower:	1,000hp (746kW)	1,000hp (746kW)	1,000hp (746kW)
Max speed:	75mph (121km/h)	90mph (145km/h)	75mph (121km/h)
Coupling type:	Inner - Link Outer - Buck-eye	Inner - Link Outer - Buck-eye	Inner - Link Outer - Buck-eye
Multiple restriction:	1951, 1957, 1963, 1966 SR EMUs	1951, 1957, 1963, 1966 SR EMUs	1951, 1957, 1963, 1966 SR EMUs
Door type:	Slam	Slam	Slam

* Seating varied on some sets, depending on layout
A few sets were reformed with a mix of SR and BR design vehicles

Right Top: *Four-car Electro Pneumatic Brake (4EPB) sets emerged in both SR and BR designs. The SR design units numbered in the 50xx and 51xx series emerged from Eastleigh Works at the end of 1951, following the final 4SUB sets off the production line. Fitted with more modern control equipments and then state-of-the-art EP brakes, each set was formed of two DMBS cars and one Compartment Trailer and one Open Trailer, with total seating for 386. The first line to see the SR EPBs was the Guildford New Line, with following sets going to all three operating divisions. The final set, No. 5260, emerged from Eastleigh Works in 1957. Towards the end of the 1950s further fleets of EPB stock were ordered, and this time a BR exterior coach design was used, with 70 sets built numbered in the 53xx series. When built all SR and BR design sets were finished in BTC green livery, small yellow warning panels and later full yellow ends were applied, with all sets after 1969 emerging in BR rail blue with full yellow ends. Painted in BR green with a full yellow warning end, set No. 5046 is illustrated working on the Eastern section. This set still sports a whistle, mounted above the driver's front window.* CJM-C

Below: *The slab fronted design of the BR EPB is shown in this image of set No. 5320 receiving maintenance inside Chart Leacon depot, in Ashford. In the main the BR design units operated on the Eastern section with just a handful working Central and Western section duties. No. 5320 stands next to a 4CEP unit and both are in green livery.* CJM-C

Class 415 – 4EPB

Above & Below: *After many years in BR green livery both the SR and BR EPB fleets were painted in all-over BR rail blue, and following internal refurbishment standard blue and grey colours were applied. The EPB sets working on the Eastern section were maintained at Slade Green depot, while those working on the Central section received maintenance at Selhurst. On the Western section Wimbledon Park (later East Wimbledon) was responsible for fleet upkeep. In the upper view we see rail-blue liveried set No. 5250 working in the Gravesend area, while the view below shows BR design set No. 5325 working on the Central section at Croydon. When painted in blue/grey colours the sets gained their running numbers on both sides of the cab, applied above the front windows. Both:* CJM

Above: *Between 1979-81 a major refurbishment project was undertaken on the EPB fleet with both BREL Eastleigh and BREL Horwich undertaking major rebuilding work. In the main this project called for the upgrading of coach interiors and the opening out of the remaining compartment vehicles. Interiors were redecorated using new materials, new lighting was installed and solid steel luggage racks fitted in place of the strung type. The refurbished sets were classified as 415/4 and renumbered in the 54xx series. Refurbished sets operated mainly in the Central section. Set No. (41)5436 is seen on shed at Selhurst.* CJM

Right Middle: *Under the TOPS renumbering system the original BR design 53xx units became class 415/6 and were renumbered in the (41)56xx series. Sporting NSE-livery, set No. 5626 is seen at Ramsgate depot.* CJM

Right Bottom: *Towards the end of the EPB operation, Slade Green depot and Network SouthEast agreed to the repainting of two sets into heritage liveries. Set No. 5001 was repainted into 1950s green with a small yellow warning panel, while set No. 5176 was repainted into 1970s rail blue. The pair are seen 'on shed' at Slade Green. Note that both sets sport a central headlight.* CJM

Class 416 – 2EPB

	SR design	BR design	Tyneside design
Class:	416/1	416/2	416/2
Number range:	6301-6334	6202-6279	5781-5795
Former number range:	5651-5684	5701-5779	-
Alpha code:	2EPB (2-car Electro Pneumatic Brake)	2EPB (2-car Electro Pneumatic Brake)	2EPB (2-car Electro Pneumatic Brake)
Introduced:	1953	1953-56	1956
Built by:	BR Eastleigh	BR Eastleigh	BR Eastleigh
Formation:	DMBS+DTS	DMBS+DTS	DMBS+DTS
Vehicle numbers:	DMBS - 14557-14590 DTS - 16101-16134	DMBS - 65300-65435 DTS - 77500-77578	DMBS - 65311-65325 DTS - 77100-77114
Set length:	129ft 6½in (39.48m)	132ft 8¼in (40.44m)	132ft 8¼in (40.44m)
Vehicle length:	64ft (19.51m)	64ft (19.51m)	64ft (19.51m)
Height:	12ft 9½in (3.90m)	12ft 9½in (3.90m)	12ft 9½in (3.90m)
Width:	9ft 3in (2.82m)	9ft 3in (2.82m)	9ft 3in (2.82m)
Seating:	Total - 178S DMBS - 84S DTS - 94S	Total - 186S DMBS - 84S DTS - 102S	Total - 176S DMBS - 74S DTS - 102S
Internal layout:	2+3	2+3	2+3
Gangway:	No	No	No
Toilets:	Not fitted	Not fitted	Not fitted
Weight:	Total - 70 tons DMBS - 40 tons DTS - 30 tons	Total - 71 tons DMBS - 40 tons DTS - 31 tons	Total - 71 tons DMBS - 40 tons DTS - 31 tons
Brake type:	Air (EP/Auto)	Air (EP/Auto)	Air (EP/Auto)
Bogie type:	SR 40ft	Mk3D	Mk3D
Power collection:	660-750V dc third rail	660-750V dc third rail	660-750V dc third rail
Traction motor type:	2 x EE507	2 x EE507	2 x EE507
Horsepower:	500hp (373kW)	500hp (373kW)	500hp (373kW)
Max speed:	75mph (121km/h)	75mph (121km/h)	75mph (121km/h)
Coupling type:	Inner - Link Outer - Buck-eye	Inner - Link Outer - Buck-eye	Inner - Link Outer - Buck-eye
Multiple restriction:	1951, 1957, 1963, 1966 SR EMUs	1951, 1957, 1963, 1966 SR EMUs	1951, 1957, 1963, 1966 SR EMUs
Door type:	Slam	Slam	Slam
Note:			Originally used on Tyneside electrified system around Newcastle

Below: *To operate alongside both the SR and BR design 4EPB sets were two-car versions, allowing 2, 4, 6, 8, 10 or 12-car trains to be formed. The two-car sets were formed of a DMBT (later DMBS) and a Driving Trailer Third (Driving Trailer Second); no brake vehicle was provided in the trailer car. Seating was for 178 on the SR design sets and 186 on the BR designed stock. Originally all were painted green, which later changed to BR rail blue and then blue and grey. In their early days on the Western section, two 2EPBs depart from Surbiton bound for Waterloo; a DTS coach is nearest the camera.* CJM-C

Refurbished
416/4
6401-6426
62xx series
2EPB (2-car Electro Pneumatic Brake)
Refurbished: 1986
BR Eastleigh
DMBS+DTS
DMBS - From 416/2 fleet
DTS - From 416/2 fleet
132ft 8¼in (40.44m)
64ft (19.51m)
12ft 9½in (3.90m)
9ft 3in (2.82m)
Total - 186S
DMBS - 84S
DT S - 102S
2+3
No
Not fitted
Total - 71 tons
DMBS - 40 tons
DTS - 31 tons
Air (EP/Auto)
Mk3D
660-750V dc third rail
2 x EE507
500hp (373kW)
75mph (121km/h)
Inner - Link
Outer - Buck-eye
1951, 1957, 1963, 1966
SR EMUs
Slam

Above: *In August 1963, the 15 Tyneside EPBs were transferred to the Southern Region, allocated to the Western section. They were quickly modified to standard BR design EPB stock, but were always identifiable by having a large guards brake van. Led by its DTS, ex-Tyneside set No. 5786 passes Surbiton in 1983 painted in blue and grey livery.* CJM

Below: *A good comparison between a BR and SR designed EPB. On the left is BR designed two-car No. 5761 seen from its DTS end, while on the right is an SR-design DMBS from set No. 5029.* CJM

Right Bottom: *In 1986-87 a major refurbishment project was undertaken on the BR-designed EPBs, bring their interiors up to date, using modern materials and installing modern lighting. The upgraded sets were classified 416/4 and renumbered in the 64xx series. At the same time, a number of the SR design sets were upgraded. Some sets were also given 'barred' windows for operation over the North London line through Hampstead Heath Tunnel where clearances were restricted. The facelifted sets were repainted in blue/grey and given their revised TOPS number above each cab front window, as shown on window bar fitted No. 6321 near Willesden Junction. This blue and grey-liveried set has its DMBS leading* CJM

Class 419 – MLV & TLV

Number range:	(41)9001-(41)9010	68201-68206
Former number range:	68001-68010	-
Alpha code:	1MLV (1-car Motor Luggage Van)	1TLV (1-car Trailer Luggage Van)
Introduced:	1959	Rebuilt - 1968
Built by:	BR Eastleigh	Rebuilt - Selhurst
Formation:	MLV	TLV
Vehicle numbers:	68001-68010	68201-68206
Vehicle length:	67ft 1in (20.44m)	58ft 11in (17.96m)
Height:	12ft 9½in (3.90m)	12ft 9in (3.89m)
Width:	9ft (2.77m)	9ft 3in (2.82m)
Seating:	None	None
Internal layout:	Open - 2 luggage compartments	Open - 2 luggage compartments
Gangway:	No	Fitted - plated over
Toilets:	Not fitted	Not fitted
Weight:	45 tons	32 tons
Brake type:	Air (EP/Auto), also fitted with Vacuum exhauster for hauling vacuum brake fitted stock	Air (EP/Auto)
Bogie type:	Mk 3B	B4
Power collection:	660-750V dc third rail and traction battery (around 20 mins power)	-
Traction motor type:	2 x EE507	-
Horsepower:	500hp (373kW)	-
Max speed:	90mph (145km/h)	90mph (145km/h)
Coupling type:	Buck-eye	Buck-eye
Multiple restriction:	1951, 1957, 1963, 1966 SR EMUs	-
Door type:	Double leaf slam	Double leaf slam
Special features:	Authorised to haul vacuum or air brake trailing load of up to 100 tons	Through SR 27 wire jumper fitted. Converted back to BG stock, mainly from 1976 into HST *en-parts* wagons

Below: *Following the Kent Coast electrification and the use of EMUs on the London-Dover boat trains the luggage capacity offered on CEP/BEP stock was inadequate to cope with demand. Originally two single-car Motor Luggage Vans (MLVs) were built, followed by a further eight. The MLVs has a full width cab at each end like an EPB or HAP unit, with two luggage compartments and a small guards office. In addition to drawing third rail power, traction batteries were provided for operation away from a live rail supply, for up to around 20 minutes with a full battery. A vacuum brake exhauster was also fitted to enable the hauling of a light vacuum brake fitted van train. The MLVs were fitted with standard EMU draw gear. No. 68007 is seen leading a Dover to Victoria boat train through Headcorn in 1977.* CJM

Above: *Painted in BR rail blue with a full yellow end, MLV No. 9003 (68003) is seen at Strawberry Hill from its traction battery end; these were housed in the six hinged boxes directly behind the cab side door. Access to the two luggage compartments was by three pairs of bi-parting hinged doors on either side. Note the vacuum pipe to the left of the buck-eye coupling.* CJM

Right Middle: *When the London & South East operating division was formed and the 'Jaffa cake' livery introduced, several of the MLVs were painted in this scheme to match the CEP stock operating passenger services. Two of the brown, orange and grey-liveried MLVs, with No. 9010 (68010) at the front, are seen at Ramsgate depot, the home allocation for the fleet.* CJM

Right Bottom: *The six Selhurst converted Trailer Luggage Vans (TLVs) were introduced in 1968 after luggage traffic again increased on the London-Folkestone/Dover route. The vehicles were BGs through wired with 27-wire SREMU jumper cables, high level air pipes and electro-pneumatic brakes. In reality the TLVs saw little service and were stored within about six years. The vehicles were later again rebuilt as barrier and HST* en-part *vehicles for use on the Western Region. A TLV is seen coupled between the MLV and CEP passenger stock on this boat train in 1970.* CJM-C

Class 420/422 – 4BIG

Class:	As built - 420 Facelifted - 422
Original number range:	7039-7058
TOPS number range:	2101-2112, 2201-2262
Alpha code:	4BIG (4 Buffet Intermediate Guards)
Introduced:	7031-7048 - 1965-66 7049-7058 - 1970
Built/rebuilt by:	BR York
Formation:	DTCL+MBS+TRB+DTCL
Vehicle numbers:	DTCL - 76112-76129, 76561-76570 MBS - 62053-62070, 62277-62286 TRB - 69301-69318, 69330-69339 DTCL - 76112-76129, 76561-76570
Set length:	265ft 8½in (80.99m)
Vehicle length:	64ft 9½in (19.75m)
Height:	12ft 9¼in (3.89m)
Width:	9ft 3in (2.81m)
Seating:	Total - 42F/120S/40U DTCL - 18F/36S, MBS - 56S TRB - 40U, DTCL - 24F/28S
Internal layout:	First - Compartment, Standard/Unclassified - 2+2
Gangway:	Throughout
Toilets:	DTCL - 2
Weight:	155.5 Tons DTCL - 35.5 tons, MBS - 49 tons TRB - 35 tons, DTCL - 36 tons
Brake type:	Air (Auto/EP)
Bogie type:	Power - Mk4 Trailer - B5 (SR)
Power collection:	750V dc third rail
Traction motor type:	4 x EE507
Horsepower:	1,000hp (740kW)
Max speed:	90mph (145km/h)
Coupling type:	Buck-eye
Multiple restriction:	1951-66 SR EMU
Door type:	Slam
Special features:	7036-7048 fitted with electric parking brake
Notes:	Most saloons rebuilt as Class 421 stock

Below: *To provide catering facilities for trains formed of new 4CIG stock, originally on the Victoria to Brighton line and latterly on the Waterloo to Portsmouth Harbour route, a fleet of 4BIG (4-Car Buffet Intermediate Guards) sets was built. Eighteen sets (7031-48) were constructed in 1965-66 for use on the Brighton line, fitted with a unique electric parking brake system rather than the traditional handbrake wheel. The sets were basically a 4CIG with a full length buffet car replacing the TS coach. The buffet, with a sizeable kitchen and serving area at one end, seated 40 being officially unclassified. When replacement stock for the COR sets in use on the Waterloo to Portsmouth route was authorised, an updated version of the CIG/BIG fleet was ordered with a further ten 4BIG units (Nos. 7049-7058) introduced in 1970. All CIG and BIG sets were constructed at the BR workshops in York and were the first of the SR unit designs to have a central power car with both driving cars being trailers. Painted in later NSE livery, TRB No. 69337, one of the 1970 built vehicles, is seen at Brighton Lovers Walk.* CJM

Above: *When originally introduced, the 18 Brighton line sets emerged in BR multiple unit green livery, off-set by a small yellow front end warning panel. Sets were repainted into standard main line blue and grey from the late 1960s and, when the second tranche of sets for the Portsmouth line emerged, these were introduced in blue and grey colours. Original Portsmouth line set No. 7051 is seen passing Earlswood with a Victoria to South Coast service in 1981. The buffet car is the third vehicle from the front.* CJM

Below: *With the renumbering of Southern EMUs into the TOPS classification system the BIG stock became Class 420 (unrefurbished sets) and Class 422 (refurbished sets). Towards the end of their operating days a number of sets were placed in traffic with the buffet cars isolated, in reality working as a three-car set. With buffet car facilities locked out of use, set No. 2259 painted in NSE colours approaches Northam Junction with a stopping service from Eastleigh to Bournemouth in 1998.* CJM

Class 421 – 4CIG, 3CIG, 3COP

Class:	-	421/3
Number range:	7301-7438	1701-1753
Former number range:	-	7301-7336*
Alpha code:	4CIG (4 **C**orridor **I**ntermediate **G**uards)	4CIG (4 Corridor Intermediate Guards)
Introduced:	1964-70	1964-70
Built by:	BR/BREL York	BR/BREL York
Rebuilt by:	-	-
Formation:	DTCL+MBS+TS+DTCL	DTCL+MBS+TS+DTCL
Vehicle numbers:	DTCL - 76076-76111, 76581-76610, 76717-76787, 76859 MBS - 62017-62052, 62287-62316, 62355-62425, 62430 TS - 70695-70730, 70967-70996, 71035-71106 DTCL - 76076-76111, 76581-76610, 76717-76787, 76859	DTCL - 76026-76129 MBS - 62017-62070 TS - 70695-71770 DTCL - 76022-76093
Set length:	265ft 8½in (80.99m)	265ft 8½in (80.99m)
Vehicle length:	64ft 9½in (19.75m)	64ft 9½in (19.75m)
Height:	12ft 9¼in (3.89m)	12ft 9¼in (3.89m)
Width:	9ft 3in (2.82m)	9ft 3in (2.82m)
Seating:	Total - 42F/192S DTCL - 18F/36S MBS - 56S TS - 72S DTCL - 24F/28S	Total - 42F/192S DTCL - 18F/36S MBS - 56S TS - 72S DTCL - 24F/28S
Internal layout:	First - Compartment Standard - 2+2	First - Compartment Standard - 2+2
Gangway:	Throughout	Throughout
Toilets:	DTCL - 2	DTCL - 2
Weight:	Total - 157.5 tonnes DTCL - 35.5 tonnes MBS - 56 tonnes TS - 31.5 tonnes DTCL - 35 tonnes	Total - 157.5 tonnes DTCL - 35.5 tonnes MBS - 56 tonnes TS - 31.5 tonnes DTCL - 35 tonnes
Brake type:	Air (Auto/EP)	Air (Auto/EP)
Bogie type:	Power - Mk4 Trailer - B5 (SR)	Power - Mk4 Trailer - B5 (SR)
Power collection:	750V dc third rail	750V dc third rail
Traction motor type:	4 x EE507	4 x EE507
Horsepower:	1,000hp (740kW)	1,000hp (740kW)
Max speed:	90mph (145km/h)	90mph (145km/h)
Coupling type:	Buck-eye	Buck-eye
Multiple restriction:	1951-66 SR EMU	1951-66 SR EMU
Door type:	Slam	Slam
Special features:	7301-7336 fitted with electric parking brake	

421/4	421/5	421/7
1801-1891	1301-1322, 1392-1399+,	1401-1411
7337-7438	73xx, 74xx series	2203-2261 (4BIG)
4CIG (4 Corridor Intermediate Guards)	4CIG (4 Corridor Intermediate Guards)	3COP (3 Coastway OPen)
1970-72	1970-72	As COP - 1997-98
BR/BREL York	BR/BREL York	BR/BREL York
-		Wessex Eastleigh
DTCL+MBS+TS+DTCL	DTCL+MBS+TS+DTCL	DTSOL+MBS+DTSOL
DTCL - 76108-76859 MBS - 62282-62340 TS - 70968-71106 DTCL - 76576-76860	DTCL - 76561-76723 MBS - 62277-62361 TS - 70967-71929 Series, plus 70229-71832 DTCL - 76571-76294	DTCL - 76563-76800 MBS - 62279-62388 DTSOL - 76573-76821
265ft 8½in (80.99m)	265ft 8½in (80.99m)	200ft 3in (61.04m)
64ft 9½in (19.75m)	64ft 9½in (19.75m)	64ft 9½in (19.75m)
12ft 9¼in (3.89m)	12ft 9¼in (3.89m) (ex-CEP vehicles 12ft 6in (3.81m)	12ft 9¼in (3.89m)
9ft 3in (2.82m)	9ft 3in (2.82m)	9ft 3in (2.82m)
Total - 42F/192S DTCL - 18F/36S MBS - 56S TS - 72S DTCL - 24F/28S	1301-1322 Total - 42F/192S 1392-1399 DTCL - 18F/36S MBS - 56S 1301-1322 - TS - 72S 1392-1399 - TS - 64S DTCL - 24F/28S	Total - 42F/184S DTSOL - 60S MBS - 58S + 1 tipup DTSOL - 60S
First - Compartment Standard - 2+2	First - Compartment Standard - 2+2	Standard - 2+2
Throughout	Throughout	Throughout
DTCL - 2	DTCL - 2	DTSL - 2
Total - 157.5 tonnes DTCL - 35.5 tonnes MBS - 56 tonnes TS - 31.5 tonnes DTCL - 35 tonnes	Total - 157.5 tonnes DTCL - 35.5 tonnes MBS - 56 tonnes TS - 31.5 tonnes (Ex CEP vehicles 33.8 tonnes) DTCL - 35 tonnes	Total - 126 tonnes DTSL - 35.5 tonnes MBS - 56 tonnes DTSL - 35 tonnes
Air (Auto/EP)	Air (Auto/EP)	Air (Auto/EP)
Power - Mk4 Trailer - B5 (SR)	Power - Mk6 Trailer - B5 (SR) or Mk4 (CEP)	Power - Mk4 Trailer - B5 (SR)
750V dc third rail	750V dc third rail	750V dc third rail
4 x EE507	4 x EE507	4 x EE507
1,000hp (740kW)	1,000hp (740kW)	1,000hp (740kW)
90mph (145km/h)	90mph (145km/h)	90mph (145km/h)
Buck-eye	Buck-eye	Buck-eye
1951-66 SR EMU	1951-66 SR EMU	1951-66 SR EMU
Slam	Slam	Slam
Set 1812 fitted with Central Door Locking (CDL) and cup & cone equipment	'Greyhound' sets with extra field weakening for Portsmouth line use	For use on Coastway line

Class 421 – 4CIG, 3CIG, 3COP

Class:	421/7	421/9
Number range:	1497-1498	1901-1908
Former number range:	1883 & 1888	7301-7336 series
Alpha code:	3CIG (3 Corridor Intermediate Guards)	4-CIG (4 Corridor Intermediate Guards)
Introduced:	As 3CIG 2004	-
Built by:	BR/BREL York	BR/BREL York
Rebuilt by:	SWT Wimbledon	-
Formation:	DTCOL+MBS+DTSOL	DTSL+MBS+TS+DTCL
Vehicle numbers:	DTCOL - From main fleet MBS - From main fleet DTSOL - From main fleet	DTSL - From main fleet MBS - From main fleet TS - From main fleet DTCL - From main fleet
Set length:	200ft 3in (61.04m)	265ft 8½in (80.99m)
Vehicle length:	64ft 9½in (19.75m))	64ft 9½in (19.75m)
Height:	12ft 9¼in (3.89m)	12ft 9¼in (3.89m)
Width:	9ft 3in (2.82m)	9ft 3in (2.82m)
Seating:	Total - 170S DTCOL - 60S MBS - 56S DTSOL - 54S	Total - 24F/210S DTSL - 54S MBS - 56S TS - 72S DTCL - 24F/28S
Internal layout:	Standard - 2+2	First - Compartment Standard - 2+2
Gangway:	Throughout	Throughout
Toilets:	DTSOL - 2	DTCL/DTSL - 2
Weight:	Total - 126 tonnes DTSL - 35.5 tonnes MBS - 56 tonnes DTSL - 35 onnes	Total - 157.5 tonnes DTCL/DTSL - 35.5 tonnes MBS - 56 tonnes TS - 31.5 tonnes DTCL - 35 tonnes
Brake type:	Air (Auto/EP)	Air (Auto/EP)
Bogie type:	Power - Mk4 Trailer - B5 (SR)	Power - Mk6 Trailer - B5 (SR)
Power collection:	750V dc third rail	750V dc third rail
Traction motor type:	4 x EE507	4 x EE507
Horsepower:	1,000hp (740kW)	1,000hp (740kW)
Max speed:	90mph (145km/h)	90mph (145km/h)
Coupling type:	Buck-eye	Buck-eye
Multiple restriction:	1951-66 SR EMU	1951-66 SR EMU
Door type:	Slam	Slam
Special features:	Brockenhurst-Lymington sets	Fitted with Mk6 power bogies

Left: *The CIG fleet built in 1970 to replace pre-war stock was introduced painted in the then standard blue and grey main line colours, as demonstrated here in set No. 7421 seen passing Surbiton on 28 August 1978 with a semi-fast Portsmouth Harbour to Waterloo service. First class accommodation on the CIG fleet was provided by a DTC at each end of the formation, one end having three and the other four compartments of six seats. Set No. 7421 is shown from the four first compartment end.* CJM

Right Top: *York Works built 138 four-car Corridor Intermediate Guards (4CIG) sets for Central and Western section use between 1964 and 1970. These were main line sets with low-density seating and fewer external passenger doors. The first batch, 7301-7336, emerged in 1964 for use on the Brighton line; these were fitted with electric parking brakes and operated with the phase one 4BIG units. When the Waterloo to Portsmouth line was modernished a further batch of CIGs numbered 7337-7366 was introduced. To allow the complete withdrawal of older pre-war stock a further batch of CIGs numbered 7337-7437 was authorised, plus one replacement set, No. 7438, covering a written off CEP unit. The Brighton line sets were introduced in BR green which was later changed to blue/grey colours. The 1970 sets were all delivered in blue and grey livery. Over the years considerable refurbishment and reformation of this fleet took place with a number of temporary and short formed sets introduced for specific purposes and routes. All CIG stock was withdrawn as part of the modernisation of the south Thames routes under privatisation. Two units were retained under the Community Rail scheme (Nos. 1497/98) for use on the Lymington Pier branch for several years painted in heritage colours. NSE-liveried set No. 1309, one of the faster acceleration 'greyhound' sets, departs from Southampton.* CJM

Right Middle: *Eleven Class 421/7s were formed by Connex South Central to operate Coastway services; these were former 4BIG sets with the buffet car removed and the interior opened out to improve passenger accommodation. Set No. 1401 is illustrated.* CJM

Below: *Like many of the Southern Region main line EMU classes, some of the 4CIG (Class 421) sets were repainted into London & South East colours or 'Jaffa cake' livery in 1985. Electric parking brake fitted phase 1 set No. 1703 is seen at BREL Eastleigh Works awaiting a test run on 18 September 1985.* CJM

Class 423, 427, 480 – 4VEP, 4VEG, 4VOP, 8VAB

	As built	Rebuilt condition	
Class:	423/0	427	423/4
Number range:	3001-3194	7901-7912	(42)3401-(42)3591
Former number range:	7701-7894	7788-7799	3001-3194 (7701-7894) series
Alpha code:	4VEP (**V**estibule **E**lectro **P**neumatic)	4VEG (**V**estibule **E**lectro **G**atwick)	4VEP (**V**estibule **E**lectro **P**neumatic)
Introduced:	1967-74	Converted - 1978	1967-74
Built/rebuilt by:	BR/BREL York	BR/BREL York Converted - Selhurst	BREL Eastleigh
Formation:	DTCL+MBSO+TSO+DTCL	DTCL+MBSO+TSO+DTCL	DTCL+MBSO+TSO+DTCL
Vehicle numbers:	DTCL - 76230-76942 MBSO - 62121-62475 TSO - 70781-71155	DTCL - 76505-76528 MBSO - 62249-62260 TSO - 70939-70950	From original fleet From original fleet From original fleet
Set length:	265ft 8½in (80.99m)	265ft 8½in (80.99m)	265ft 8½in (80.99m)
Vehicle length:	64ft 9½in (19.75m)	64ft 9½in (19.75m)	64ft 9½in (19.75m)
Height:	12ft 9¼in (3.89m)	12ft 9¼in (3.89m)	12ft 9¼in (3.89m)
Width:	9ft 3in (2.82m)	9ft 3in (2.82m)	9ft 3in (2.82m)
Seating:	Total - 48F/232S DTCL - 24F/38S MBSO - 58S TSO - 98S DTCL - 24F/38S	Total - 48F/208S DTCL - 24F/34S MBSO - 50S TSO - 90S DTCL - 24F/34S	Total - 36F/266S DTCL - 18F/46S MBSO - 76S TSO - 98S DTCL - 18F/46S
Internat layout:	First - compartment Standard - 2+2/2+3	First - compartment Standard - 2+2/2+3	First - compartment Standard - 2+2/2+3
Gangway:	Throughout	Throughout	Throughout
Toilets:	DTCL - 1	DTCL - 1	DTCL - 1
Weight:	Total - 148ton 4cwt DTCL - 34ton 5cwt MBSO - 49 ton TSO - 30ton 14cwt DTCL - 34ton 5cwt	Total - 151 tonnes DTCL - 35 tonnes MBSO - 49.5 tonnes TSO - 31.5 tonnes DTCL - 35 tonnes	Total - 151 tonnes DTCL - 35 tonnes MBSO - 49.5 tonnes TSO - 31.5 tonnes DTCL - 35 tonnes
Brake type:	Air (Auto/EP)	Air (Auto/EP)	Air (Auto/EP)
Bogie type:	Powered - Mk6 Trailer - B5 (SR)	Powered - Mk6 Trailer - B5 (SR)	Powered - Mk6 Trailer - B5 (SR)
Power collection:	750V dc third rail	750V dc third rail	750V dc third rail
Traction motor type:	4 x EE507	4 x EE507	4 x EE507
Horsepower:	1,000hp (740kW)	1,000hp (740kW)	1,000hp (740kW)
Max speed:	90mph (145km/h)	90mph (145km/h)	90mph (145km/h)
Coupling type:	Buck-eye	Buck-eye	Buck-eye
Multiple restriction:	1951-66 stock, 73/1, 33/1	1951-66 stock, 73/1, 33/1	1951-66 stock, 73/1, 33/1
Door type:	Slam	Slam	Slam
Special features:		Converted back to VEP fleet after introduction of Gatwick Express stock	
Notes:			

423/8	423/9	480
(42)3801-(42)3810	(42)3901-(42)3919	8001
3001-3194 (7701-7894) series	3001-3194 (7701-7894) series	
4VEP (**V**estibule **E**lectro **P**neumatic)	4VOP (**V**estibule **O**pen **P**neumatic)	8VAB (**V**estibule **A**utobrake **B**uffet)
1967-74	1999	1967-68
BR Chart Leacon	Adtranz Chart Leacon	Modified - Bournemouth/Selhurst
DTCL+MBSO+TSO+DTCL	DTSL+MBSO+TSO+DTSL	DTCL+MBSO+DTCL+DTCL+ MBSO+TRB+MBSO+DTCL
From original fleet From original fleet From original fleet	From original fleet From original fleet From original fleet	DTCL - 76373-76376 MBSO - 62200/02/03 TRB - 1759§
265ft 8½in (80.99m)	265ft 8½in (80.99m)	531ft 5in (161.98m)
64ft 9½in (19.75m)	64ft 9½in (19.75m)	64ft 9½in (19.75m)
12ft 9¼in (3.89m)	12ft 9¼in (3.89m)	12ft 9¼in (3.89m)
9ft 3in (2.82m)	9ft 3in (2.82m)	9ft 3in (2.82m)
Total - 36F/266S DTCL - 18F/46S MBSO - 76S TSO - 98S DTCL - 18F/46S	Total - 314S DTSL - 70S MBSO - 76S TSO - 98S DTSL - 70S	Total - 96F/299S/23Unclassified DTCL - 24F/38S MBSO - 58S DTCL - 24F/38S DTCL - 24F/38S MBSO - 31S TRB - 23Unclassified MBSO - 58S DTCL - 24F/38S
First - compartment Standard - 2+2/2+3	First - compartment Standard - 2+2/2+3	First - compartment Standard - 2+2/2+3 Buffet - 2+1
Throughout	Throughout	Throughout
DTCL - 1	No	DTCL - 1
Total - 151 tonnes DTCL - 35 tonnes MBSO - 49.5 tonnes TSO - 31.5 tonnes DTCL - 35 tonnes	Total - 151 tonnes DTCL - 35 tonnes MBSO - 49.5 tonnes TSO - 31.5 tonnes DTCL - 35 tonnes	Total - 323 tons DTCL - 34ton 5cwt MBSO - 49 tons DTCL - 34ton 5cwt DTCL - 34ton 5cwt MBSO - 48 tons TRB - 39 tons MBSO - 49 tons DTCL - 34ton 5cwt
Air (Auto/EP)	Air (Auto/EP)	Air (Auto/EP)
Powered - Mk6 Trailer - B5 (SR)	Powered - Mk6 Trailer - B5 (SR)	Powered - Mk6 Trailer - B5 (SR) TRB - Commonwealth
750V dc third rail	750V dc third rail	750V dc third rail
4 x EE507	4 x EE507	12 x EE507
1,000hp (740kW)	1,000hp (740kW)	3,000hp (2,220kW)
90mph (145km/h)	90mph (145km/h)	90mph (145km/h)
Buck-eye	Buck-eye	Buck-eye
1951-66 stock, 73/1, 33/1	1951-66 stock, 73/1, 33/1	1951-66 stock, 73/1, 33/1
Slam	Slam	Slam
Porterbrook owned sets	Converted for South London 'Metro' services, open layout, no first class or toilets	Disbanded 1974 after extra REP sets were delivered, reverted to VEP stock § Former loco-hauled vehicle

Class 423, 427, 480 – 4VEP, 4VEG, 4VOP, 8VAB

Left Top: *The main fleet on long-distance outer-suburban traction on the Southern Region from 1967 was 4 Vestibule Electro Pneumatic (4VEP) units, built at York (Derby built the intermediate vehicles for the first 20 sets) and numbered from 7701 to 7894. The first 20 sets went to the newly electrified Waterloo-Bournemouth line and were the first Southern units fitted with AWS. The sets were laid out in high-density style with first class seating provided in compartments in the DTC vehicles. Over the years a number of reforms and upgrades took place, the most significant being the reducing of the size of the original guards van in the MBSO vehicle and inserting two extra bays of seats. Sets delivered up to 1971 were in all-over BR rail blue, after which blue-grey colours were adopted as standard. Bournemouth line set No. 7703 is illustrated; note that the buck-eye is in the lowered position.* CJM-C

Left Middle: *Painted in blue-grey livery, later built set No. 7847 is seen calling at West Byfleet station with a Guildford to Waterloo stopping service on 8 April 1980.* CJM

Below: *The VEP stock remained the mainstay of operations on Connex and South West Trains after rail privatisation until replacement 'Electrostar' and 'Desiro' stock was introduced. Painted in NSE livery and with its enlarged passenger accommodation in the MBSO vehicle, refurbished set No. (42)3516 passes St Denys bound for Southampton on 20 March 1995.* CJM

Right Top: *Class 423 (4VEP) interior, showing later design of moquette. Seating was provided in the high-density 2+3 style with an external door to each seating bay. Metal above seat luggage racks were provided. Coach ventilation was gained by passenger controlled sliding hopper windows.* CJM

Right Middle: *When introduced the MBSO vehicles seated 58 in six bays with the rest of the coach occupied by a guards office and large luggage van. With declining cargo being carried by passenger trains, it was agreed that during refurbishment at Eastleigh - the luggage van would be halved in size and the area at the end of the coach rebuilt to accommodate two seating bays. This modification is seen on car No. 62200. In modified condition the MBSO seated 76 standard class passengers.* CJM

Below: *Under the privatisation banner and ownership by lease companies the VEP sets became the property of Porterbrook and Angel Trains, with privatised operator liveries carried. Here a South West Trains variant of the NSE colours is shown on set No. (42)3466 at Basingstoke. This set has had its original opening quarter lights removed from the saloon windows in the leading vehicle.* CJM

Class 423, 427, 480 – 4VEP, 4VEG, 4VOP, 8VAB

Above: *In 1978 the growth in passenger numbers and luggage being transported on the London Victoria to Gatwick Airport route required extra luggage accommodation. This was achieved by modifying 12 VEP units into VEG (Vestibule Electro Gatwick) sets and inserting extra luggage stacks, reducing the seating by 24 per train. The sets were renumbered in the 79xx series and Rapid City Link London-Gatwick branding was also applied. After the introduction of Gatwick Express stock, the VEG units returned to VEP status. Set No. 7904 is illustrated.* CJM

Below: *To cover for a shortage of stock on the electrified Waterloo-Bournemouth line in 1968, when VEP sets 7739, 7741 and 7742 were delivered they were reformed by Selhurst into an eight-car unit; the set consisted of a three- and five-car set formed DTC+MBS+DTC / DTC+MBS+TRB+MBS+DTC. In the middle of the five-car set, a former loco-hauled buffet car, No. 1759, wired for MU operation, was inserted. The set was numbered 8001 and remained in operation until extra REP/TC stock was delivered in 1974. In 1971 the set is seen passing West Byfleet with a Bournemouth-Waterloo service.* CJM

'Networker Classic' Class 424

Below: Adtranz embarked on a major project in 1997 to produce a lower cost option to replace the existing slam door passenger stock operated on the South London former Southern Region networks. They devised the 'Networker Classic' which was a rebuild of existing Class 421 4CIG DTC 76112, one of the original phase 1 vehicles replacing the entire bodywork above the frame with a 'Networker' style body. Running and control gear would have remained from the original vehicle, but everything else above the frame would have been new, meeting the latest Group Standards. One demonstrator vehicle was built at Derby Litchurch Lane and classified 424; the demonstrator was set out in the 2+3 style offering 77 seats. Passenger access was by bi-parting sliding doors at the one third and two third positions. The coach was used as a demonstrator at Derby and did operate over the main line to take part in a display to the Government and passenger user groups at London Victoria. The vehicle is seen at Derby Litchurch Lane. The plan was never furthered and No. 76112 was broken up in 2012. CJM

Number range:	424001, car 76112
Former unit number:	1761
Alpha code:	Not issued
Introduced:	Originally - 1965 Rebuilt - 1997
Built/rebuilt by:	Originally - BR York Rebuilt - Adtranz Derby
Formation:	DSO
Vehicle length:	20.66m (67ft 9¼in)
Height:	3.78m (12ft 4¾in)
Width:	2.80m (9ft 2¼in)
Seating:	77S
Internal layout:	2+3 high-density
Gangway:	Within set
Toilets:	Not on demonstrator
Weight:	31 tonnes
Brake type:	Air (EP/Auto)
Bogie type:	B4
Power collection:	750V dc third rail
Traction motor type:	Not fitted
Horsepower:	Not applicable
Max speed:	100mph (161km/h)
Coupling type:	Tightlock
Multiple restriction:	Not authorised on demonstrator
Door type:	Sliding
Notes:	Demonstration vehicle

Class 430 – 4REP

Class:	430
Amended class:	432
Original number range:	3001-3015
Revised number range:	2001-2015
Alpha code:	4REP (4-car Restaurant Electro Pneumatic)
Introduced:	1966, 1974
Built by:	BR/BREL York
Formation:	DMS+TRB+TBF+DMS
Vehicle numbers:	DMS - 62142-62162, 62476-62482 (even numbers) TRB - 69319-69329, 69022-69025 TBF - 70801-70811, 71156-71159 DMS - 62141-62161, 62477-62483 (odd numbers)
Set length:	265ft 5¼in (80.91m)
Vehicle length:	DMS - 64ft 9in (19.74m) TRB/TBF - 64ft 6in (19.66m)
Height:	12ft 9½in (3.90m)
Width:	9ft 3in (2.82m)
Seating:	Total - 24F/128S/23U DMS - 64S TRB - 23U TBF - 24F DMS - 64S
Internal layout:	First - Compartment Standard - 2+2 Unclassified - 2+1
Gangway:	Throughout
Toilets:	TBF - 1
Weight:	Total - 173.5 tonnes DMS - 51.5 tonnes TRB - 35 tonnes TBF - 35.5 tonnes DMS - 51.5 tonnes
Brake type:	Air (EP/Auto)
Bogie type:	DMS - Mk6 TRB, TBF - B5
Power collection:	660-750V dc third rail
Traction motor type:	8 x EE546B of 400hp (298kW)
Horsepower:	3,200hp (2,386kW)
Max speed:	90mph (145km/h)
Coupling type:	Buck-eye
Multiple restriction:	1951, 1957, 1963, 1966 SR EMUs with loading restriction on third rail due to high power consumption
Door type:	Slam
Special features:	SR cab-signalling in 'odd' numbered driving cars (later isolated)

Below: *With electrification of the Bournemouth line south from Pirbright Junction to Bournemouth in 1967 came the need for some special EMUs. The service onwards from Bournemouth to Weymouth as well as Southampton Docks was not to be electrified, but through services needed to be maintained. The answer came in building a fleet of high-powered tractor units and a fleet of trailer control sets which could operate under electric conditions as far as Bournemouth. Onwards to Weymouth the trailer units would be powered by a Class 33, operating in a push-pull mode and driven from the driving cab of the TC unit. In 1966 a fleet of 11 high-output four-car Restaurant Electro Pneumatic (4REP) sets plus three three-car and 28 four-car Trailer Control (TC) sets were built by York. The sets were all painted in BR rail blue and allocated to Bournemouth depot. Usually trains were formed with the REP tractor set at the London end and either one or two TC sets on the country end. The REP sets were formed of two high-powered driving cars, which were new built vehicles. The buffet cars were, however, rebuilds of loco-hauled RBs originally built in 1961. These were modified for EMU operation but much of their internal fittings remained the same. The other intermediate vehicle, a Trailer Brake First, was rebuilt from loco-hauled Mk1 CK stock. In 1974 four additional REP sets were built at York, and again the driving motor cars were new built while the intermediate coaches were loco-hauled rebuilds. In the view below we see buffet car No. 69320 from set 3002. This was the first York buffet rebuild, the first vehicle being upgraded at Eastleigh. Later the REP sets were renumbered from their original 30xx series to the 20xx number range.* CJM

Above: *With 3,200 installed hp (2,386kW), the REP fleet was able to reach speeds in excess of 100mph (160km/h) and on the rare occasion of a REP working alone some very spirited running could be seen. In July 1981, REP No. 3002 leads two 4TC sets towards Pirbright Junction with a semi-fast Bournemouth to Waterloo service.* CJM

Below: *After renumbering into the TOPS numeric sequence of (43)2013 an eight-car REP/TC formation heads away from Worting Junction on 27 April 1987 with the 09.33 Weymouth to Waterloo service. Note the NSE branding on the side of the REP.* CJM

Class 442 – 5WES

	As built	Refurbished
Number range:	442401-442424	442401-442424
Alpha code:	5WES (**WES**sex electric)	-
Introduced:	1988-1989	-
Refurbished	-	2009-2010
Built by:	BREL Derby	-
Refurbished by:	-	Wolverton Works
Formation:	DTFL+TSOL(A)+MBRSM+TSOL(B)+DTSL	DTSO(A)+TSO+MBC+TSOW+DTSO(B)
Vehicle numbers:	DTFL - 77382-77405 TSOL(A) - 71818-71841 MBRSM - 62937-62960 TSOL(B) - 71842-71865 DTSL - 77406-77429	DTSO(A) - 77382-77405 TSO - 71818-71841 MBC - 62937-62960 TSOW - 71842-71865 DTSO(B) - 77406-77429
Vehicle length:	DTFL/DTSL - 75ft 11½in (23.15m) TSOL/MBRSM - 75ft 5½in (23m)	DTSOL - 75ft 11½in (23.15m) TSO, MBC, TSOW - 75ft 5½in (23m)
Height:	12ft 6in (3.81m)	12ft 6in (3.81m)
Width:	8ft 11¾in (2.74m)	8ft 11¾in (2.74m)
Seating:	Total - 50F/248S DTFL - 50F TSOL(A) - 80S MBRSM - 30S TSOL(B) - 76S DTSL - 78S	Total - 24F/318S DTSO(A) - 74S TSO - 76S MBC - 24F/28S TSOW - 66S DTSL - 74S
Internal layout:	First - 2+1 Standard - 2+2	First - 2+1 Standard - 2+2
Gangway:	Throughout	Throughout
Toilets:	TSOL-1	TSO-2, TSOW-1
Weight:	Total - 202.84 tonnes DTFL - 39.06 tonnes TSOL(A) - 35.26 tonnes MBRSM - 54.10 tonnes TSOL(B) - 35.36 tonnes DTSL - 39.06 tonnes	Total - 206.1 tonnes DTSO(A) - 38.5 tonnes TSO - 37.5 tonnes MBC - 55.0 tonnes TSOW - 37.8 tonnes DTSO(B) - 37.3 tonnes
Brake type:	Air (EP/auto)	Air (EP/auto)
Bogie type:	Power - BR Mk6 Trailer - BREL T4	Power - BR Mk6 Trailer - BREL T4
Power collection:	750V dc third rail	750V dc third rail
Traction motor type:	4 x EE546 of 402hp (300kW)	4 x EE546 of 402hp (300kW)
Horsepower:	1,608hp (1,200kW)	1,608hp (1,200kW)
Max speed:	100mph (161km/h)	100mph (161km/h)
Coupling type:	Outer - buck-eye Inner - Bar	Outer - buck-eye Inner - Bar
Multiple restriction:	Within type	Within type
Door type:	Single-leaf sliding plug	Single-leaf sliding plug
Owner:	Angel Trains	Angel Trains

Right Above & Right Below: *With the extension of the electrification from Bournemouth to Weymouth in the mid 1980s came the order for replacement rolling stock, in the form of 24 five-car Wessex Electric (5WES) sets, built by BREL Derby and based on the latest Mk3 coach design. In many respects these were the pinnacle of modern EMU construction offering high quality interiors, swing plug doors and an exceptional ride quality. The five-car sets seated 50 first and 248 standard class passengers in the low-density 2+1 and 2+2 style. The first 13 sets were built with two luggage cages either side of the guards office in the MBRSM coach. Later builds were fitted with a seating snug adjacent to the buffet which was retro-fitted to the earlier built sets. Originally painted in NSE livery, the sets were later transferred to South West Trains. With standardisation on South West Trains with 'Desiro' stock, the Class 442s were withdrawn in 2007 and in 2008 were heavily rebuilt at Wolverton for redeployment on the new joint Southern/Gatwick Express Brighton line operation. The rebuild saw major internal changes with the two driving cars becoming driver standards and the intermediate motor coach becoming a composite vehicle. Sets were repainted in a new Gatwick Express livery. In the upper view set No. 2411 is seen at Waterloo with its DTSL coach leading, while the view below shows set No. 2403 in full South West Trains livery passing Vauxhall. Both:* CJM

5-8

Class 444 – 'Desiro'

Number range:	444001-444045
Introduced:	2003-04
Built by:	Siemens Transportation SGP, Austria
Formation:	DMSO+TSO(A)+TSO(B)+TSRMB+DMCO
Vehicle numbers:	DMSO - 63801-63845 TSO(A) - 67101-67145 TSO(B) - 67151-67195 TSRMB - 67201-67245 DMCO - 63851-63895
Vehicle length:	77ft 3in (23.57m)
Height:	12ft 1½in (3.7m)
Width:	8ft 9in (2.74m)
Seating:	Total: 35F/299S DMSO - 76S TSO(A) - 76S TSO(B) - 76S TSRMB - 47S DMCO - 35F/24S
Internal layout:	First 2+1 Standard 2+2
Gangway:	Throughout
Toilets:	TSO, TSRMB - 1
Weight:	Total - 221.8 tonnes DMSO - 51.3 tonnes TSO(A) - 40.3 tonnes TSO(B) - 36.8 tonnes TSRMB - 42.1 tonnes DMCO - 51.3 tonnes
Brake type:	Air, regenerative
Bogie type:	Siemens SGB5000
Power collection:	750V dc third rail
Traction motor type:	1TB2016-0GB02 three-phase
Output:	2,682hp (2,000kW)
Max speed:	100mph (161km/h)
Coupling type:	Outer - Dellner 12 Inner - Semi-auto
Multiple restriction:	Class 444 and 450
Door type:	Single-leaf sliding plug
Construction:	Aluminium
Special features:	Air conditioned, PIS
Owner:	Angel Trains
Operator:	South West Trains

Below: *South West Trains totally modernised its outer suburban and main line operations in 2003-07 with the introduction of Class 444 and 450 'Desiro' stock, removing the last slam door stock from service on the former Southern Region Western section. For long distance main line duties, a fleet of 45 five-car Class 444 sets was built in Austria and tested in Germany before being shipped to the UK via the Channel Tunnel. The 45 sets have main line configuration with all open saloons and external doors feeding vestibules rather than going directly into the passenger section of the vehicles. The '444s' seat 35 first and 299 standard class passengers, with first class accommodation usually in the London end driving car. The sets are nominally based at Northam Traincare Depot, but receive service exams at most SWT depot facilities. The sets are usually concentrated on the Waterloo to Weymouth and Portsmouth routes. The driving controls and front end layouts are the same as on the outer suburban Class 450 stock. In this view we see set No. 444009 from its DMSO end, while on the right Class 450 'Desiro' set No. 450117 shares the frame, clearly showing the near identical design of the front ends.* CJM

Right Bottom: *While a small buffet counter is provided at one end of the TSRMB coach, the vehicle coupled to the driving car housing first class accommodation, the 444 formed trains usually have a trolley perambulating the length of the train and many consider the buffet area is taking up space which could be used for seating. With its first class vehicle leading, identified by the light blue dots at cant rail height, set No. 444013 awaits departure from Bournemouth with a Waterloo bound service.* CJM

Above: *The South West Trains Class 444 fleet is painted in the Stagecoach main line white livery, off-set by blue and red with swirl ends. Set No. 444024 passes through the 'up' main line platform at Surbiton on 6 November 2006 with a Portsmouth Harbour to Waterloo service.* CJM

Right: *The middle vehicle of a Class 444 formation is a TSO with seating for 76 in the 2+2 style. At one end bicycle stowage space is provided. Car No. 67157 is illustrated.* CJM

Class 445 & 446 – 4PEP & 2PEP

Class:	445 originally 461+	446 originally 462+
Number range:	4001-4002	2001
Former number range:	-	-
Alpha code:	4PEP (4-car **P**rototype **E**lectro **P**neumatic)	2PEP (2-car **P**rototype **E**lectro **P**neumatic)
Introduced:	1971	1972
Built by:	BREL York	BREL York
Formation:	DMS+MS+MS+DMS	DMS+DMS
Vehicle numbers:	DMS - 64301 & 64303 MS - 62427 & 62426 MS - 62428 & 62429 DMS - 64302 & 64304	DMS - 64300 DMS - 64305 - -
Set length:	264ft 10in (80.72m)	132ft 5in (40.36m)
Vehicle length:	DMS - 64ft 11½in (19.8m) MS - 65ft 4¼in (19.93m)	DMS - 64ft 11½in (19.8m)
Height:	11ft 6½in (3.58m)	11ft 6½in (3.58m)
Width:	9ft 3in (2.82m)	9ft 3in (2.82m)
Seating:	Total - 280S DMS - 68S MS - 72S MS - 72S DMS - 68S	Total - 136S DMS - 68S DMS - 68S - -
Internal layout:	2+2	2+2
Gangway:	Within set	Within set
Toilets:	Not fitted	Not fitted
Weight:	Total - 140 tons DMS - 35 tons MS - 35 tons MS - 35 tons DMS - 35 tons	Total - 70 tons DMS - 35 tons DMS - 35 tons - -
Brake type:	Air, EP/rheostatic	Air, rheostatic
Bogie type:	4001 - BT5, 4002 - Mk6	Mk6
Power collection:	750V dc third rail	750V dc third rail
Traction motor type:	16 x GEC	8 x GEC
Horsepower:	1,600hp (1,193kW)	800hp (596.6kW)
Max speed:	75mph (121km/h)	75mph (121km/h)
Coupling type:	Inner - Bar Outer - Scharfenberg	Inner - Bar Outer - Scharfenberg
Multiple restriction:	Within type only	Within type only
Door type:	Bi-parting sliding	Bi-parting sliding
Notes:	+ When originally built, BREL papers showed the driving cars classified as Class 461 and the intermediate non driving cars Class 462	

Left: *Towards the end of the 1960s a major need was foreseen for replacement suburban EMU stock and the BRB launched a design programme to establish new state-of-the-art design principles. For this, three prototype trains (two four-car and one two-car) were ordered from York Works. Classified as PEP, the trains were a culture change; two pairs of passenger activated bi-parting sliding doors were on each side of each coach, automatic Scharfenberg couplings were fitted incorporating physical, air and electrical connections, and no guards van was provided. The guard would use one of the unoccupied driving cabs as his office. The two four-car sets were delivered to the Southern Region at Wimbledon in 1971, painted in BR rail blue. The two-car set in unpainted aluminium emerged the following year. On the Southern the sets operated on the Waterloo to Chessington, Hampton Court and Shepperton lines. The silver two-car set leads a four-car at Wimbledon in 1974.* CJM

Above & Below: *The PEP stock paved the way for the development of the production 1972-design EMUs of Classes 313, 314, 315, 507 and 508. It was very much a design tool and numerous modifications were carried out on vehicles at different times, with a number of reformations to test equipment. The first main line running for the PEP was on the Farnham to Alton line in the summer of 1972, where the above view was recorded of set No. 4001. At this time the main passenger saloon windows did not have opening quarter lights, all ventilation being of the forced air type, but modified windows were soon fitted. In the view below, set No. 4001 is seen with its modified side windows at Waterloo awaiting to depart with a Hampton Court service. For its operational trials PEP stock was allocated to Wimbledon Park depot. After its testing period was complete on the Southern the two-car set went to Scotland to pave the way for the introduction of Class 314 stock, while the four-car sets entered departmental service at the Railway Technical Centre, Derby. Both:* CJM

Class 450 – 'Desiro'

Class:	450/0	450/5
Number range:	450001-450042, 450071-450127	450543-450570
Former No. range	-	450043-450070
Introduced:	2002-07	As 450/5 2008-09
Built by:	Siemens Duewag, Germany, and Siemens SGP, Austria	Siemens Duewag, Germany, and Siemens SGP, Austria
Modified by:		Bournemouth SWT depot
Formation:	DMSO(A)+TCO+TSO+DMSO(B)	DMSO(A)+TSO+TSO+DMSO(B)
Vehicle numbers:	DMSO(A) - 63201-242/271-300/701-710/901-917 TCO - 64201-242/271-300/851-860/921-937 TSO - 68101-142/171-200/801-810/901-917 DMSO(B) - 63601-642/671-700/751-760/921-937	DMSO(A) - 63243-63270 TSO(A) - 64243-64270 TSO(B) - 68143-68170 DMSO(B) - 63643-63670
Vehicle length:	66ft 9in (20.4m)	66ft 9in (20.4m)
Height:	12ft 1½in (3.7m)	12ft 1½in (3.7m)
Width:	9ft 2in (2.7m)	9ft 2in (2.7m)
Seating:	Total - 24F/242S + 13 tip up DMSO(A) - 70S TCO - 24F/32S + 4 tip up TSO - 61S + 9 tip up DMSO(B) - 79S	Total - 240S + 11 tip up DMSO(A) - 64S TSO(A) - 56S + 4 tip-up TSO(B) - 56S + 7 tip up DMSO(B) - 64S
Internal layout:	First - 2+2F Standard - 2+2 & 2+3	2+2 & 2+3
Gangway:	Throughout	Throughout
Toilets:	TCO - 1, TSO - 1	TSO - 1
Weight:	Total - 172.2 tonnes DMSO(A) - 48.0 tonnes TCO - 35.8 tonnes TSO - 39.8 tonnes DMSO(B) - 48.6 tonnes	Total - 171.9 tonnes DMSO(A) - 48.0 tonnes TSO(A) - 35.5 tonnes TSO(B) - 39.8 tonnes DMSO(B) - 48.6 tonnes
Brake type:	Air, regenerative	Air, regenerative
Bogie type:	Siemens SGP SF5000	Siemens SGP SF5000
Power collection:	750V dc third rail	750V dc third rail
Traction motor type:	4 x 1TB2016 0GB02 three-phase	4 x 1TB2016 0GB02 three-phase
Output:	2,682hp (2,000kW)	2,682hp (2,000kW)
Max speed:	100mph (161km/h)	100mph (161km/h)
Coupling type:	Outer - Dellner 12 Inner - Semi-auto	Outer - Dellner 12 Inner - Semi-auto
Multiple restriction:	Class 444 and 450	Class 444 and 450
Door type:	Bi-parting sliding plug	Bi-parting sliding plug
Construction:	Aluminium	Aluminium
Owner:	Angel Trains	Angel Trains
Operator:	South West Trains	South West Trains
Special features:	Air conditioned, CCTV, PIS	Air conditioned, CCTV, PIS
Sub class variations:	Standard unit	High Capacity standard class sets

Left: *In common with Siemens policy, all new trains are tested on the builder's test track at Wildenrath, Germany, before delivery to the UK; this ensures any problems are fully sorted out before the expensive transit to the UK is undertaken. To cope with the South West Trains 'Desiro' testing, one of the test tracks at Wildenrath had to be equipped with BR Southern Region style third rail power equipment. The first Class 450 is seen on the test track in spring 2002.* CJM

Right Top: *A total of 127 four-car Class 450 sets were built by Siemens in Germany between 2002-2007 to replace the remaining slam-door stock in use on South West Trains. Based on the 'Desiro' platform, the sets seat 24 first and 242 standard class passengers. First class seating is in the 2+2 style in an intermediate vehicle, while standard class seating is in a mix of 2+2 and 2+3. Passenger access is by two pairs of bi-parting sliding-plug doors on either side of each coach. All '450s', along with the Class 444s, are based at Northam depot near Southampton, but receive maintenance at all SWT depots. The '450s' carry the SWT/Stagecoach outer suburban blue livery, with standard swirl ends. Sets are gangwayed throughout and fully automatic Dellner couplers are fitted with physical, pneumatic and electrical connections. Set No. 450031 is seen in the 'up' slow platform at Woking.* CJM

Right Middle: *First class seating is located in the intermediate Trailer Composite Open coach which also houses a guards office. First class seating is for 24, with power for laptops and overhead reading lights.* CJM

Below: *To cater for increased standard class patronage on the Waterloo-Windsor lines a batch of 28 Class 450s was modified in 2008-09 as standard class only, with increased standing room; these sets, known as High Capacity 450s, are classified as 450/5 and have the HC letters above the unit numbers on vehicle ends. Set No. 450552 is illustrated.* CJM

Class 455

As built

Class:	455/7	455/8	455/9
Number range:	455701-455750	455801-455874	455901-455920
Introduced:	1984-85	1982-84	1985
Built by:	BREL York	BREL York	BREL York
Formation:	DTSO(A)+MSO+ TSO+DTSO(B)	DTSO(A)+MSO+ TSO+DTSO(B)	DTSO(A)+MSO+ TSO+DTSO(B)
Vehicle numbers:	DTSO(A) - 77727-77811 (odds) MSO - 62783-62825 TSO - 71526-71568 DTSO(B) - 77728-77812 (evens)	DTSO(A) - 77579-77725 (odds) MSO - 62709-62782 TSO - 71637-71710 DTSO(B) - 77580-77726 (evens)	DTSO(A) - 77813-77852 (odds) MSO - 62826-62845 TSO - 71714-71733 DTSO(B) - 77814-77852 (evens)
Vehicle length:	DTSO - 65ft ½in (19.83m) MSO - 65ft 4½in (19.92m) TSO - 65ft 4½in (19.92m)	DTSO - 65ft ½in (19.83m) MSO - 65ft 4½in (19.92m) TSO - 65ft 4½in (19.92m)	DTSO - 65ft ½in (19.83m) MSO- 65ft 4½in (19.92m) TSO - 65ft 4½in (19.92m)
Height:	DTSO/MSO - 12ft 1½in (3.7m) TSO - 11ft 6½in (3.58m)	12ft 1½in (3.7m)	12ft 1½in (3.7m)
Width:	9ft 3¼in (2.82m)	9ft 3¼in (2.82m)	9ft 3¼in (2.82m)
Seating:	Total - 318S DTSO(A) - 74S MSO - 84S TSO - 86S DTSO - 74S	Total - 316S DTSO(A) - 74S MSO - 84S TSO - 84S DTSO(B) - 74S	Total - 316S DTSO(A) - 74S MSO - 84S TSO - 84S DTSO(B) - 74S
Internal layout:	2+3	2+3	2+3
Gangway:	Throughout	Throughout	Throughout
Toilets:	Not fitted	Not fitted	Not fitted
Weight:	Total - 130.1 tonnes DTSO(A) - 29.5 tonnes MSO - 45.6 tonnes TSO - 25.5 tonnes DTSO(B) - 29.5 tonnes	Total - 132 tonnes DTSO(A) - 29.5 tonnes MSO - 46 tonnes TSO - 27 tonnes DTSO(B) - 29.5 tonnes	Total - 132 tonnes DTSO(A) - 29.5 tonnes MSO - 46 tonnes TSO - 27 tonnes DTSO(B) - 29.5 tonnes
Brake type:	Air (Westcode)	Air (Westcode)	Air (Westcode)
Bogie type:	DTSO - BREL BT13 MSO - BREL BP27 TSO - BREL BX1	DTSO - BREL BT13 MSO - BREL BP20 TSO - BREL BT13	DTSO - BREL BT13 MSO - BREL BP20 TSO - BREL BT13
Power collection:	750V dc third rail	750V dc third rail	750V dc third rail
Traction motor type:	4 x EE507 of 250hp (186kW)	4 x EE507 of 250hp (186kW)	4 x EE507 of 250hp (186kW)
Horsepower:	1,000hp (746kW)	1,000hp (746kW)	1,000hp (746kW)
Max speed:	75mph (121km/h)	75mph (121km/h)	75mph (121km/h)
Coupling type:	Outer - Tightlock, Inner - Bar	Outer - Tightlock, Inner - Bar	Outer - Tightlock, Inner - Bar
Multiple restriction:	Class 455 and 456	Class 455 and 456	Class 455 and 456
Door type:	Bi-parting sliding	Bi-parting sliding	Bi-parting sliding
Construction:	Aluminium body/steel frame	Aluminium body/steel frame	Aluminium body/steel frame

Left: *The Class 455s brought new standards of driving cabs to the BR Southern Region, a massive improvement on the SUB and EPB designs, which in many cases did not have either AWS or even a speedometer. The cab of set No. 5808 is illustrated soon after delivery. The electronic brake controller is on the left side, with the master switch and power controller operated by the driver's right hand. Brake and speed gauges are on the inclined panel with switch gear on the facia panel and desk. The door control buttons on this example have been plated over.* CJM

Right Top, Middle & Bottom: *Introduced from 1982 as Southern Region suburban replacement stock for withdrawn SUB and EPB designs, the Class 455s became the standard local train design on the Central and Western sections, and remain the backbone of these operations today, operated by the privatised railway in a much refurbished and upgraded condition. The first batch of Class 455s off the York production line was 74 four-car Class 455/8 sets which used the Class 210/317 front end design with warning horns at roof height. Seating was for 316 standard class passengers in the 2+3 style, using low back seats. The sets were unique to the Southern Region, having Tightlock couplings, Westcode brakes and passenger activated, crew controlled sliding doors. The sets experienced huge teething troubles and entry into full passenger service was delayed. At first sets were all allocated to the Western section, based at Wimbledon, but as further sets were delivered the first batch of Class 455/8s was transferred to Selhurst for Central section use. The next batch of Class 455s to emerge was 43 Class 455/7s. These were built as three-coach sets, taking one Trailer Second Open from each of the Class 508s, which were at the same time transferred north to the Merseyrail system as three-car sets. This augmentation of the sets saw a different body profile on the TSO coach, very reminiscent of the days of augmented SUB stock on the Southern. The Class 455/7s incorporated the newer design of rounded cab roof and improved Group Standard light clusters. The final batch of Class 455s to be built was 20 Class 455/9s delivered in 1985, which had revised ventilation. In the top view is standard as delivered Class 455/8 No. 5856 at East Wimbledon depot. The middle image shows Class 455/7 No. 5743 departing from New Malden bound for Waterloo. The original Class 508 TS is the third vehicle of the formation and identifiable by its lower roof profile. The bottom image shows one of the final Class 455/9 sets, No. 5906, departing from Wimbledon bound for Effingham Junction via Epsom. All:* CJM

Class 455

Class:	455/7	455/8	455/9
Number range:	455701-455750	455801-455874	455901-455920
Introduced:	1984-85	1982-84	1985
Refurbished:	2003-07	2003-08	2004-07
Built by:	BREL York	BREL York	BREL York
Refurbished by:	Bombardier Ashford	(Southern) Alstom Eastleigh (SWT) Bombardier Ashford	Bombardier Ashford
Formation:	DTSO(A)+MSO+ TSO+DTSO(B)	DTSO(A)+MSO+ TSO+DTSO(B)	DTSO(A)+MSO+ TSO+DTSO(B)
Vehicle numbers:	DTSO(A) - 77727-77811 (odds) MSO - 62783-62825 TSO - 71526-71568 DTSO(B) - 77728-77812 (evens)	DTSO(A) - 77579-77725 (odds) MSO - 62709-62782 TSO - 71637-71710 DTSO(B) - 77580-77726 (evens)	DTSO(A) - 77813-77852 (odds) MSO - 62826-62845 TSO - 71714-71733 DTSO(B) - 77814-77852 (evens)
Vehicle length:	DTSO - 65ft ½in (19.83m) MSO - 65ft 4½in (19.92m) TSO - 65ft 4½in (19.92m)	DTSO - 65ft ½in (19.83m) MSO - 65ft 4½in (19.92m) TSO - 65ft 4½in (19.92m)	DTSO - 65ft ½in (19.83m) MSO- 65ft 4½in (19.92m) TSO - 65ft 4½in (19.92m)
Height:	DTSO/MSO - 12ft 1½in (3.7m) TSO - 11ft 6½in (3.58m)	12ft 1½in (3.7m)	12ft 1½in (3.7m)
Width:	9ft 3¼in (2.82m)	9ft 3¼in (2.82m)	9ft 3¼in (2.82m)
Seating:	Total - 236S + 8 tip-up DTSO(A) - 50S + 4 tip up MSO - 68S TSO - 68S DTSO - 50S + 4 tip up	Total - Southern 307S,+ 3 tip-up SWT - 236S + 8 tip-up Southern Sets DTSO(A) - 74S MSO - 84S TSO - 75S + 3 tip up DTSO(B) - 74S South West Trains Sets DTSO - 50S + 4 tip up MSO/TSO - 68S	Total - 236S + 9 tip-up DTSO(A) - 50S + 4 tip up MSO - 68S TSO - 68S DTSO(B) - 50S + 5 tip up
Internal layout:	2+3	2+3	2+3
Gangway:	Throughout	Southern - Within set SWT -Throughout	Throughout
Toilets:	Not fitted	Not fitted	Not fitted
Weight:	Total: 133.4 tonnes DTSO(A) - 30.8 tonnes MSO - 45.7 tonnes TSO - 26.1 tonnes DTSO(B) - 30.8 tonnes	Southern: 149.1 tonnes SWT: 131.7 tonnes DTSO(A) - 33.6 tonnes MSO - 47.9 tonnes TSO - 34.0 tonnes DTSO(B) - 33.6 tonnes South West Trains sets DTSO(A) - 29.5 tonnes MSO - 45.6 tonnes TSO - 27.1 tonnes DTSO(B) - 29.5 tonnes	Total: 131.8 tonnes DTSO(A) - 30.7 tonnes MSO - 46.3 tonnes TSO - 28.3 tonnes DTSO(B) - 26.5 tonnes
Brake type:	Air (Westcode)	Air (Westcode)	Air (Westcode)
Bogie type:	DTSO - BREL BT13 MSO - BREL BP27 TSO - BREL BX1	DTSO - BREL BT13 MSO - BREL BP20 TSO - BREL BT13	DTSO - BREL BT13 MSO - BREL BP20 TSO - BREL BT13
Power collection:	750V dc third rail	750V dc third rail	750V dc third rail
Traction motor type:	4 x EE507 of 250hp (186kW)	4 x EE507 of 250hp (186kW)	4 x EE507 of 250hp (186kW)
Horsepower:	1,000hp (746kW)	1,000hp (746kW)	1,000hp (746kW)
Max speed:	75mph (121km/h)	75mph (121km/h)	75mph (121km/h)
Coupling type:	Outer - Tightlock, Inner - Bar	Outer - Tightlock, Inner - Bar	Outer - Tightlock, Inner - Bar
Multiple restriction:	Class 455 and 456	Class 455 and 456	Class 455 and 456
Special features:	CCTV	CCTV	CCTV
Door type:	Bi-parting sliding	Bi-parting sliding	Bi-parting sliding
Construction:	Aluminium body/steel frame	Aluminium body/steel frame	Aluminium body/steel frame
Owner:	Porterbrook	Eversholt, Porterbrook	Porterbrook

Right Top: *All Class 455s came under the control of Network SouthEast from the mid-1980s, when a limited facelift and re-livery into NSE red, white and blue livery took place. By this time Class 455/8s Nos. 5801-5846 were operating on the South Central section and 5847-5874, plus all Class 455/7s and all Class 455/9s, were working on the Western section. Set No. 5809 in NSE livery is seen on the Central side at Clapham Junction on 13 April 1989.* CJM

Right Middle: *After privatisation the entire SWT batch of Class 455s was fully refurbished by Bombardier at Ashford, with a totally new interior devised, using high-back seats, increased standing room, a passenger information system and CCTV. The sets emerged in the SWT local lines red livery as shown on Class 455/7 No. 5725 at Clapham Junction.* CJM

Below: *The 46 Class 455/8s operated by Connex, later Southern, have received major refurbishing by Alstom at Eastleigh, which has included the removal of the front gangway and inserting a driving cab air conditioning system. Interiors have been fully refurbished with new high-back 3+2 seats. Cab ends also now sport larger headlights on both sides of the cab and a joint tail/marker light above. Set No. 455822 is illustrated in Southern green and white livery.* CJM

Class 456

Number range:	456001-456024
Introduced:	1990-91
Built/rebuilt by:	BREL York
Formation:	DMSO+DTSO
Vehicle numbers:	DMSO - 64735-64758 DTSO - 78250-78273
Vehicle length:	65ft ½in (19.83m)
Height:	12ft 4½in (3.77m)
Width:	9ft 3in (2.82m)
Seating:	Total: 152S DMSO - 79S DTSO - 73S
Internal layout:	2+3
Gangway:	Within set
Toilets:	DTSOL - 1 (out of use)
Weight:	Total - 72.5 tonnes DMSO - 41.1 tonnes DTSO - 31.4 Tonnes
Brake type:	Air (Westcode)
Bogie type:	Powered - BREL P7 Trailer - BREL T3
Power collection:	750V dc third rail
Traction motor type:	2 x GEC507-20J of 250hp (186kW)
Horsepower:	500hp (370kW)
Max speed:	75mph (121km/h)
Coupling type:	Outer - Tightlock Inner - Bar
Multiple restriction:	Class 455 and 456
Door type:	Bi-parting sliding
Construction:	Aluminium alloy/steel underframe
Owner:	Porterbrook

Below: *To allow greater flexibility in rostering stock, NSE ordered a fleet of 24 two-car Class 456s for delivery in 1990-91 for use on the Central section of the Southern Region. The sets incorporated a revised version of the then current Class 321 style cab end, which had to include nose mounted control and air connections for compatibility with Class 455s. The two-car sets allowed 2, 4, 6, 8, 10 and 12 car trains to be formed. Each Class 456 consisted of one Driving Motor Standard Open and one Driving Trailer Standard Open, with a total of 152 standard class seats. When delivered the sets were painted in NSE livery, then under privatisation all were repainted into Southern green and white. These sets are scheduled to transfer to South West Trains at the end of 2013 and will be refurbished in keeping with that operator's Class 455s. In Southern livery, set No. 456012 is seen from its DTS coach at Clapham Junction.* CJM

Below: *In 1989, as part of the 'Networker' train development project, four of the former Class 210 DMU coaches were taken over by NSE and rebuilt at the RTC Derby as a traction development unit. After a period of testing on the former Southern Region, based at Strawberry Hill, from where it worked over the Shepperton line, the set was returned to the Engineering Development Unit (EDU) at Derby and further modified as a Class 316 test bed for 'Networker' ac traction development. Two redundant vehicles from the Class 457 are seen dumped at Eastleigh Works.* CJM

Class:	457
Number:	457001
Introduced:	As Class 210: 1981 As Class 457: 1989
Built by:	BREL Derby
Rebuilt by:	RTC Derby & Strawberry Hill
Formation:	DMS+TS+TS+DMS
Vehicle numbers:	DMS - 67300 (60300/54000) TS - 67400 (60400/57000) TS - 67401 (60401/57001) DMS - 67301 (60301/54001)
Vehicle length:	DMS 65ft 0½in (19.83m) TS - 65ft 4in (19.92m)
Height:	12ft 3½ (3.75m)
Width:	9ft 3in (2.81m)
Seating:	No seats fitted - development train
Internal layout:	Test equipment
Gangway:	Throughout
Toilets:	Not fitted
Weight:	Total - 119.7 tonnes DMS - 32 tonnes TS - 26.8 tonnes TS - 28.9 tonnes DMS - 32 tonnes
Brake type:	Air, EP
Bogie type:	Power - BREL BP20 Trailer - BREL BT13
Traction package:	'Networker' development
Horsepower:	1,140hp (850kW)
Max speed:	90 mph (145km/h)
Coupling type:	Tightlock
Multiple restriction:	Not fitted
Door type:	Double leaf sliding
Special features:	Development train, later converted to Class 316 No. 316999 for ac traction development

Class 458 – JOP

	As built 458/0	Modified as 5-car sets 458/5
Number range:	458001-458030	458501-458536
Alpha code:	4-JOP (Juniper Outer-suburban Porterbrook)	5-JOP (Juniper Outer-suburban Porterbrook)
Introduced:	New: 1999-2002	Refurbished: 2013-2014
Built by:	Alstom, Washwood Heath, Birmingham	
Refurbished by:	-	Wabtec, Doncaster and Loughborough
Formation:	DMCO(A)+TSO+MSO+DMCO(B)	DMSO(A)+TSO+MSO+TSO+DMSO(B)
Vehicle numbers:	DMCO(A) - 67601-67630 TSO - 74001-74030 MSO - 74101-74130 DMCO(B) - 67701-67730	DMSO(A) - 67601-67630 TSO - 74001-74030 MSO - 74101-74130 TSO - ? DMSO(B) - 67701-67730
Vehicle length:	DMCO - 69ft 6in (21.16m) TSO, MSO - 65ft 4in (19.94m)	DMSO - 69ft 6in (21.16m) TSO, MSO - 65ft 4in (19.94m)
Height:	12ft 3in (3.77m)	12ft 3in (3.77m)
Width:	9ft 2in (2.80m)	9ft 2in (2.80m)
Seating:	Total: 24F/255S + 6 tip-up DMCO(A) - 12F/63S TSO - 54S + 6 tip up MSO - 75S DMCO(B) - 12F/63S	Total: ?S DMSO(A) - ? TSO - ? MSO - ? DMSO(B) - ?
Internal layout:	First - 2+2 Standard - 2+3	First - 2+2 Standard - 2+2
Gangway:	Throughout (no unit to unit access)	Throughout
Toilets:	TSO, MSO - 1	TSO, MSO - 1
Weight:	Total: 169.5 tonnes DMCO(A) - 46.4 tonnes TSOL - 34.6 tonnes MOS - 42.1 tonnes DMCO(B) - 46.4 tonnes	Total: - tonnes DMSO(A) - 46.4 tonnes TSOL - 34.6 tonnes MOS - 42.1 tonnes TSO - DMSO(B) - 46.4 tonnes
Brake type:	Air, regenerative	Air, regenerative
Bogie type:	Alstom ACR	Alstom ACR
Power collection:	750V dc third rail	750V dc third rail
Traction motor type:	6 x Alstom of 361hp (270kW)	6 x Alstom of 361hp (270kW)
Horsepower:	2,172hp (1,620kW)	2,172hp (1,620kW)
Max speed:	100mph (161km/h)	75mph (121km/h)
Coupling type:	Outer - Tightlock Inner - Semi-auto	Outer - Tightlock Inner - Semi-auto
Multiple restriction:	Within class only	Within class only
Door type:	Bi-parting sliding plug	Bi-parting sliding plug
Special features:	Air conditioned, PIS	Air conditioned, PIS
Construction:	Steel	Steel
Owner:	Porterbrook	Porterbrook

Right Top: *The first new trains ordered by Stagecoach/South West Trains were 30 Alstom 'Juniper' sets for delivery in 1999. The sets were from the standard Alstom 'Juniper' product platform, but had to be redesigned as SWT required end corridor connections, which resulted in a rather ugly exterior design. The 30 sets, based at Wimbledon, were not that well accepted and many technical issues prevented them from giving a good return on investment. By 2005 most were stored after the introduction of the Class 450 'Desiro' sets, but in 2006 owner Porterbrook made an investment in the fleet to return it to operation. The sets, normally used on the Waterloo to Reading and Guildford-Ascot corridor. Fitted with sliding plug doors they seated 24 first and 255 standard class passengers. In 2011 it was announced that following the withdrawal of the similar Class 460 Gatwick Express sets, their vehicles would be heavily rebuilt to strengthen the 30 Class 458s into five-car trains and at the same time create six extra five-car sets from the spare Class 460 vehicles. In 2013 this major rebuild was being undertaken at Wabtec Doncaster and Loughborough. The sets will start to return to traffic at the end of 2013 will be for standard class only occupancy and outshopped in the SWT outer suburban blue livery. During the modification work the sets maximum speed will be reduced from 100mph (161km/h) to 75mph (121km/h) and they will be modified to allow coupling to 'Desiro' stock. Set No. 458012 is seen at Waterloo, leading an eight-car formation to Reading.* CJM

Below: *The rebuilding of the redundant Class 460 Gatwick Express vehicles into extra 458 stock was awarded to Wabtec, which rebuilt all the intermediate vehicles at its Doncaster site, with the former streamlined driving cars being dealt with at the former Brush plant in Loughborough who were geared to deal with the heavier engineering. The work called for one extra vehicle to be added to each Class 458, and the building of six new sets, Nos. 458531-536, which will include the totally rebuilt ex streamlined driving cars, now fitted with new window spaces and sporting a new front end. One of the former 460 intermediate vehicles is seen being worked on at the Doncaster site in April 2013.* CJM

Class 460 – 8GAT

Number range:	460001-460008
Alpha code:	8 GAT (8-car GATwick)
Introduced:	1999-2001
Built by:	Alstom, Birmingham
Formation:	DMFL+TFO+TCO+MSO+MSO+TSO+MSO+DMSO
Vehicle numbers:	DMFL - 67901-67908, TFOL - 74401-74408 TCOL - 74411-74418, MSO - 74221-74228 MSO - 74431-74438, TSOL - 74441-74448 MSO - 74451-74458, DMSO - 67911-67918
Vehicle length:	DMFL, DMSO - 69ft 1½in (21.05m)+ TFO, TCO, MSO, TSO - 65ft 4¾in (19.94m)
Height:	12ft 4½in (3.77m)
Width:	9ft 2¼in (2.80m)
Seating:	Total - 43F/299S DMFL - 10F, TFO - 25F, TCO - 8F/38S, MSO - 58S, MSO - 58S, TSO - 33S, MSO - 58S, DMSO - 54S
Internal layout:	2+1F/2+2S
Gangway:	Within set
Toilets:	TFO - 1, TCO - 1, TSO - 2
Weight:	Total - 319.4 tonnes DMFL - 42.7 tonnes, TFO - 34.5 tonnes, TCO - 35.9 tonnes, MSO - 42.5 tonnes MSO - 42.8 tonnes, TSO - 35.2 tonnes, MSO - 40.5 tonnes, DMSO - 45.3 tonnes
Brake type:	Air (rheostatic)
Bogie type:	Alstom ACR
Power collection:	750V dc third rail
Traction motor type:	10 x Alstom T3517 3-phase of 362hp (270kW)
Horsepower:	3,620hp (2,700kW)
Max speed:	100mph (161km/h)
Coupling type:	Outer and between cars 4/5 Scharfenberg 330* Inner - Bar
Multiple restriction:	Not authorised
Door type:	Bi-parting sliding plug
Construction:	Steel
Owner:	Porterbrook

+ Length does not include GRP nose cone
* When delivered Tightlock couplers were fitted

Below: *The 1990s modernisation of the Gatwick Express operation between London Victoria and Gatwick Airport led to the introduction of some of the most stylish electric multiple units ever to operate in the UK. Built as part of the Alstom 'Juniper' family, these eight-car sets with streamlined outer ends were based on the same shell fabrication as the Class 458, and were introduced to operate the 15min-interval dedicated airport express service. Each set had one driving car set aside for luggage, with a small coupé for 10 first class passengers at the inner end. This vehicle had a roller shutter side door to the luggage compartment. All other vehicles had two pairs of sliding plug doors on each side feeding directly into the saloon areas. In addition to the driving cars, which are motored, three intermediate MSOs were included giving a top speed of 100mph (161km/h). These sets were constructed as two half trains of four carriages, with the non-driving 'inner' end of each half portion powered; in addition the vehicle behind the driving motor standard (country end) was also powered. Trains were painted in the Gatwick Express and later advertising liveries. From late 2010 these sets started to go into warm store, being replaced on the Gatwick Express service by modified Class 442s. In 2013 the vehicles were being totally rebuilt at Wabtec Doncaster and Brush Loughborough to augment South West Trains' Class 458s to form five-car commuter services and introduce five extra sets. The units' distinctive cab ends were thus lost as the rebuilt trains were fitted with Class 458 style slab ends. A brand new Gatwick Express Class 460 is seen inside its home depot at Stewarts Lane in 2000.* CJM

Above: *The Class 460s were introduced to replace the Class 73 and Mk2 loco hauled stock which operated the intensive route from the mid 1980s. The '460s' were well liked, but gave little flexibility to the operators of the joint Gatwick Express/ Southern franchise, so in recent years have been replaced. During the introductory phase of the Class 460s, set No. 04 (460004) is seen at Gatwick with its Driving Motor First Luggage van on the London end.* CJM

Below: *While the UK rail industry has never largely adopted on-train advertising, the lucrative airport market has attracted some prime airline advertisers to pay for entire train branding. One such operater was Emirates Air, who funded branding of several sets in the mid 2000s. In the main this was tastefully applied and the core white colour was retained. Set No. 06 (460005) is seen passing a SWT Class 455 near Clapham Junction in 2008.* CJM

Class 465 & 466 'Networker'

Class:	465/0	465/1
Number range:	465001-465050	465151-465197
Original number range:	-	-
Year introduced:	1991-93	1993
Year modified:	-	-
Built by:	BREL / ABB York	BREL / ABB York
Modified by:	-	-
Formation:	DMSO(A)+TSO+ TSOL+DMSO(B)	DMSO(A)+TSO+ TSOL+DMSO(B)
Vehicle numbers:	DMSO(A) - 64759-64808 TSO - 72028-72126 (even numbers) TSOL - 72029-72126 (odd numbers) DMSO(B) - 64809-64858	DMSO(A) - 65800-65846 TSO - 72900-72992 (even numbers) TSOL - 72901-72993 (odd numbers) DMSO(B) - 65847-65893
Vehicle length:	DMSO - 68ft 6½in (20.89m) TSO, TSOL - 65ft 9¾in (20.06m)	DMSO - 68ft 6½in (20.89m) TSO, TSOL - 65ft 9¾in (20.06m)
Height:	12ft 4½in (3.77m)	12ft 4½in (3.77m)
Width:	9ft 3in (2.82m)	9ft 3in (2.82m)
Seating:	Total - 348S DMSO(A) - 86S TSO - 90S TSOL - 86S DMSO (B) - 86S	Total - 348S DMSO(A) - 86S TSO - 90S TSOL - 86S DMSO (B) - 86S
Internal layout:	2+3 high-density	2+3 high-density
Gangway:	Within set	Within set
Toilets:	TSOL - 1	TSOL - 1
Weight:	Total - 133.6 tonnes DMSO(A) - 39.2 tonnes TSO - 27.2 tonnes TSOL - 28 tonnes DMSO(B) - 39.2 tonnes	Total - 136 tonnes DMSO(A) - 39.2 tonnes TSO - 27.2 tonnes TSOL - 28 tonnes DMSO(B) - 39.2 tonnes
Brake type:	Air (rheostatic)	Air (rheostatic)
Bogie type:	Powered - Adtranz P3 Trailer - Adtranz T3	Powered - Adtranz P3 Trailer - Adtranz T3
Power collection:	750V dc third rail	750V dc third rail
Traction motor type:	8 x Hitachi asynchronous+	8 x Hitachi asynchronous+
Horsepower:	3,004hp (2,240kW)	3,004hp (2,240kW)
Max speed:	75mph (121km/h)	75mph (121km/h)
Coupling type:	Outer - Tightlock Inner - Semi-auto	Outer - Tightlock Inner - Semi-auto
Multiple restriction:	Class 465 and 466	Class 465 and 466
Door type:	Bi-parting sliding plug	Bi-parting sliding plug
Construction:	Aluminium	Aluminium
Owner:	Eversholt	Eversholt
Sub-class differences:	BREL / ABB phase 1 train	BREL / ABB phase 2 train

+ Originally fitted with Brush TIM970 traction motors

Left: *Painted in Network SouthEast red, white and blue, phase 2 BREL/ ABB set No. 465162 is seen on the approaches to London Bridge. All the BREL/ABB-built sets originally had Brush traction motors, but in the mid-2000s these were changed to Hitachi units in the quest for better reliability and ease of maintenance. Each Class 465/0 or 465/1 seats 348 standard class passengers in a mix of 2+2 and 2+3 styles.* CJM

465/2	465/9
465235-465250	465901-456934
-	465201-465234
1991-93	1991-93
-	2005
Metro-Cammell, Birmingham	Metro-Cammell, Birmingham
-	Wabtec, Doncaster
DMSO(A)+TSO+ TSOL+DMSO(B)	DMCO(A)+TSOL+TSO+DMCO(B)
DMSO(A) - 65734-65749 TSO - 72787-72817 (odd numbers) TSOL - 72788-72818 (even numbers) DMSO(B) - 65784-65799	DMC0(A) - 65700-65733 TSOL - 72719-72785 (odd numbers) TSO - 72720-72786 (even numbers) DMCO(B) - 65750-65783
DMSO - 68ft 6½in (20.89m) TSO, TSOL - 65ft 9¾in (20.06m)	DMCO - 68ft 6½in (20.89m) TSO, TSOL - 65ft 9¾in (20.06m)
12ft 4½in (3.77m)	12ft 4½in (3.77m)
9ft 3in (2.82m)	9ft 3in (2.82m)
Total - 348S DMSO(A) - 86S TSO - 90S TSOL - 86S DMSO (B) - 86S	Total - 24F / 302S DMCO(A) - 12F / 68S TSO - 76S TSOL - 90S DMCO (B) - 12F / 68S
2+3 high-density	First - 2+2 Standard - 2+3
Within set	Within set
TSOL - 1	TSOL - 1
Total - 136 tonnes DMSO(A) - 39.2 tonnes TSO - 27.2 tonnes TSOL - 28 tonnes DMSO(B) - 39.2 tonnes	Total - 138.2 tonnes DMCO(A) - 39.2 tonnes TSOL - 30.3 tonnes TSO - 29.5 tonnes DMCO(B) - 39.2 tonnes
Air (rheostatic)	Air (rheostatic)
Powered - SRP BP62 Trailer - SRP BT52	Powered - SRP BP62 Trailer - SRP BT52
750V dc third rail	750V dc third rail
8 x Alstom G352AY	8 x Alsthom G352BY
3,004hp (2,240kW)	3,004hp (2,240kW)
75mph (121km/h)	75mph (121km/h)
Outer - Tightlock Inner - Semi-auto	Outer - Tightlock Inner - Semi-auto
Class 465 and 466	Class 465 and 466
Bi-parting sliding plug	Bi-parting sliding plug
Aluminium	Aluminium
Angel Trains	Angel Trains
Metro-Cammell built train	Refurbished 465/2 with first class

Below: *The modernisation of the Kent suburban network by Network SouthEast took place in the 1990s when four-car EMUs were ordered from BREL/ABB and Metro-Cammell. These were of the same general structural design as the Class 165 DMU fleet and became known as the 'Networker' fleet. A total of 147 four-car sets were built in three batches: 97 by BREL/ABB and 50 by Metro-Cammell. The sets are almost identical with a few detail differences, mainly involving the interior design. A slow delivery followed many technical issues, but the fleet soon revolutionised rail travel on the Kent inner and outer-suburban network, introducing driver only operation, rapid acceleration and spacious train interiors. Originally sets were painted in NSE red, white and blue, but following privatisation and operation by Connex and later SouthEastern Trains these operators' liveries have been applied. A fleet of 34 of the original Metro-Cammell build were refurbished in 2005 for longer distance services. First class seating was added in each driving car, and these sets were reclassified as 465/9. The Class 465/0, 465/1 and 465/2 fleets are allocated to Slade Green, while the 465/9 sub class is allocated to Gillingham. All units have pressure ventilation. In recent years refurbishment has been carried out with all units now carrying SouthEastern white livery, and some front end modifications had to be made after introduction to stop the risk of 'train surfers'. Painted in full SouthEastern livery, first class seating fitted Class 465/9s No. 465902 is illustrated at London Bridge.* CJM

Class 465 'Networker'

Above: *In as-delivered condition without anti surfer covers and a cab-end handrail, the pioneer of the Metro-Cammell (Alstom)-built 'Networker' fleet, No. 465201, is seen inside the works test hall on delivery in 1991. The 50 strong fleet of Class 465/2s took some two years to complete.* CJM

Below: *Displaying SouthEastern white and yellow livery, BREL/ABB set No. 465005 arrives at New Eltham with a stopping service from Charing Cross to Dartford on 31 November 2007. Due to high patronage, the majority of SouthEastern local services are now formed of eight cars all day, with passengers frequently having to stand due to a shortage of seating.* CJM

Class 466 'Networker'

Below: *For low patronage branch line use and to augment formations to either six or ten carriages, Network SouthEast ordered a batch of 43 two-car 'Networker' sets from GEC-Alstom at Washwood Heath, Birmingham in 1993-94. These are basically a two-car version of the Class 465/2 breed, except that one driving car does not have traction equipment and is thus a Driving Trailer Standard Open (DTSO). These coaches also contain a small toilet compartment (the only 'Networker' driving cars so fitted). The two-car sets are allocated to Slade Green and were originally painted in NSE colours, which later gave way to South Eastern Trains white livery. The units can be seen throughout the SET operating area; all have now had their original front handrails removed and are fitted with anti-surfer angled plates above the buffer beam, in a similar manner to the Class 465s. Displaying SouthEastern white and yellow livery, set No. 466030 is illustrated.* CJM

Number range:	466001-466043
Introduced:	1992-94
Built by:	GEC-Alstom, Birmingham
Formation:	DMSO+DTSO
Vehicle numbers:	DMSO - 64860-64902 DTSO - 78312-78354
Vehicle length:	68ft 6½in (20.89m)
Height:	12ft 4½in (3.77m)
Width:	9ft 3in (2.82m)
Seating:	Total - 168S DMSO - 86S DTSO - 82S
Internal layout:	2+3 high
Gangway:	Within set
Toilets:	DTSO - 1
Weight:	Total - 72 tonnes DMSO - 40.6 tonnes DTSO - 31.4 tonnes
Brake type:	Air (rheostatic and regenerative)
Bogie type:	Powered - Adtranz P3 Trailer - Adtranz T3
Power collection:	750V dc third rail
Traction motor type:	4 x Alstom G352AY of 375hp (280kW)
Horsepower:	1,500hp (1,120kW)
Max speed:	75mph (121km/h)
Coupling type:	Outer - Tightlock, Inner - Semi-auto
Multiple restriction:	Class 465 and 466
Door type:	Bi-parting sliding plug
Construction:	Aluminium
Owner:	Angel Trains

Class 482

Number range:	482501-482510
Former number range:	-
Alpha code:	Not allocated
Introduced:	1993
Built by:	ABB Derby
Formation:	DMSO + MSO
Vehicle Numbers:	DMSO - 65501-65510 MSO - 67501-67510
Train length:	108ft 11¾in (33.20m)
Vehicle length:	53ft 3¾in (16.25m)
Height:	9ft 4¾in (2.87m)
Width:	8ft 11in (2.72m)
Seating (2-car set)	Total - 72S DMSO - 36S MSO - 36S
Internal layout:	Transverse
Gangway:	No, end emergency doors
Toilets:	Not fitted
Weight:	Total - 47.5 tonnes DMSO - 23.75 tonnes MSO - 23.75 tonnes
Brake type:	Air (rheostatic)
Power collection:	600-630V dc third rail
Traction motor type:	4 x 57.6hp (43kW) dc Brush traction motors per car
Horsepower (2-car set):	461.3hp (344 kW)
Max speed:	60mph (97km/h)
Coupling type:	Inner - semi permanent Outer - Wedgelock
Multiple restriction:	Within type
Door type:	Bi-parting sliding

Built as part of LUL Central Line replacement order
Sets later sold to LUL and line transferred to Central Line control

Below: *Network SouthEast was granted funds to modernise the Waterloo & City line in the early 1990s, and chose to use a follow-on order for Central Line LUL stock, then under construction by ABB Derby. A fleet of ten two-car trains was ordered, each consisting of a driving car and a motor standard open, requiring two half trains to be coupled together to form a service train. Modernisation of the short line from Waterloo to Bank took place in 1993 with a lengthy period of closure, while the old 1940-built stock was removed and the new trains lifted in by crane and commissioned. The sets were painted in a revised version of NSE colours of grey body with blue doors and cab end off-set by a red, white and blue strip. Each half train provided seats for 72. The new stock commenced operation on 19 July 1993 and was operated by NSE until 1 April 1994 when the line was transferred to London Underground and became part of the Central Line operation. Soon afterwards the BR class prefixed numbers were removed and LUL branding applied. In the view below, two two-car sets, Nos. 482503 and 482504, are seen on the test track at ABB Derby.* CJM

Above: *The old depot at the Waterloo end of the Waterloo & City line, built for the first stock used on the line in 1898, had to be totally rebuilt for the new state-of-the-art trains; this required new pits, jacks and testing equipment, which for a period in mid 1993 had to deal with both the new trains and the then current 1940-built stock. Seen on 28 May 1993, new set No. 482502 stands adjacent to 1940 car No. S53.* CJM

Right: *For the Waterloo-based main line drivers who were responsible for operating the Waterloo & City line until its transfer to London Underground, the new 1993 stock was a culture change from the previous 1940 sets, which in place of a brass spring loaded power controller and straight Westinghouse brake had a computer age cab with a pull-out joint power and brake controller operated by the driver's right hand.* CJM

Class 483

Number range:	(483)001-(483)009 (last three digits carried)
Former number range:	Ex-LUL 1938 stock
Introduced originally:	1938
Introduced on Isle of Wight:	1989-90
Built by:	Metro-Cammell
Rebuilt by:	BRML Eastleigh
Formation:	DMSO(A)+DMSO(B)
Vehicle numbers:	DMSO(A) - 121-129 DMSO(B) - 221-229
Vehicle length:	DMSO - 52ft 9in (16.15m)
Height:	9ft 5½in (2.88m)
Width:	8ft 8½in (2.65m)
Seating:	Total: 82S DMSO(A) - 40S DMSO(B) - 42S
Internal layout:	2+2, bench
Gangway:	Within set, emergency end doors
Toilets:	Not fitted
Weight:	Total - 54.8 tonnes DMSO(A) - 27.4 tonnes DMSO(B) - 27.4 tonnes
Brake type:	Air (Auto/EP)
Bogie type:	LT
Power collection:	660V dc third rail
Traction motor type:	4 x Crompton Parkinson/ GEC/BTH LT100
Horsepower:	670hp (500kW)
Max speed:	45mph (72.5km/h)
Coupling type:	Wedgelock
Multiple restriction:	Within type only
Door type:	Bi-parting and single sliding
Construction:	Steel
Owner:	South West Trains

Below: *The remaining railway system operated on the Isle of Wight has always been a little world of its own in terms of trains used, and today the line which operates from Ryde Pier Head to Shanklin is no exception. Electrified by British Railways Southern Region in the mid-1960s to oust steam traction from the Island, no normal railway stock could be used due to gauge clearances. To provide the system with 'new' trains BR purchased a fleet of redundant 1927 London Underground tube stock and rebuilt this for use on the isolated network. This stock became life-expired in the late 1980s and Network SouthEast then purchased yet more second hand, but in Isle of Wight terms 'modern' stock, this time dating back to 1938! This stock was rebuilt at BRML Eastleigh into twin power-car sets which can either operate in two- or four-car formations. Each two-car set can seat 82 standard class passengers. All sets are allocated to Ryde St John's Road depot, which is also the main administration base for the isolated network. The sets have LU-style group and longitudinal seats with crew-operated sliding doors. After delivery in NSE colours, the fleet was painted in 'dinosaur' livery for a period, but now sports mock London Transport red. Set No. 001 is seen in as delivered NSE livery at Brading.* CJM

Above: *Painted in the rather dubious 'dinosaur' livery, set No. 008 is seen in a dilapidated condition at Ryde St John's Road on 23 March 2007 working a Shanklin to Ryde Pier Head service. This set appears to have lost its destination indicator and train numbers.* CJM

Below: *In 2008 a start was made to apply London Underground historic deep red livery to the remaining operational six sets. No. 004 is illustrated shunting into Ryde St John's Road depot.* CJM

Class 485 & 486 – 4VEC & 3TIS

Class:	485	486
Number range:	041-046	031-036
Former number range:	Ex LUL	Ex LUL
Alpha code:	4VEC	3TIS
Introduced:	1967 (on BR), 1923-31 (on LU)	1967 (on BR), 1923-31 (on LU)
Originally built by:	Metro-Cammell, Union Car, Cammell Laird	Metro-Cammell, Union Car, Cammell Laird
Rebuilt by:	BR Stewarts Lane	BR Stewarts Lane
Formation:	MBSO+TSO+DTSO+MBSO	MBSO+TSO+DTSO
Vehicle numbers:	MBSO - 1-25 series TSO - 41-49, 92-96 series DTSO - 26-36 series MBSO - 1-25 series	MBSO - 1-25 series TSO - 41-49, 92-96 series DTSO - 26-36 series -
Set length:	207ft 11in (63.37m)	156ft 5½in (47.69m)
Vehicle length:	MBSO - 54ft 8½in (16.68m) TSO - 49ft 9¼in (15.17m) DTSO - 50ft 2¼in (15.30m)	MBSO - 54ft 8½in (16.68m) TSO - 49ft 9¼in (15.17m) DTSO - 50ft 2¼in (15.30m)
Height:	9ft 6in (2.89m)	9ft 6in (2.89m)
Width:	8ft 8in (2.64m)	8ft 8in (2.64m)
Seating:	Total - 132S MBSO - 26S TSO - 42S DTSO - 38S MBSO - 26S	Total - 106S MBSO - 26S TSO - 42S DTSO - 38S -
Internat layout:	2+2, transverse	2+2, transverse
Gangway:	No, emergency end doors	No, emergency end doors
Toilets:	Not fitted	Not fitted
Weight:	Total - 94 tonnes MBSO - 29 tonnes TSO - 19 tonnes DTSO - 17 tonnes MBSO - 29 tonnes	Total - 65 tonnes MBSO - 29 tonnes TSO - 19 tonnes DTSO - 17 tonnes -
Brake type:	Air (EP/Auto)	Air (EP/Auto)
Bogie type:	LT design, Z and V	LT design, Z and V
Power collection:	630V dc third rail	630V dc third rail
Traction motor type:	4 x EE	2 x EE
Horsepower:	960hp (716kW)	480hp (358kW)
Max speed:	45mph (72km/h)	45mph (72km/h)
Coupling type:	Ward	Ward
Multiple restriction:	Class 485 and 486 only	Class 485 and 486 only
Door type:	Sliding	Sliding

Below Left: *The 1967 modernisation on the Isle of Wight saw the introduction of 12 former London Underground trains formed of 1923-31 'Standard' tube stock, which were totally rebuilt at Stewarts Lane into six four- and six three-car units classified as 4VEC and 3TIS units. Usually a train was formed of one set of each class giving total accommodation for 238 seated passengers; occasionally single sets operated, especially on the Ryde Pier 'shuttle'. When converted the sets were finished in rail blue off-set by yellow warning ends; this later gave way to blue grey colours and from the mid 1980s NSE red, white and blue was applied with the Island Line branding until modernisation in 1989. Three-car set No. 035 is seen at Sandown in mid 1972 .* CJM

Right Top: *After the VEC and TIS sets were repainted in blue and grey livery they started to receive their full TOPS prefixed running numbers, applied to the lower panel below the non-driving front cab window. An amount of reforming was also done around this time to keep the best vehicles in traffic in operational sets. Class 485 (4VEC) No. 485043 approaches Sandown with a service from Ryde in June 1985.* CJM

Below: *When Network SouthEast was formed in the mid 1980s, it inherited the VEC and TIS sets, with Chris Green promising to modernise the line as soon as funds were available. This came in 1989, but in the interim period some internal cleaning was done and sets were painted in NSE red, white and blue colours. One of the last operational sets, No. 485043, is seen at Brading. Note that when compared with the above view of the same unit, some front end work has been carried out.* CJM

Class 487

	Driving Cars	Trailers
Number range:	S51-S62	S71-S86
Former number range:	-	-
Introduced:	1940	1940
Built by:	English Electric	English Electric
Vehicle numbers:	S51-S62	S71-S86
Vehicle length:	49ft 1¾in (14.98m)	49ft 1¾in (14.98m)
Height:	9ft 7in (2.92m)	9ft 7in (2.92m)
Width:	8ft 7¾in (2.64m)	8ft 7¾in (2.64m)
Seating:	40S	52S
Internal layout:	2+2, longitudinal	2+2, longitudinal
Gangway:	No, emergency end doors	No, emergency end doors
Toilets:	Not fitted	Not fitted
Weight:	23 tons	19 tons
Brake type:	Air (Westinghouse)	Air (Westinghouse)
Bogie type:	Special	Special
Power collection:	600V dc third rail	-
Traction motor type:	2 x EE500	-
Horsepower:	380hp (283kW)	-
Max speed:	35mph (56km/h)	35mph (56km/h)
Coupling type:	Ward	Ward
Multiple restriction:	Within class only	Within class only
Door type:	Sliding	Sliding

Below: *The Southern Railway operated Waterloo & City Line, which was originally opened as an electric railway by the London & South Western Railway in 1898, was modernised in 1940, when a fleet of new English Electric stock was built by Dick Kerr, consisting of 12 double-ended motor cars and 16 trailers, enabling formations of one, two or five cars to operate. The stock had air operated sliding doors with a mix of 2+2 and longitudinal seating; a five car train seated 236, with ample space for another 300 standing. All the motor cars had their power bogie end facing Bank. When delivered sets were painted in Southern green with silver ends and doors. Later BR rail blue was applied, again with silver end and doors. After the formation of Network SouthEast, red, white and blue livery was applied with grey ends. The Waterloo & City stock was unusual in that is carried a red light on both front and back, with no white marker light. The sets were equipped with brass whistles rather than horns and did not have windscreen wipers as they did not usually operate outdoors. Sets were maintained in the depot complex at Waterloo, with sets being lifted out from the line in Waterloo North Sidings and hauled to a major works for classified attention. On the left we see an intermediate trailer car painted in Network SouthEast colours, while below is a five car set in as delivered condition in green and silver livery.* CJM / CJM-C

Above: *In the summer of 1977, one of the Waterloo & City Driving Motor cars, No. S58, was operated over the main line between Farnham and Alton during the development of new speedometer equipment. This was one of the only times the sets had ever worked under their own power away from the Waterloo & City line. The car is seen at Farnham on 27 September 1977. During the course of these tests, if it started to rain the vehicle had to be put inside Farnham shed immediately as they did not have windscreen wipers.* CJM

Right Middle: *Viewed from its non-powered end, motor car No. S57 is seen inside the depot at Waterloo painted in NSE livery on 11 March 1992.* CJM

Right Bottom: *The very last 1940 Waterloo & City train operated over the Waterloo to Bank and return line on 28 March 1993, powered by motor cars S60 (Bank end) and S56 (Waterloo end). The train is seen in the platform at Waterloo after arrival on the final journey before the set worked into the carriage sidings and the removal of the stock began. NSE were quite surprised by the dozens of enthusiasts who had travelled from all corners of the country to witness the last passenger carrying working of a Waterloo & City train.* CJM

Class 488

Class:	488/2	488/3
Number range:	(48)8201-(48)8210	(48)8301-(48)8319
Former number range:	From Mk2f stock	From Mk2f stock
Introduced originally:	1973-74	1973-74
Introduced as 488:	1983-84	1983-84
Originally built by:	BREL Derby	BREL Derby
Rebuilt by:	BREL Eastleigh	BREL Eastleigh
Formation:	TFOLH+TSOLH	TSOLH+TSOL+TSOLH
Vehicle numbers:	TFOLH - 72500-72509 TSOLH - 72617-72644 (series)	TSOLH - 72602-72647 (series) TSOL - 72701-72719 TSOLH - 72602-72647 (series)
Vehicle length:	66ft 0½in (20.12m)	66ft 0½in (20.12m)
Height:	12ft 9¼in (3.89m)	12ft 9¼in (3.89m)
Width:	9ft 3in (2.82m)	9ft 3in (2.82m)
Seating:	Total - 41F/48S TFOLH - 41F TSOLH - 48S	Total - 144S TSOLH - 48S TSOL - 48S TSOLH - 48S
Internal layout:	First - 2+1 Standard - 2+2	Standard - 2+2
Gangway:	Throughout	Throughout
Toilets:	TFOLH, TSOLH, TSOL - 1	TFOLH, TSOLH, TSOL - 1
Weight:	Total - 70 tonnes TFOLH - 35 tonnes TSOLH - 35 tonnes	Total - 105 tonnes TSOLH - 35 tonnes TSOL - 35 tonnes TSOLH - 35 tonnes
Brake type:	Air (auto/EP)	Air (auto/EP)
Bogie type:	B4	B4
Power:	From loco/GLV	From loco/GLV
Max speed:	90mph (145km/h)	90mph (145km/h)
Coupling type:	Inner - Bar Outer - Buck-eye	Inner - Bar Outer - Buck-eye
Multiple restriction:	Within type, GLV, Class 73	Within type, GLV, Class 73
Door type:	Slam	Slam
Special features:	CDL	CDL

Below and Below Right: *For the radical modernisation of the Airport Express link between London Victoria and Gatwick Airport in 1984 came the conversion of a maximum of 10 'new' train sets. Passenger accommodation was to be provided in modified Mk2f loco-hauled stock, upgraded to EMU standards at BREL Eastleigh. Two sub-classes were formed of 488/2, which were two-car sets formed with one first class and one standard class vehicle, and 488/3, which were three-car sets formed of all standard class accommodation. The two- and three-car sets were semi-permanently coupled together. To suit the powering Class 73 and GLV, high level control and air connections were provided. When in use, trains would usually be formed of one or two of the three-car sets and one of the two-car formations. Internally the stock was heavily rebuilt for its Railair Link use, with reduced numbers of seats and lots of luggage room; standard class seating was in the 2+2 style, while first class was 2+1. Traction was to be provided by Class 73s. To provide driving facilities at the remote end, 10 Gatwick Luggage Vans (GLVs) were converted from withdrawn Class 414 HAP DMBS vehicles at Eastleigh and given the 489 classification. To form the new GLVs, the shells were gutted, new body panelling installed and the former passenger area converted to a luggage van, accessed by three pairs of double-leaf hinged doors. A modern driving cab was fitted as was a small guards office. Painted in Executive or InterCity colours and branded Railair Link, the trains entered service in 1983, later being taken over by the Gatwick Express train operator. The Class 488/489 formations continued in operation until replaced by Class 460 stock between 2000-05. The stock was always based at Stewarts Lane. On the left we see two-car Class 488/2 No. 8201 inside Stewarts Lane electric multiple unit shed viewed from its first class end.* CJM

Class 489 – 1GLV

Below: *In usual operation, the Gatwick Express stock worked every 15 minutes between Victoria and Gatwick, with the journey taking around 30 minutes. Trains were usually formed with the Class 73 at the country (Gatwick) end of the formation. GLV No. 9102, car No. 68501, is seen at Gatwick Airport showing the privatised Gatwick Express livery and branding.* CJM

Number range:	(48)9101-(48)9110
Alpha code:	1GLV (Gatwick Luggage Van)
Introduced originally:	1959 (as HAP DMB)
Introduced as GLV:	1983-84
Built/rebuilt by:	BR/BREL Eastleigh
Formation:	1GLV (**G**atwick **L**uggage **V**an)
Vehicle numbers:	68500-68509
Vehicle length:	63ft 11½in (19.49m)
Height:	12ft 8¾in (3.88m)
Width:	9ft 3in (2.82m)
Seating:	None
Internal layout:	Luggage space only
Gangway:	Non driving end only
Toilets:	Not fitted
Weight:	40.5 tonnes
Brake type:	Air (Auto/EP)
Bogie type:	Mk4
Power collection:	750V dc third rail
Traction motor type:	2 x EE507
Horsepower:	500hp (373kW)
Max speed:	90mph (145km/h)
Coupling type:	Buck-eye
Multiple restriction:	1951, 1957, 1963 and Gatwick Express stock
Door type:	Twin-leaf slam

Class 491 & 492 – 3TC & 4TC

Class:	491	492
Amended class:	438	438
Number range:	401-434	301-303
TOPS number range:	8001-8034	-
Former number range:	Converted from loco-hauled Mk1s	Converted from loco-hauled Mk1s Reformed to 432-434
Alpha code:	4TC (4-car **T**railer **C**ontrol)	3TC (3-car **T**railer **C**ontrol)
Introduced:	1966, 1974	1966
Built/rebuilt by:	BR York	BR York
Formation:	DTSO+TFK+TBSK+DTSO	DTSO+TBSK+DTSO
Vehicle numbers:	DTSO - 76271-76332/76944-76948 TFK - 70844-70871/71162-71167 TBSK - 7-812-70843/71160-71161 DTSO - 76270-76330/76943-76947	DTSO - 76325-76329 (odd numbers) TBSK - 70840-70842 DTSO -76326-76330 (even numbers)
Set length:	265ft 4¼in (80.57m)	198ft 3½in (60.43m)
Vehicle length:	DTSO - 64ft 9in (19.74m) TFK/TBSK - 64ft 6in (19.66m)	DTSO: 64ft 9in (19.74m) TBSK - 64ft 6in (19.66m)
Height:	12ft 9½in (3.90m)	12ft 9½in (3.90m)
Width:	9ft 3in (2.82m)	9ft 3in (2.82m)
Seating:	Total - 42F/160S DTSO - 64S TFK - 42F TBSK - 32S DTSO - 64S	Total - 160S DTSO - 64S TBSK - 32S DTSO - 64S
Internat layout:	First - Compartment, Standard - Compartment, 2+2,	Standard - Compartment, 2+2
Gangway:	Throughout	Throughout
Toilets:	TBSK, TFK - 1	TBSK - 1
Weight:	Total - 134.1 tons DTSO - 32.5 tons TFK - 33.5 tons TBSK - 35.6 tons DTSO - 32.5 tons	Total - 100.5 tons DTSO - 32.5 tons TBSK - 35.5 tons DTSO - 32.5 tons
Brake type:	Air (EP/Auto)	Air (EP/Auto)
Bogie type:	B5	B5
Power collection:	From external supply, either 4REP, or Class 33/1, 73/1 or 74	From external supply, either 4REP, or Class 33/1, 73/1 or 74
Traction motor type:	-	-
Horsepower:	-	-
Max speed:	90mph (145km/h)	90mph (145km/h)
Coupling type:	Buck-eye	Buck-eye
Multiple restriction:	1966 stock, Classes 33/1, 73/1 and 74 locos	1966 stock, Classes 33/1, 73/1 and 74 locos
Door type:	Slam	Slam

Left: *In late 1991 two 4TC sets were transferred to the NSE operated Premier Charters operation and part refurbished being painted in BR blue for charter train operation. No. 410 is seen at Bournemouth depot on 25 October 1991. As part of the development of bogies for the Channel Tunnel rolling stock a six-car TC set was formed in 1994 operated by the Eurostar development team, painted in red/blue livery and numbered 8007. Two TC sets were later operated by London Underground for surface line use.* CJM

Above and Right: *To operate alongside the 4REP tractor units on the 1967 Waterloo-Bournemouth electrification came two fleets of Trailer Control (TC) stock, 28 four-car sets and three three-car sets. All vehicles were converted from existing loco-hauled Mk1 stock at York Works. The TC sets operated with power from the REP unit between London and Bournemouth, from where a push-pull modified Class 33/1 would attach to the country end of the train and haul one or two TC sets through to Weymouth. On the return the Class 33 would propel the train back to Bournemouth for re-attachment to a REP tractor unit. The TC sets fitted with 1966 style high-level air pipes and connections could operate with Class 33/1s, 73/1s and 74s. The TC sets were also deployed on some Southampton Dock traffic and in later years on the Waterloo-Salisbury route. In 1987 the three 3TC sets were augmented with an extra TFK to make four-car sets (432-434), while three extra four-car sets were modified and numbered 429-431. As built sets were painted in BR blue; this later gave way to blue/grey and after the formation of Network SouthEast their red, white and blue colours were applied. In the 1990s renumbering into the six digit TOPS system took place, with numbers in the 80xx series applied.* CJM

Class 501

Number range:	501135-501189
Former number range:	-
Alpha code:	Not isued
Introduced:	1957-58
Built by:	BR Eastleigh
Formation:	DMBS+TS+DTBS
Vehicle numbers:	DMBS - 61133-61189 TS - 70133-70189 DTBS - 75133-75189
Set length:	181ft 9in(55.4m)
Vehicle length:	DMBS - 57ft 5in (17.5m) TS - 57ft 1in (17.4m) DTBS - 57ft 5in (17.5m)
Height:	12ft 8in (3.86m)
Width:	9ft 6in (2.9m)
Seating:	Total - 256S amended to 242S DMBS - 74S TS - 108S, later amended to 94S after opening out of compartments DTBS - 74S
Internal layout:	Compartment and 2+3
Gangway:	No
Toilets:	Not fitted
Weight:	Total - 106 tons DMBS - 47 tons TS - 29 tons DTBS - 30 tons
Brake type:	Air (EP/Auto)
Bogie type:	Mk2
Power collection:	630V dc third rail
Traction motor type:	4 x 185hp (138kW) GEC
Horsepower:	740hp (552kW)
Max speed:	60mph (96km/h)
Coupling type:	Screw
Multiple restriction:	Within class only
Door type:	Slam

Set numbers not carried, formations usually kept with last two numbers the same

Below: *The original London area L&NWR electrification was up for modernisation in 1957-58, when a fleet of EPB style units was ordered from Eastleigh Works. These three-car non gangwayed units were to operate the Euston to Watford dc line services, the branch from Watford to Croxley Green, as well as the then Richmond to Broad Street North London Line route. Each set was formed of a DMBS, an intermediate Trailer Second and a Driving Trailer Brake Second. The 57 sets were originally based at Croxley Green depot, but later sets were maintained at Willesden DED. The driving cars had their accommodation in seven 3+2 bays, while the intermediate trailer was a compartment coach. In later years the intermediate TS was converted to an open saloon following pressure placed on the railway about passenger safety. When new the sets were painted in green livery; later yellow warning ends were applied and from the late 1960s rail blue was applied. Some sets that received overhauls in the 1980s were given a coat of blue/grey livery. In the view below, the pioneer set of the fleet is seen, viewed from its DMBS vehicle. Note the window bars applied to this fleet; this was due to the very limited clearances of Hampstead Heath Tunnel, where just a slight hang from the window could lead to a person coming into contact with the tunnel structure.* CJM

Above: *Although built at Eastleigh Works at the same time as the EPB stock, the front end appearance of these sets was very different and incorporated a unique multiple jumper arrangement. Screw couplings were used and ground level air pipes. These sets also sported a two-character alpha-numeric route display and had a single red lamp on the end for tail identification. A three-car set with its DTMS nearest the camera is seen near Kew.* CJM

Below: *The 'Watford' stock, as the fleet became known, was given the Class 501 number under TOPS, but no unit or set numbers were carried. Vehicles were usually referred to by coach number, and it was usual to find sets formed of vehicles ending in the same last two digits. The Class 501s were withdrawn from service in May 1985 and replaced by Class 416 EPB stock. Set '187 is seen near Bushey.* CJM

Class 502

Vehicle type:	DMBS	TS	TC	DTC
Number range:	28311-28369	29545-29594	29812-29820	29866-29899
Introduced:	1939-41	1939-41	1939-41	1939-41
Built by:	LMS Derby	LMS Derby	LMS Derby	LMS Derby
Vehicle length:	66ft 6in (20.27m)	66ft 6in (20.27m)	66ft 6in (20.27m)	66ft 6in (20.27m)
Height:	12ft 8in (3.86m)	12ft 8in (3.86m)	12ft 8in (3.86m)	12ft 8in (3.86m)
Width:	9ft 5in (2.87m)	9ft 5in (2.87m)	9ft 5in (2.87m)	9ft 5in (2.87m)
Seating:	88S	102S	53F/29S	53F/29S
Internat layout:	Standard - 2+3	Standard - 2+3	First - 2+2 Standard - 2+3	First - 2+2 Standard - 2+3
Gangway:	No	No	No	No
Toilets:	No	No	No	No
Weight:	41 tons	24 tons	24 tons	25 tons
Brake type:	Air	Air	Air	Air
Bogie type:	?	?	?	?
Power collection:	630V dc third rail	630V dc third rail	630V dc third rail	630V dc third rail
Traction motor type:	4 x EE 235hp (175kW)	-	-	-
Horsepower:	Total - 940hp (701kW)	-	-	-
Max speed:	70mph (113km/h)	70mph (113km/h)	70mph (113km/h)	70mph (113km/h)
Coupling type:	Screw	Screw	Screw	Screw
Multiple restriction:	Within type	Within type	Within type	Within type
Door type:	Bi-parting sliding	Bi-parting sliding	Bi-parting sliding	Bi-parting sliding
Notes:			Downgraded to TS and seated 82S, or rebuilt as DTs	

Below: *Built for the Liverpool to Southport line by the LMS at Derby Works in 1939-41, a total of 152 vehicles of this design in four types were constructed, with 34 three-car and 25 two-car trains formed to replace worn out Lancashire & Yorkshire sets. Although no set numbers were ever carried and vehicles were referred to by coach numbers, the sets remained quite constant. The sets had air operated sliding doors and seating was arranged in the 3+2 style. The sets were fitted with screw couplers and conventional side buffers. When introduced the sets were painted in LMS maroon; this later gave way to BR green, BR rail blue and towards the end of their operating lives BR blue and grey was applied. An LMS maroon-liveried set, with DMBT 28317 nearest the camera, is seen at Meols Cop depot soon after delivery. This is a three-car set. Note the heavy duty shoe gear.* CJM-C

Above: *Carrying BR branding, a five-car set of what became Class 502 stock is seen on a Southport to Liverpool working in the late 1950s. It was usual operating practice to form trains with a power car at the outer ends.* CJM-C

Right: *With MerseyRail bodyside branding, a three-car set painted in 1960s rail blue with full yellow ends is shown. The train is led by car No. M29869M, an original Driving Trailer Composite, now declassified.* CJM

Below: *Horwich Works was always responsible for the classified repairs of the Class 502 stock. Sets overhauled from 1978 emerged in blue-grey colours as shown on this three-car set mounted on accommodation bogies.* CJM

Class 503

	1938 stock	1956 stock
Former number range:	-	-
Alpha code:	Not issued	Not issued
Introduced:	1938	1956
Built by:	DMBS - Metro-Cammell TC (later TS) - 29702-12 - BRCW, 29713-20 - Metro-Cammell DTS - BRCW	DMBS - Metro-Cammell TC (later TS) - 29821-32 - BRCW, 28933-46 - Metro-Cammell
Formation:	Original - DMBS+TC+DTS Modified - DMBS+TS+DTS	Original - DMBS+TC+DTS Modified - DMBS+TS+DTS
Vehicle numbers:	DMBS - 28671-28690 TC(TS) - 29702-29720 DTS - 29271-29289	DMBS - 28371-28394 TC(TS) - 29821-29846 DTS - 29131-29156
Set length:	176ft 11in (53.9m)	176ft 11in (53.9m)
Vehicle length:	DMBS/DTS - 58ft 0in (17.68m)	DMBS/DTS - 58ft 0in (17.68m)
Height:	11ft 10¼in (3.61m)	11ft 10¼in (3.61m)
Width:	9ft 11in (3.02m)	9ft 11in (3.02m)
Seating:	Total - Original - 15F/166S Modified - 180S DMBS - 58S TC - 15F/40S Rebuilt TS - 54S DTS - 68S	Total - Original - 15F/166S Modified - 180S DMBS - original - 58S, - modified with emergency door - 56S TS - 54S DTS - 66S
Internal layout:	First - 2+1 Standard - 2+2	First - 2+1 Standard - 2+2
Gangway:	Original - No Modified - Emergency end doors	Original - No Modified - Emergency end doors
Toilets:	No	No
Weight:	Total - 77 tons DMBS - 36 tons TC (TS) - 20 tons DTS - 21 tons	Total - 77 tons DMBS - 36 tons TC (TS) - 20 tons DTS - 21 tons
Brake type:	Air (EP/Auto)	Air (EP/Auto)
Bogie type:	Single bolster	Single bolster
Power collection:	650V dc third rail	650V dc third rail
Traction motor type:	BTH	BTH
Horsepower:	540hp (403kW)	540hp (403kW)
Max speed:	70mph (113km/h)	70mph (113km/h)
Coupling type:	Screw	Screw
Multiple restriction:	Within class only	Within class only
Door type:	Bi-parting sliding	Bi-parting sliding

Minor structural differences exist between two builds

Above and Left Bottom: *The LMS ordered 19 three-car EMUs in 1938 for the Wirral & Mersey Lines to replace older L&Y built stock. A further 24 units were built in 1956-57 to near identical design. Both builds were constructed by the private sector, with Metro-Cammell building all driving cars and a small number of intermediate vehicles and Birmingham Railway Carriage & Wagon building the balance of intermediate vehicles. Originally sets were set out for first and third class occupancy, with first class seating provided for 15 in the intermediate vehicle; this was later declassified and the sets were third (second) class only. When introduced these sets were very much state-of-the-art, with automatic couplers and air operated sliding doors, more reminiscent of the London Underground network. The original LMS built sets were finished in LMS maroon, but this later gave way to BR green and subsequently BR rail blue. The sets built in the 1950s emerged in BR green livery, and yellow warning ends were later applied. Following the opening of the tunnel sections of the Liverpool suburban network, sets were modified to incorporate an emergency door in the cab ends. Bottom left we see an LMS liveried set led by car No. 28698 a DMBS vehicle. The image above shows a 1956 built set with car M28371M, a DMBS type coach, leading. Both:* CJM-C

Below: *Showing BR rail blue livery and Merseyrail bodyside branding, a three-car set led by Driving Trailer Second No. M29145M with a Garston destination board in the non-driving front window is seen at Cressington station in July 1978.* CJM

Class 504

Number range:	No set numbers carried
Former number range:	-
Alpha code:	Not issued
Introduced:	1959
Built by:	BR Wolverton
Formation:	DMBS+DTC
Vehicle numbers:	DMBS - 65436-65461 DTC - 77157-77182
Set length:	133ft 3½in (40.63m)
Vehicle length:	63ft 11½in (19.5m)
Height:	12ft 7in (3.83m)
Width:	9ft 3in (2.82m)
Seating:	Total - As built - 16F/162S Total - Modified - originally 186S, then reduced to 178S DMBS - 84S As built - DTC 16F/78S, Modified - DTS - 102 then reduced to 94S
Internal layout:	2+3
Gangway:	No
Toilets:	Not fitted
Weight:	Total - 83 tons DMBS - 50 tons DTS - 33 tons
Brake type:	Air (EP/Auto)
Bogie type:	Gresley
Power collection:	1,200V dc side contact third rail
Traction motor type:	4 x EE 141hp (105.1kW)
Horsepower:	564hp (421kW)
Max speed:	70mph (113km/h)
Coupling type:	Buck-eye
Multiple restriction:	Within class only
Door type:	Slam

Below: *These unique 26 two-car units, built by BR Wolverton Works in 1959 to modernise the Manchester to Bury route, were fitted with side contact third rail power collection, as the voltage used was 1,200V dc, rather than the more conventional 600-750V dc in other areas. The sets were built to the late 1950s standard EMU profile, as used on such types as the AM4 and AM5 fleets. The Bury sets, as they became known, seated 16 first and 162 third class passengers as built; this was later amended to 186 standard class with the DTC vehicle becoming a DTS. These sets were fitted with power collection shoes on the outer ends of the DMBS vehicle and on both ends of the DTS car, with high-voltage power passing to the power car via a protected bus-cable. Sets were painted in BR multiple unit green, offset by a cream body band. Buck-eye couplers and high level air and multiple control jumpers were provided. Sets were based at Bury depot. These units remained in operation until 1991 when the Manchester Victoria to Bury route was transferred to light rail operation, being worked as part of the Manchester Metrolink project. In the view below at Radcliffe Central a Bury bound train has its DMBS leading.* CJM-C

Above: *The first unit of the built, with DMBS No. M65436 leading, is seen at Wolverton Works ready for delivery to Manchester. The drop-head buck-eye couplings are in the lowered position and no power collection shoe gear is attached. This picture gives a clear view of the Gresley-design bogies.* CJM-C

Below: *BR green livery, later with yellow warning ends, gave way to BR rail blue with full yellow ends from the late 1970s. Subsequently some sets were repainted in standard BR blue grey colours and a number were repainted into Manchester area orange and brown. Rail blue-liveried DMBS No. M65446 leads a two-car set into Bury in 1981.* CJM

Class 506

Number range:	No set numbers carried
Former number range:	-
Alpha code:	Not issued
Introduced:	1954
Built by:	Metro-Cammell and BRCW
Formation:	Original formation - DMBS+TC+DTS Revised formation - DMBS+TS+DTS
Vehicle numbers:	DMBS - 59401-59408 TC/TS - 59501-59508 DTS - 59601-59608
Set length:	177ft 10in (54.20m)
Vehicle length:	DMBS - 60ft 4½in (18.40m) TS - 55ft 0½in (16.78m) DTS - 55ft 4½in (16.88m)
Height:	12ft 8¼in (3.87m)
Width:	9ft 3in (2.82m)
Seating:	Original Total - 24F/150S DMBS - 52S TC -24F/38S DTS - 60S Modified Total - 174S DMBS - 52S TS - 62S DTS - 60S
Internal layout:	2+2
Gangway:	No
Toilets:	Not fitted
Weight:	Total - 104ton 9cwt DMBS - 50ton 12cwt TS - 26ton 8cwt DTS -27ton 9cwt
Brake type:	Air (EP/Auto)
Bogie type:	Single bolster
Power collection:	1,500V dc overhead
Traction motor type:	EE
Horsepower:	432hp (4322kW)
Max speed:	75mph (121km/h)
Coupling type:	Screw
Multiple restriction:	Within class only
Door type:	Bi-parting sliding

Below: *The eight Glossop line three-car EMUs, later classified as 506, were built by Metro-Cammell and BRCW in 1954 to operate on the Manchester Piccadilly to Glossop line, with a triangular junction between Dinting and Hadfield. The sets were originally ordered by the LNER in 1938 and thus took their numbering. When introduced, these sets had both first and third (later second) class passenger accommodation and in design were very similar to the AL6 Class 306 sets operated on the Great Eastern section of the Eastern Region. As introduced the first class seating was provided in the intermediate TC vehicle with 24 higher-quality first class seats. These vehicles were later modified to all third/second class with a three-car set in that form seating 174. Taking power at 1,500V dc from the overhead, these sets were confined to their intended route; technically they could have operated over the Pennines to Sheffield but this was never the case, and the sets concentrated on the Manchester Glossop/Hadfield line for their entire life. Passenger access was by bi-parting air-operated sliding doors, two pairs on each side of each vehicle. The power collection pantograph was mounted above the driving cab/guards van of the DMBS vehicle. Painted in green as delivered livery, two three-car sets are illustrated working in multiple, with DMBS M59405 leading.* CJM-C

Above: *The Manchester-Glossop sets had a unique multiple control and jumper system , allowing the fleet members to only operate with themselves. Nose end mounted control jumpers, a screw coupling and buffer beam mounted air connection were fitted. The sets used electro-pneumatic braking. Route description was by four white lights displayed on the front under the non driving window. A red central tail light was also fitted. A three-car set is seen departing from Hadfield.* CJM-C

Below: *From the late 1960s, repaints were in BR rail blue, then in the early 1980s blue and grey started to appear in the short time before the sets were withdrawn on 7 December 1984. Blue and grey liveried set No. '04 with its DTS nearest the photographer is seen at Dinting on 3 September 1980.* CJM

Class 507

Number range:	507001-507033	
Introduced:	1978-80	
Built/rebuilt by:	BREL York/Alstom Eastleigh	
Formation:	BDMSO+TSO+DMSO	
Vehicle numbers:	BDMSO - 64367-64399 TSO - 71342-71374 DMSO - 64405-64437	
Vehicle length:	BDMSO/DMSO - 64ft 11½in (19.80m) TSO - 65ft 4¼in (19.92m)	
Height:	11ft 6½in (3.58m)	
Width:	9ft 3in (2.82m)	
Seating:	As built Total - 230S BDMSO -74S TSO - 82S DMSO - 74S	Refurbished Total - 186S BDMSO - 56S TSO - 74S DMSO - 56S
Internal layout:	2+2	
Gangway:	Within set (emergency end doors)	
Toilets:	Not fitted	
Weight:	Total - 98 tonnes BDMSO - 37 tonnes TSO - 25.5 tonnes DMSO - 35.5 tonnes	
Brake type:	Air (EP/rheostatic)	
Bogie type:	BX1	
Power collection:	700-750 V dc third rail	
Traction motor type:	8 x GEC G310AZ of 110hp (82.12kW)	
Horsepower:	880hp (657kW)	
Max speed:	75mph (121km/h)	
Coupling type:	Outer - Tightlock Inner - Bar	
Multiple restriction:	Class 507 and 508/1 only	
Door type:	Bi-parting sliding	
Construction:	Body - aluminium, Frame - steel	
Special features:	CCTV	

Below: *As part of the modernisation of the Liverpool suburban electrified railway a fleet of 33 three-car Class 507 sets were built to the 1972 design sets (based on the PEP) between 1978-80. As built the sets seated 230 standard class passengers in the 2+3 open layout. Following refurbishment and the installation of improved 2+2 seating the overall train capacity has now been reduced to 186. Each set is formed of two near identical Driving Motor Standard Open cars, housing all the power and control equipment, flanking a Trailer Standard Open. When constructed sets were finished in the then standard blue and grey livery, offset by yellow warning ends. Blue and grey-liveried set No. 507004 is illustrated passing Birkenhead North EMU depot on 1 April 1995.* CJM-C

Above & Below: *Following privatisation and considerable local government input, the Class 507s and the similar 508s have been refurbished. The sets now sport revised front ends with large headlights on either side and a joint marker/ tail light, together with a roof level marker light meeting the latest Group Standards. In the view above, set No. 507001 is illustrated at Hillside on 8 September 2011. The revised low-density interiors on both the MerseyRail Class 507s and 508s have been well accepted by the public; their dark brown moquette, high-back seats, yellow grab poles and a good passenger information system are a far cry from the original interiors of these sets. Both:* John Binch

Class 508

Class:	508/1	508/2	508/3
Number range:	508101-508143	508201-508212	508301-508303
Former No. range:	508001-508043	508101/5/6/7/9/13 16/19/21/29/32/33	508102/135/142
Originally built:	1979-80	1979-80	1979-80
Introduced:	As 508/1 - 1984-85	As 508/2 - 1998	As 508/3 - 2002-03
Originally built:	BREL York	BREL York	BREL York
Refurbished by:	BRML Eastleigh	Alstom Eastleigh	Alstom Eastleigh
Formation:	As built: DMSO+TSO+TSO+BDMSO Revised: DMSO+TSO+BDMSO	DMSO+TSO+BDMSO	DMSO+TSO+BDMSO
Vehicle numbers:	DMSO - 64651-64691 TSO - 71485-71525 (TSO - 71526-71568) BDMSO - 64694-64734	DMSO - 64649-64681 series TSO - 71483-71515 series BDMSO - 64692-64724 series	DMSO - 64650-64690 series TSO - 71484-71524 series BDMSO - 64693-64733 series
Vehicle length:	DMSO - 64ft 11½in (19.80m) TSO - 65ft 4½in (19.92m)	DMSO - 64ft 11½in (19.80m) TSO - 65ft 4½in (19.92m)	DMSO - 64ft 11½in (19.80m) TSO - 65ft 4½in (19.92m)
Height:	11ft 6½in (3.58m)	11ft 6½in (3.58m)	11ft 6½in (3.58m)
Width:	9ft 3in (2.82m)	9ft 3in (2.82m)	9ft 3in (2.82m)
Seating:	Total (as built) - 312S DMSO - 74S TSO - 82S, TSO 82 BDMSO - 74S Total (present) 186S DMSO - 56S TSO - 74S BDMSO - 56S	Total - 219S DMSO - 66S TSO - 79S BDMSO - 74S	Total - 222S DMSO - 68S TSO - 86S BDMSO - 68S
Internal layout:	2+2 (originally 2+3)	2+3 high-density	2+3 high-density
Gangway:	Within set, emergency end doors	Within set, emergency end doors	Within set, emergency end doors
Toilets:	Not fitted	Not fitted	Not fitted
Weight:	Total - 99.3 tonnes DMSO - 36.0 tonnes TSO - 26.7 tonnes BDMSO - 36.6 tonnes	Total - 99.0 tonnes DMSO - 36.0 tonnes TSO - 26.5 tonnes BDMSO - 36.5 tonnes	Total - 99.1 tonnes DMSO - 36.0 tonnes TSO - 26.5 tonnes BDMSO - 36.6 tonnes
Brake type:	Air (Westcode/rheostatic)	Air (Westcode/rheostatic)	Air (Westcode/rheostatic)
Bogie type:	BX1	BX1	BX1
Power collection:	750V dc third rail	750V dc third rail	750V dc third rail
Traction motor type:	8 x GEC G310AZ	8 x GEC G310AZ	8 x GEC G310AZ
Horsepower:	880hp (657kW)	880hp (657kW)	880hp (657kW)
Max speed:	75mph (121km/h)	75mph (121km/h)	75mph (121km/h)
Coupling type:	End - Tightlock, Inner - Bar	End - Tightlock, Inner - Bar	End - Tightlock, Inner - Bar
Multiple restriction:	Class 507 and 508/1	Within sub class only	Within sub class only
Special features:	CCTV	-	CCTV
Door type:	Bi-parting sliding	Bi-parting sliding	Bi-parting, sliding
Construction:	Body - aluminium	Body - aluminium	Body - aluminium

Right Top: *A total of 43 four-car Class 508s were built in 1979-80 for BR Southern Region to operate on the Western section on suburban lines radiating from Waterloo. The sets were a stop-gap until purpose-built Class 455s were introduced, at which time the 43 sets, reduced to three-car formation, were transferred north to the MerseyRail network. The removed TS was inserted in the second tranche of 43 Class 455/7s. As built the four-car 508s seated 312 standard class passengers in the 2+2 and 2+3 mode with low-back seats, and bi-parting passenger doors were provided. All sets were delivered in blue and grey livery and on the Southern were based at East Wimbledon depot. No. 508018 is seen passing Hampton Court Junction.* CJM

Right Middle Upper: *After transferring to MerseyRail, a number of sets became spare and 12 were transferred back south to operate for Connex SouthEastern on branch line duties. These sets were reclassified as Class 508/2s, and all are presently out of service stored. Set No. 508203 is seen at London Bridge.* CJM

Right Middle Lower: *The 27 remaining Class 508s working on the MerseyRail system have all been refurbished and like the Class 507s now sport low-density 2+2 high-back seating, front ends have been modified to incorporate new light clusters and a high level marker light has been added. Seating on these sets today is for 186 standard class passengers. Set No. 508139 is seen at Ellesmere Port.* Murdoch Currie

Right Bottom: *In 2002-03, three off-lease Class 508s were taken over by Silverlink and modified to operate alongside the Class 313 dual power sets on the Euston to Watford route; these were reclassified as 508/3 and renumbered 508301-508303. These sets were dc only and had to operate a captive roster to ensure they were not required to operate from the overhead power supply. Externally the sets were repainted in Silverlink mauve, green and white colours. All are currently stored, but in summer 2013 discussions were rife as to the re-instatement of these sets into use for Transport for London. Set No. 508303 is seen at Willesden Junction.* CJM